mHealth Innovation
Best Practices from the Mobile Frontier

Edited by

Rick Krohn, MA, MAS

David Metcalf, PhD

Editors of the HIMSS Books Best-Seller

mHealth:
From Smartphones to Smart Systems

HIMSS Mission
To globally lead endeavors optimizing health engagements and care outcomes through information technology.

© 2014 by Healthcare Information and Management Systems Society (HIMSS). All rights reserved. No part of this publication may be reproduced, adapted, translated, stored in a retrieval system, or transmitted in any form or by any means, electronic, mechanical, photocopying, recording or otherwise, without the prior written permission of the publisher.

Printed in the U.S.A. 5 4 3 2 1

Requests for permission to make copies of any part of this work should be sent to:
Permissions Editor
HIMSS
33 West Monroe Street, Suite 1700
Chicago, IL 60603-5616
matthew.schlossberg@himssmedia.com

The inclusion of an organization name, product or service in this publication should not be considered as an endorsement of such organization, product, or service, nor is the failure to include an organization name, product or service to be construed as disapproval.

ISBN: 978-1-938904-61-5

For more information about HIMSS, please visit www.himss.org.

About the Editors

Rick Krohn, MA, MAS
Rick Krohn is an expert in healthcare corporate strategy and strategic marketing, business development, corporate communications, technology product development and commercialization. Mr. Krohn has served as president of HealthSense since 1998. His 27 years of industry experience spans the healthcare, telecommunications, education, banking and technology spaces. He is the author of more than 100 articles on a wide range of healthcare subjects, and has written two health industry texts. In addition to writing, Mr. Krohn has delivered presentations at national healthcare conferences sponsored by VHA, Premier, AMGA, ACHE, MGMA, HIMSS, mHIMSS, NMHCC, AIC and others about strategic business, technology, and operations issues in healthcare. Mr. Krohn has earned degrees from Towson University, American University and The Johns Hopkins University. He is the co-editor, with David Metcalf, PhD, of the HIMSS Books best-seller *mHealth: From Smartphones to Smart Systems* (2012). Further information about Mr. Krohn may be found on his web site, www.healthsen.com.

David Metcalf, PhD
David Metcalf has more than 20 years' experience in the design and research of web-based and mobile technologies converging to enable learning and healthcare. Dr. Metcalf is director of the Mixed Emerging Technology Integration Lab (METIL) at the University of Central Florida's Institute for Simulation and Training. The team has built mHealth solutions, simulations, games, eLearning, mobile and enterprise IT systems for Google, J&J, VA, the U.S. military and UCF's College of Medicine among others. Recent projects include Lake Nona's Intelligent Home prototype and Significant Technology, a mobile university tool kit. Dr. Metcalf encourages spinoffs from the lab as part of the innovation process. In addition to research and commercial investments, he supports social entrepreneurship in education and health. Dr. Metcalf continues to bridge the gap between corporate learning and simulation techniques and non-profit and social entrepreneurship. Simulation, mobilization, mobile patient records and medical decision support systems, visualization systems, scalability models, secure mobile data communications, gaming, innovation management and operational excellence are current research topics. Dr. Metcalf frequently presents at industry and research events shaping business strategy and use of technology to improve learning, health and human performance. For more information see http://metillab.com. He is the co-editor, with Rick Krohn, MA, MAS, of the HIMSS Books best-seller *mHealth: From Smartphones to Smart Systems* (2012).

About the Contributors

Corey Ackerman is President and Chief Operating Officer of Happtique and manages all operations. Prior to Happtique, Mr. Ackerman spent nine years as legal counsel for GNYHA Ventures' portfolio companies, including its healthcare group purchasing and consulting businesses. He also provided support for all aspects of contracting and regulatory compliance, including HIPAA. Prior to joining GNYHA Ventures, Mr. Ackerman worked on corporate and securities matters for start-up and telecommunications companies at Mintz Levin.

Ellen Badinelli is founder and CEO of ScanAvert Inc. and an early promoter of mobile delivery of personal health information. She is a Strategic Partnership for Industrial Resurgence (SPIR) grant recipient from the State University of New York (SUNY), where she earned her BS (Oneonta campus). Ms. Badinelli has held leadership positions within scouting, BSA, GSA, special education PTA, and currently serves on FINRA [NASD] Board of Arbitrators. ScanAvert has received acclaim, press, and most recently recognition by *Fast Company*, as 2013's World's Most Innovative Companies. Its first-generation/kiosk service won IEEE's 2nd Place CCNC Consumer Application of the Year in 2006, and was CEWIT's Featured Developer in 2005.

Samuel Benefour is a social development worker with over 20 years' experience in implementing and managing a variety of sexual and reproductive health and other public health-related interventions in Ghana. He holds BA and MA degrees from the University of Ghana, Legon. Since 2006, Mr. Benefour has worked with Family Health International and the Academy for Educational Development in HIV prevention–to-care continuum interventions targeted at key populations. His innovative idea of reaching key populations with HIV strategic messages through the use of text messaging has created opportunities for those populations in accessing appropriate health and related services.

James BonTempo, MS, is the Director of ICT & Innovation at The Johns Hopkins Bloomberg School of Public Health's Center for Communication Programs. He is also a Core Faculty member at the Foundation for Advancement of International Medical Education and Research. Since 1995, Mr. BonTempo has worked in Information and Communication Technology (ICT) across the commercial, academic and non-profit sectors. A recognized thought-leader in ICT for international development, with experience across Africa and Asia, he has managed and led the design, development, implementation and evaluation of health ICT systems for workforce development, service delivery, behavior change, monitoring and evaluation.

Keith Boone is a Standards Geek for GE Healthcare, which represents GE to various SDOs, develops health IT standards, and teaches and promotes them in the industry. He has been working in health IT for more than a decade and as a software developer and implementer of standards for more than three decades. Mr. Boone is the author or editor of numerous health IT standards, including the HITSP C32, HL7 CCD®

and the HL7 CCDA, and also The CDA™ Book, a text on the HL7 Clinical Document Architecture standard.

Jeffrey L. Brandt, BSCS, GC-BMI, began his career in mobile telecom and location-based technologies, transitioning to online payment services as Senior Software Engineer at CyberCash/Verisign. The advent of the iPhone and graduate work at Oregon Health & Sciences University in medical informatics led him to develop the first secure personal health record for the iPhone and Android. Mr. Brandt also contributed to several HIMSS books and publications, including the privacy and security, interoperability and standards sections of the mHIMSS *Mobile Health IT Roadmap*. He also contributed the security and compliance chapter to HIMSS Books' *mHealth: From Smartphones to Smart Systems* (2012). Mr. Brandt has spoken on security and interoperability at many events, including the Annual HIMSS Conference & Exhibition in 2012 and 2013. Mr. Brandt is currently a consultant and informatics advisor.

Noel Chandler, BA, is the CEO and Co-Founder of Mosio, a mobile messaging company specializing in two-way text messaging communications used in clinical research, health and event services. Winner of the Mobile category at South by Southwest in 2008, Mosio's client list includes McKesson, the American Hospital Association, Quintiles, Blue Cross, Kaiser Permanente, CareWire, HHS.gov, Albert Einstein College of Medicine, BrdsNBz National and Young Moms Connect. Mr. Chandler served for seven years as a U.S. Trends Editor for The Futures Company, an international strategic insights and innovation consultancy. Prior to Mosio, he was the founder of, and remains a partner at Attack!, one of the leading experiential marketing agencies in the United States.

Nana Fosua Clement is a social development management person with 16 years' experience managing HIV interventions. Her expertise ranges from conducting baseline surveys to developing behavior change strategies for sustained behavior change, project implementation and management, and conducting project evaluations. She has provided technical assistance to a broad coalition of stakeholders, including governmental agencies, civil societies and non-governmental organizations. Ms. Clement is currently working with FHI360 Ghana as the Associate Director, Technical for the USAID Ghana SHARPER Project, where she provides technical leadership related to AIDS prevention, care and community empowerment for key populations and people living with HIV; guides strategic thinking and planning in new technical areas; and manages service delivery through sub-awards and direct implementation. Ms. Clement is fluent in English, four local dialects and conversational in French.

Will Comerford, who has a prior background in journalism and creative writing, is the Content Director with Physicians Interactive. He has written and developed medical content for innovative online and mobile applications for more than 10 years, including work for the National Kidney Foundation, CCG Metamedia and WebMD. His work has been the recipient of multiple industry awards, including Aegis, Hermes and Webby.

Joshua L. Conrad, PharmD, is Director of Patient Safety and Clinical Utility at Epocrates Inc., an athenahealth company. Dr. Conrad received his doctorate in pharmacy, summa cum laude, from Nova Southeastern University (NSU), where he subsequently completed a specialty residency in drug information. Before joining Epocrates, he served on the faculties of the colleges of pharmacy at NSU and Auburn University. In his current role, Dr. Conrad is responsible for ensuring the accuracy, quality and clinical utility of Epocrates' mobile medical references and tools.

Gladys Damalin is the Program Operations Manager on the SHARPER project of Family Health International (FHI360), Ghana. She holds an MPHIL in Clinical Psychology from the University of Ghana, Legon. Ms. Damalin has more than 10 years of progressive professional experience working with international NGOs and private management institutions. Prior to joining FHI360, she worked on USAID's project Focus Region Health Project (FRHP) where she was a member of the team of specialists that provided technical assistance and support to the MOH/GHS. She also worked as Senior Program Officer for the OICI/USAID program. Specific competencies and experiences acquired over the years include capacity strengthening, project management, advocacy, community mobilization, strategic planning and program design, among others.

Meredith Puleio DuBoff, MBA, has more than seven years of experience in global health and social innovation. As an independent consultant, Ms. DuBoff supports clients with new business development, technical writing, and project implementation, focusing on the areas of mobile health, social enterprise and socially responsible business practices. Previously, at Georgetown University's Institute for Reproductive Health, Ms. DuBoff was a core member of the team that developed and tested the mHealth innovation CycleTel™, an SMS-based family planning service. Ms. DuBoff holds an MBA from Georgetown University, and a BA in International Affairs from George Washington University.

Lynne A. Dunbrack, MBA, MS, is Research Vice President at IDC Health Insights. Ms. Dunbrack provides in-depth coverage of the connected health market, including consumer engagement and a range of technologies such as mobile health, remote health monitoring, virtual or online care, machine-to-machine (M2M), and health information exchange. She has more than 25 years of experience in healthcare. Prior to joining IDC, Ms. Dunbrack was a consultant for MA-SHARE, LLC, one of the nation's first live clinical data exchange initiatives. She was also Director of Product Management at NaviMedix Inc. (now NaviNet) and served as the Director of HIPAA Compliance. Ms. Dunbrack holds a BA from the College of the Holy Cross, and an MBA and MS from Boston University's Graduate School of Management.

Dave Dushyant is a graduate student at the New Jersey Institute of Technology (NJIT) where he studied Computer Science with a focus on software development, design and data analytics. Mr. Dushyant holds a bachelor of science in computer science and business from NJIT, is a member of The National Society of Collegiate Scholars, and a First Place Recipient of the Capstone Challenge for his work with ScanAvert Inc.

Doug Elwood, MD, MBA, is a board-certified physician and entrepreneur. He has published numerous peer-reviewed articles and presented worldwide as an innovation thought leader on patient care, technology, policy, gaming and leadership. Dr. Elwood co-founded an mHealth company in 2009, acts as an executive advisor for multiple emerging companies, works as a digital/innovation strategy lead for a major biopharmaceutical firm, and is on faculty at the Rusk Institute of Rehabilitation.

John Fessler, MBA, has helped healthcare organizations align technology to achieve results and has served in various leadership positions, including CEO of Santech. Santech provides better health through tailored mobile messaging solutions used by health systems, health plans and other healthcare organizations.

Travis Froehlich is the Associate Vice President of Corporate Communications for GNYHA Ventures, the business arm of the Greater New York Hospital Association. He manages strategic communications projects, event planning and social media. Previously, Mr. Froehlich held positions at Western Wisconsin Technical College and the School of the Art Institute of Chicago.

Ross Gensler is Marketing Team Lead and Business Enhancement Guru for Sonic Boom Wellness. He is tasked with spreading the awesomeness that is the Sonic Boom program — sharing innovative developments, client case studies and personal Sonic success stories from individual members. Professionals have lots to read throughout the day; his team focuses on making vital wellness information as entertaining as possible.

Douglas Goldstein is an innovator and eFuturist who delivers the latest intelligence and insights on how emerging technology, science and wisdom can improve health. As a speaker and author, he motivates and inspires people to apply knowledge from his keynotes and workshops to create the future. As an innovation executive and leader on the forefront of transformation, Mr. Goldstein delivers strategies and solutions for leaders in the fitness, health, healthcare and life sciences industries.

Travis Good, MD, MBA, MS, is an expert, speaker and commentator on healthcare technology and social media. His mission is to improve healthcare for providers and consumers through intuitive technologies, making both sides of care more enjoyable and efficient. He has worked in IT consulting, founded an NGO, founded an international mHealth company, helped healthcare organizations with technology decisions, written industry blogs and spoken nationally on health technology. He serves as Editor for HIStalkConnect, an industry blog. He's co-founder of Catalyze, which offers compliant cloud-based software for the healthcare industry.

Kimberly Green has more than 20 years' experience in public health management, policy development and research. She specializes in HIV prevention and care systems and policy development, working with key populations, mHealth/ICT, ART adherence and retention in care, prevention with positives, palliative care, community and home-based care, youth and orphans and vulnerable children interventions, and intervention development, implementation and evaluation. She is the author of several technical reports, articles, training curricula and presentations. She has worked with FHI 360 for nearly 10 years, first in Vietnam as part of the regional platform and now in Ghana as Chief of Party. While with FHI 360, she has provided HIV and sexual and reproductive health technical assistance and capacity building support to local organizations and governments implementing programs in Asia and Africa.

Gautam Gulati, MD, MBA, MPH, is the Chief Medical Officer and Head of Product Innovation for Physicians Interactive Holdings, where he leads a world-class team to ideate, design, build, and deploy disruptive solutions for a health audience. In addition to his executive role, he serves as an Adjunct Professor of Medical Innovation and Entrepreneurship at The Johns Hopkins University Carey Business School, sits on numerous company boards, and speaks at a variety of events around the world. Over the years, Dr. Gulati has earned an impeccable reputation for his ability to transform organizations to meet the future innovative demands of the health industry. Along this journey, he has been dubbed both a "health hooligan" and "physician artist," encapsulating the creative characteristics that allow him to meld his various vantage points as a clinician, executive, designer, professor, advisor, entrepreneur, speaker and technology advocate.

Evan Harary is a student at The Johns Hopkins University, majoring in International/Global Studies. As Corporate Communications Intern for GNYHA Ventures, Mr. Harary managed the content development and submission of Chapter 25.

Jeffrey T. Heckman, DO, is a board-certified physician and the Medical Director of the Regional Amputation Center at VA Puget Sound Health Care System, where he coordinates care for veterans with limb loss in a large portion of the western United States. He has presented his innovative patient care approaches internationally, including a novel, personalized amputee care kit, dynamic peer support program with social networking, mobile health and patient engagement strategies.

Susan C. Hull, MSN, RN, is a nursing executive and thought leader with national and international reach, passionate about co-creating technology-enabled innovations, transforming health and care eco-systems to dramatically improve population health and well being. Ms. Hull is the Founder and CEO of WellSpring Consulting, supporting healthcare organizations and communities in the United States and Canada since 1994 to strengthen their capacity for innovation in services, products and impact. She recently served as Chief Health Informatics Officer for Diversinet, Vice President for Elsevier's CPM Resource Center, and serves on the NeHC Consumer e-Health Advisory Board and ONC's FACA Consumer Technology Standards Workgroup.

Leslie Isenegger is Senior Vice President of Corporate Communications for GNYHA Ventures, overseeing marketing and communications for all business affiliates and subsidiaries, including Happtique. Before joining GYNHA Ventures, Ms. Isenegger led communications for the Greater New York Hospital Association and held positions at the Centers for Medicare & Medicaid Services (CMS) as a speechwriter, the CMS Office of Legislation, as well as the Advisory Board Company/National Journal Group.

Anand K. Iyer, PhD, MBA, is President and Chief Operating Officer of WellDoc Inc. Dr. Iyer is a pioneer in the domain of wireless technology and strategy, and a leader in its application within the mobile health industry. A type-2 diabetes patient himself, he oversees product and services development at WellDoc. With a doctorate in image pattern recognition, he also leads the company's data science efforts in the domains of informative, predictive and adaptive modeling to further improve patient outcomes and reduce healthcare costs, by utilizing real-time data from WellDoc's clinical and behavioral science-driven mHealth platforms.

Michelle Jacobs has worked as a communications executive at several Fortune 100 companies, where she produced award-winning publications, web sites and videos. Ms. Jacobs currently serves as Director of Editorial Services for GNYHA Ventures.

Robert Jarrin is a Senior Director of Government Affairs for Qualcomm Inc. Mr. Jarrin's areas of responsibility include federal wireless health policy, healthcare legislative affairs, FDA regulation of converged medical devices, FCC healthcare efforts, CMS telehealth reimbursement, and ONC regulation of health IT. Externally, Mr. Jarrin chairs the Advisory Council to mHIMSS, leads the American Telemedicine Association (ATA) Policy A-Team on Telehealth and Meaningful Use, is the U.S. Chair for the Trans-Atlantic Business Council (TBC) eHealth Policy Sub-Working Group, Co-Chairs the Telecommunications Industry Association (TIA) Health IT Working Group, co-leads the FCC mHealth Task Force (MTF) and serves on the Scientific Advisory Board of Medical Automation. Mr. Jarrin frequently speaks at public conferences, federal workshops and hearings. He is on the faculty of the George Washington University School of Medicine and Health Sciences as an Adjunct Assistant Professor of Emergency Medicine, and provides lectures on mHealth and medical device regulations for Case Western Reserve University, Case School of Engineering. Mr. Jarrin holds a BA degree in Government and Politics from the University of Maryland at College Park and a JD from Northeastern University School of Law.

Georges E. Khalil, MPH, is a doctoral candidate in Health Communications at the University at Buffalo, and a doctoral fellow in Cancer Prevention at the MD Anderson Cancer Center. His research interests include the study of digital games for health promotion and disease prevention. In particular, he is interested in the evaluation of games for health and the identification of gaming features responsible for health games' success.

Tina Koro, MPH, is the Product Manager for Santech and develops much of the message content and messaging applications used by healthcare organizations. Her e-mail address is ckoro@santechhealth.com.

Kelly L'Engle, PhD, MPH, is a Health Behavior and Education Scientist with over 20 years of experience in the health sector. Since 2007, Ms. L'Engle has been with FHI 360, where she leads reproductive health research in developing countries. Ms. L'Engle is FHI 360's leading expert on mHealth communication technologies and research, and she is highly proficient in developing, testing and evaluating health communication materials and interventions. Ms. L'Engle has expertise in research and evaluation, adolescent health, higher risk populations, substance use, HIV and family planning communication, digital and social media, and knowledge management.

Elizabeth Lyons, PhD, MPH, is an Assistant Professor in the Institute for Translational Sciences at the University of Texas Medical Branch. Her research concerns the use of technology to increase motivation for behaviors related to energy balance (that is, physical activity, sedentary behavior and food intake). She is particularly interested in the power of narrative and character identification to increase motivation and self-efficacy. Though most of her research is on commercially available video games, she also studies other media that include characteristics of video games, such as activity monitors and their competitive mobile applications.

Sandra C. Maliszewski, MSN, JD, MBA, is Director of the Health App Certification Program at Happtique, and has more than 25 years of healthcare experience, having worked as a registered nurse, family nurse practitioner and licensed midwife in hospitals and private practice. She is also a seasoned healthcare attorney with extensive experience in corporate compliance, ethics, and HIPAA program development and management, risk management, clinical integration and quality initiatives. In her role at Happtique, Ms. Maliszewski runs the Health App Certification Program, working with testing partners and advisory groups.

Thomas (Tom) Martin is a doctoral candidate at the University of Delaware School of Public Policy. His dissertation is focused on the valuation of mobile healthcare applications for providers and the impacts of regulatory change on existing policies. Mr. Martin has served as project lead for numerous IT implementations and mobile app developments while working for the not-for-profit HIMSS and Fortune 100 companies. In addition, he provided input on Happtique's certification process for mobile health applications and the FCC's mHealth Taskforce recommendations to Chairman Genachowski on ways to improve mHealth policy. Mr. Martin is an instructor at Georgetown University in the School of Continuing Studies Technology Management Program. He has authored numerous blogs and articles on the role of research in understanding the impacts of mHealth technology, increasing access to clinically underserved communities by way of technology, and the impacts of policy change. Mr. Martin's research interests include the use of cost/benefit analysis, comparative effectiveness, and other economic valuations within the healthcare setting.

Gregg Masters, MPH, is co-founder and chief executive of HealthInnovationMedia.com, curators of ACOWatch.com, JustOncology.com, IllustratorsJournal.com, and HealthGeek.tv. The company also produces Internet audiocasts, including *This Week in Health Innovation*, *This Week In Accountable Care* and *This Week in Oncology* on the BlogTalk Radio Network. Mr. Masters consults on social media strategy for healthcare organizations and has served in senior management strategist positions for both flagship and development stage healthcare ventures.

Brian Mayrsohn, MS, is a medical student at UCF College of Medicine. He graduated with a BA from Vanderbilt University and a Masters in Nutrition from Columbia University. His research evaluates health games' effectiveness in driving behavior change. He served as Director of Business Development for Metro Physical and Aquatic Therapy and is a Scout for the business incubator StartUp Health Academy. As co-founder of Healthcare Innovations, he challenges healthcare professionals to think differently about practicing medicine and encourages cross-disciplinary collaboration and entrepreneurship. As a clinician, he plans to utilize sensors, health games and mobile technology to tailor medicine to his patients.

Robert B. McCray is Co-Founder, President and CEO of the Wireless-Life Sciences Alliance, Chairman of Alliance Healthcare Foundation, Special Advisor to Triple-

Tree LLC, Member of Midmark Corporation Board of Directors, Member of Board of Directors of CONNECT and an active advisor to several companies. Mr. McCray leverages more than 25 years of experience as a business owner, senior operating executive, and legal and transactional advisor to private and public companies. Mr. McCray has served as President, COO and an early investor in Digital On-Demand Inc., a retail services technology company that operates under the brand name Red-DotNet in chains, including Barnes & Noble, Best Buy, Blockbuster and Fred Meyer. Previously, he served as Chairman, President and CEO of HealthCap Inc., a venture-capital-backed physician practice management company that returned 90 percent CAGR to its investors. Mr. McCray also served as managing director of Caremark Physician Resources, directing its formation during its initial high-growth years prior to its sale to MedPartners Inc. He also co-founded OnCall Medicine Inc., a medical house calls company. Prior to his success as a business operator, he was a Managing Partner in his law firm, and a partner in a predecessor and transactional legal and consulting services to the healthcare industry for more than 20 years.

Muhammad Nauman, MD, MS, has 13 years of experience in research, IT and the healthcare environment. Dr. Nauman completed his medical diploma at Dow University of Health Sciences and worked as an ICU and ER physician. He was involved in the identification of molecular basis of X-chromosome inactivation at The Johns Hopkins University and the determination of the effects of lack of sleep on acute illness and trauma at Good Samaritan Hospital. Dr. Nauman currently serves in the Board of Directors at the HIMSS Greater Chicago Chapter (GCC HIMSS). He also is an instructor with American Heart Association and a member of All Pakistani Physicians of North America. He received the Health Innovation Award, a graduate scholarship from GCC HIMSS, and was a presenter at the fifth annual health IT event. He has also participated in different conferences in different roles including the AMIA 2013 Annual Conference, IHE NA Connectathon 2013, HIMSS13 and RSNA 2013. He recently finished his graduate studies in health informatics and consults in different projects involving EHR, PHR and mobile health applications.

Malinda Peeples, MS, RN, CDE, is Vice President of Clinical Advocacy at WellDoc Inc. Ms. Peeples, an informatics nurse specialist and certified diabetes educator, coordinates clinical outreach, grant and research programs, and professional organization activities at WellDoc. Previously, Ms. Peeples served as president of the American Association of Diabetes Educators, where she advanced the strategic direction of the organization to incorporate behavior change as a key outcome of diabetes education. As a research fellow in healthcare informatics at The Johns Hopkins School of Medicine, she developed taxonomy of chronic disease patient education that has been applied to mobile messaging content.

Joanne Peter, MBChB, MPhil, is Deputy Director of the Mobile Alliance for Maternal Action (MAMA). She joined MAMA as the in-country lead for MAMA South Africa, where she helped define and launch a suite of mobile services that now provides health information to almost 100,000 low-income mothers. Previously, Dr. Peter spent four years at Google.org, where she focused on using technology to address global health challenges and managed $20 million in grant funding. Dr. Peter was awarded her medical degree cum laude from the University of Cape Town and read for an MPhil in Development Studies as a Rhodes Scholar at Oxford University.

Tommaso Piazza, PhD, graduated summa cum laude in Managerial Engineering in Palermo, Italy, where he also completed a doctorate in Production Management in 2004. In 2001, he joined the University of Pittsburgh Medical Center (UPMC) Italy. In 2006, he became CIO of UPMC Italy and ISMETT with the goal of ISMETT becoming one of the first paperless hospitals in Europe. In 2010, it had reached Stage Six in the HIMSS EMR Adoption Model. He is actively cooperating with AISIS (Italian Association of CIO) and serves in the governing council of HIMSS Analytics Europe.

Steven R. Steinhubl, MD, is a Professor and the Director of Digital Medicine at Scripps Translational Science Institute (STSI) and a cardiologist at the Scripps Clinic in LaJolla, CA. He is a Purdue-trained engineer who then received his MD at St. Louis University, followed by an Internal Medicine residency at David Grant USAF Medical Center and General and Interventional Cardiology training at the Cleveland Clinic. Dr. Steinhubl has been principal investigator or helped lead more than a dozen large-scale, international randomized trials, and has authored nearly 200 peer-reviewed manuscripts, as well as numerous book chapters and abstracts.

Stacey Succop, MPH, PMP, has been working in global health for more than 10 years. The majority of her research and project work has focused on family planning, reproductive health and HIV prevention. Currently a Research Associate in the Social and Behavioral Sciences Department at FHI 360, she has served as Project Manager since 2012 for a portfolio of mHealth projects, including Mobile for Reproductive Health (m4RH). Ms. Succop earned a BA from Duke University and an MPH from the University of North Carolina at Chapel Hill Gillings School of Public Health, with a certificate in Global Health.

Marilyn Teplitz, MBA, FHIMSS, is the founder and principal of MGT Associates, LLC, a global management consulting firm providing B2B strategic and product business consulting to healthcare, life science, medical device and software companies. Worldwide clients range from startups to Fortune 100 companies including Avnet Technology Solutions, Encore Health Services, iSirona, McKesson and Wipro. Ms. Teplitz held senior management positions with Siemens Medical, McKesson, Ernst & Young, Motorola and Dignity Health where she introduced new products, improved operations and provided strategic consulting for businesses in the United States and globally. She holds an MBA from Wharton Business School and is a HIMSS Fellow.

Randy L. Thomas, FHIMSS, is a Service Line Executive for Encore Health Resources. Ms. Thomas has more than 25 years' experience in health IT with a focus on analytics and the re-use of data to support the performance improvement efforts of healthcare organizations. Having served in a variety of leadership roles in strategic consulting and product management, Ms. Thomas offers a seasoned perspective on how to drive measurable results through the use of business intelligence in healthcare. Ms. Thomas is the Service Line Executive for Health Analytics at Encore Health Resources. A HIMSS Fellow since 2002, Ms. Thomas received the Spirit of HIMSS Award in 2003 and the HIMSS 2004 John A. Page Outstanding Service Award.

William. C. Thornbury, Jr., MD, was a pharmacist that returned to study medicine at the University of Louisville, graduating summa cum laude. He completed work with Harvard Medical School at The Cambridge Hospital, and his post-doctoral training includes both General Surgery and Family Medicine. Dr. Thornbury's academic interest involves Lean systems in healthcare. His research includes the clinical application of mobile eVisit technology, and he is considered one of the world's leading authorities. He is the founder of Me-Visit Technologies, a company pledged to pioneer solutions to improve healthcare delivery and lower costs. Dr. Thornbury is an actively practicing physician, and has been named by his peers as the Citizen Doctor of the Year in Kentucky.

Siadeyo M.W. Torgbenu is a Program Officer at FHI 360 — Ghana, working in mHealth interventions. In this position, Ms. Torgbenu facilitates information communication technologies interventions to promote the health and well-being of PLHIV and key populations. She has an MSc Public Health in Health Promotion from Leeds Metropolitan University, United Kingdom, and her work in health promotion in the last decade revolves around using qualitative methods to advance health education (especially HIV) and development.

Heather Vahdat, MPH, has served as the co-investigator for m4RH since its inception and was actively involved in the development of message content as well as designing the architecture for message development. In addition, she led a project to adapt global family planning checklists for provision via mobile phone applications. She has served as the primary technology expert for mHealth projects at FHI 360 with experience in developing logic models and content for delivery via SMS, USSD, and mobile applications across multiple platforms. Ms. Vahdat has served as co-investigator for mobile technology studies including m4RH and ECINFO. She is a founding member of the mHealth Working Group and currently serves on the advisory board. Ms. Vahdat received her MPH from the University of North Carolina at Chapel Hill.

Giovan Battista Vizzini, MD, completed post-graduate studies in gastroenterology and hepatology at the University of Palermo in 1985. In 1999, he joined the University of Pittsburgh Medical Center (UPMC) Italy as attending physician in ISMETT. In 2002, he was appointed Chief of the Hepatology and Gastroenterology Unit of ISMETT, and in 2003, became Director of the Department of Medicine. His main fields of clinical and scientific interest are transplant hepatology, clinical epidemiology, evidence-based medicine, medical education and health IT. He has published more than 60 scientific articles in peer-reviewed journals and more than 40 books chapters.

Samuel Wambugu, MPH, is a public health specialist with 13 years of progressive experience in designing public health programs and implementing monitoring and evaluation systems of donor-funded programs with experience working in Kenya, South Africa, Liberia and Ghana. His experience includes designing studies, rolling them out according to design, and analyzing findings from evaluations and packages results for use in programming. He is passionate in the use of emerging mHealth tools and platforms. Mr. Wambugu holds an MPH specializing in Demography and Population Studies and is a Microsoft-certified professional (MCP) in database management.

Table of Contents

Acknowledgements xviii

Foreword xix
By Robert B. McCray

Introduction xxiv
By Rick Krohn, MA, MAS, and David Metcalf, PhD

Part I: mHealth and the Rise of Consumerism

Chapter 1: The mHealth Ecosystem 3
By Rick Krohn, MA, MAS, and David Metcalf, PhD

Chapter 2: Will the Convergence of Mobile and Consumer Engagement
Technologies Lead to Better Health Outcomes? An Analysis 11
By Lynne A. Dunbrack, MBA, MS

Chapter 3: Mobile Messaging and Behavioral Change: A Case Study 19
By John Fessler, MBA, and Tina Koro, MPH

Chapter 4: Using Mobile Texting to Change Social Behavior: A Case Study 29
By Noel Chandler, BA, and Marilyn Teplitz, MBA, FHIMSS

Chapter 5: Empowering Mobile Technology for Healthier Dietary Practices:
A Case Study 37
By Ellen Badinelli and Dave Dushyant

Chapter 6: Remodeling the Paradigm in Patient Engagement to Personalize
Interventions: An Analysis 45
By Doug Elwood, MD, MBA, and Jeffrey T. Heckman, DO

Chapter 7: Blue Button — Empowering Consumers for Shared Decision Making
and Improved Health: A Case Study 57
By Susan C. Hull, MSN, RN

Part II: The Drivers of Innovation

Chapter 8: The Drivers of mHealth Innovation 79
By David Metcalf, PhD

Chapter 9: Mobile Games for Health 85
By Brian Mayrsohn, MS, and Georges E. Khalil, MPH

Chapter 10: A Research-Driven Computer and Mobile Game for Health:
A Case Study 95
By Georges E. Khalil, MPH; Brian Mayrsohn, MS; and David Metcalf, PhD

Chapter 11: Zombies, Run! A Case Study 103
By Brian Mayrsohn, MS, and Elizabeth Lyons, PhD, MPH

Chapter 12: Toshiba America Medical Systems: A Case Study 111
  By Ross Gensler

Part III: The Intersection of Mobile Health & Traditional Medicine

Chapter 13: mHealth and Traditional Medicine: Collaboration and Collision 119
  By Rick Krohn, MA, MAS, and David Metcalf, PhD

Chapter 14: Effective Engagement with Mobile Messaging: A Case Study 125
  By Travis Good, MD, MBA, MS

Chapter 15: Mobile Prescription Therapy: A Case Study 131
  By Malinda Peeples, MS, RN, CDE, and Anand K. Iyer, PhD, MBA

Chapter 16: Getting Smart About Wellness Data: An Analysis 143
  By Randy L. Thomas, FHIMSS

Chapter 17: Home Monitoring After Liver Transplantation: A Case Study 149
  By Giovan Battista Vizzini, MD, and Tommaso Piazza, PhD

Part IV: mHealth as a Business

Chapter 18: Managing mHealth Innovation 159
  By Rick Krohn, MA, MAS, and David Metcalf, PhD

Chapter 19: The Business of mHealth 165
  By Rick Krohn, MA, MAS, and David Metcalf, PhD

Chapter 20: Implications of a Mobile-to-Mobile Online Delivery Model: A Case Study 173
  By William C. Thornbury, Jr., MD

Chapter 21: mHealth: Helping Doctors Treat the Underinsured: A Case Study ... 181
  By Joshua L. Conrad, PharmD

Part V: Standards, Security & Policy

Chapter 22: Mobile Health IT Standards 189
  By Keith Boone

Chapter 23: Mobile Security 199
  By Jeffrey L. Brandt, BSCS, GC-BMI

Chapter 24: Approaches to Policy: Organizational and Regulatory Perspectives in Mobile Health 215
  By Thomas Martin and Robert Jarrin

Chapter 25: Health App Certification: Frontline Lessons from the Self-Regulation Movement: An Analysis 223
  By Corey Ackerman and Sandra C. Maliszewski, MSN, JD, MBA, with Travis Froehlich, Evan Harary, Leslie Isenegger, and Michelle Jacobs

Chapter 26: Evaluating the Quality of mHealth Apps: A Case Study 233
By Muhammad Nauman, MD, MS

Part VI: Global Perspectives

Chapter 27: mHealth — A Global Perspective 249
By Rick Krohn, MA, MAS, and David Metcalf, PhD

Chapter 28: Using Mobile Technology to Educate and Empower Low-Income
Mothers and Families: A Case Study 255
By Joanne Peter, MBChB, MPhil

Chapter 29: Using Mobile Phones to Provide Critical Family Planning
Information in Africa: A Case Study 263
By Kelly L'Engle, PhD, MPH; Stacey Succop, MPH, PMP; and Heather Vahdat, MPH

Chapter 30: Improving Lives Through Mobile Phones in Ghana: A Case Study ... 273
By Kimberly Green; Nana Fosua Clement; Siadeyo M.W. Torgbenu; Gladys Damalin; Samuel Benefour; and Samuel Wambugu, MPH

Chapter 31: Brothers for Life's Mixed-Media Campaign Improves Voluntary
Male Medical Circumcision Services in South Africa Using a Mobile Information
Platform: A Case Study 279
By James BonTempo, MS, and Meredith Puleio DuBoff, MBA

Part VII: The Future of mHealth

Chapter 32: Where Mobile Health Technologies Are Needed in Healthcare 287
By Steven R. Steinhubl, MD

Chapter 33: Next-Generation Solutions in mHealth 297
By David Metcalf, PhD

Chapter 34: Designing an Open, Collaborative Platform to Transform
Productivity in an Era of Anywhere, Anytime Care: A Case Study 305
By Gautam Gulati, MD, MBA, MPH, and Will Comerford

Chapter 35: Innovation Cure for mHealth Barriers 315
By Douglas Goldstein and Gregg Masters, MPH

Chapter 36: Looking Ahead: An mHealth Roundtable Discussion 329
By Rick Krohn, MA, MAS, and David Metcalf, PhD

APPENDIX A
mHealth Apps: Functional Comparisons 337
By Muhammad Nauman, MD, MS

APPENDIX B
MAMA Community Spotlights 345
By Joanne Peter, MBChB, MPhil

Index 349

Acknowledgements

A book of this description is the product of many hands, and I would first like to thank the book's contributors — essayists, case study authors, thought leaders and my co-editor David Metcalf for their participation. I would also like to thank the staff of HIMSS and our HIMSS editor, Matt Schlossberg for their forbearance in shepherding this project to completion. Finally, I would like to thank my friends and family, and particularly my son Nick, without whose support and encouragement the writing of this book would not have been possible.

—*Rick Krohn*

I would like to thank all of the authors, editors, peer-review team and publishing team at HIMSS Books and mHIMSS, and the many other advisors, experts and contributors to this work. Your efforts speak for themselves in the quality of this volume. Special thanks to Matt Schlossberg from HIMSS Books for his tireless collaboration to drive the schedule and quality. Rick Krohn, it has been a pleasure working with you again on this second mHealth book.

Daily, I am thankful for my teams at both UCF College of Medicine and the Institute for Simulation and Training, Mixed Emerging Technology Integration Lab. The knowledge sharing and direct projects that informed my early understanding of mHealth has been invaluable. In particular, I'd like to thank Dean Deborah German, Jeanette Schrieber, Dr. Jonathan Kibble, Dr. Juan Cendan, Josue Rodas, the UCF College of Medicine Healthcare Innovation Club, UCF Mobile Makers, Dr. David Rogers, Angela Hamilton, Mike Eakins, Devon Veller, Colin Forward, A.J. Ripin and the rest of the METIL team. Our friends and sponsors from Lake Nona Institute/Medical City, the U.S. Military, VA, Johnson & Johnson and throughout the mHealth ecosystem rallied around this effort to make it successful.

Most of all, I thank my lovely wife, Katy, and sons, Adam and Andrew, for their patience and teaching me about health on a daily basis, whether mobile-enabled or not. Finally, I thank Jesus Christ for the abilities and opportunities to make this book possible.

—*David Metcalf*

Foreword

Top-Down Technology Needs Bottom-Up Demand

By Robert B. McCray
Co-Founder, President and CEO, Wireless-Life Sciences Alliance

What is the state of mHealth? When will this market mature? How close is the inflection point when the market for mHealth products and services will deliver measurable returns to patients, consumers, payers and investors?

These questions are in the minds of entrepreneurs, investors, providers, patients and consumers. By whatever name[1] it is called, mHealth's status has moved from "what is it?" to "when will it produce outcomes?" Expectations are high. Some may be unattainable. Technology innovation is not the impediment to meeting expectations. We have an *adoption* issue.

Institutions and consumers are slow to adopt tech-enabled solutions for common diseases if changes in workflow or behavior are required. Moreover, much of the waste in healthcare spending[2] is accounted as revenue to thousands of organizations whose leadership, employees, owners and policy representatives are incentivized to maintain the status quo insofar as they benefit.

Nonetheless, key elements necessary to the disruption of the *healthcare* market and creation of the *health* market are in place. Like energy, automobiles, retail and other industries, the healthcare sector will not be able to permanently sustain overpriced products and services for phantom or avoidable demand. Like those industries, the disruption of *healthcare* and creation of the *health* market will be driven by consumers who are equipped with digital knowledge and tools and motivated by passion, self-interest and economics. As with other industries, "outsiders" help consumers start the disruption and smart industry insiders will adapt to succeed. Non-adapters will fail.

What are the elements of connected healthcare disruption?
- Transparency and knowledge. It is now government policy to make information about the cost and quality of healthcare products and services available to the public.[3] Digital technologies and the Internet make it as easy to deliver this information in impactful ways to consumers as it is to deliver any other form of content.
- Economics. Consumers are increasingly responsible for a rising portion of their own healthcare costs.[4] Employers cannot sustain the cost of healthcare for

their employees and retirees. Governments are going broke due to the cost of healthcare.[5]
- Consumer demand. People want health. From time to time they need healthcare (though perhaps not as much as they previously thought). Consumers hate paying for healthcare, but as they are being forced to accept financial responsibility they gravitate to the resources that are affordable and convenient, features that are rarely associated with government or the healthcare sector. A massive shift in popular thinking about healthcare is underway that will generate the bottom-up, consumer-driven demand for the institutional and policy changes necessary to enable consumers to get what they want.
- Technology. Technology innovation, which is a top-down process, is creating the tools that will deliver what consumers want. It is offering ways to measure outcomes, improve quality, make diagnosis less expensive and personalize therapeutic approaches to increase the likelihood of success.

While the process is slow and the results will not be perfect, I take it as a given that healthcare will be improved due to the application of these forces. Waste will be reduced as diagnosis becomes more organized, therapies are more personalized and unnecessary services are avoided. mHealth will play an important role in this development of a connected healthcare system as it enables the long-recognized value of making healthcare more patient-centric and continuous.

mHealth is equally important to the much larger opportunity that I envision — the establishment of the connected health market.

Connected health focuses on the goal (health) more than a specific product or service (healthcare). It recognizes that the best solution to a health problem may not be more healthcare. It empowers individuals and families to take charge of their own health and avoid the need for healthcare services. This is the big shift in thinking that drives change. The addressable market that is related to this shift is the one-half (or more — estimates range to 70 percent) of healthcare spending that is caused by lifestyle/behavior. mHealth tools are key to this shift because they connect users to data, knowledge, coaching and all the support services that help people to maintain healthier lifestyles.

The healthcare sector will not create the market that reduces the demand for its own products and services. Hospitals and doctors are focused on treating illness and injury where people are "patients." They do not understand "consumers."

We can look to the history of other business sectors to understand the elements that will drive the creation of a new market and transform an old one. The common elements are knowledge of better products or approaches to meeting a set of needs, the technology to deliver them, and the energy of consumer movements that demand access to the new market and pay for them. This demand in turn fuels investor interest, entrepreneurs and policy changes.

The energy industry is an example. Prior to the 1970s, U.S. energy policy was driven by a primary goal of simply producing or acquiring more power supply. Then a shift in our thinking occurred and energy costs as a percentage of GDP peaked in 1981 at almost 14 percent of GDP, but declined to 6 percent in 1998 during a long period of continuous growth in the U.S. economy.[6]

What happened to drive this success? Starting in the 1970s, economists and environmentalists created a change in our thinking to focus on increasing the *output* of energy use (HVAC, lighting and productive capacity) rather than just energy capacity. This established the conservation and clean-tech sectors and achieved virtually steady state spending (as a percent of GDP) on energy for 40 years while the GDP increased 400 percent.

Compare this success with healthcare spending which as a percentage of GDP doubled over this period while chronic disease more than doubled[7] and the percentage of the population that is uninsured grew by approximately 60 percent.[8]

The auto industry is another example of success. Compared to those built and sold in the 1970s, cars today are safer, better equipped, more fuel efficient, cleaner and more fun to drive. At the same time, they are cheaper in real dollar terms (compare a 1970 Volkswagen beetle with a Toyota Prius). In the 1970s the competition from better and cheaper foreign vehicles began the destruction of the U.S. auto industry. Citizen movements (Ralph Nader for safety, MADD for impaired driving) accelerated these market forces and drove the adoption of key policy changes and expectations. Industry was pleased to respond to these developments with new products and services and ultimately the U.S. auto sector joined in, completing its "creative destruction."

Knowledge of a better way to achieve a desired goal fueled by the self-interest and passion of consumers led to the adoption of the laws, financing and regulatory features that enabled our progress in energy and automobiles (and entertainment, consumer electronics, retailing, publishing and a host of other sectors).

However, skeptics will suggest that these forces cannot work in healthcare where the expertise is so unbalanced and because of the weak results of programs for healthy behavior change. Prevention and wellness programs historically underperform against expectations and this has lead to a common belief that we should not expect substantial reductions in healthcare demand from favorable population-level changes in behavior. This is short sighted. We are already benefiting from such changes in population behavior.

Consider driving safety. The technology of cars makes them more likely to avoid an accident (ABS brakes) and safer in a crash (airbags and rigid structures). However, two major changes in public behavior have also contributed to the decreased rate of fatal traffic accidents: 1.) seat-belt usage increased from zero to 75 percent today; and 2.) drunk driving is no longer socially acceptable.[9]

Another example involves smoking and lung cancer. The U.S. smoking rate at the beginning of the 1970s was over 40 percent. Today it is less than 20 percent.[10] This smoking reduction has led to a 40 percent decrease in lung cancer rates.[11] That is, 40 percent of the demand for healthcare services related to lung cancer has been eliminated through changes in behavior. This was a consumer-driven achievement supported by policy (place restrictions), taxes (applied to ad campaigns and healthcare) and culture (led by the entertainment industry, smoking became unwelcome and uncool in many homes).

All the same elements are at play in connected health empowered by mHealth technologies. Multiple web sites are delivering information about the quality and cost of healthcare to consumers.[12] Early adopters of medical and consumer technologies that enable personal measurement of activity, vital signs and other data that may be relevant to health (the "quantified self" movement) are demanding more personal control over their health and a more personalized healthcare system. Thought leaders such as Dr. Eric Topol and Dr. Donald Berwick are articulating the insider's case for the transformation of healthcare.

The beginnings of smart consumer spending can be seen in the "engaged health consumer" who is willing to spend her own money on products and services that she believes will lead to a more healthful life. The supplement industry and brands such as Whole Foods, Lulemon, Garmin and Nike are winners in this market. For these people, health is personal, it is "cool" to be concerned about personal health. They may be strong influencers within their communities. An mHealth device has been anointed by an arbiter of fashion as "A list" technology for fashion insiders.[13] In a recently reported study, chain restaurants that reduced their calorie counts improved same store sales by 5 percent, while chains that did not do so suffered declines of 5 percent.[14]

The promise of mHealth is that it will enable a shift in our culture that reverses the growth of obesity, diabetes, heart disease and other behavior-driven chronic diseases. It has a critical role to serve in the education and empowerment of consumers to become engaged in their own health and to empower them to take greater control of their own healthcare.

mHEALTH INNOVATION: BEST PRACTICES FROM THE MOBILE FRONTIER delivers a comprehensive overview of the landscape of relevant issues including innovation, adoption, outcomes and regulation. Editors Rick Krohn and David Metcalf have assembled a diverse group of authors from among the creators of the new and better health world that we collectively envision. I have personally worked with many of them. These are important voices to which the reader should listen.

Rob McCray
San Diego

REFERENCES

1. Note on terminology. Multiple terms are used to describe the influence of technology on healthcare. Commonly used adjectives include *mobile* or *m*, *digital*, *wireless*, and *electronic*. The author prefers *connected health* as the term which best describes the source of value derived from the convergence of technology and healthcare, including mobile communications infrastructure, digitized information, big data, cloud-based systems and behavioral economics. It is also relevant to the human dimension of the matter. Technology is an enabler; good health is the goal.

2. National Research Council. *The Healthcare Imperative: Lowering Costs and Improving Outcomes: Workshop Series Summary*. Washington, DC: The National Academies Press, 2010.

3. CMS. Medicare Provider Charge Data 2011. Available at: www.cms.gov/Research-Statistics-Data-and-Systems/Statistics-Trends-and-Reports/Medicare-Provider-Charge-Data/index.html. Accessed September 12, 2013.

4. OECD. Key Indicators, OECD Health Data 2012. Available at: http://stats.oecd.org/index.aspx?DataSetCode=HEALTH_STAT. Accessed September 12, 2013.

5. Chernew ME, Baicker K, Hsu J. The spector of financial Armageddon—healthcare and federal debt in the United States. *New England Journal of Medicine*; 2010; 362: 1166-1168.

6. Energy Information Administration. Annual Energy Review 2011. Available at: www.eia.gov/totalenergy/data/annual/pdf/aer.pdf. Accessed September 12, 2013.

7. DeVol R, Bedroussian A. An unhealthy America: the economic burden of chronic disease. Milken Institute. Available at: www.milkeninstitute.org/healthreform/pdf/AnUnhealthyAmericaExecSumm.pdf. Accessed September 12, 2013.

8. Health Insurance Coverage Trends, 1959 – 2007, Estimates from the National Health Interview Survey, National Health Statistics Reports Number 17, July 2009. Available at: www.cdc.gov/nchs/data/nhsr/nhsr017.pdf. Accessed September 12, 2013.

9. In 2011, the rate of alcohol-impaired driving fatalities per 100,000 population was 3.2, representing a 65 percent decrease since 1982, according to The Century Council, a trade group. Available at: www.centurycouncil.org/drunk-driving/drunk-driving-statistics. Accessed September 12, 2013.

10. National Center for Health Statistics. Health, United States, 2007. With chart book on trends in the health of Americans. Hyattsville, MD: National Center for Health Statistics; 2007. Available at: www.cdc.gov/nchs/data/hus/hus07.pdf. Accessed September 12, 2013.

11. U.S. Department of Health & Human Services. The Health Consequences of Smoking. A Report of the U.S. Surgeon General. 2004.

12. www.zocdoc.com, www.castlighthealth.com, patientfusion.com, www.nerdwallet.com.

13. Malle C. Vogue. September 2013. Available at: www.vogue.com/vogue-daily/article/band-of-insiders-how-the-nike-fuelband-became-the-a-lists-chicest-accessory/#1. Accessed September 12, 2013.

14. Hudson Institute, Lower-Calorie Foods, It's Just Good Business. February 2013.

Introduction

It's not often that we get to witness, let alone recognize, a watershed moment in U.S. healthcare. But that moment is upon us. At incredible speed and with an uncharacteristic display of industry innovation, mobile healthcare has within a few short years been catapulted to healthcare's center stage. Mobile health (described here as mHealth) is an anomaly among health IT solutions — it's cheap, scalable and accessible, it is highly configurable and endlessly adaptive, and most importantly — it is highly effective. Few technologies have the potential to radically alter the processes of traditional healthcare in so many areas — clinical workflows and healthcare delivery, patient engagement and consumerism among others — as mobile solutions. Mobile is inserting itself into ever more granular aspects of everyday living, with healthcare providing a seemingly limitless template for mobile innovation.

mHealth and its wellspring of industry innovation isn't just a disruptive force in healthcare — it's a *displacement* force that is reinventing healthcare delivery. mHealth is personalizing healthcare by virtue of its convenience, connectivity, clinical and economic coherence. Its organizing principle is alignment — alignment of the inputs to healthcare — the verticals, the venues, the spectrum of caregivers, the technologies, the workflows — within an integrated, interoperable system architecture that is efficient and accessible. In sum, the cascading effect of mHealth innovation is changing the way that each of us experience healthcare.

mHealth innovation is being driven by the tech sector, by the never-ending search for efficiency and cost savings in an industry riddled with waste, by a surge in entrepreneurship unbound by healthcare's formidable barriers to entry, by a vision of healthcare delivery viewed through a retail lens, by the need to discover new ways to improve healthcare access and quality, and by overwhelming demand from consumers.

The tools of mobile computing — smartphones and PDAs, tablet PCs, patient monitoring devices, and an avalanche of apps among them — are opening new vistas of opportunity for clinical collaboration and public health. It's an evolutionary cycle — telemedicine, voice recognition and home monitoring have been around for years, but the current wave of mHealth product innovation is being driven by the convergence of form, function, a burst of entrepreneurship and favorable economics. mHealth devices have made dramatic leaps forward in terms of cost, bulk, weight, durability and performance, and there are thousands of mobile apps for healthcare already on the market, with more on the way. They include e-prescribing, medical calculators, decision support tools, personal health records, health and fitness apps, and patient medical and eligibility queries, for starters.

But mHealth innovation is more than just a technology play — it's about transforming healthcare at a foundational level. These solutions support new treatment modalities, such as accountable care organizations (ACO), health information exchanges (HIE) and patient-centered medical homes. They recast the terms of healthcare delivery by extending the reach of the healthcare enterprise, by reinventing diagnostic and treatment processes, and by creating new provider-patient touch points. And significantly, mHealth is democratizing healthcare, giving people the ability to understand and play an active role in addressing their health issues. mHealth provides a mechanism for healthcare consumers — patients with both temporary and chronic health issues as well as the healthcare conscious, the family caregiver and the "worried well" — to become responsible stewards of their own health.

And after an uncertain beginning, mHealth is becoming a viable economic proposition. During its rapid ascendancy, the main economic driver of mHealth has been the consumer and the primary class of solution: the retail app. That market dynamic is now shifting, as mHealth proves its worth. Payers are increasingly reimbursing providers for services like eVisits, and rewarding members for behavioral change and self-care via mobile tools. Healthcare facilities are imbedding mobile solutions into their operations, producing benefits in resource efficiency, patient engagement and satisfaction, clinical quality and cost savings. Providers are using mHealth tools to supplement staff resources, to manage patients more effectively, and to create brand preference. Governments are employing mHealth tools to promote population health, to increase access to underserved populations, and to address critical health issues. Finally, consumers and patients with chronic conditions are becoming increasingly accountable for their own health, and are willing to pay for mHealth tools that allow them to more effectively manage and maintain their health status.

Perhaps most tellingly about the value of mHealth is the fact that it is a global phenomenon, with some of the most innovative solutions being deployed in the developing world, or "global south." As detailed in a later chapter, in general terms, global south has a dearth of healthcare resources and populations who are at risk for many diseases that are largely unknown in the developed world. What these countries do have are widely distributed wireless networks and access to cheap mobile devices. Leveraging mobile communications and pervasive mobile access (mainly via feature phones), mHealth solutions have been deployed for wellness and prevention, chronic disease management, eVisits, field staff management and much more. This phenomenon illustrates the central features of mHealth innovation — almost limitless opportunities to reshape healthcare and an immediate global impact.

This is a hinge moment in healthcare — a golden opportunity to reinvent care delivery to cure the industry's ills and deliver a quantum leap in both clinical quality and outcomes. And this transformation is not being led by a select group of visionaries or healthcare pioneers — it's happening right now, across the broad expanse of healthcare, by those at the point of care — the provider, the patient and the consumer.

We have only scratched the surface of mHealth's potential to reshape healthcare delivery and the cumulative health of entire populations. At the point of care, in the home, in the field, on the fly, mHealth is fundamentally changing the way that healthcare occurs. Since the writing of our first book on mHealth two years ago, the landscape has changed dramatically. With the rush of pilot programs and early promise also comes false hopes and unmet expectations that cannot be ignored. How do we evaluate the effectiveness of programs? Do we assign greater weight to health outcomes and evidence, ROI/cost savings or elegant technology solutions? How do we know which innovations might succeed? Our editorial focus has been to follow the natural market curves of emerging technologies and seek out examples that show evidence of the potential to have health outcomes impact; meet the Triple Aim of better, faster and cheaper care; and scale far beyond pilot stage in a sustainable way. We are on a precipice that requires delicate balance to keep moving fast with the industry and emerging technologies, while measuring and validating examples. In these pages, with many voices, it is our intent to demonstrate how global healthcare is undergoing a seismic shift — a new paradigm — via mHealth innovation.

mHealth Innovation: Best Practices from the Mobile Frontier is organized around seven major topics that are shaping the roadmap of mHealth innovation. They are: the mHealth ecosystem and its principle features; the drivers of mHealth and their impact on the course of innovation; the intersection of mHealth and traditional medicine; the business of mHealth; mHealth standards and regulation; a global perspective on mHealth; and finally a look ahead at mHealth's future. With an array of contributors, each topic area includes a leading discussion, guest analysis and case studies. It is our hope that mHealth Innovation: Best Practices from the Mobile Frontier will create awareness and inspire innovation within the healthcare community, and spark creative thinking about healthcare's problems — and possible mHealth solutions.

Rick Krohn, MA, MAS
David Metcalf, PhD

Part I
mHealth and the Rise of Consumerism

Chapter 1

The mHealth Ecosystem

By Rick Krohn, MA, MAS, and David Metcalf, PhD

For the past 100 years, the U.S. healthcare system has been constructed around the hospital as its central figure — a care model that has been a study in inefficiency (Fig. 1-1). Reactive, waste-ridden, unevenly performing and economically nonsensical, we are now faced with a stark truth: the U.S. healthcare system in its current incarnation, a system of facility-based, wildly expensive, hopelessly fragmented, episodic care is insufficient to the task of improving our nation's health. Healthcare demographics aren't in our favor either. An aging population, clinical staff shortages, cost inflation, and uneven quality are leading us toward a potential healthcare tsunami. New estimates from the Office of the Actuary at the Centers for Medicare and Medicaid Services (CMS) project that aggregate healthcare spending in the United States will grow at an average annual rate of 5.8 percent for 2012-22, or 1 percentage point faster than the expected growth in the gross domestic product (GDP). The healthcare share of GDP by 2022 is projected to rise to 19.9 percent from its 2011 level of 17.9 percent. In

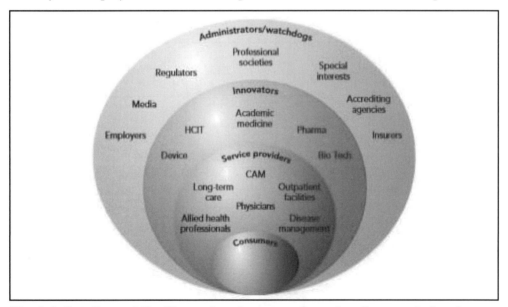

Fig. 1-1: Our Current Healthcare Landscape — Complex, Fragmented and Antiquated.

(From Deloitte Center for Health Solutions, 2010. Used with permission.)

other words, healthcare as a percentage of GDP is growing, while healthcare inflation exceeds the CPI rate, and is well ahead of the average wage increase.

What is needed to reverse this trend is a healthcare delivery model with a greater array of provider-patient touch points; with more active patient engagement and empowerment; with better care coordination; with a bias toward wellness and prevention; with tools for self care; with a recalibration of incentives; and with the capability of achieving behavioral change across the spectrum of healthcare stakeholders. The true promise of mHealth is a balance between emerging technologies and process innovations coupled with evidence of outcomes in health/quality, cost, and efficiency, and unlocking the power of mobile through global scalability that matches the potential impact that so many mobile devices can deliver (Fig. 1-2). Imagine any phone in someone's hand becoming their "hPhone" and unlocking access to the best information wellness and treatment have to offer.

The conceptual framework for this new model of care is patient-centered healthcare — it's become an industry mantra — a catchphrase to describe the forces that are transforming the industry, whether they are coming from Washington, from payers, providers, patients or consumers. Taken in part, these forces are nibbling at the edges of a wholesale restructuring of healthcare delivery. But viewed in their entirety, these forces do constitute a sea change in healthcare — the first major shift in healthcare delivery since the introduction of Medicare. The ultimate aim — a patient-centered healthcare ecosystem.

In a general context, a patient-centered ecosystem describes the interplay of many factors, including the environment, personal attributes and relationships, cultural influences, technology and health resources that affect individual health status. The idea of an ecosystem in which the patient lies at the solid center envisions an environment of comprehensive, high-quality, convenient, affordable, personalized and accessible care. In this ecosystem patients and consumers are empowered through education, knowledge and tools to be their own health managers. And in a radical departure

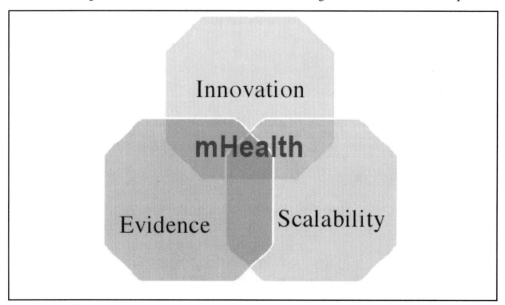

Fig. 1-2: Components of an mHealth Ecosystem.

from traditional medicine, the ecosystem places a primary emphasis on education, health promotion, wellness and prevention, as well as self-management (Fig. 1-3).

It's a compelling idea: by aligning the inputs to healthcare finance and delivery, everyone can benefit — not least the patient. Payers can benefit by incenting wellness, prevention, behavior change and early interventions (and in so doing, cut costs) as part of a program to shift provider reimbursement methodology from volume of services performed to value delivered (as measured by outcomes, readmits, etc.). Providers can benefit from efficient care coordination, from patient satisfaction, and from financial incentives tied to pay-for-performance. Patients benefit from better care and from a more active role in their own health management. This construct translates seamlessly to the mobile space.

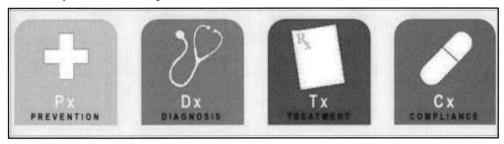

Fig. 1-3: The mHealth Patient Continuum.

Taken one step further, an *mHealth ecosystem* is about extending access and remote connectivity within the industry — it's about engagement among providers, with patients and consumers, with payers and employers, public health and social services — with every healthcare industry stakeholder. In both clinical and business applications, mHealth is aimed at the creation of a connected healthcare ecosystem through the integration of mobile communication, transactions and knowledge. This community includes payers, providers, consumers, vendors and telecommunications. It harnesses the collective power of enabling technology, efficient resource allocation, clinical decision support and persistent patient care. And at its heart, the mHealth ecosystem addresses healthcare's most intractable problems — unsustainable cost inflation and uneven clinical quality.

The mHealth ecosystem is characterized by innovation in care delivery, robust care teams and heightened clinical collaboration, an epidemiological health perspective (including population health, prevention and wellness), utilitarian technology solutions and consumerism. Most importantly, it is about recasting the terms of healthcare delivery by placing the patient in the solid center. "Nothing about me, without me" captures the conceptual framework of a healthcare ecosystem in which the patient is the central figure. In the mHealth ecosystem, information is now portable, personalized and participatory, making it a perfect complement to the patient-centric model of healthcare — unbound by age, location or economic strata. In the mHealth ecosystem, information isn't pushed or pulled; it's shared persistently and pervasively. Healthcare information is shared in real-time between providers, patients and consumers in bilateral flows, but can include a larger universe of stakeholders including payers, employers, public health, social services, researchers, solutions providers, partners, supply chain and more. That industry dynamic is currently in play, but it has yet to achieve maturity. Fig. 1-4 describes the ever-growing touchpoints in the mHealth ecosytem.

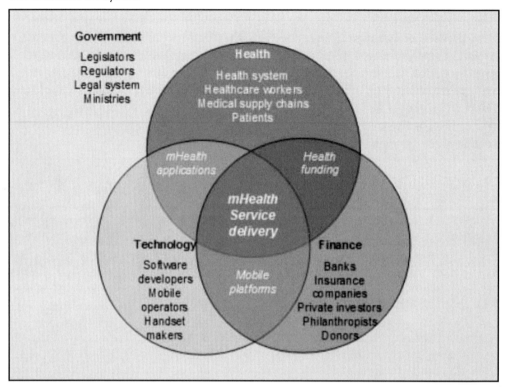

Fig. 1-4: The mHealth Ecosystem is Created through the Collision of Three Sectors — Health, Technology and Finance — with the Backdrop of Government Policy and Regulation.

For the mHealth ecosystem to reach its fullest expression, the number one issue that must be addressed is defining, attracting and retaining the customer — and that customer might be a government agency, an insurer, a hospital system, a provider, a patient or a consumer. The mHealth end user is unlike the traditional buyer of healthcare services, because where traditional healthcare is sold on a B2B or B2C basis, mHealth is largely a retail market. It must be sold on the strength of one or more of these qualities — connectivity, clinical collaboration, convenience and cost. And we're still in the opening stages of mHealth market development — it's worth noting that we are still climbing the curve of the hype cycle. Fig. 1-5 describes the forces that are influencing both the image and reality of the mHealth market, both now and in the coming months.

Although clinicians — mainly doctors and nurses — account for a proportion of mHealth market growth, the primary driver to date has been the consumer. They are not just buying smartphones and tablets in stores and online, they're buying apps, medical devices and services. But in healthcare, direct-to-consumer has had a mixed record of success. For several years, an ongoing problem obstructing the patient-centric model of healthcare has been getting the healthcare consumer — not only the

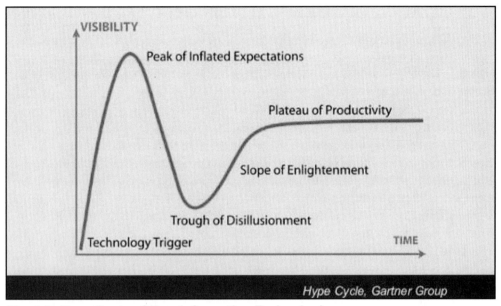

Fig. 1-5: Hype Cycle of New Information Technologies.

patient with issues, but the enlightened public as well — actively engaged in digital health. To date the patient portal hasn't proven to be the form horse of consumer engagement, and neither has the personal health record (PHR). Why? Because in the main consumers choose to avoid the tedium of entering and maintaining their own health data. That user experience is not taking shape in the mobile space, in part due to the digital convergence — the intersection of the professional and personal applications of mobile that is a growing phenomenon. The user — the provider, the patient, the consumer — is comfortable with mobile devices and apps, appreciates the convenience of their use, and is easily engaged in the collection and sharing of their health data. As a result, the healthcare consumer is gravitating towards the center of the care process. It is this trend — grassroots demand across the healthcare spectrum — that will sustain the continued growth of the mHealth ecosystem.

However, we're not there yet. It's going to take a wholesale restructuring of healthcare delivery to achieve an mHealth ecosystem. That includes culture change on the part of payers, providers and patients; a new definition of clinical "value" based on mass personalization of the care experience; partnerships that deliver collaborative, coordinated care; and team-based care delivered through new care systems, including PCMH, the ACO and HIE. It's going to take a realignment of payment incentives tied to the shift from volume to value as the primary metric of reimbursement, with attendant tools to measure and manage. It's going to take interoperability and connectivity of information systems and information channels. And finally, it all must translate into improved operating efficiencies and bottom line revenue in order to succeed. The mHealth ecosystem is still in a formative stage and some prime determinants — standards, security layers, compliance and regulation — will have a heavy influence on the adoption curve and the proliferation of mHealth solutions.

THE CATALYST OF THE mHEALTH ECOSYSTEM: INNOVATION

mHealth is premised on the notion that healthcare is not restricted by its traditional boundaries, and that technologies, processes and roles in healthcare can be architected in wholly new ways. In an industry that has been hidebound for decades in an antiquated philosophy of healthcare delivery, that's a truly novel idea. It's a huge challenge: healthcare has lagged far behind other industries in the application of technology solutions, and has been seemingly incapable of removing the silos of information care, and stakeholders that create barriers to change. In fairness, the industry is not homogenous (like banking or retail) and presents enormous barriers to wholesale restructuring — from finance to asset allocation. And the record of technology solutions in healthcare doesn't inspire confidence — when solutions like EMR, CPOE and e-prescribing have been introduced, they often fail to live up to their advance billing. The widespread industry skepticism about technology's ability to cure healthcare's ills is founded on a mixed historical record, so what does this bode for mHealth?

First, it must be noted that mHealth is simply unlike any other class of healthcare technology. For the most part, mHealth solutions don't rely on expensive proprietary technology sourced from a single vendor — so they do not require a sizable, irreversible capital investment. And unlike other technology solutions whose foremost purpose is to digitize manual processes, mHealth is oriented around re-engineering processes with technology acting as an enabler. That's a critical distinction — mHealth is not about technology as the solution, it's about technology as a component part of a process solution.

mHealth is also distinctive in two of its foundational attributes — connectivity and communication. Whereas many technology solutions are standalone or M2M, mHealth is unique in its capability to create connectivity among healthcare's stakeholders, for care coordination, for patient engagement, for resource allocation, for chronic disease management, for self care, for population health and wellness, for event response — the list keeps growing. It creates channels of communication that are pervasive and persistent, and remove the silos of information, care and access as barriers to efficient service delivery.

mHealth is unique in its ability to capture, store and communicate healthcare information at the point of care, across platforms, among a host of devices, and all in real-time. It makes healthcare an ongoing process, removes barriers to provider/patient communication and collaboration, and democratizes both access to and management of care. It also allows patients and consumers to act as stewards of their own care, in concert with the provider community, with affinity groups and with family members. As patients and consumers take ownership of their care via mHealth tools, they become more accountable for the outcomes of their health management. That's a key objective of patient-centered care — to make the healthcare consumer an active participant in maintaining his or her own health.

mHealth is characterized by four attributes — connectivity, clinical collaboration, convenience and cost — that make the user experience engaging across the spectrum of healthcare services. mHealth is endlessly adaptive and scalable, which makes solution development possible from the most discrete app to a global solution. And from a business perspective, mHealth addresses the critical components of success with innovation — the linkage between product or service excellence and economic rationality (Fig. 1-6).

Finally, mHealth leverages existing consumer electronics, public communication and network infrastuctures. It makes use — efficient use — of commercial devices, most notably mobile phones, whether they are smartphones or feature (text and voice) phones. It communicates with people where they are, with tools they can use, at an acceptable cost. And it taps into the widespread development of mobile networks, even in the poorest countries, to make broadcast engagement a realistic prospect.

That combination of availability and affordability makes mHealth solutions viable,

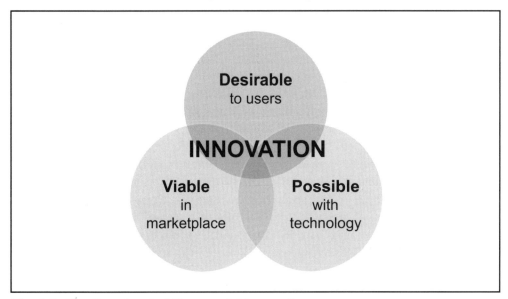

Fig. 1-6: The Construct of Successful Innovation.

in terms of cost and access, to entire populations, regardless of economic strata, geographic isolation or technological sophistication.

It is these "brand identifiers" of mHealth that make it such a rich template for innovation. And because the universe of healthcare services is so broad, and the gaps in care so great, there is an elegant need-meets-opportunity aspect to mHealth's growth and diversification. mHealth solutions can be conceptualized, developed, pressure tested and commercialized within a matter of months. The barriers to entry are remarkably low. Often these solutions are developed outside the mainstream of health IT, on a shoestring, by entrepreneurs with little direct healthcare experience. These startups — or upstarts — have brought fresh thinking, inter-industry and interdisciplinary experience to the task of making healthcare transactions — knowledge, education, treatment, prevention and finance — more efficient. It's this wellspring of new thinking being applied to old problems that is making mHealth the rising star of health IT. And the result: mHealth innovation is emerging as the single most transformative force in healthcare today.

Returning to the theme of the mHealth ecosystem, it can be readily understood that innovation is shaping the ecosystem in terms of process, location, interoperability and impact. The tools of mHealth have already established a firm foothold in areas such as wellness and chronic disease management, but they are growing organically into more diverse areas such as remote patient management, telehealth and mobile wallet. It is forward reaching in areas such as mobile imaging, augmented reality and body area networks. And the application of mHealth to gaps in care — from engaging the underserved and treating specific disease indications, to broadcasting educational and prevention messages to entire populations, is rapidly expanding the scope — and what is possible — within the mHealth ecosystem.

mHealth innovation isn't just shaping the ecosystem via groundbreaking technologies — it is also leveraging complimentary technologies. There are huge opportunities to bolt together boutique solutions within a mobile architecture. Several independent health technologies illustrate this point. Real-time location systems (RTLS) are being merged with mobile devices to accelerate patient throughput, manage staff, monitor at-risk family members and schedule utilization of high-value equipment. Speech recognition tools are being employed via mobile devices for documentation, charge capture, scheduling and notes. Mobile video conferencing mated with robotics has spawned a new market segment — telepresence. In each case — RTLS, speech recognition and video and all boutique health technologies — are innovating to perform in a mobile environment. mHealth solutions are being designed with the user experience in mind. For example, there are now biometric monitors that capture data via earbuds, mHealth coaches that intuitively modify care plans as new data is obtained, and non-invasive diabetes testing and reporting tools. We are constantly learning about new applications of mHealth solutions, of ways that healthcare delivery is being reinvented via mHealth solutions, and ways that mHealth is being married with complementary technologies to fundamentally alter healthcare's workflows, economics and the patient experience.

If we're looking for a window into the future of the mHealth ecosystem, we should reference the avalanche of progressive, innovative tools that are now in the developmental stage — tools like body area networks; integrated voice, text and video; mobile diagnostics; and advanced telemedicine. We should reference the insertion of mHealth throughout the fabric of healthcare, within discrete populations like long-term care, behavioral and correctional health, and with increasingly granular solutions aimed at second- and third-tier health issues. We should note the growing catalogue of mHealth customers — the consumer, the patient, and increasingly, the payer and provider. And finally, we should look internationally at the way mHealth has been a leapfrog technology in establishing a wireless healthcare delivery infrastructure in countries with a skeletal healthcare industry. Linking these to the Venn triumvirate in Fig. 1-2 — innovation, evidence and scalability — will unlock the promise of mHealth. Watch for these common themes to emerge throughout this book.

CHAPTER 2

Will the Convergence of Mobile and Consumer Engagement Technologies Lead to Better Health Outcomes? An Analysis

By Lynne A. Dunbrack, MBA, MS

Managing chronic conditions accounts for approximately 75 percent of all healthcare costs in the United States.[1] Since most chronic conditions are exacerbated by lifestyle choices, such as diet, exercise, smoking or substance abuse, if we are to bend the cost curve we need to engage consumers to take better care of themselves and make better health decisions. Prior attempts by healthcare organizations to reach consumers through web sites, reminders sent via print or interactive voice response (IVR) systems, or other forms of mass communication have had modest success at best.

Consumer engagement is challenging because a one-size-fits-all approach simply will not work. There are all types of consumers — from the blissfully unaware of their health status to the quantified-self consumer who dutifully records every step walked, morsel of food eaten, or hour slept and how well. Some consumers are not only managing their own health, but also their children's as well as elderly parents'. These consumers are often referred to as the "Sandwich Generation" and typically are the women in the family. Consumers living with a severe chronic condition or experiencing a health event such as pregnancy might be ready to take action. And then there are the consumers dwelling in a state of denial who do not want to change their behavior. Thus, to be effective, consumer engagement must entail the "five rights." It needs to (1) reach the right consumer, (2) at the right time, (3) with the right message, (4) for the right reason, and (5) on the right channel.

With cellphone use nearly ubiquitous — 91 percent of American adults use a cellphone and 55 percent of those phones are smartphones, according to Pew Internet surveys — that channel is increasingly a mobile device.[2] Mobile communication enables healthcare organizations to reach consumers wherever they are and according to their preferences, whether it's an e-mail message to someone who moves between fixed and mobile devices, a text message for a younger consumer who eschews phone and e-mail, or a voice call for someone who wants to talk with a live person.

THE CONVERGENCE OF mHEALTH AND TELEHEALTH

Consumers are becoming increasingly reliant on their mobile devices. It has been suggested by industry pundits and psychologists alike that consumers are becoming "addicted" to their mobile devices. On average, consumers look at their phones more than 150 times a day to check for messages, e-mail, news and alerts or missed voice calls; play games; watch videos; interact with their social network via Facebook; or share photos via Instagram. There is even a term for this relentless need to check-in — fear of missing out or "FOMA," originally coined by consumer behavior and brand strategy expert Dan Herman, PhD. Why not leverage this "addiction" to the mobile device and turn it into a channel for the delivery of a variety of telehealth services through a single pane of glass?

Opportunities to improve consumer engagement through the use of mobile technology include:

Text reminders. The most basic form of mobile communication is the SMS text message. Its use has grown exponentially because of the convenience, speed and ease of use. IDC forecasts that both multimedia message services (MMS) and short message services will continue to grow reaching more than 3.4 trillion messages per year by 2016.[3] Text messages can be used to send reminders, education and inspirational messages, and provide an opportunity for consumers to report symptoms or request to engage directly with a health coach by entering a keyword like "crave" or "lapse" if, for example, they are enrolled in a smoking cessation program. Clinical studies have shown that well-constructed texts for health programs can be effective and produce positive outcomes. For example, according to a randomized controlled trial conducted by researchers at the George Washington University School of Public Health and Health Services, 34 percent of text2quit users quit smoking after four weeks in the program.[4] Compare this to less than 5 percent of consumers who are able to quit without help. Voxiva, the developers of text2quit, also provides text services for maternal health (text4baby), children's health (text4kids), wellness (text4health) and diabetes (care4life).

Mobile health applications. There are tens of thousands of mobile health applications available on the public app stores of Apple, Blackberry, Google and Microsoft, as well as those available for download directly from healthcare organizations or other health-related web sites. These applications cover the gamut of health topics: fitness, health and wellness, weight loss, smoking cessation, mental health, women's and men's health, managing specific diseases like diabetes or asthma, the list goes on.

Forward-thinking payers and providers have deployed mobile apps for their members or patients, and even the community at large. Typical apps include mobile access to the healthcare organization's web site or member/patient portal. Michigan-based Priority Health was one of the first health plans to offer a mobile version of its member ID card. Members can view information about their PCP, add physicians to their contact list, and use click-to-call to dial their physician offices or customer support. Other common apps offered by healthcare organizations show wait times at the hospital's emergency room and provide the ability for consumers to search for nearby urgent care centers.

Remote health monitoring. Increasingly, remote health monitoring devices are becoming connected devices that can transmit biometric readings via Bluetooth and cellular connectivity. Machine-to-machine transmission ensures the veracity of the data (i.e., the consumer did not fudge or cherry-pick results to share with his clinician). The mobile device and the accompanying mobile health application serve as the data gateway, transmitting biometric readings to a back-end clinical system for further analysis and generation of alerts to the consumer, clinicians, or family caregivers as the situation warrants it. IDC Health Insights research findings suggest that more than one third of consumers who use a mobile phone are somewhat (23.3 percent) or extremely interested (13.6 percent) in a device that notified their provider.[5]

Convergence is also happening at the device level with cellular technology built into remote health monitoring devices. One such example is the Telcare Blood Glucose Meter (BGM), one of the first cellular-powered glucometers. Telcare BGM can automatically upload blood glucose readings wirelessly to Telserve, an FDA-cleared clinical data repository. After each blood test, a personalized message appears on the Telcare BGM providing clinical feedback and coaching at the teachable moment. MyTelcare.com is a patient portal that can be accessed from a PC, Mac or smartphone. Telcare BGM users can view their readings in an easy-to-read graphical format, print reports, as well as provide their physicians, care team, friends and family caregivers secure access to the portal. A provider portal offers a dashboard to help clinicians monitor their diabetic patients, and allows them to send customized messages to their patients using the Telcare service. An optional free smartphone application, MyTelcare Diabetes Pal App, is available in the Apple App Store and Google Play to consumers who use Telcare BGM, as well as other brands of glucometers. The mobile application helps consumers better manage their diabetes by tracking readings, nutrition, activity and notes. It can also send reminders to test. Early results from deployments are showing meaningful reductions in A1c levels and average daily blood glucose readings, as well as high levels of satisfaction from patients, their care teams and providers.

Wearable devices. Tapping into the quantified self movement is the growing popularity of health and fitness devices that can be wirelessly connected via Bluetooth to a mobile health application or used with a USB connection. As wearable devices with a variety of built-in sensors, they make it easy for consumers to keep track of the number of steps walked and distance covered, calories consumed and expended, body mass index (BMI), heart rate, blood pressure, and the duration and quality of sleep. Form factors include armbands, wrist bands, watches and clip-on devices which can feature lights or digital readout displays to show daily progress made towards certain objectives (e.g., number of steps walked, calories expended) and even provide inactivity alerts for deskbound consumers.

Healthcare organizations are exploring using wearable devices for a variety of cases such as health coaching, health and wellness programs, 30-day readmission mitigation, and even predicting length of stay for surgical patients. In January 2013, Cigna announced a pilot program using BodyMedia's armband and health coaching with four of its U.S. employer health plan customers to help manage 1,600 at-risk employees, reduce the risk of diabetes and improve the health of those with the disease. The Mayo Clinic ran a clinical trial testing the use of a consumer-grade accelerometer to measure patient mobility (e.g., ability to ambulate) during hospital recovery after cardiac surgery. Patients wore a FitBit to monitor how many steps they walked each day after their surgery. While not surprising that those patients who were able to ambulate sooner and further had shorter lengths of stay, there was a significant difference between patients identified as early as the second recovery day — who would be able to transition home independently and who would need to be discharged to a skilled nursing facility or home with healthcare. The researchers conclude that functional measures of recovery will be inevitable with changing reimbursement models, expanding accountable care organizations, and bundled payments.[6] The use of wearable devices provides not only an opportunity to measure recovery progress, but also to gauge discharge disposition.

Games for health. Health games and health gamification, while related, are not interchangeable terms. Highly interactive, health games combine entertainment with health education and employ game theory and game mechanics to create an engaging and enjoyable experience to drive or change specific behaviors. Gamification — a business strategy that is enabled by technology, not a technology itself, emerged from the computer and video game industry.

Many of the same game mechanics found in conventional games can be used effectively in mobile health games. Consumer progress toward a health objective is measured by achievement through the collection of points or movements through levels; bonuses are awarded for completing a task or goal. Accountability is created through public measurement of progress (or progression dynamic in game mechanic parlance) through a set of tasks or steps towards a health objective. These public measurements can include status, leaderboards and streaks. Consumers, especially competitive consumers, will stay engaged with the game and "play to win" to avoid scenarios that create some sense of loss of status (i.e, loss aversion dynamic). Infinite game play, where there is an emphasis on maintaining a positive state, is particularly useful in health games because there is no real stopping point for continuing healthy behaviors. Major healthcare organizations such as Humana, Kaiser and Optum offer healthcare games — both mobile and web-based — to appeal to consumers of all ages.

Socially connected health and wellness. There is a growing body of evidence that consumers' health status is influenced both positively and negatively by not only the company they keep, but their friends' friends as well. In their compelling research, social scientists Nicholas A. Christakis, MD, PhD, MPH, and James Fowler, MA, PhD, reveal how one's social networks can influence behavior and perceptions of norms resulting in social contagion, even among people who do not directly know each other. Connecting mobile health apps to social media sites like Facebook or Twitter help foster a sense of community among consumers using these tools to better manage their health. Consumers increasingly look to their social networks for health advice and information.

Health and wellness trackers can also be used in conjunction with mobile health applications to provide additional tools and opportunities for health coaching, and make it possible for consumers to share their success (and failed attempts) as they work toward achieving their health objectives. Biometric readings can also be shared with the consumer's social network via Facebook posts or Twitter feeds. Thus, the consumer's social network serves as cheerleaders, providing encouragement and holding their friends accountable for sticking with their health programs. BodyMedia,

FitBit, JawBone, Nike and Withings devices provide consumers the option of sharing some or all of their achievements on either Facebook or Twitter or both. FitBit takes it one step further and helps consumers discover who among their Facebook friends are also using FitBit and connects them.

Challenges and Recommendations

The use of mobile technology combined with various connected health technologies is still in the early stages for most providers and payers. One of the biggest challenges facing healthcare organizations today, but one that will ultimately drive investment in consumer engagement initiatives, is the shift from fee-for-service to value-based reimbursement. This is a turbulent time for healthcare organizations as they straddle two diametrically opposed reimbursement strategies and need to invest in new technologies to transform their care delivery models.

Healthcare organizations must first invest in analytics, health information exchange and a population management tool to support the evolving care and reimbursement models of accountable care and patient-centered medical homes. Once these underlying technologies are in place, healthcare organizations will also be positioned to pursue consumer engagement initiatives, which will require not only these key technologies, but also mobile and connected health technologies.

When evaluating mobile solutions for consumer engagement, healthcare organizations should consider the following recommendations:

Define the problem to be solved, because it's not all about the "gadget." The first step healthcare organizations should take is to clearly articulate the objective of the mobile consumer engagement initiative. Many consumer engagement initiatives fail because of a disproportionate focus on the device (whether it's a mobile device or other connected health technology). Healthcare organizations must also identify the problem that they are trying to solve first before embarking on the search for a technology solution. Otherwise, they risk selecting the wrong technology.

Remember the "Five Rights;" consumer engagement is not a one-size-fits-all strategy. Healthcare organizations would do well to remember the "Five Rights" of consumer engagement as they develop their consumer engagement strategies. The ability to segment and microsegment consumers will require investment in analytic tools. Multidisciplinary teams will be required to formulate a consumer engagement strategy that is compelling, be on target with its messaging for the different consumer segments that comprise the population, and offer the appropriate combination of mobile and other connected health technologies.

Develop "sticky" mobile health solutions that fit into the workflow of consumers. Mobile health applications that can be readily incorporated into consumers' daily living activities (e.g., grocery shopping, navigating a menu for healthy food choices, even sleep), are easy to use, and provide value to the consumer are more likely to be perceived as indispensible and not abandoned after a few tries. Consumer abandonment is a real risk for mobile health applications. Various industry studies reveal that consumers will download and use a general mobile application a few times before they stop using it, even if they paid to download the application.

Establish an enterprise app store to curate mobile health applications. It is easy for both consumers and clinicians to become overwhelmed by the sheer volume of mobile apps available today on public app stores. Healthcare organizations should consider establishing their own enterprise app stores to curate mobile health applications on behalf of consumers and clinicians. If it's easy for physicians to find mobile health apps "endorsed" by a healthcare organization, they are more likely to recommend them to their patients. Like other connected health technologies, consumers are more willing to use a mobile app if their physicians recommend one. Mobile-savvy physicians are beginning to recommend mobile applications to their patients according to the IDC Health Insights' 2013 *Connected Health Physician Survey*. Nearly one out of five (19.2 percent) of physician respondents recommended a mobile app related to managing chronic conditions or health and fitness, and 2.6 percent of respondents recommended a specific mobile app to their patients.[7]

Link mobile apps and clinical systems. Most mobile health applications on public app stores are standalone applications that provide access to health information or basic health guidance at the point that the consumer needs it. But more sophisticated mobile applications aggregate, analyze, and transmit data from remote health monitoring and health and fitness devices. These converged mobile health/remote health monitoring applications will provide clinicians insights into their patients' health status beyond the "four walls" of the institution including social health issues — such as mood or feelings of depression — that can positively or negatively influence health outcomes. The challenge is that they create another siloed data source of patient information. Population health management initiatives will require the ability to integrate clinically relevant consumer source data with the appropriate health IT system (e.g., EMR, care management, population health management or clinical data repository). Data should be collected via machine-to-machine (M2M) transmission to ensure accuracy and assuage clinicians' concern about the veracity of consumer-sourced data and analytic tools applied to make relevant filtered data available (e.g., out of normal range readings, trends and other relevant clinical data).

CONCLUSION

The widespread adoption of mobile technology and the variety of ways consumer use this technology beyond voice and e-mail will have a profound impact on consumer engagement strategies over the next five years as innovation continues to accelerate. Consumer engagement will be enhanced by providing telehealth services through a mobile device consumers regularly carry and constantly check throughout the day. Mobile health applications that combine remote monitoring or health and fitness tracking, along with social networking opportunities, will form the nexus of converged mHealth and telehealth initiatives, further blurring the lines between the two. Numerous studies have shown that consumers who are actively engaged and manage their health will have better outcomes than consumers who do not play an active role in addressing their health issues.

REFERENCES

1. CDC. Chronic diseases: the power to prevent, the call to control. National Center for Chronic Disease Prevention and Health Promotion. 2009. Available at: www.cdc.gov/chronicdisease/resources/publications/aag/pdf/chronic.pdf.

2. Pew Internet Spring Tracking Survey. April 17-May 19, 2013.

3. *U.S. Mobile Messaging 2012–2016 Forecast* (IDC #236137, August 2012).

4. Abroms L, Ahuja M, Kodl Y, Windsor R. Text2Quit: results from a pilot of an interactive mHealth quit smoking program. Available at: www.text2quit.com.

5. *Smarter Healthcare is Connected Healthcare* (IDC # DR2012_T7_LD, March 2012).

6. Cook DJ, Thompson JE, Prinsen SK, Dearani JA, Deschamps C. Functional Recovery in the Elderly After Major Surgery: Assessment of Mobility Recovery Using Wireless Technology. *The Annals of Thoracic Surgery*. 1 September 2013 (volume 96 issue 3 Pages 1057-1061 DOI: 10.1016/j.athoracsur.2013.05.092).

7. *Physician Attitudes Toward Connected Health Strategies* (IDC Health Insights #HI243258, September, 2013).

CHAPTER 3

Mobile Messaging and Behavioral Change: A Case Study

By John Fessler, MBA, and Tina Koro, MPH

ABSTRACT

"Drugs don't work in patients who don't take them."
– C. Everett Koop, MD
Surgeon General of the United States, 1982-1989

This quote speaks to a larger dilemma that is a key driver of healthcare costs in the United States and around the world. Poor health behaviors, including non-adherence to prescribed medications, unhealthy diet, and lack of exercise lead to preventable conditions that comprise as much as 75 percent of healthcare costs in the United States alone.[1] Healthcare organizations are struggling with effective ways to support patients and members adopt healthier behaviors today just as much as they did when C. Everett Koop was surgeon general in the 1980s.

Mobile phones, and particularly smartphones, offer an opportunity to modify behavior. Through the use of biometric and other sensors that are embedded or attached to the phone, individuals can receive immediate feedback on conditions ranging from blood glucose to blood pressure. Numerous devices track physical activity and have platforms to monitor and reward progress at the individual and group level, as well as leverage various forms of social networks. Mobile phones also offer the ability to provide personalized, tailored messaging to improve behavior. Mobile messaging programs can complement and extend traditional health coaching programs or be delivered on a stand-alone basis. A mobile messaging program can be offered at a fraction of the cost of a health coach, along with the convenience of 24/7 availability. This chapter will describe the opportunity associated with mobile messaging programs, common success factors, and how to implement mobile messaging programs.

OPPORTUNITY

Mobile messaging programs are used to improve a wide variety of health behaviors, and fall into three categories: adherence, chronic care management, and prevention and wellness, as shown in Table 3-1.

Table 3-1: Mobile Messaging Programs are Used to Improve a Wide Variety of Health Behaviors.

Adherence	Chronic Care	Prevention and Wellness
Medication	Diabetes	Obesity
Appointment Reminders	Respiratory/COPD	Smoking Cessation
Immunizations	Cardiac Care	Screenings and Tests
Care Management	Hypertension	Maternal and Child Health
		Health Coaching
		Health Tips

A number of studies have shown mobile messaging can be an effective tool to improve health behavior and outcomes in all three of these categories. For example, research indicates that text messages are effective in improving preventive behaviors, such as adhering to medical appointments, as well as in clinical care, such as improving diabetes care management.[2,3] Text messaging has also been proven to be effective in treating obesity, as evidenced by the first study published of its kind by Kevin Patrick, MD, at the University of California, San Diego, and Co-Founder of Santech.[4] The text message intervention, called mDiet, resulted in significantly more weight lost compared to those who did not receive the program.

Meta-analyses of text messaging interventions directed toward improved health outcomes showed improvements in a variety of disease prevention and disease management behaviors, including smoking cessation and diabetes self-management, with effects sustained and across different ages, ethnicities and nationalities.[5,6]

The use of mobile phones and mobile messaging systems provides a platform to deliver behavioral programs that are convenient and straightforward. Research on success factors identified interactivity and tailoring of messaging content as critically important.[6] Our experience at Santech, a mobile messaging company specializing in behavior change, has also led us to conclude that successful programs have the following traits in common:

- Sound behavioral change design.
- Personalization and tailoring.
- User engagement.
- Integrated solutions.
- Advanced messaging capabilities.

Sound Behavioral Change Design

Before explaining how behavioral change can be designed into effective mobile messaging solutions, it is important to describe key behavioral change concepts. Much of behavior change is built on Social Cognitive Theory (SCT) and the techniques derived from that framework are in wide use by psychological professionals, including health coaches. SCT explains how people acquire and maintain certain behavioral patterns, while also providing the basis for intervention strategies.[7] Evaluating behavioral change depends on three factors: environment, people and behavior. SCT provides a framework for designing, implementing and evaluating programs.

While SCT involves a number of techniques, a meta-analysis found the following techniques most successful:

- Goal setting: Setting goals that are realistic and measurable with a reasonable duration in order to better align cause with effect is critical. A weight loss goal of two pounds per week is more effective than a goal to lose 25 pounds in three months.
- Self efficacy: Improving one's confidence and abilities to achieve his or her goal directly correlates to the likelihood of success. Setting realistic goals, rewarding small accomplishments and providing encouragement have proved successful.
- Self monitoring: Establishing a measurement and feedback loop that is timely and provides insight into cause and effect is important. Studies have shown that the simple act of regularly measuring one's weight has resulted in effective weight loss.

These principles help to inform the content of messages that provide education and support for the individual. Another critical component is the behavioral design framework developed by B.J. Fogg at Stanford University. The framework is depicted in Fig. 3-1.

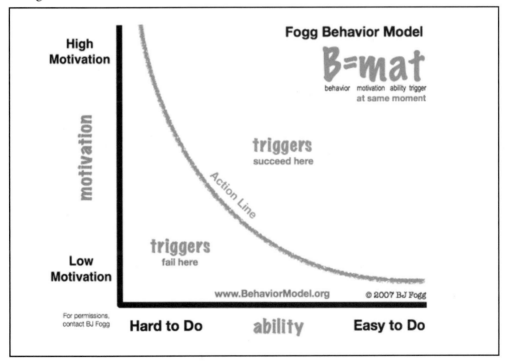

Fig. 3-1: The Behavioral Design Framework.

Adopting a new behavior or stopping an existing behavior is driven by a trigger or call-to-action that acts as the catalyst for the change in behavior. An example would be a message to remind an individual to take his or her medication or attend a scheduled appointment. Whether a trigger will lead to the targeted behavior is a function of the user's ability and motivation. The easier or simpler the targeted behavior, the more likely a trigger will result in the behavior being achieved. Similarly, the more motivated someone is to change their behavior, the more likely a trigger will achieve the desired behavior.

In the context of mobile messaging, sound behavioral design involves developing messages that have a specific action, and either build on motivation or improve ability. In the case of medication adherence, messages that not only remind users to take their medication, but also reinforce a core motivational driver like faith or staying healthy, are more effective. Similarly, messages that provide tips to make it easier to routinely take one's medication, like linkage to an already established habit, are more effective than messages that are more general in nature.

Personalization and Tailoring

Once grounded in sound behavioral design, a messaging platform or intervention needs to be tailored and personalized. Sending messages about sugar-sweetened beverages to someone who does not drink them is not only ineffective, but also reduces the impact of other messages that are relevant. Messages must be based upon known characteristics and preferences available in a user's profile for maximum effect. A user's profile can be updated from registration at intake, through user response to interactive messages, and by automated interface to electronic medical records (EMR) and other data repositories as well as biometric sensors. Automated interfaces are usually supported through web services.

Once updated, the user profile can be used to tailor and personalize the message. Personalization uses values that are tied directly to the user and can be demographic, medical and behavioral in nature. For example the user profile in the messaging system may store the user's first name, their weight goal, and their progress over the last week collected either through self-reporting or via updates from a wireless weight scale. A personalized message, as depicted in Table 3-2, would appear as follows:

Table 3-2: Personalized Messaging.

Programmed message	Message delivered to user
[First name] you gained/lost [weight change] last week and are [goal value] to your goal weight of [goal weight].	John, you lost 1 pound last week and are 10 pounds from your goal weight of 170 pounds.

For maximum effectiveness, a message needs to be both personalized and tailored. Tailoring involves message content that takes into account the context and characteristics of the user. Using the personalized weight message in Table 3-2, tailoring would take into account different outcomes, as depicted in Table 3-3.

Future messaging can also be tailored based upon progress with message frequency, and content modified for those who have gained versus lost weight.

User Engagement

For a mobile health messaging application, engagement can be measured based upon the response rate to interactive messages. The mDiet study showed improved weight loss overall and better results for those who were actively engaged than those who were not. Using sound behavioral change design and appropriate tailoring and personalization will go a long way toward improving the user experience and driving engagement. In addition, gamification techniques, particularly the use of rewards, can also play an important role.

Table 3-3: Tailoring a Personalized Message.

Outcome	Message delivered to user
Gained one pound	John, you gained one pound last week but can still get to 170 pounds, you are only 12 pounds away. Think of what you can change to get back on track.
Lost 2 pounds	John, you lost two pounds last week, congrats! You are 9 pounds away to your goal of 170 pounds. Keep it up!

When designing rewards for a mobile health messaging intervention, consideration needs to be taken to avoid reporting bias. For example, with a medication adherence application that uses interactive messaging to determine whether the user has missed a dose and the reasons thereto, it is important to reward the participant's responding, not the response. The reward system should prevent a response bias that would reward the user only for responding in the "desired" way: for example, that they hadn't missed a dose. Instead, it is important to also reward responses that are critical to intervention tailoring and behavior modification success, such as reasons or barriers for a missed dose. Rewarding such responses to program messages encourages users to provide the information necessary to tailor message plans to address individual behavior change barriers in the future. Rewards should be based upon message response rates, not on the response outcomes.

Integrated Solutions

Integration of mobile health messaging applications can come in two forms: systems integration and program integration. Systems integration involves linking disparate data from existing databases to update and inform the user profile that is then used to tailor and personalize program messages. Data may come from biometric sensors, EMR, personal health records and health risk assessments. The messaging platform needs to have the flexibility to consume structured and unstructured data (free-form text) using web services. In the case of Santech, a set of APIs to capture data incorporated into the user's profile are available. Santech also consumes other organizations' APIs like those published by the 2Net Platform for biometric sensor data by Qualcomm Life.

Systems integration allows for a mobile messaging platform to incorporate varied data sets when updating a user profile and delivers a highly tailored and personalized user experience, while program integration involves linkage with existing care management and wellness programs to maximize effectiveness. Although mobile messaging programs can be delivered standalone, they can also help to maximize the effectiveness of an existing program. Examples include reinforcement of chronic care management programs like cardiac rehabilitation or diabetes management; extending or supplementing health coach programs for smoking cessation, obesity, hypertension and other lifestyle conditions; and medically supervised weight loss. Any post-discharge care treatment plan can be complemented with a mobile messaging application. For example, in a large health system, a mobile messaging application to support cardiac rehabilitation patients was integrated into the educational component of their cardiac rehabilitation program. Patients found it much easier to adhere to their care management therapy with mobile messaging reminders and support.

Advanced Messaging Capabilities

The technology that enables effective mobile health messaging applications needs to apply sophisticated algorithms and utilize advanced messaging capabilities to deliver the optimal user experience and support improved health behavior. Algorithms are used to deliver the appropriate tailored, personalized message to the user; it's been found that advanced messaging capabilities result in the best impact. Examples of advanced messaging capabilities include:

- Keywords: Keywords are unique words within an application that support an automated response when the user texts or otherwise messages that keyword. For example, the keyword "craving" can be used for a smoking cessation program that provides a response to the user for a specific action to help combat a craving for a cigarette in the moment. Sophisticated systems can also personalize the message and track previous messages so that a new message is sent each time the keyword is invoked.
- Message time outs: Interactive messages that are awaiting a response can be timed out and re-sent. Sophisticated systems can also alter the language of the re-sent message.
- Personalization fields: Messages can be personalized with values that are associated with the user's profile as previously described in personalization and tailoring above.
- Multiple-level interaction: Messages can be interactive at multiple levels. Subsequent message content and frequency can also be updated and tailored based upon message responses.
- Message response call backs: Message responses can be captured and updated in a user profile that tailors future messages and can also be forwarded to third-party systems through web services. Examples include updating patient scheduling systems if the patient indicates that he or she cannot make an appointment, or forwarding a message to a health coach or other professional to review and act upon.
- Unsolicited message response and call back: The personalized, tailored nature of effective mobile health messaging programs can often lead to the user sending messages that are not expected by the system, which we call unsolicited messages. Capabilities for handling these types of user-generated messages need to be flexible enough to meet different client requirements and protocols ranging from a system standard response such as: "This is an automated system and messages are not reviewed. If this is a medical emergency, please contact your medical provider or call 911," to a personalized response such as forwarding the message to a health professional for review.
- Multimedia: The saying "a picture is worth a thousand words" certainly applies when communicating concepts like portion size or physical exercise. Messag-

ing platforms that support images as well as text for standard SMS delivery, or images and video when delivering through a mobile app or mobile web, can be important to create an impactful message.

SMS VS. MOBILE APPLICATION

A critical consideration in the design and rollout of a mobile health messaging application is the transmission modality. Mobile health messaging applications have traditionally been delivered through SMS, but as smartphones continue to gain traction, a mobile messaging application that has a similar user experience as SMS becomes a viable option. A mobile application can have a very similar user experience as SMS with the user receiving a push notification supported by Andriod, or IOS indicating there is a message for them to review. The message can be encrypted and requires the user to enter his or her password before accessing their message. An encrypted message could contain personal health information (PHI) and be structured to be compliant, whereas standard SMS messages need to avoid PHI. Besides PHI and HIPAA compliance, there are a number of other considerations that should be evaluated. Advantages of a mobile app include:

- The limitation of 160 characters per message no longer applies. Although as a general rule, the more succinct the message the better; removing this limitation does improve flexibility.
- Messages can imbed other content like video and mobile web links. Messages can be part of a more comprehensive app and link to other apps.
- SMS message fees that may be charged by the user's cellphone carriers and SMS delivery fees charged by carriers and SMS aggregators are not applicable.

On the other hand, there are constraints that need to be evaluated:

- A mobile app is limited to smartphones while SMS supports substantially all cellphones, both feature phones and smartphones. Although smartphones are widespread, there is still a significant minority who did not have a smartphone at the end of 2013, with a concentration among older and less affluent individuals. These may be important demographics for the intended mobile health messaging application.
- A mobile application has a steeper learning curve and therefore lower adoption rates than SMS. Although a mobile app can be designed to be highly intuitive, the user needs to download the app and register his or herself before use, which can be a barrier to adoption for novel users.

OTHER IMPLEMENTATION CONSIDERATIONS

Besides determining the appropriate modality, the approach for enrolling users and the frequency of messaging are important considerations. For mobile health messaging programs that are delivered through a mobile application, enrollment involves downloading the application and completing any registration information needed at intake. For SMS programs, enrollment can be accomplished through a number of approaches. A user can text a keyword and in turn respond to one or a series of messages to complete registration. A user could also complete a profile through the web (either mobile or standard) and complete registration by replying to an interactive message, a process called opting in. Finally, registration could be initiated through the messaging system capturing the registration information that is communicated to another system through web services, with opting in accomplished through response to a message sent from the messaging system.

All SMS enrollment options for U.S.-based applications need to comply with the guidelines established by the Mobile Marketing Association, which requires the user to opt in for mobile messaging from their mobile device, and that the user is clearly informed how to automatically terminate by texting stop keywords to the program.

Finally, message frequency needs to consider user burden. Giving the user the ability to adjust the frequency of messaging through keywords or modifying his or her profile may be critical in some applications.

IMPLEMENTING A MOBILE HEALTH MESSAGING APPLICATION

In summary, key steps for implementing a mobile health messaging application are as follows:

Determine the target behavior and demographic for the mobile health messaging application. The target behavior is an important consideration as it can range from a specific action for a specific time (appointment reminder), to a sustained discreet action (medication adherence), to a sustained combination of a number of actions (chronic care management and lifestyle like obesity and diabetes). The more sustained and complex the targeted behavior, the longer the duration and frequency of messages needed.

1. Determine the best modality — mobile application or standard SMS.
2. Develop the message content to support the targeted behavior using a sound behavioral framework.
3. Determine how to best incorporate interactive messaging to sustain engagement.
4. Develop approach to sustain and monitor engagement.
5. Develop approaches to measure outcomes and user engagement. Develop user feedback for continuous improvement.

CONCLUSION

The widespread use of mobile phones provides an unprecedented opportunity to instantaneously reach the vast majority of the population in the United States. When implemented correctly, mobile messaging can be an effective and cost-efficient solution to drive behavior change and improve health outcomes in both prevention and disease management. To be successful, mobile messaging programs should at a minimum utilize theoretically sound behavior change principles, engage users without creating participation burden, and employ algorithms to maximize personalization and tailoring of messaging plans in an automated fashion.

Given the staggering proportion of healthcare costs attributed to conditions that could be prevented with better health behaviors, along with the robust body of literature indicating effectiveness in improving a wide range of health outcomes at a low cost, mobile messaging interventions are becoming an increasingly appealing solution for health systems, health payers, wellness organizations, pharmaceutical companies and more. Mobile messaging is establishing itself as one of the tools healthcare companies have in their arsenal to prevent and manage disease, and improve health at a population level.

REFERENCES

1. Department of Health and Human Services, 2010.
2. Car J, Gurol-Urganci I, de Jongh T, Vodopivec-Jamsek V, Atun R. Mobile phone messaging reminders for attendance at healthcare appointments. *Cochrane Database System Rev.* 11(7);2012.
3. Hussein W, Hasan K, Jaradat A. (2001). Effectiveness of mobile phone short message service on diabetes mellitus management, the SMS-DM study. *Diabetes Research Clinical Practice.* 94(1);2001.
4. Patrick K, Raab F, Adams M, Dillon L, Zabinski M, Rock L. et al. A text message-based intervention for weight loss: randomized controlled trial. *Journal of Medical Internet Research.* 11(1); 1-9;2009.
5. Fjeldsoe B, Marshall A, Miller Y. (2009). Behavior change interventions delivered by mobile telephone short-message service. *American Journal of Preventive Medicine.* 36(2); 165-73;2009.
6. Lewis H, Kershaw T. Text messaging as a tool for behavior change in disease prevention and management. *Epidemiologic Reviews.* 32(1); 56-69;2010.
7. Bandura A. *Self-Efficacy: The Exercise of Control.* 1997. New York: W. H. Freeman.

CHAPTER 4

Using Mobile Texting to Change Social Behavior: A Case Study

By Noel Chandler, BA, and Marilyn Teplitz, MBA, FHIMSS

ABSTRACT

Mobile communication has arguably had a bigger impact on humankind in a shorter period of time than any other invention in human history.[1]

The use of text messaging to communicate as a means of changing social behavior is now a proven method, especially for reaching teens in the United States, and women and teens in developing countries. Mobile communication, especially texting, can support the following social behavior programs:

- Disseminating information
- Progress tracking/monitoring
- Surveys and data capture
- Alerts, notifications
- Training of front-line workers
- Advocacy and outreach

REACHING TEENS

The Pew Internet Project is an initiative of the Pew Research Center, a nonprofit, nonpartisan "fact tank" that provides information on the issues, attitudes and trends shaping America and the world. The Project studies the social impact of the Internet. Its first survey, in March 2000, covered the general role of the Internet and e-mail in people's lives. The data in this section is from the Pew Research Center's primary research on teens' (ages 12-17) technology use. These findings are based on a nationally representative phone survey of 802 parents and their 802 teens ages 12-17. It was conducted between July 26 and September 30, 2012. Interviews were conducted in English and Spanish and on landline and cellphones. The margin of error for the full sample is ± 4.5 percentage points.

Teens' use of cellphones is a harbinger of broader social change. About 25 percent of teens in the United States are "cell-mostly" users, using their phones in preference to a shared or tethered device, such as a laptop or desktop. About three in four (74 percent) teens are "mobile Internet users" who say they access the Internet on cellphones, tablets and other mobile devices at least occasionally, as compared with 55 percent of adults who are mobile Internet users.[2]

Of the 78 percent of teens who have cellphones, more than half own smartphones.[3] Forty-five percent of teens own smartphones, which is nearly twice the number of teen smartphone owners from just two years prior (23 percent).[4] More interesting, however, is that 34 percent of older teen girls (ages 14-17) are cell-mostly users compared with 24 percent of older teen boys, even though boys and girls are equally likely to be smartphone owners.[5]

Teens who are in lower socioeconomic groups are just as likely — and in some cases more likely than those living in higher income and more highly educated households — to use their cellphone as a primary point of access.

Teens with highly educated parents or with parents in the highest income bracket are more likely to have cellphones. However, teens living in the lowest-earning households (under $30,000 per year) are just as likely as those living in the highest-earning households ($75,000 or more) to own smartphones (39 percent vs. 43 percent). Older teens are more likely than younger teens to have cellphones and those phones are more likely to be smartphones. Rural teens are significantly less likely to have a smartphone than urban or suburban teens.[6]

Ownership of smartphones versus regular phones does not vary by race, ethnicity or income. However, Latino teens and white teens whose parents earn less than $30,000 annually or are not college-educated are all less likely to know if their phone is classified as a smartphone.[7]

Teens use text messaging as the main method of communication with all people in their lives:[8]

- Sixty-three percent say that they text to communicate with others every day.
- Forty-nine percent of teens send and receive text messages with friends every day, consistent with 2011 rates.[9]
- Thirty-nine percent of teens make and receive voice calls on their mobile phones every day.
- Thirty-five percent of all teens socialize with others in person outside of school daily.
- Twenty-nine percent of all teens exchange messages daily through social network sites.
- Twenty-two percent of teens use instant messaging daily to talk to others.
- Nineteen percent of teens talk on landlines with people in their lives daily.
- Six percent of teens exchange e-mail daily.

An increasing trend among teens is their preference to text more and use instant messaging and e-mail less. Nearly two in five teens say they never or cannot exchange instant messages, and another 39 percent of teens say they never exchange e-mail. Talking on a landline is also proving less popular, with 20 percent of teens saying they never or cannot talk on a landline.[10]

Texting and Hotlines and Helplines

Mosio is an award-winning mobile software company founded in 2007 by Noel Chandler, CEO, and Jay Sachdev, CTO. Mosio's solutions enable health professionals,

counselors and information specialists to communicate with consumers via two-way text messaging and mobile web services in several main areas:
- Health prevention services.
- Patient engagement in clinical trials.
- Healthcare communication services.

The company has responded to increasing market demands for adding text messaging to pre-existing communication channels, such as hotlines or helplines. They have found:
- Sixty percent added SMS to a telephone hotline or helpline.
- Forty percent added it to a web site of information only or Q&A via e-mail.
- Anecdotally, Mosio heard from some organizations that they wanted to add text messaging because their hotline call volumes had gone down. This is confirmed by the Pew Research Center report on "Teens, Smartphones and Texting."
- All were looking for new ways of being relevant to the younger demographic, or to be accessible on-the-go to a larger segment of the population.
- Because of the time-shifting element of texting (texting doesn't technically have to happen in real-time), text messaging is easier to staff and manage than a "live" voice line or online chat service.

Based on Mosio's research and database, most (86 percent) hotlines/helplines are using text messaging for Q&A. Fifteen percent use it for outbound text messaging to communicate tips and advice alerts about sexual health. Approximately 20 percent target sexual health specifically with the rest being open to sexual health and social issues, such as relationships, dating, health, anti-bullying, etc. Less than 5 percent are currently using it for surveys, but there is growing interest in using it for research or to gather feedback.

Because the primary demographic is teens, questions on sexual health are not only regarding the act itself, but include issues regarding relationships (healthy vs. controlling, abusive), social pressure, body awareness, myths vs. facts, etc.

Short Codes vs. Virtual Texting Numbers
There are two methods by which health educators can communicate using text messaging:
1. *Keywords with Short Codes*: a five- or six-digit number approved by the mobile carriers for text messaging. Users text a special word (keyword) to the number to begin the communication process.
2. *Virtual Texting Numbers:* a 10-digit (in the United States and Canada) number enabling users to text back and forth with educators in the same way they do with friends and family.

Initially, Mosio began its support for hotlines/helplines by providing clients with a keyword, but discovered:
- Many young adults use free texting apps which cannot text to short codes.
- Other young adults who can text from their phones have short code blocking (parental controls at the billing/plan level).
- The mobile carriers seem to have gotten more lax in how they define the use of virtual texting numbers (10-digit numbers) versus short codes. Virtual numbers need to be peer to peer (one-on-one), so depending on the program

(local vs. national), Mosio works with clients to decide which is best for their organization.
- Short codes in other countries are typically a premium service making virtual numbers a better method for two-way interaction.

Text Speak and Time-Shifting
- Mosio has an 800-plus term "text speak" translator, so health educators can quickly translate any acronyms teens use that may not make sense to them.
- Young adults are masters of time-shifting. While some inquiries are simple, single question-and-answer replies, others are threaded conversations that go on for hours, or even days.
- Mosio's two-way text messaging platform was created to make it efficient for clients to receive and respond to text messages in a contact center environment.
- Some Mosio clients started out using a mobile phone, but quickly found that it was difficult to keep up, manage collaboration or quickly gather statistics about usage and reports to show the effectiveness of the medium.

ADOLESCENT PREGNANCY PREVENTION CAMPAIGN OF NORTH CAROLINA

In the early 1980s, the United Way in Charlotte, NC, formed a work group to find solutions for the area's rapidly rising teen pregnancy rates. The Adolescent Pregnancy Prevention Campaign of North Carolina (APPCNC) was founded in 1985. A year later, the North Carolina General Assembly launched a state-funded partnership leveraging APPCNC to support pregnancy prevention projects across the state. It worked. After six years, North Carolina reversed the teen pregnancy rate, starting an overall decline that is still continuing.

In the late 2000s, APPCNC kicked off the BrdsNBz Text Message Warm Line, using mobile technology. In 2009, the North Carolina General Assembly passed the Healthy Youth Act. For the first time since the mid-1990s, public schools must provide students with health information that is medically accurate and age-appropriate. Furthermore, the law gives local school boards broad authority to use proven curricula and provide a full range of parent-and-science-supported information.

In 2010, the Centers for Disease Control and Prevention selected APPCNC to serve as one of eight organizations in the United States to demonstrate the impact of a broad, community-wide initiative to lower teen pregnancy rates. The initiative is called Gaston Youth Connected, and it is already providing important lessons for the rest of the state. In 2011, APPCNC launched the WISE initiative to increase schools' capacity to provide effective sex education that meets local needs. APPCNC continues to be successful at driving down teen pregnancy rates. As of 2010, incidence of teen pregnancy in North Carolina was 53 percent lower than it was in 1990.

Mobile Technology
APPCNC began BrdsNBz with a simple text-in/text-out response capability. In 2012, however, the mobile provider stopped offering the service and recommended Mosio as a provider. The technology provides a web-based dashboard for the health educa-

Chapter 4: Using Mobile Texting to Change Social Behavior: A Case Study

tors to manage incoming and outgoing texts, statistical reports on demographics, usage, types of questions, etc. BrdsNBz is now able to handle clients with significantly larger numbers of teens.

APPCNC presents BrdsNBz to teens, providing them with a keyword to text. Once a teen submits a question and receives a reply, BrdsNBz follow up with a survey, asking for the teen's satisfaction with the experience, as depicted in Figs. 4-1 and 4-2.

Fig. 4-1: Health Educators Receive and Respond to Questions on a Secure, Web-Based Dashboard, Accessible via Computer, Tablet or Smartphone.

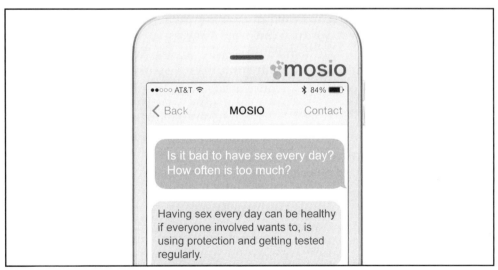

Fig. 4-2: Users Send Text Messages from their Mobile Phones and Engage in Two-Way 'Textchat' Conversations.

INTERVIEW: KENNON JACKSON, JR., MA (APPCNC), AND BETH CARLS (ONESEVENTEEN MEDIA), BRDZNBZ TEXT MESSAGE WARM LINE

1. How has implementing text messaging changed how you work with clients in communicating with young adults?

In 2009, APPCNC sought to engage youth "on their turf." Until that time, our organization worked directly with service providers. We surveyed parents to obtain information about their thoughts regarding sexual health, but the conclusions we drew were secondhand and anecdotal at best. Text messaging allowed our organization to collect information from adolescents through BrdsNBz. By creating a two-way dialogue between our health educators and the adolescents they serve, BrdsNBz provided a new stream of data and information from adolescents in the form of their questions about sexual health and related topics.

Text messaging has also given our organization a better opportunity to analyze the information we collect from adolescents by conducting quantitative and qualitative analyses. Using BrdsNBz to collect text messaging data was the best decision that APPCNC ever made to further its mission of improving the lives of adolescents.

2. You have deployed services to a number of different clients. What aspects are the same and what are different in how each organization uses the medium?

The lowest common denominator for our BrdsNBz clients is text messaging. Each BrdsNBz licensee has a similar request: to obtain more information about their adolescent target population with respect to sexual health and related topics. Most licensees also want additional data about why adolescents are using text messaging to obtain information about sexual health and related topics as opposed to taking advantage of opportunities to get the information in school or at after-school or community-based programs. BrdsNBz taps into the need to use a salient means of communication with adolescents that's already in place and widely used by youth: text messaging.

In terms of differences, the size and scope of the deployment can vary from one licensee to the next. Some groups that BrdsNBz work with are small, community-based nonprofits, while others operate from state departments of health. Some BrdsNBz licensees choose to utilize the BrdsNBz Evaluation Module to capture outcome-based changes in health behaviors. The ability to market and provide outreach opportunities for BrdsNBz also differs from one licensee to the next. Some BrdsNBz licensees work exclusively through their own marketing and outreach activities, while other licensees utilize the local school system, peer health educators and partner organizations to "spread the word" about BrdsNBz. Some licensees even choose to use billboards, PSA's and bus advertising. Because of the differences in how each BrdsNBz licensee actuates their marketing plan, utilization can vary from one implementation to the next.

3. Did you get the results you expected before starting to offer text messaging? Anything unexpected that worked out positively?

BrdsNBz was the product of the need to collect additional data from adolescents about sexual health and related topics. Before BrdsNBz was launched, adolescents were reluctant at best to offer information about their sexual health because they felt that the information was personally identifiable and "not private." Because BrdsNBz is anonymous, the service has provided a platform where adolescents can share some of their most intimate questions via text message with trained health educators, who can then provide them with a medically accurate and up-to-date response to their question(s).

Since 2009 BrdsNBz has collected a substantial number of questions about sexual health and related topics in seven different states, thus informing the sexual health demographics of adolescents in a cross-section of differing physical, political and health-oriented environments.

4. Anything that didn't work as expected or needed improvement?

Sustainability continues to be an issue for any organization dealing with adolescent sexual health. Based on APPCNC's years of experience, BrdsNBz has helped its licensee organizations tap into more reliable and sustainable streams of funding for multi-year implementations of the service. In terms of marketing, some licensees actuate the BrdsNBz marketing plan in full. BrdsNBz has identified, however, that working with schools — both at a district and individual level — can sometimes be difficult, as policies around sexual health and technology vary from one school (system) to the next — even within a single state.

BrdsNBz relies on the agreement to its terms and conditions during the opt-in process as a means of verification. Over the past four years, primarily due to mobile number portability, relying on mobile number area code and exchange has become a less reliable means of tracking BrdsNBz utilization for geo-location purposes.

REFERENCES

1. Minges M. Maximizing mobile: information and communications for development. The World Bank, 2012: 11.
2. Madden M, Lenhart A, Duggan M, Cortesi S, Gasser U. Teens & Technology (Pew Research Center) March 13, 2013, 2.
3. *Ibid.*
4. Fitzgerald T. Wanna reach teens? use the phone. *Medialife Magazine*, April 18, 2013 Available at: www.medialifemagazine.com/wanna-reach-teens-use-the-phone.
5. Madden M, et. al., Teens & Technology: 2.
6. *Ibid*, 7.
7. Lenhart A. Teens, smartphones and texting. Pew Research Center, March 9, 2012: 2.
8. *Ibid*, 16-17.
9. *Ibid*, 10.
10. *Ibid*, 17.

CHAPTER 5

Empowering Mobile Technology for Healthier Dietary Practices: A Case Study

By Ellen Badinelli and Dave Dushyant

ABSTRACT

For more than 40 million Americans, making responsible dietary choices can be daunting, requiring consumers to be tethered to one or several dietary guidance web sites. ScanAvert allows the consumer to specify one or multiple dietary criteria important to them/their family in one single site/application.

Consumers download the service app on their Android or iPhone, and follow the prompts to register their dietary profile, either on the handset or the web site, choosing among allergy, prescriptions, illnesses/conditions and nutritional allowances menus. This establishes a family's profile or dietary filter. There is also a custom diet feature for users to create their own algorithm in addition to those listed on the diets/dietary restrictions menu.

Unlike most apps, whereby all information resides within the programmed app, ScanAvert is a web-enabled app, continuously feeding information to and from the Internet. This was a deliberate choice to allow for interoperability between devices and several authorized users, including family, physicians, healthcare providers and facilities.

THE PROBLEM/CHALLENGE

For the 40 million Americans who must decipher labels, making responsible dietary choices can be daunting, requiring being tethered to a dietary guidance web site, or flipping back and forth through several if your family has more than one dietary issue. Some web sites offer lists of approved substances/products, and/or off-limits, while others allow you to scan or enter the barcode and receive a fixed "rating" that one product is "better" than another based on that company's criteria dictated by their chosen authority. This "one size fits all" approach fails to recognize that a student running track requires more carbohydrates in his diet than a sedentary adult or diabetic.

Likewise, diet soda is often a "better" choice for someone on a diet, but not someone with Phenylketonuria (PKU) who must avoid aspartame.

ScanAvert allows the consumer to specify one or multiple dietary criteria important to them or their families in a single site/application. The following examples are a sample of the vital information the app delivers: a parent is alerted that "spelt" is harmful to his wheat allergic child; a pregnant woman purchasing Advil is alerted that it is not recommended for pregnant women in their last trimester; a customer managing diabetes is alerted that the carbohydrate grams per serving of his chosen cereal exceed the dietary limits he established in his profile; the customer purchasing grapefruit juice is alerted that it is contra-indicative of his prescription, Lipitor, or the performance of his child's prescribed antibiotic.

Inherent in the registration process is a single site where all prescriptions, allergies, illnesses and other conditions are housed as well as all products scanned; and is the framework of an electronic medical record (EMR). While shopping histories are maintained largely for commercial gain, never before have they been classified by more meaningful criteria and harnessed for consumer benefit. ScanAvert answers the simple question: "Is this product safe for ME/MY FAMILY? If not, show me what is."

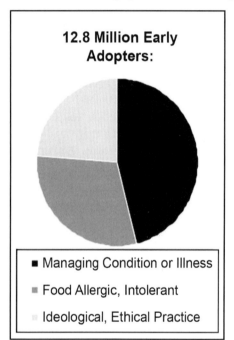

Fig. 5-1: 12.8 Million Early Adopters.

There are an estimated 40 million Americans, or 12.8 million heads of household, if we adjust the consumer base by the average family size — 3.2 (U.S. Census) — who must make dietary choices, as follows:

1. Consumers managing conditions, illnesses, or diseases who wish to avoid substances that exacerbate symptoms include: Celiac disease patients (500,000 Americans, est. Celiac Disease Center) must adhere to a gluten-free diet, PKU patients, (300,000 Americans, est. PKUnews.org) must avoid aspartame and protein in large quantities and also require a method to monitor dietary intake. The Feingold Diet prescribed to treat ADD/ADHD and Autism recommends the avoidance of salicylates and food additives/preservatives found in dyes, gluten and fruits, among other substances. Diabetics (17.9 million Americans, est. American Diabetes Assoc. diagnosed; another 7 million estimated undiagnosed) must monitor/limit their consumption of substances based on carbohydrate grams per serving, among other nutritional substances for weight management.

2. The number of consumers with food allergies/intolerance who must avoid substances that could cause a harmful reaction is estimated to be approximately 12.5 million Americans, according to the Food Allergy & Anaphylaxis Network (FAAN). Composition of products is not listed alphabetically, so even informed allergic consumers must read the label several times to ensure the product is compatible.

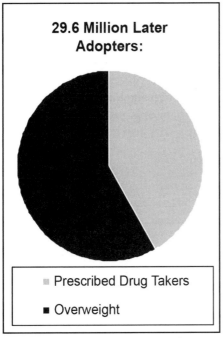

Fig. 5-2: 29.6 Million Later Adopters.

According to the Food Allergy Initiative (FAI), the allergic consumer spends 29 percent more time in their store performing this task. Furthermore, if the consumer has more than one food allergy concern — and studies show this is the case — and each of the "Big 8" food allergies has multiple terms that indicate the presence of that allergen, the task can be daunting. ScanAvert translates all terminology used in labels to indicate the presence of the same underlying allergen, and delivers decisive compatibility/incompatibility information.

3. Approximately 12 million American consumers (Mintel) adhere to ideological and ethical practices (e.g. Kosher, Hindu, vegan, vegetarian, and organic) and must avoid products with certain ingredients or that have been derived in certain procedures. Ideological consumers seek to purchase products of companies that adhere to their preferred practices and policies. This group of consumers is also technologically and ideologically active and expected to grow in number as concerns over artificial additives and preservatives, genetically modified crops and other ethical preferences continue to grow in commercial appeal. "Organic" and "natural" products now constitute more than 13 percent of U.S. grocery purchases.

The U.S. Census reports that over half of Americans take prescription drugs daily, including 82 million between the ages of 20-59. According to National Institute of Health (NIH), an estimated 31.4 percent of adults are classified as obese. Sixty-six percent of adults or 111 million and 17 percent of children are overweight.

These individuals may not currently be studying and interpreting labels for better dietary choices, however 69 percent of them report following some form of diet, but without knowledge or information of what their daily allowances should be (International Food Information Council).

THE SOLUTION

Sources for prescription, allergy, and food label data information have existed for years, but in databases that were separated like silos. A service was needed that pulled all this information together to deliver compatibility results — and with a simple user interface if it was to be adopted by the public. ScanAvert was created to fill that void and provide a simple means of detecting unwanted or desired ingredients for dietary adherence and avoidance of harmful reactions. As an added service, ScanAvert auto-notifies subscribers if a product in their scanning history is recalled, a potentially life-saving service.

ScanAvert translates synonymous terminology used in food labels for each of the "Big 8" food allergies, as provided by FAAN and prescription leaflet information obtained from patientassistance.com.

ScanAvert released its free dietary compatibility service in July 2009 on Android. By word of mouth, it attracted enough users for a beta test, nearly 500 downloads, half of whom have dietary restrictions and a need for such a service. A substantial number downloaded the app thinking it was a price checker. To prevent users from downloading the app without first reading its description, ScanAvert decided to charge a fee. This barrier proves pivotal in securing valid and reliable user data, as the paid users that download the app are those with dietary restrictions, conditions/illness, or taking prescriptions, the intended user base. Top dietary restrictions/requirements were MSG free, gluten-free, pregnant/nursing. The most common drugs were Lipitor, Adderall, and aspirin; while the most common dietary allowances monitored were calories, carbohydrates, calcium and calories from fat, proving that if you provide simple-to-use tools, consumers *will* use them (Figs. 5-3, 5-4 and 5-5). ScanAvert reported the high number of Adderall prescriptions identified from females at Health2.0's Fall 2009 conference. These beta user findings are validated by Harvard School of Public Health which reports identical findings in November of 2011, and Medco's study released March 2012. Gluten-free remains in the top identified dietary restrictions, and the majority of the allowances have remained consistently in the top three, which is encouraging news that subscribers are monitoring the most important nutritional information from a diet perspective. While the top three prescriptions have changed, indicating we are expanding to a more varied user base as we approach 5,800 subscribers, the psychotropic drugs Zoloft, Adderall, and Prozac remain commonly reported as well.

An Industry in Need of a Revolution

While the above reflects the societal problem that needs to be solved, and the sizeable opportunity based on the magnitude of the population making uninformed dietary

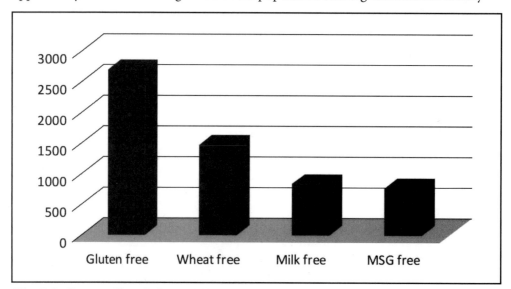

Fig. 5-3: Current Top-Selected User Diets.

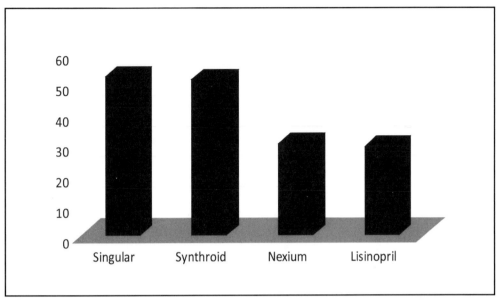

Fig. 5-4: Current Top-Selected User Prescriptions.

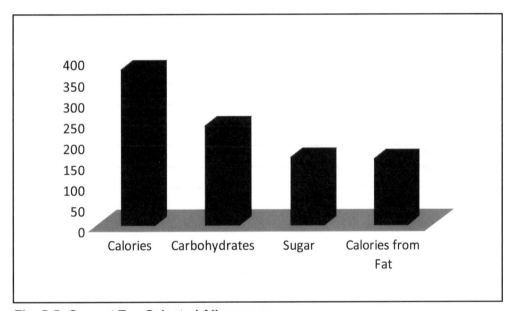

Fig. 5-5: Current Top-Selected Allowances.

choices and poor dietary practices, a larger problem exists within the medical community itself — a reluctance to consider solutions by innovators outside the medical profession. This may be due to comfort, or concern that any communication, mobile or otherwise, increases liability exposure, and therefore requires medical training. This is a credible concern and the mHealth industry must pressure the Department of Health & Human Services to grant protection from liability for solution providers, many of which are small businesses and could not survive the burden of costly litigation. Failure to lobby and secure such protection means many innovations will never be brought to public domain.

A larger obstacle looms in how we can afford to provide such solutions. Many mHealth companies that were funded a few years ago are trying to determine sustainable income now that the hype and honeymoon is over. An industry long entrenched in financial support from insurers, payees and employers must pivot to find other means of revenue, as more employers push retiree benefits they used to fund to national managed care. This will require the medical community to seek partners with ROI that is retail-driven, while still remaining HIPAA compliant, and is likely the industry's biggest challenge. Indeed, ScanAvert began as a free app, switched to a paid app, and is now back to being a free service. Additional tools are being developed for health professionals and facilities.

Striving for Simplicity

ScanAvert developed a simple intuitive user interface that would simplify the task of finding compatible products, even for households with several dietary/health issues, but found that we still needed to train users, and promptly set up our help desk. We also found subscribers skipped the registration process, neglecting to agree to the terms and conditions, which would bounce them out of the app, or they failed to follow the instructions or view the tutorials. We found that many of the users who experienced problems rarely contacted us for assistance, but instead took to social media to vent. In response, we recently re-released the app for free, which would remove the registration prompts that caused so many problems, and created dissatisfaction among users. Despite positive publicity, and critical acclaim of colleagues, press, industry trade groups, the user community trumps them all, it simply wasn't simple enough. An important retail lesson was learned; the *customer is always right*.

Constant Pivot

"The only thing constant is change." While ScanAvert auto-notifies subscribers of product recalls for any product in their scanning history, this service has resulted in an influx of e-mail from consumers across the country reporting suspected product contamination and inquiring of other reports. Answering these inquiries took up almost as much time as our mobile app so we created a database that sorts complaints by region, product and manufacturer to more readily identify common sources in the supply chain for improved food safety.

CONCLUSION

While the medical community has come a long way in the last two years, the conversation is still slanted; mHealth is defined as *patient engagement*, and that is where it all goes awry and why electronic medical records have dismal adoption rates. Rarely does one identify herself first as a "patient." In the hierarchy of descriptions, before patient comes wife, husband, parent, doctor, accountant, lawyer, Catholic, Jewish, vegan, sword swallower, etc. Even the language with which medical information is published and imparted requires a PhD in Latin and chemistry to decipher. It's written by those and for those with a medical pedigree, and not the audience for which it is intended. It is urgent that we change the conversation topic from *patient engagement* to *consumer engagement*, which means we must approach mHealth by making it as intuitive and simple as possible if our work is to achieve scalability required for any meaningful effect. The hand that rules the supermarket cart, the cupboard, physical activities and doctors' appointments, is the arbiter of all healthy — and unhealthy — behaviors and we must appeal to her/him. We must recognize and accept that healthcare has ceased to be a profession; it is now a commodity, bought and sold like any other.

CHAPTER 6

Remodeling the Paradigm in Patient Engagement to Personalize Interventions: An Analysis

By Doug Elwood, MD, MBA, and Jeffrey T. Heckman, DO

ABSTRACT

The healthcare system at times resembles the bulk and obdurate position of an immovable object. One topic that has garnered a considerable amount of attention for its ability to potentially improve the system is patient engagement. Five years ago we set out to understand, as physicians and researchers, how we might better appreciate the different components of health interactions and therefore influence patient engagement. Concurrent with technology trends ongoing in the market, we focused our energy on newer methods of communication and delivery, principally mobile health; however, we also included social media, engagement gaming approaches, and real-time digital tools at the point of care. Through a series of independent studies, we delved specifically into the notion of streamlining the delivery process for physicians to provide individualized information for patients, which the patients could then further personalize for themselves. We wanted to extend beyond seeing patients as static subjects and more as dynamic partners in care. We focused on limiting secondary complications in diabetes and improving functional independence, and looked ahead to a world of "prescribable apps." Our research adds to the tremendous amount of work done in this space and helps demonstrate that technology can act as an enabler to improve patient engagement and outcomes.

INTRODUCTION

The idea that healthcare delivery as it currently stands in the United States must change seems ubiquitous: the outcomes of health populations are too poor, the costs are too high, and the experience of patients are too often diminished by ineffective information delivery and/or communication. The force toward improvement has a momentum that is unmistakable; yet, it is butting up against an enormous system with a litany of deficiencies and inconsistencies. Potential solutions to improving the system often bring to mind the paradox "What happens when an unstoppable force meets an immovable object?" There are many who believe that the unstoppable force toward patient engagement might finally be enough to at least shape the immovable object that is our current health paradigm.

Patient engagement is defined as many things by many people. The broadest, and simplest definition is involving patients in their care. The concept that patients should play a role in their care is not new, but the conversation around patient engagement has become increasingly sophisticated, and in some instances reached a fever pitch, in recent years. It has broadened in scope to topics like patient-centered care and activated patients among others, with major publications on the issue, and even organizations developed to address it (among other topics) like the Patient-Centered Outcomes Research Institute.[1-9] There are many indications to believe that improving patient engagement will in fact offer tremendous benefits toward reducing costs and improving outcomes.[10-14]

The research presented in this paper emanates from that thinking. As practicing physicians, we recognized early in our career the need for patients to better understand their care, their medications, their plan and their support systems. Our own jobs entailed a vast number of responsibilities set against a paucity of time and with limited resources at our disposal, which challenged our ability to effectively and consistently intervene in a viable manner. After years of witnessing patients lost in the milieu of our health system, we decided to try and understand it better and to see if we could improve it, not just for patients but for physicians as well. Over the next five years we conducted numerous studies, working with thousands of patients in a concerted effort to pinpoint potential solutions and to provide them in an individualized manner. Studies included assessing hospitalized patients in real-time to elucidate their expectations and concerns, one of the country's first and largest studies on the use of iPads in clinical care by both physicians and patients, and the creation of both an engagement gaming app and an online social program.

Our work was unique in the following ways. First, it involved mobile health, which is focused on mobile devices as delivery vehicles (and is, even today, a nascent field). Second, it directly measured the impact along several variables of point-of-care digital/mHealth interventions, involving both practitioners and patients. Third, it combined multiple new approaches into one cohesive front to better understand each individually. And finally, we coalesced these three points under the umbrella of value, not of use. We wanted the ability to personalize education, communications and interventions for individuals in a seamless manner that vastly improved the user experience. Ultimately, we envisioned a world that has already started to come to fruition, one in which apps are prescribed by physicians that are relevant for specific patients, allowing patients to individualize them in a way that mirrors their evolution within the health system. Most importantly, we saw these apps taking into account as much as possible a term we call "life-centered care," a concept that expands the more common one used these days, "patient-centered care," to capture the importance of context and the impact of an individual's lifestyle on personal health status.

The pages that follow highlight some of the details of this journey, and we hope they both contribute to the massive amount of work on this topic and provide a glimpse of what the future of healthcare portends.

CHALLENGE

Throughout our careers as rehabilitation physicians specializing in care for persons with disabilities, we have been cognizant of the importance of providing education, information resources, and guidance to assist with specific diagnoses and treatment plans. However, we have found barriers and challenges to providing optimal personalized care to patients in the current healthcare climate. First and foremost, the most prominent form of communication we have for patients is paper-based. Office visits are short and paper materials are often missing and/or in short supply, hampering workflow. Additionally, paper materials are by definition static snapshots, and are not designed to change over time as patients' needs evolve.

Although the Internet provides a tremendous advance by offering patients the ability to access information — 72 percent now using it for health information — there remains a large gap.[1] Consumers often find themselves lost in a fragmented information distribution network, struggling to align the information they find online with their own unique health conditions, and losing contextual balance in the process.[1,15-20]

Likewise, electronic medical records (EMR) do not provide materials for our patients (and will not for some time despite the surge from Meaningful Use), the web is too scattered on the whole to be valuable in an individual clinical encounter, and external materials provided by organizations are almost always too vague; are focused on one point of the care continuum like initiation; or make assumptions that are not accurate in a real-time setting.[1,15,21-23] Even when we do identify a piece of content that can help, it is difficult to share it effectively, to provide different content to different patients, and to initiate any sort of broader conversation with the other stakeholders in that patient's health ecosystem (caregiver, pharmacist, nurse or allied health providers).

Compounding all of this is the fact that physicians get barely any (most would say none) training on segmenting patients and identifying key factors about patients related to literacy, activation or engagement triggers. Simultaneously, doctors are increasingly expected to provide this education and are being compensated on factors related to outcomes and patient satisfaction. This is a challenging situation with great opportunity for improvement.[23]

On the other side of the examination table, patients face all the challenges doctors do related to finding relevant information, but they are amplified by the fact that patients have to leave the office/hospital and actually find ways to follow their treatment plan, if they even are cognizant of what it is. Information provided by physicians or on the Internet almost always focuses on one point in time rather than evolving with the patient, and is not individualized enough to provide real direction or guidance. There are few materials that take into account a patient's real life (job, family, finances, neighborhood, etc.) or their background (race, ethnicity, age, etc.), and little (to any) coordination among stakeholders involved in their care.[15-20]

Not surprisingly, patients increasingly turn to other patients for help and advice. The Internet has greatly expanded this capability and patients are taking advantage. It is important when considering patient engagement not to make false assumptions about patients requiring some wake-up call; there are in fact a vast number of individuals who are very inquisitive and seek knowledge, and who want to control their health. The system unfortunately is not wholly prepared for this group, or for those who require a bit of a nudge (or shove) to move forward in their care.

For our studies, we used these problem statements and the backdrop of all the great work that has been done to this point, to guide us as we created our tools, understanding that both sides of the conversation are stressed and therefore ripe for positive action.

DESIGN

From 2008–2013, we conducted numerous studies to examine different variables around patient engagement. We focused our studies on mHealth, digital, point of care, and personalized outreach that extends to a patient's life outside of the doctor visit. Table 6-1 provides a summary of our different approaches. Our design evolved over time: in 2008, we captured data in real-time in an inpatient clinical setting; in 2009 we added a comprehensive online social approach; in 2010, we were one of the first programs in the country to provide iPads to staff and begin identifying how they were being used for training, education and patient care; and in 2011, we created an engagement game.

Throughout this time period, we also consistently evaluated how physicians use mobile devices in real-time clinical settings, progressing in our sophistication of what was in our mobile toolbox and how it was being shared with patients. In sum, we prospectively evaluated more than 2,500 patients, thousands of physician-patient encounters, and hundreds of individual patient experiences with the various interventions. We focused on multiple specialties and different settings (inpatient, outpatient, peer support groups) and across a broad demographic. In fact, a majority of our patients and more than half of our physicians were over 50 years of age and were late adopters of technology. Patients also overwhelmingly had multiple co-morbid chronic conditions. A large percentage had diabetes, one of the most devastating diseases in our healthcare system with regard to costs and secondary complications. It was the diabetic continuum that we narrowed on to see if we might help curtail secondary complications and help patients maintain functional independence, improving quality of life through increased activity, peer support, and better education/preparation for next steps.

We based our research on the following core questions:
1. Who were the patients at a demographic/social level that came to our clinics?
2. Where were they on their healthcare continuum (e.g., newly diagnosed, well into treatment)?
3. How did they prefer to receive information from their healthcare provider?
4. What interventions within our toolkit motivated patients to action?
5. How can physicians use tools within their workflow and how do they favor channels, content and delivery of those tools to patients?

6. How can the two, physicians and patients, be matched in a common approach to allow a seamless initiation and follow-through?
7. How can we facilitate information individualization and relevancy over time?

Table 6-1: Summary of Studies.

Problem	Date	Design	Methods	General Results
Lack of patient awareness and education during inpatient hospitalization leads to frustration, anxiety, longer patient stays and inappropriate readmissions. [24]	2008	Prospective, multi-specialty patient study on 1,000+ patients.	Interviewed more than 1,000 patients in real-time with a 30-question survey related to their care. Questions measured expectations vs. reality of their stay.	Patient expectations and reality do not match. Patients expect to be more informed and receive guidance through their inpatient hospitalization. They also need a lot more input that is personalized to their journey and knowledge level, and reflects their real-time questions and challenges.
Physician ACGME training has been confined mostly to classroom and simulated patient environments, not real encounters. Physicians are therefore not completely trained to respond to individual patient personalities. [25]	2008	Prospective assessment using professionalism surveys to understand prospect of real-time interventions on hundreds of patient encounters, as well as feedback on education and ACGME guidelines.	Used third party to follow patient encounters and obtain real-time feedback from patients, staff, and residents on actual interactions.	Real-time 360 degree view adds tremendous value to conversation for physicians and patients, and allows a more complete rendering of thoughts, opinions and perceptions of both parties. Real-time feedback allows physicians to adapt and respond accordingly when providing personalized communication to patients.
Patients have a difficult time understanding necessary steps they are supposed to take throughout their treatment journey and how best to obtain information that is relevant to their specific needs. They do not feel they get this information from physicians or other healthcare staff. [26-27]	2009	Prospective assessment using social approach initiated to help more than 80 patients understand various aspects of their journey in a personalized manner.	Invited half of patients to participate in program to help them with their care over a measured time period; half acted as control group and did not access the program.	Patients who had access to the online social program were able to better understand their diagnosis and treatment plan, ask more informed questions, and become "trainers" to the control group without the targeted, personalized information. They also felt that it made it easier for physicians to point them in the right direction, and most importantly, made it easy for them to find others who were also making a similar journey through their healthcare.

Table 6-1: Summary of Studies. (continued)

Problem	Date	Design	Methods	General Results
Point of Care Interactions [28]: 1. Doctors are not always readily presented with information to help them make informed, real-time decisions on best practice treatment approaches. 2. Doctors need help in preparing materials to share in real-time with patients. 3. Patients need targeted, personalized information based on their specific journey and needs.	2010-ongoing	Prospective multi-faceted study examining iPad and smartphone usage in a real-time clinical setting with many steps: 1. Basic understanding of physician usage and device ownership; 2. Physician/patient encounters: sharing information, perceptions of time spent/ needs addressed; 3. Patient satisfaction with physician device use with them; 4. Educational attainment from encounter; and 5. Different forms of digital delivery.	Variety of surveys and assessments incorporated over time to understand impact of using real-time delivery and specialized content to bolster education, awareness, and engagement. Dozens of physicians and hundreds of patients involved in study in prospective design. On many occasions, met with patients multiple times with various forms of materials.	Overall, patients greatly benefitted from the approaches. Different content led to different reactions (more interactive = better results, to a point). Doctors and patients found mobile devices to be extremely important and helpful in sharing of information and in navigating individual journeys. Patients greatly appreciated doctor initiation of programs and tie-in to broader construct. While some patients did not welcome the use of digital technology in the exam room, an overwhelming number appreciated that the physician was attempting to educate and involve them. Accordingly, their satisfaction and perception of time spent and needs addressed skyrocketed, but only with the right information. They could easily discern the basic print material that had been refurbished for the iPad vs the more dynamic and resource-laden content.
Doctors are not fully aware of: 1. The rapidity with which technology movement is occurring. 2. How to best implement mHealth technology into their clinical settings to help themselves and their patients.	2011-ongoing	Didactic sessions to help elucidate the benefits of using technology to spur patient education, awareness and engagement.	Presented at an international specialty conference with built-in surveys to understand pre-/ post- understanding of participants in this area and to gain appreciation of how best to disseminate knowledge on this subject to physicians.	Didactic sessions had great effect on physician knowledge: While the course did not provide the physicians with as much detail as they would have liked, the course did foment a baseline from which to move forward and to learn more. Importantly, the participants understood the connection between their own work approach and how best to connect that to patients, leveraging mHealth technology to accomplish this connection and increased communication in a targeted manner.

Table 6-1: Summary of Studies. (continued)

Problem	Date	Design	Methods	General Results
Patients vary in response to different engagement techniques. Specifically, gaming in health has ascended in importance but there have been few trials to understand impact in conjunction with other interventions.	2011-ongoing	Created and developed an engagement game on the iOS platform that utilized the iTunes library and tapped into various social outlets like Facebook. The phone's accelerometer captured movement and measured activity.	Used surveys in conjunction with the game to understand impact of using the engagement tool in many different facets of their care, and understanding of how to live healthier and adhere to their treatment.	Patients responded very well to the game. They made a connection between the game and their health and became teachers quickly. They wanted it to include even more information and to be tied more closely with other elements of their care.

METHODS

For our prospective trials, we used a variety of validated scales to measure different metrics associated with the respective interventions. We captured both pre- and post-intervention results in nearly all cases pertaining to attitude, perceptions, expectations and satisfaction. We tested knowledge in certain cases and correlated many of our findings with outcomes. Metrics such as falls, activity level and office visits were recorded, providing valuable insight into our overarching mission. We were overall less concentrated at this stage to understand the long-term impact of the interventions, though we continue to monitor them, focusing more on identification and using technology (predominantly mHealth) as the enabler.

We used clinical settings for both the exchange of information and the implementation of interventions, and captured data through mobile devices and some remote monitoring where applicable. A summary of methods is provided in Table 6-1. Whether on rounds, in the clinic, or in support groups, we used trained assistants to work with the patients and introduced doctors at appropriate times.

Our largest study consisted of combining many of these efforts into one. We met with more than 200 patients and initiated an engagement program involving and activated by physicians. Due to budget constraints, we did not utilize a completed platform, however, we made all resources available and easily accessible for patients. Physicians met with these patients in a routine clinical visit, and then based on a quick assessment of where patients were in their care path, pointed them to specific interventions based on the research previously conducted by our team. The main ones included the engagement game, the social network, digital point-of-care tools, a virtual peer support group, and others. Patients were then able to take this "digital prescription" and adopt the interventions they felt to be most relevant, starting with the actual clinic visit. Importantly, this sequence started and ended with the physician, who would track the patient's progress on the next visit with any of the interventions and where applicable, building off the ones that resonated most with that patient.

RESULTS

Results for most of the studies are summarized at a high level in Table 6-1. Specifically, Table 6-2 provides a more thorough review (note: some results have been shared on an ongoing basis throughout our research; however, these data extend those numbers and add new endpoints).

Table 6-2: Summary of Studies–Results.

	Patient Satisfaction	Real-Time Point of Care Tools	Patient Needs and Time Spent	Physician Needs	Instructional Course	Gaming
Result	1. A majority of patients' hospital experiences differed significantly from what they expected. 2. Areas specifically targeted were plans for home care, discharge process and understanding of diagnosis. 3. Patients desire (and expect) more education and information that is relevant to their individual point in care. 4. Real-time information and education pulsed along the continuum of care could dramatically influence the satisfaction and experience of hospitalized patients.	Patient satisfaction with digital point-of-care tools is reflected as follows: • Print 30 percent • Print on iPad 30 percent • Interactive 55 percent • Interactive with resources 75 percent • Interactive with resources shared by physician 90 percent	With digital toolkit, patient responses on the perceived time spent with physicians and the fulfillment of their needs were improved as follows: • Routine visit 55 percent/ 40 percent • Sharing information at baseline with toolkit 70 percent/ 60 percent • Augmented sharing 85 percent/ 80 percent • Knowledge of both medications and diagnosis increased over 20 percent.	• 95 percent of physicians reported improved access to real-time information. • 90 percent felt it facilitated information distribution. • 90 percent reported improved self-education. • 85 percent reported broadening of patient interactions. • 75 percent felt available web sites/ apps did not maximize the capabilities of the devices or fully address their needs.	• 95 percent reported a more thorough understanding of use cases for mobile technology. • 85 percent reported a more thorough understanding of how to integrate into daily patient care. • 80 percent of physicians reported an "excellent" rating on course objectives. • 65 percent would like more information on how to use.	After completing the game, patients reported (scale: 1 not at all, 5 very much): • Empowered 4.3 gamers vs. 2.3 control; • Connected to Peers 4.7 vs 2.5; • Part of a Group 4.2 vs 3.1 • Motivated to Improve 4.6 vs 2.4 • Average number of falls decreased in one year period from 1.7 to .9 per month • Activity level, as measured by going for a walk more than 2 blocks increased from average of 1.5 to 2.2. • 80 percent appreciated the connection more between games and health.

In our most recent and robust study, we found the following to be statistically significant ($p<.05$) pre to post intervention:
- 65 percent of patients were more satisfied with their physician's approach to providing additional helpful information after the physician initiated the program and provided the patient with choices.
- 80 percent of patients appreciated the physician attempts to share education.
- 47 percent of patients felt more informed to manage their disease.
- 43 percent of physicians felt their patients would improve their self-care.

- 70 percent of physicians felt more confident that their patients had the right information.
- 85 percent of physicians agreed that the tool's flexibility and relevance were beneficial features.
- 68 percent of physicians saw the connection between prescribable apps and our approach.

A significant ($p<.001$) number of physicians felt they had provided better education to patients after the process than before; likewise, patients overwhelmingly stated that the approach was helpful. A proportion of both physicians and patients did not feel this toolkit was useful for three main reasons: 1.) They viewed technology as a barrier to communication/understanding (17 percent); 2.) They did not own devices (14 percent); and 3.) They did not understand the purpose of the program (2 percent). There was no correlation to demographics, though there was a slight skew to patients over 80 falling into the group who did not feel the approach was meaningful.

These results are also captured by many testimonials including the following two quotes, one from a patient and one from a physician:

Patient Smytha: "*I have undergone a lot of surgeries for my amputation and have been in the hospital many, many times because of them. It was not until now that I felt like my doctors understood the challenges I was going through and had a clue how to address them. Just by providing the choices and giving me the resources that were right FOR ME – I can't thank Dr. Heckman enough!*"

Doctor Bonder: "*The women I see on a daily basis deal with a multitude of issues: physical, social and emotional. The ability to help them navigate their care in a seamless manner has tremendously increased their feelings of control and satisfaction with their situation. This is more than a placebo effect; this represents a great step forward in understanding the individuality of patients and how physicians can best identify and provide personalized information and resources that do not interrupt our workflow.*"

CONCLUSION

To observers of the health system, the idea that it is an immovable object might seem a fitting analogy, despite the recent surge to reform it. Indeed, the healthcare delivery system is facing an important cusp in its trajectory. Achieving the Triple Aim (better outcomes, reduced costs and higher satisfaction) is an admirable goal and will entail scrutiny of social systems, care plans and numerous other factors. Mobile technology is an enabler in this conversation; consequently, knowledge attained by our work and others will help the healthcare system to improve personalized care. Our results are simply another step in the quest to improve the dynamic of health delivery, and to uncover better methods of providing physicians and patients the right information at the right time. Perhaps the push toward patient engagement will prove an unstoppable force that can disrupt the paradox.

The authors would like to thank all of the staff, physicians and patients who participated in these studies over the years. Specifically, we would like to point out the great contributions of the following: Dr. Jaclyn Bonder, Geoff Hall, Dr. Alex Moroz, Kathleen O'Rourke, Dave Norfleet, Dr. Matthew Diamond and Jeffrey Yip.

REFERENCES

1. http://pewinternet.org/Reports/2013/Health-online.aspx. Accessed July 28, 2013.
2. Fowler F, Gerstein B, Barry M. How patient centered are medical decisions? *JAMA*. July 2013; 173(13): 1216-1221.
3. Greene J, Hibbard J, Sacks R, et al. When seeing the same physician, highly activated patients have better care experiences than less activated patients. *Health Affairs*. 2013; 32(7): 1299-1305.
4. Chase D, Christensen K, Tritle B, et al. (2013) *Engage!*. HIMSS.
5. http://content.healthaffairs.org/content/32/2.toc. Accessed July 28, 2013.
6. Topol E. (2013) *The Creative Destruction of Medicine*. Basic Books.
7. Blanch-Hartigan, D. An Effective Training to Increase Accurate Recognition of Patient Emotion Cues, *Pt Ed and Cnsl*, Vol. 89, No. 2, Nov 2012, pp 274–280.
8. Goetz T. (2011) *The Decision Tree*. New York: Rodale Books.
9. Smih S, Curtis L, Wardle J, et al. Skill set or mind set? Associations between health literacy, patient activation and health. *PLoS One*. 2013; 8(9): e74373.
10. Forbat L, Cavless S, Knighting K, et al. Engaging patients in health care: an empirical study of the role of engagement on attitudes and action. *Patient Educ Couns*. Jan 2009; 74(1): 84-90.
11. www.healthaffairs.org/healthpolicybriefs/brief.php?brief_id=86. Accessed August 1, 2013.
12. www.ncbi.nlm.nih.gov/pmc/articles/PMC1337906/pdf/cmaj00069-0061.pdf. Accessed August 1, 2013.
13. www.forbes.com/sites/davechase/2012/09/09/patient-engagement-is-the-blockbuster-drug-of-the-century/. Accessed August 1, 2013.
14. www.hl7standards.com/blog/2012/08/28/drug-of-the-century/. Accessed August 1, 2013.
15. Hesse B, Moser R. Surveys of Physicians and Electronic Health Information. *NEJM*. 2010; 362: 859-860.
16. Routh J, Gong E, Cannon G, et al. Does a controversial topic affect the quality of urologic information on the Internet? *Urology*. 2011; 78: *1051-1057*.
17. Gabarron E, Fernandez-Luque L, Armayones M, et al. Identifying measures used for assessing quality of YouTube videos with patient health information: A review of current literature. *Interact J Med Res*. Jan-Jun 2013; 2(1): e6.
18. Eastman P. Cancer Patients Increasingly Confused by Internet Health Information; Trust in Physicians Growing. *Oncology Times*. June 2010; 32(11): 43-44.
19. Wong L, Hanmu Y, Margel D, et al. Urologists in cyberspace: A review of the quality of health information from American urologists' web sites using three validated tools. *Can Urol Assoc J*. Mar-Apr 2013; 7(3-4): 100–107.
20. Hungerford D. Internet access produces misinformed patients. *Orthopedics*. Sept 2009; 32(9).
21. Scullard P, Peacock C, Davies P. Googling children's health: reliability of medical advice on the internet. *Arch Dis Child*. 2010; 95: 580–582.
22. Erdem S, Harrison-Walker L. The role of the Internet in physician-patient relationships: the issue of trust. *Bus Hor*. 2006; 387-393.
23. http://mashable.com/2012/06/15/online-medical-searches. Accessed August 12, 2013.
24. Elwood D, Heckman J, Bonder J, et al. Assessing patient expectations and concerns in a Physical Medicine and Rehabilitation unit: A real-time snapshot. *PM&R*. June 2010; 2(6): 521-527.
25. Bonder J, Heckman J, Elwood D, et al. Implementation of peer review into a Physical Medicine and Rehabilitation program and its effect on professionalism. *PM&R*. Feb 2010; 2(2): 117-124.
26. Heckman J, Bonder J, Elwood D. Evaluating the efficacy of a hospital-based multidisciplinary amputee support group. *PM&R*. Sept 2009; 1(9): S194.

27. Heckman J, Elwood D, Beltran J. Evaluating the efficacy of an informational portal for amputee rehabilitation. Association of Academic Physiatrists.

28. Elwood D, Diamond M, Heckman J, et al. Mobile Health: Exploring attitudes among Physical Medicine and Rehabilitation physicians toward this emerging element of health delivery. *PM&R*; July 2011; 3(7): 678-680.

Chapter 7

Blue Button — Empowering Consumers for Shared Decision Making and Improved Health: A Case Study

By Susan C. Hull, MSN, RN

In 2010, the U.S. Department of Veterans Affairs (VA) included a Blue Button icon on its My HealtheVet patient portal to indicate to veterans a way to securely download their health information electronically.[1] Since then, the use of the Blue Button has expanded beyond the VA to other government agencies and private sector and non-profit organizations. More than 1.7 million unique veterans, Department of Defense (DoD), and Centers for Medicare & Medicaid Services (CMS) beneficiaries have used the Blue Button to download their health data[2] through the My HealtheVet web site, the VA Mobile Blue Button, Tricare Online, and CMS MyMedicare.gov; with more than 8 million Blue Button views since inception.

Additionally, under the leadership of the Department of Health & Human Services' Office of the National Coordinator (ONC), a voluntary pledge community was launched in 2011, catalyzing a larger group to increase awareness of health data and educate consumers to make it easier for individuals and caregivers to have secure, timely and electronic access to their health information. More than 500 federal, state, private sector and non-profit entities, including payers, providers, health exchanges, labs, pharmacies, health information technology vendors, Regional Extension Centers, states, research institutes, associations, consumer advocacy groups and mobile health innovators have taken what is now known as the Blue Button Pledge[3], inspiring a movement to experiment and learn how to effectively engage and empower consumers in accessing personal health information.

In 2012, responsibility for encouraging broader use of Blue Button and enhancing its technical standards[4] was transferred to the ONC's Consumer eHealth Program. "On the simplest level, Blue Button is a literal 'button' that lets consumers get their health information online… it's also becoming a rallying cry for change, a shorthand way of referring to the growing reality and future potential of consumer and patient engagement supported by better health information and tools," says Lygeia Ricciardi,

Director of ONC's Office of Consumer eHealth.[5] The vision is that any consumer in any healthcare setting in America will be able to view, download, use and share their personal health data from any provider, hospital, pharmacy or other data holder through web and health apps. The hope is that the Blue Button symbol will become as ubiquitous and understood as other concepts like the Energy Star and Recycling symbols, created by the federal government and now widely used by the private sector.

Members of the Blue Button Pledge Program include "data holders," such as healthcare providers and systems, payers, health information exchanges, labs and pharmacies, which together reach more than 100 million Americans, and agree to offer them electronic access to their own health information. Members of this group include the Cleveland Clinic, Partners Healthcare, Aetna, United, the New York eHealth Collaborative, Quest and Walgreens. "Non data holder" members, such as Microsoft, Oracle and Humetrix agree to build useful tools for consumers that enable them to take action with their data, and spread the word about the importance of Blue Button and health engagement. These include associations and entrepreneurs, such as AARP, the American Cancer Society and the CEO Alzheimer's Association. As year three of the program unfolds, pledging organizations are being asked to make good on their pledge to make it easier for individuals and their caregivers to have secure, timely and electronic access to their health information; to encourage individuals to use this information to improve their health and care; and to engage and empower individuals to be partners in their health through information technology.[6]

Policy levers are also fueling the movement. Recent clarification to the Health Insurance Portability and Accountability Act (HIPAA) clarifies that when a patient's information is stored electronically, patients have the right to obtain an electronic copy and to have that copy sent at their request to another person or entity, like a doctor, a caregiver, a personal health record or mobile health app.[7] The recently modified Clinical Laboratory Improvement Amendments (CLIA) supports access of completed lab tests directly to consumers upon request. This CMS-CDC-OCR rule[8] amends the 1988 CLIA regulations, and specifies that, upon a patient's request, the laboratory may provide access to test reports that, using the laboratory's authentication process, can be identified as belonging to that patient. Subject to conforming amendments, the rule retains the existing provisions that provide for release of test reports to authorized persons and, if applicable, the individuals (or their personal representative) responsible for using the test reports and, in the case of reference laboratories, the laboratory that initially requested the test. In addition, this rule also amends the HIPAA Privacy Rule to provide individuals the right to receive their test reports directly from laboratories by removing the exceptions for CLIA-certified laboratories and CLIA-exempt laboratories from the provision that provides individuals with the right of access to their protected health information.

"Blue Button is a *movement* for patient engagement; a *mode* for consumers to get their health information from providers and other sources electronically; and a *mechanism*, for providers to meet Meaningful Use Stage 2 view, download and transmit requirements," says Ellen Makar MSN, RN, Senior Policy Advisor, ONC's Office of Consumer e-Health.[9] Novel web and mobile Blue Button applications and services are emerging to help people aggregate data from multiple sources and use their health data to better understand their health condition or manage their care, including portal and personal health record (PHR) solutions, mobile health wallets, in-case-of-emergency apps and other applications.

Related efforts encouraging easier and more complete electronic access to health records that have traditionally been off limits to patients are creating additional momentum. OpenNotes[10] is a national movement and large-scale action research project that encourages clinicians to invite patients to read their clinical visit notes online. As a proof of concept, it is hoped that giving patients access to their health data can be mutually beneficial for both patients and providers, and result in better communication and outcomes for patients. Patients with access to their clinical notes reported feeling more in control of their healthcare, had better understanding of their medical issues, and were more likely to take their medications as prescribed.[11] At the conclusion of the study, no doctors elected to stop sharing visit notes. The effort has recently been expanded to other clinical providers, inpatient and outpatient settings and may have some interesting use cases that will complement Blue Button.

The Health Record Banking Alliance (HRBA)[12] is encouraging pilots to demonstrate how consumer-controlled health records, including Blue Button records, can be compiled and stored in secure repositories and become a platform for affordable nationwide exchange of health information. William Yasnoff, MD, PhD, Founder and President of the HRBA, and former senior advisor to HHS on national health information infrastructure, stated, "Hundreds of efforts around the country to share information between unaffiliated providers continue to fail. Their technical architectures and lack of consumer control greatly limit their value, and thus their potential business models."

THE CHALLENGE: BLUE BUTTON SPREAD, INTEROPERABILITY AND SCALE

1. Adoption of personal health information technologies like Blue Button requires significant cultural shifts for data liberation, engagement and shared-decision making. A growing cadre of U.S. patients — alternatively called "consumers," "caregivers" or "health citizens" — are engaging in their own health and healthcare, and the health of people they care for in historically unprecedented ways through the use of personal health information technology (PHIT). Laying a timely foundation for the Blue Button movement, adoption of PHIT is enabled by the convergence of social and economic forces,[13] including a growing dependency on digital and mobile technologies in everyday life; expectations for real-time access to traditional and virtual health services; increasing clinical and financial responsibilities for patients; pressure on providers to transition from episodic to value-based and population health focused care; and significant regulatory and legislative mandates.

As detailed in *Engage! Transforming Healthcare Through Digital Patient Engagement* (HIMSS Books, 2013),[14] PHIT can bolster patient engagement by enabling people to better understand their health and health conditions; obtain access to their own health data in real-time or near real-time; improve communications with their doctors and providers; take more responsibility for their own health and health outcomes; improve their experience of interacting with the healthcare system; inform and educate their families and caregivers and get support about health and healthy behaviors from family, friends, caregivers, and health professionals. Blue Button has the potential to meet and complement these types of engagement needs. We are still learning as an industry about effective engagement, shared care planning, adherence and outcomes.

Healthcare providers and payers have historically been organized to protect and control, rather than liberate patient access to personal health information, and data liquidity has been constrained both culturally and technologically.[15] While a growing number of healthcare organizations provide patients with access to information via web-based patient portal systems, the idea of enabling all available personal health information to be combined into single and/or aggregated electronic files that can be viewed, downloaded and transmitted (and/or printed) by consumers, and directed by consumers, is novel.

While the Blue Button concept at its core is a simple idea that solves the critical problem of single and standardized data access, it will require cultural shifts for consumers and providers to successfully support placing control of data and information in patients' hands. Enabling the idea of "consumer empowerment" to take on real and practical meaning in multiple settings of care, including the patient's home or neighborhood, and across care settings, is a fundamental shift. The ultimate goal for Blue Button is not simply getting consumers to access their health data through PHIT; rather these tools need to be tailored to the needs, preferences, mobile lifestyle and motivators for consumers to access, use, and manage their health through shared decision-making.

"Placing the patient in full control of their personal health information is disruptive to the culture of medicine, which continues to harbor lingering professionalism and paternalism. In effect, the Blue Button has cracked open the vault of the medical record."[16]

2. Awareness and consumer demand is low despite apparent early interest in Blue Button. Current exposure to and experience with Blue Button is low for consumers outside of the VA, DoD and CMS. The VA is evolving their learning with the My HealtheVet (MHV) Patient-Centered Redesign Program, recognizing they are part of the "PHR paradox," where interest is high, yet adoption is low.[17] MHV is an interdisciplinary team under the Office of Informatics and Analytics that works with the Office of Information & Technology (OIT), other VA and Veterans Health Administration (VHA) offices, Department of Defense, Medicare, Indian Health Services (HIS) and personal health record (PHR) private sector partners, including Kaiser, Mayo, Cleveland Clinic and consumer health informatics communities. The redesign efforts will allow veterans to share all or part of their personal health information with their healthcare providers, both inside and outside the VA, as well as with family, caregivers or other individuals of their choosing. Other innovations are expected to expand the number of products and resources available to veterans within the VA's My HealtheVet PHR to improve and increase co-management and advocacy through Blue Button.

In an effort to increase awareness of Blue Button, the ONC has developed a three-pronged, multi-faceted approach known as the "Three A's" — Access, Action and Attitudes — to empower individuals to become engaged and active in their health through health information technology. Consumer eHealth tools are changing the nature of how providers and patients interact and share decision making, while broadening our definition of consumers to encompass patients, families and caregivers.[18] ONC has continued to build relevant content on its Health IT.gov web site,[19] including a series of patient videos and testimonials featuring the value of access to and action with health information.

ONC recently conducted focus group testing to inform the development of public service announcements (PSAs) that will be part of a nationwide Blue Button communications campaign scheduled to launch in early 2014. The centerpiece of the campaign is a new tool — the Blue Button Connector (www.healthit.gov/bluebutton) — that helps people find out which providers offer Blue Button and what apps and tools exist to help people use their information once they get it. The campaign[20] is intended to promote the concept of Blue Button, which surveys show is very appealing to folks, and address the general lack of awareness about Blue Button. The PSAs will feature family and caregivers, as well as provider and consumer-focused messages.

Tracking consumer adoption rates of Blue Button is early and likely, will be challenging. Some data reflects actual use, and other estimates market sizing and potential adoption. Highlights include:

- In October 2011, McKesson's Relay Health Division won the VA-sponsored Innovation Initiative (VAi2) Blue Button for ALL Americans[21] contest by adding Blue Button functions to the patient portals it offers through its 200,000 physician and 2,000 hospital clients. The contest was designed to encourage widespread Blue Button use and assure that all veterans had access to their Blue Button health data, regardless of whether they sought care from the VA or from a private non-VA healthcare provider.
- Walgreens, with 8,000 stores located within five miles of 75 percent of the U.S. population, has embraced Blue Button with both desktop computer and mobile apps that provide customers with a downloadable PDF file of all their prescriptions, among other things.
- The U.S. Office of Personnel Management has asked all health insurance carriers (more than 200 serving approximately 8 million federal employees, members of Congress, their families and retirees) participating in the Federal Employees Health Benefit Program (FEHBP) to add Blue Button functionality to personal health record systems (PHR) on their web sites.
- Veterans, Tricare military members and Medicare beneficiaries can use Blue Button through their federal patient portals. Cross-agency collaboration continues, and a monthly Blue Button Common Core Metrics Report provides statistics of use for VA, DoD and CMS. As of August 2013, more than 1.7 million unique veterans, DoD and CMS beneficiaries have already used Blue Button to download their health data[22] through the My HealtheVet web site, the VA Mobile Blue Button, Tricare Online and CMS My Medicare.gov; with more than 8 million Blue Button views since inception.
- Private payers announced their support with member reach projections. Aetna offered Blue Button to more than 36 million members. United Healthcare plans to support nearly 26 million of its enrollees to access their PHR with the click of the Blue Button.[23]

3. Provider adoption is low and may reflect the lack of a strong business case for sharing information with patients and concerns about privacy, security and consumer-mediated exchange. Current exposure to and experience with Blue Button is low with front-line clinicians, providers, payers, HIEs, pharmacies and vendors who are early in the development of pilots and education initiatives. As more health information becomes digital, through adoption of EHR technology fueled by the CMS EHR Meaningful Use Incentive Programs, it will become easier for patients and caregivers to access their information electronically. Meaningful Use Stage 2 requirements that went into effect October 1, 2013, for eligible hospitals and January 1, 2014, for eligible providers require that certified EHR technology enable patients with a way to view online, download and transmit (VDT) their health records for a minimum of 5 percent of patients. Meeting these requirements may stimulate adoption of Blue Button, although additional outreach is needed to educate the vendor and provider community about the value of adding and implementing the BlueButton+ guidelines to their solutions.

Healthcare provider organizations are also in the early stages of developing comprehensive patient engagement strategies, and Blue Button initiatives may or may not be explicitly linked. The National eHealth Collaborative (NeHC) Consumer Engagement Survey of CMIOs[24] indicates 59 percent of healthcare organizations report that their consumer engagement and health IT strategies are evolving, while 33 percent report that their strategy is not clear at all. According to NeHC CEO Kate Berry, "Effectively leveraging health IT to engage with patients and consumers will lead to better healthcare outcomes. Our survey shows that a majority of organizations believe in the strategic importance of consumer engagement yet their strategies are understandably nascent."

During a recent AMIA Fellows Debate,[25] the question of whether health information exchange organizations should "shift their principal focus to consumer-mediated exchange in order to facilitate the rapid development of effective, scalable and sustainable health information infrastructure" was debated. Debaters recognized that both provider and consumer-mediated exchange are needed, one propelling and maturing the other. Cultural barriers exist, including provider concerns about the liability of relying on data from other providers and unsolicited data from consumers. Another challenge is a lack of commonly accepted approaches to identify and authenticate patients when they request access to their health information.[26]

Will the Blue Button movement create an ecosystem of apps and tools that allow consumers to circumvent traditional silos by mediating their own exchange? How will we support consumers to manage and reconcile the many sources of potential Blue Button health information as they interact across settings? These and other questions will need to be addressed to build provider and consumer confidence, trust and adoption.[27]

Current Blue Button approaches are largely centered on the provider/payer to patient relationship and workflows, making current electronic data available as a *push* to consumers. As consumers begin to mediate their own exchange, *pull* and aggregate health data from multiple settings (providers, payers, retail pharmacies, and care settings across the continuum) and multiple sources (including sensors, patient generated health data, provider entered data, claims data), new approaches for privacy, security, consent and data segmentation are needed. Patients as consumers may want to authorize any app they choose, and incorporate those prescribed by a provider, a pharmacist, a dietitian, physical therapist or themselves. Consumers may want to manage their preferences, and choose their circle of sharing, dynamically over time. Consumers will want to have reliable ways of tracking the source of data, where and when it has been shared, and data provenance much the way they do banking and other personal information. Sense making and shared decision making needs for the consumer are different than for the provider or payer and will need to be addressed.

4. Technical guidance and framework is in place for BlueButton+, yet standards are voluntary. Technical standards and the development community are also evolving. The VA's initial rollout of Blue Button enabled patients to view their health information online and download or print in either an ASCII text or PDF format to share with their healthcare providers, caregivers and others they trust in a technically straightforward, but bare bones way. Today, veterans can download and share their data either in print or as an electronic file on a flash drive, for example. New efforts in 2014 will give veterans the ability to send their health records as a file attachment using secure messaging and to send a health summary (VA CCD) electronically to a non-VA provider or system via DIRECT.

The recent release of implementation guidelines called Blue Button Plus (BlueButton+)[28] serve as a blueprint for providers, payers and third-party developers to facilitate the structured and secure transmission of personal health data on behalf of an individual consumer. Through a public-private collaborative process run through the ONC's Standards & Interoperability (S&I) Framework Initiative, 68 volunteer organizations have worked to build off of Meaningful Use (MU) Stage 2 requirements and develop this voluntary implementation guidance. These guidelines go above and beyond what is strictly required by MU, and are consistent with and build off those requirements.

The implementation guide for data holders/providers and for third-party applications advances Blue Button as the symbol for patient access to their own health data, and BlueButton+ as the preferred way to enable patients to get their records in a human- and machine-readable format and send them wherever they choose. This enables a consumer to do everything from printing a physical copy to sharing it with a third-party application. BlueButton+ guidelines enable organizations to standardize the structure and transport of health information and electronic health records to support the use of more sophisticated tools that allow consumers to better share their Blue Button information with others they trust and plug them into apps and tools. Of interest, these guidelines make it easier for consumers to get automatic updates to their health records (e.g. "set it and forget it").[29] (See Fig. 7-1).

The S&I Framework efforts are catalyzing and supporting a diverse development community, and are encouraging pilots to test bi-directional push and pull of consumer's Blue Button data across multiple care settings, with interfaces as light as possible to facilitate mobile solutions. Utilizing the Blue Button REST API[30] using OAuth2 and the recently released open source C-CDA parsing code for iOS,[31] a demo of the API[32] the "Good Health Clinic" is a reference implementation of a Blue Button Data Holder. Other resources include C-CDA to JSON Parser[33]; a C-CDA Scorecard[34];

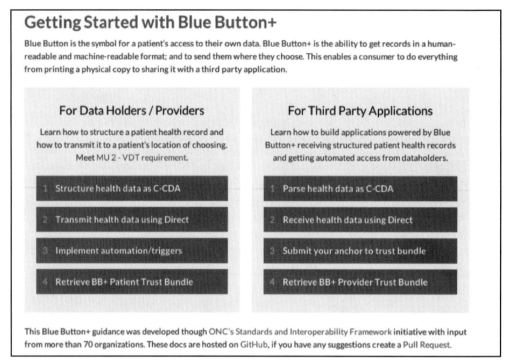

Fig. 7-1: Getting Started — BlueButton+ Implementation Guide.

and C-CDA generation helpers and tools, including Model Driven Health Tools to generate a C-CDA.[35] The BlueButton+ RESTful Pilots Workgroup[36] is convening a core group of BlueButton+ community members who are interested in actively piloting the BlueButton+ RESTful API. This workgroup is intended to provide a regular forum for discussion, troubleshooting and matchmaking between BlueButton+ Pilot WorkGroup organizations.

The Blue Button development community recognizes that Blue Button will thrive as an ecosystem play. As Dr. Josh Mandel recently reflected, "We're hashing out the details of an OAuth2-based framework that puts patients in control over when and how apps can fetch health data. An important question has been, how can we enable an ecosystem where thousands of apps connect to providers across the country in a trusted way?"[37]

Emerging technology, innovation and policy are intertwined. "A key aspect of this infrastructure is app registration, or a process by which data holders know which apps exist (and hence which apps a patient can authorize).[38] The S&I framework deliberations are uncovering needs for a both decentralized protocol for OAuth2 Dynamic Registration, that allows apps to register with BlueButton+ implementers in a fully automated fashion; as well as a centralized process, e.g. Trust bundle-based registration, where app developers apply for membership in a national "trust bundle" that each BlueButton+ implementer would rely on.

5. Blue Button innovators are hampered with a lack of data flow and relevant research, yet are creating momentum with novel challenges and code-a-thons. Like a chicken-and-egg problem, demonstrating the impact of patient access to health data on engagement, behavior change and shared decision making is largely in the early experimental stage, especially that which is explicitly linked to Blue Button. There currently are not enough consumer apps and tools to help consumers meaningfully engage and use their health data (including Blue Button), and the information flow is needed to create an app market and vice-versa. There is a growing evidence base that demonstrates the positive impact of consumers having e-access to health data but that additional research is needed to evaluate the impact on patient satisfaction and outcomes, as well as evaluation of the impact on provider practices, e.g. on call volume and practice efficiencies since gains could be made in this area as a result of streamlining some of these processes.[39]

A new breed of behavior enhancing applications (BEA) are changing how consumers manage their fitness, health and mobile lifestyle and are informing needs for preference-sensitive Blue Button solutions. The ubiquitous availability of mobile phones, and increasing rate of what has been slow adoption of smartphones and tablets is radically changing how consumers acquire information, track behaviors and choose to share that information with their social network and care teams. The adoption of mobile for life and health management is changing how we transform systems of care and leverage technology to meet patients where they are to improve care and health outcomes, and lower cost. There are approximately 5.9 billion mobile subscribers, 87 percent of the world population. The pervasiveness of mobile devices also allows providers to connect and engage patients in a personal and meaningful way outside the walls of clinics and hospitals to impact patient behaviors for improved health, a meaningful application of Blue Button.[40]

BEAs are being built collaboratively with developers, clinicians and behavior scientists and hold the potential to enhance human behavior.[41] For example, a BEA accessible on a smartphone, tablet or PC, as well as in your car and on home appliances ensures maximum exposure. The ability to combine patient interactive decision aids, health monitoring and location awareness with sensing require a team science approach to innovation, helping patients do the right thing at the right time. These BEAs may contribute to the Blue Button ecosystem innovating to garner market acceptance and desired outcomes.

A series of Blue Button and PHR design challenge events, code-a-thons, crowdsourced feedback and funding[42] are also moving the market forward, inviting Blue Button innovators in the public and private sector, including those with experience in developing BEAs. For example, the D+ Collab/Patient Record challenge invited designers across the country to reimagine the patient (personal) health record. Over 230 responded and inspired us with their submissions, with the showcase and framework open to others to innovate further on through GitHub.[43] Another effort called the Blue Button Co-Design Challenge,[44] sponsored by the ONC, HealthTech Hatch and Health 2.0, sought to engage patients and developers to work together to build applications that use BlueButton+ functionality to address salient patient problems. This effort engaged patients to crowdsource the winning application ideas and contribute in the co-design process alongside companies and application builders.[45]

Reflecting on why code-a-thons work,[46] Leonard Kish summarized key learnings with the capstone, "Developing New Patient Engagement Drugs," after the Fall 2013 Health 2.0 pre-conference event, sponsored by ONC and Optum. "Perhaps not immediately obvious, a gaming collaboration space is incredibly appropriate for a healthcare code-a-thon for a couple of reasons. First, what code-a-thon does is create a game out of innovation, and that's a key part of why they work, people like to compete and develop mastery in a social setting. The second reason is that game designers are experts at motivating decisions and behavior. Ultimately, motivating and enabling decisions and behavior are what any healthcare program or app will need to do in a value-based care system." Figuring out how behavior is changed actually happens in the gaming environment of the event, as Kish describes the power of paying attention to the narrative, the mastery and social aspects of the event, mimicking very much how patients and consumers experience health. Two tracks focused innovators: 1.) BlueButton and Patient Generated Health Data: Crossing the Chasm Between Consumer Devices for Wellness and the Rest of the Healthcare System; and 2.) Exploring New Types of Data: Redesigning the Explanation of Benefits. Kish congratulates the winner, Mind Mentor. "It was truly inspiring, and for a 'behavioral app' to screen for disorders, then give patients a nice visual for symptoms, a physician dashboard, and integration with Validic-integrated devices like Fitbit and Withings to track what works for them. I am betting we may see a lot more of this. This was a behavioral app, I might add, that incorporated narrative, mastery and social communication for behavior change."

ACHIEVING THE TRIPLE AIM: PROMISING OUTCOMES AND CASE STUDIES

Bringing Blue Button to adoption, interoperability and scale, for more than 314 million Americans in a complex care ecosystem, with measurable outcomes toward the Triple Aim of saving time, lives, money through technology, process efficiencies and innovation will take some time. We are early, yet promising outcomes, case studies and pilots are building a strong foundation.

Patient Experience, Consumer Engagement and Clinical Outcomes
- A number of studies are underway to evaluate the Blue Button and assess its impact in the VA, and support future implementation planning. Early insights demonstrate that patients value having easier access to their data, perceive that it improves their ability to participate in their care, and makes it easier for them to share information among multiple care providers. For example, 87 percent of respondents in a recent VA survey perceived that having access to Blue Button information was helpful to their care provider in making decisions about their care. When asked what was most useful about the Blue Button, 68 percent of respondents said that having their VA personal health information in one place was most useful, while 48 percent indicated that having an electronic file of their information was useful. Twenty percent indicated that being able to share a copy of their VA personal health information with someone else was most useful.[47]
- Another study at the VA examined the experiences of physicians, nurses, and pharmacists with patients using the My HealtheVet PHR portal and secure messaging systems with the goal of developing insights into the interaction of

technology and processes of healthcare delivery taking into account the social and organizational context of healthcare delivery and the reciprocal nature of patient engagement. Drawing on an information ecology perspective, qualitative interviewing explored the vibrant dynamic among technologies, people, practices and values, accounting for both the values and norms of the participants and the practices of the local setting. While adoption of the PHR portal and its functions has been lower in utilization than desired, the addition of secure messaging revealed a multidimensional dynamic between the trajectory of secure messaging implementation and its impact on organizational actors and their use of technology, influencing workflow, practices and the flow of information. While PHRs have been a consumer-oriented tool for patients, and secure messaging a tool for providers, these have not been brought together historically in implementation efforts. The study findings suggest that engagement must be a reciprocal process. "In effect, secure messaging was the missing element of a complex information ecology and its implementation acted as a catalyst for change. Secure messaging was found to have important consequences for access, communication, patient self-report and patient/provider relationships."[48] The VA My HealtheVet PHR research agenda calls for additional research about PHRs and their use, as well as significant progress via a collaborative partnership with the VA eHealth Quality Enhancement Research Initiative (QUERI) Center established in 2010.

- A recent deployment of a mobile PHR designed specifically for diabetes patients at Howard University Hospital (HUH) Diabetes Treatment Center in DC[49] has demonstrated that patients, in this case, urban poor, who are provided access to their personal health information (PHI) via a PHR can become a more engaged patient in self-managing their health. As part of this grant, HUH launched a PHR initiative creating a patient portal using NoMoreClipboard (NMC), linking NMC to their clinical diabetes EHR, CliniPro from NuMedics. The PHR provides patients with access to their problem list, vitals (height, weight, blood pressure, BMI), medication lists, basic lab results, HbA1c results and basic demographic information. The PHR has purposely been kept the simple and focused on the treatment of diabetes. Of the 1,000 patients, 26 percent have adopted the PHR, compared to national averages of less than 7 percent. HUH's own survey has found that 70 percent of all patients have a computer. "Digging deeper into those adoption numbers an even more revealing and stunning finding comes forth. While diabetes patients are evenly split across Medicare, Medicaid and commercial insurance, adoption and use of the PHR is not. The highest adoption and use of the PHR is among Medicaid patients, who make up 87 percent of all diabetic patients at HUH using the PHR. Why the strong adoption among this sub-group? Fragmented care. Dr. Nunlee-Bland, Center Director, explained that Medicaid patients must move from one provider or clinic to another to receive treatment — there is no consistency for this group as to where they receive their care and the PHR provides this group a "medical home" for their PHI which they value." Prior to launching this project, the average HbA1c levels for patients was 8.8, and reduced to 7.6 (~14 percent drop) and is continuing to trend downward. She attributes this to the patients having access to their PHI, particularly the ability to see trending data and visualize their progress. HUH has also seen a decrease in ER visits by patients using the PHR. On the strength of this project, the center has received an NIH grant to study the impact of a mobile PHR on pre-diabetic young adults. This study is under way now including integration of the PHR with a Fitbit device.

- Jubilee Community Health, a safety net clinic in rural Paoli, IN, has demonstrated successful results of a PHR pilot program for a small group of non-compliant and uninsured diabetes patients to better manage their chronic condition. This effort is part of an ONC grant awarded to the HealthLINC and HealthBridge HIEs to help improve consumer access to healthcare information.[50] Twenty-eight diabetes patients at the clinic were provided with a NoMoreClipboard PHR and trained to actively monitor their condition by providing blood sugar measurements on a daily basis, and utilize an electronic health diary to track their symptoms and diet. The PHR was configured for smartphone access, making it easy for patients to provide data. Patients also were provided with a laminated card containing instructions on how to access and use the PHR. As patients submitted blood glucose results, they were presented with immediate feedback based on entered values. When the PHR was set up, the patient coordinator helped patients populate the PHR, and lab results were integrated into the PHR from the clinical messaging service offered by the HIE that serves the area. Thirty-eight percent of the patients remained actively engaged and regularly entered blood glucose readings. Of these patients, 28.6 percent had improved HbA1c levels and reported feeling better. Conversely, of the patients who did not remain engaged, 21.4 percent of them had no improvement or increased HbA1c levels, and one of the patients whose HbA1c level increased suffered an MI.
- A recent collaboration and study, "eHealth2go" with MedStar Health System's Diabetes Institute and Get Real Health has demonstrated positive clinical results with a set of "integrated PHR tools;" the pilot group and key functionality has been expanded to mobile.[51] A pilot study determined whether a diabetic patient portal would help its most disadvantaged Type 2 diabetes patients and their families and their providers manage this disease. MedStar patients, who were low in socioeconomic status and elderly, saw significant reduction in HbA1c (9.3 percent to 7.7 percent) and in blood glucose (181 mg/dl to 153 mg/dl) as well as positive increase in eHealth literacy levels and patient satisfaction. The study built on learning that integrated PHRs, rather than stand-alone PHRs give patients and providers meaningful connected care. They offer a single view of a patient's health story, which must include mashing up data from all data sources and clinical repositories.[52] For this study, the web-based PHR and related set of tools included One Touch glucometers uploaded directly to the portal, out-of-range alerts, visual cues, disease-specific care plans, downloads of medical records, health diaries and collaboration with care managers. New kinds of reports to the providers were beneficial, and spurred value-added communication in between office visits. This project has received numerous awards for its innovation with the Medstar population. Awards include the 2011 Micro-

soft Innovation Award and the 2011 Promising Practice Award of Excellence at the 4th American Diabetes Association Disparities Forum.

Interoperability and Exchange

- In a recent study catalyzed by an ONC Challenge grant, "Consumer-Mediated Information Exchange: An HIE-populated personal health record for cardiac revascularization patients," 100 percent of patients were provided a web-based PHR to access, manage and benefit from electronic health information exchange data for a period of six months. The web-based PHR was pre-populated with clinical data from the regional HIE, supporting participants to enter in their own health data diary, and move health data back and forth. Findings demonstrated that seniors with chronic conditions, with assistance, can and will use a PHR to engage in the management of their health. Positive engagement outcomes were observed for all 200 patients who recently underwent cardiac revascularization with an increase in their Patient Activation Measurement (PAM) scores. Improved glycemic control was achieved for the subset of patients with a history of diabetes.[53] Collaboration included diverse partners, including Parkview Physicians Group, NoMoreClipboard, Indiana Health Information Technology Inc., The Med-Web HIE, Parkview Research Center, ONC, Parkview Heart Institute, Indiana University School of Medicine-Fort Wayne, and the Midwest Alliance for Health Education. PPCG is an Indiana Challenge Grant pilot site, and continuing to study labeled ePHR-COPE (Deployment of electronic Personal Health Records post Coronary intervention — analysis of Outcomes and Patient Engagement), evaluating the impact of an electronic PHR on intermediate health outcomes as compared to national statistics of similar patients.
- A critical-access hospital, Margaret Mary Health, is sponsoring a community wide patient portal in partnership with NoMore Clipboard that is populated with HIE data. While the case study does not have results, early indications are very positive. In less than one month of the launch, 1,200 patients signed up for an account out of a town population of 6,500.[54]
- Recognizing patients have care across many settings with diverse portals, collaboration among enterprise, regional and state HIEs will be needed to support Blue Button data portability for patients. Get Real Health in partnership with the state of Arkansas HIE and Optum Insight, is reaching out to rural providers with 500 or less patients. The HIE portal can support these providers to attest for MU and can include Blue Button, within these implementations, with a rapid implementation cycle of often less than a week. The portal is being designed to also support care management and data visualization tools, and also an ecosystem of health apps.
- One effort to follow is the National Association for Trusted Exchange (NATE),[55] a consortium of states developing a scalable Trust and Policy framework that eliminates the existing barriers inhibiting the use of health information exchange while addressing legal, policy and technical barriers to optimize national exchange of health information. NATE is currently executing a PHR pilot with support from the ONC's State Health Policy Consortium (SHPC)

with two use cases: 1.) recruited providers will send structured data to a patient-subscribed NATE qualified PHR using Direct secure messaging/Blue-Button+ specifications; and 2.) patient data will be sent by the test patient from their PHR to a second provider using DIRECT secure messaging/BlueButton+ specifications. The pilot goals are to identify and overcome policy, governance and technical challenges of transporting patient data bi-directionally between untethered PHRs (patients) and providers. California, Oregon and Alaska are leading pilot projects under this program. Other member states contributing to policy development of this program include Nevada, Utah, Hawaii, North Dakota, Michigan and Florida. Expected pilot deliverables include 1.) Identify and establish minimum technical, security and privacy requirements for PHRs participating in the pilot; 2.) develop a trust mechanism known as a "trust bundle" to facilitate the determination of trust on the part of NATE participants interested in either sending and/or receiving information to/from a PHR source; and 3.) identify and support PHR vendors and providers as they provide consumers with access to their data via DIRECT-enabled exchange.

- Cloud-based platforms and communities are also onboard to support interoperability. Microsoft HealthVault can also import VA Blue Button data and Patients Like Me has made available a free open-source parser to better translate the Blue Button health data that is in ASCII text into structured data that computer programs can read and use, as part of their commitment to join the Blue Button ecosystem.[56]

Mobile Innovation

- hReader, a project of Mitre Corp. Center for Health Transformation, is a patient-centric, simple, safe, mobile health data manager that provides patients and their families with their complete health information in the palm of their hand. It leverages the hData[57] and RHEx projects,[58] and provides an applet framework to provide hyper-personalized "focused-on-me" applets to engage patients in their own health status and how they can improve. hReader's code is open source, available for free, and is related to other initiatives. hReader works in conjunction with the RESTful Health Exchange project (RHEx) Patient Data Server to provide patients with their data. RHEx interfaces with a variety of different EHR systems and acts as a secure repository for patient data. RHEx also provides a single RESTful API, which hReader uses to access the data, with successful outcomes demonstrated during 2013 HIMSS Interoperability Showcase™.[59]

- Northrop Grumman has been testing a Blue Button mobile application to work on the Apple iPhone, according to James Speros, special assistant to VA's chief technology officer.[60] Veterans nationwide will have access to mobile Blue Button capabilities for their iPhones. Other vendors are developing Blue Button apps for other smartphones and tablets, he said. The apps are not just carrying data. "They're consolidating it, graphing it and making sense of it. They're helping consumers make decisions about their diets, their medications and their exercise and how they can choose to take action so they can be healthier," Speros said in a recent webinar sponsored by HIMSS.

- iBlueButton[61] enables patients to easily access and share their health records with any providers they visit, directly from their mobile devices. Now in its fourth version, the ONC Blue Button Challenge winning solution actually is a set of mobile apps working in tandem — one for consumers and one for healthcare providers, supporting the patient to download a Blue Button or C-CDA record generated by a provider EMR or HIE system, and another app for patient-provider record exchange between Apple and Android devices at the point of care. The mobile solution works with authorized direct programmatic access to the data source, or via the Humetrix Direct BlueButton+ server. This is a BlueButton+ patient trust bundle registered application,[62] enables patients to receive their health information from any EMR certified for MU-2 V/D/T or other BlueButton+ compliant data source.
- In September 2013,[63] Humetrix announced the debut of its newest solution, ICEBlueButton (In Case of Emergency), an app also recognized as the second place winner in the summer 2013 Blue Button Co-Design Challenge. The mobile phone and tablet app allows immediate access to critical personal health information via a QR code to EMS personnel or bystanders attending to an emergency. An ICE record can be immediately accessed by anyone attending to an emergency, and a complete health record which is available to authorized EMS personnel using the EMS module of iBlueButton *Professional* app. The BlueButton+ enabled application provides automated entry of complex medical data from existing online Blue Button records and allows the consumer to easily enter their own personal information to generate a "snapshot" of their personal health records — all retrieved via a QR code scanning the individual QR code generated by the app.

RESOURCES

The ONC's Blue Button Pledge community[64] is a voluntary mechanism whereby organizations commit to advancing efforts to increase patient access to and use of their own health data to improve their health and healthcare experience. Members benefit from participation in person meetings and webinars, networking, hearing updates from the federal government, and sharing and learning best practices from others who are working to advance a common goal: to use technology to support better health, better healthcare, and lower costs, and to meet the needs defined by individual consumers.

A number of the ONC Pledge community members have created toolkits, including the Alliance for Nursing Informatics,[65] committed to inviting nurses and nurse informaticists to take the pledge, experience eHealth themselves, to improve advocacy roles. Many of the 62 ONC supported Regional Extension Centers (REC) are also offering patient engagement services to the 140,000 providers they have worked with, including emphasis on Meaningful Use requirements.

The ONC's Standards and Interoperability (S&I) Framework initiatives[66] are open to public participation and not only include Blue Button, but an array of complementary work efforts. This collaborative community of participants from the public and private sectors, are focused on providing the tools, services and guidance to facilitate the functional exchange of health information. Activities are convened using a set of integrated functions, processes, and tools that enable execution of specific value-creating initiatives. Each S&I Initiative tackles a critical interoperability challenge through a rigorous process that typically includes 1.) development of clinically-oriented user stories and robust use cases; 2.) harmonization of interoperability specifications and implementation guidance; 3.) provision of real-world experience and implementer support through new initiatives, workgroups and pilot projects; and 4.) mechanisms for feedback and testing of implementations, often in conjunction with ONC partners such as NIST.

Federal Advisory Committees (FACA), supporting ONC to meet HITECH Act mandates, has recently added two consumer eHealth focused workgroups to the two current Health IT Policy Committee (HITPC) and the Health IT Standards Committee (HITSC). The Consumer Technology Workgroup (CTWG), under HITSC, and The Consumer Empowerment Workgroup (CEWG), under HITPC, are charged with providing recommendations on standards and interoperability issues and opportunities related to strengthening the ability of consumers, patients, and lay caregivers to manage health and healthcare for themselves or others. These FACA workgroups have initially focused on Patient Generated Health Data (PGHD) and will continue to address some of the policy, technical and other challenges associated with facilitating bi-directional exchange of patient information.

The National eHealth Collaborative (NeHC) and its recent Patient Engagement Framework[67] supports organizations and vendors to develop strategies, tools and resources for patient engagement. The Roadmap and Consumer eHealth Readiness Tool (CeRT)[68] offer a blueprint, assessment and guide to progress from Inform Me, to Engage Me, to Empower Me, to Partner with Me and to Support my e-Community. Efforts are currently underway developing a complementary Patient Experience Framework,[69] with consumer and provider personas that offer starting points for developing strategies, products and solutions.

With the Blue Button Connector coming in early 2014, mHealth developers, innovators, clinicians, payers and the entire ecosystem can make a personal investment in setting access to their own health data, and continue to take an active role in educating patients about these new resources, contributing to progress in the Blue Button movement.

CONCLUSION

While patient engagement has been named as the "blockbuster drug of the century,"[70] our understanding of how to effectively engage and empower consumers supported by current and emerging personal health information technologies (PHIT) for positive outcomes, is nascent and an emerging art and science. As we push for spread, interoperability and scale with Blue Button, our success will be measured in how we are able to improve care delivery models and successfully bend the healthcare cost curve.

Blue Button is a disruptive innovation, as a technology and cultural shift in the democratization of health data. For Blue Button to achieve its goals for patient centeredness, strategic openness among data holders will be required, along with continued distributed and interoperable solutions that fit consumers' mobile lifestyles, and privacy and security needs. Consumers will want transparency in making sense of how they choose to share their personal health information, who they share it with, and also in how it flows between healthcare settings, primary medical homes, exchanges, payers and other stakeholders in the ecosystem. Adoption is early, but has great potential to catalyze the growing adoption of PHIT tools by consumers, providers and payers.

We have decades of experience building provider- and institutional-centric electronic health records, systems and tools and are still struggling as an industry with achieving a truly interoperable health system. Harmonization of standards and interoperability, from a consumer engagement viewpoint, across the mobile landscape of EMRs, PHRs, patient portals, HIEs, and diverse settings of place-based and virtual care will require new work as an industry. As we better understand patient and family centric mobility and the need for dynamic, granular and portable consent, data portability, migration, corrections and reconciliation needs will only continue to escalate. Consumers will demand tools and services that help them make sense of their health information from multiple sources and settings and assist with managing episodic care, healthcare transitions and decision making.

Centralized and decentralized approaches are needed to support consumers to mediate exchange and manage their privacy and sharing preferences across traditional and virtual care settings. Empowering consumer-mediated exchange, like the vision for Blue Button compels, recognizes that health is mobile and social, and health improvement occurs in daily and longitudinal activities in traditional care settings (within the four walls), and also in workplaces, homes and communities (outside the four walls).

The Blue Button movement is an idea for our time, with unparalleled national momentum and innovative entrepreneurial experimentation. While we understand Blue Button today to be about supporting individuals and families, we have the potential of going beyond the activated patient to the activated community, where individuals and families see themselves as citizens of healthcare and builders of health in the community, rather than merely as consumers of medical services. Blue Button aligns with the learning health system and other citizen healthcare initiatives, as a way to engage patients, families, and communities as co-producers of health and healthcare.[71]

REFERENCES

1. Woods S. Veterans Affairs Health Administration Department of Veterans Affairs: patient engagement and the bluebutton. In: Oldenburg J, Chase D, Christensen KT, Tritle B, eds. *Engage! Transforming Healthcare Through Digital Engagement*. Chicago: HIMSS Books; 2013.
2. Nazi K. Informational interview and cross agency metrics: BlueButton and CCD inception through August 2013. October 8, 2013.
3. Health IT.gov. U.S. Department of Health & Human Services. The Blue Button pledge. Available at: www.healthit.gov/patients-families/pledge-info.
4. BlueButton+ Implementation Guide web site. Available at: http://bluebuttonplus.org/history.html.
5. Ricciardi L. Kicking off National Health IT Week: the Blue Button movement. Health IT Buzz. Available at: www.healthit.gov/buzz-blog/electronic-health-and-medical-records/blue-button-movement-kicking-national-health-week-consumer-engagement.

6. Health IT.gov. U.S. Department of Health & Human Services. The Blue Button pledge. Available at: www.healthit.gov/patients-families/pledge-info.

7. *Federal Register*. Modifications to the HIPAA Privacy, Security, Enforcement, and Breach Notification Rules Under the HITECH Act and the Genetic Information Nondiscrimination Act; Other Modifications to the HIPAA Rules. Available at: www.federalregister.gov/articles/2013/01/25/2013-01073/modifications-to-the-hipaa-privacy-security-enforcement-and-breach-notification-rules-under-the.

8. *Federal Register*. CLIA programs and HIPAA Privacy Rule; patient's access to test reports (CMS-2319-F). Available at: www.federalregister.gov/regulations/0938-AQ38/clia-programs-and-hipaa-privacy-rule-patients-access-to-test-reports-cms-2319-f.

9. HHS/ONC Consumer Health IT Summit. September 16, 2013.

10. Open Notes web site. Available at: www.myopennotes.org.

11. Robert Wood Johnson Foundation. OpenNotes. Available at: www.rwjf.org/en/grants/grantees/OpenNotes.html.

12. HITECH Answers. Health record banks a platform for health information exchange. Available at: www.hitechanswers.net/health-record-banks-a-platform-for-health-information-exchange.

13. Griskewicz M. The need for personal health IT—partnering with patients to change a paradigm. Available at: http://blog.himss.org/2013/09/13/the-need-for-personal-health-it-partnering-with-patients-to-change-a-paradigm.

14. Oldenburg J, Chase D, Christensen KT, Tritle B, eds. *Engage! Transforming Healthcare Through Digital Engagement*. Chicago: HIMSS Media; 2013.

15. Nazi K. BlueButton+ implementation: a key investment. Veterans and Consumers Health Informatics Office, Office of Informatics and Analytics, Veterans Health Administration, U.S. Department of Veterans Affairs; May 30, 2013.

16. *Ibid*.

17. Nazi K. Veterans' voices: use of the American customer satisfaction index (ACSI) survey to identify my healthevet personal health record users' characteristics, needs, and preferences. JAMIA;17(2):203-211;2010.

18. Ricciardi L, Mostashari F, Murphy J, Daniel J, Siminerio E. A national action plan to support consumer engagement via eHealth. Health Aff. February 2013;32(2):376-384.

19. Health IT.gov. Patient & Families. Available at: www.healthit.gov/patients-families.

20. Garrett P. Help us put Blue Button on the Map. Health IT Buzz. Available at: www.healthit.gov/buzz-blog/health-innovation/put-blue-button-map.

21. Merrill M. RelayHealth's PHR wins blue button contest. Healthcare IT News. Available at: www.healthcareitnews.com/news/relayhealth%E2%80%99s-phr-wins-blue-button-contest; U.S. Department of Veterans Affairs. VA announces winner of 'blue button for all Americans' contest. Available at: www.va.gov/opa/pressrel/pressrelease.cfm?id=2188; RelayHealth blog. RelayHealth donating 'blue button for all Americans' prize to wounded warrior project. Available at: www.relayhealth.com/news-and-events/blog/RelayHealth-Donating-Blue-Button-For-All-Americans-Prize-to-Wounded-Warrior-Project.html.

22. Nazi K. Informational interview and Cross Agency Metrics: Blue Button and CCD Inception through August 2013, October 8, 2013.

23. OpenHealth News. Blue button goes viral: United Healthcare promotes importance of personal health records to millions of enrollees. Available at: www.openhealthnews.com/content/blue-button-goes-viral-unitedhealthcare-promotes-importance-personal-health-records-millions. July 5, 2012.

24. National Health. Available at: www.nationalhealth.org/consumer-engagement-health-information-technology-survey.

25. Halamka JD. The AMIA healthcare information exchange debate. Life as a Healthcare CIO [blog]. Available at: http://geekdoctor.blogspot.com/2012/11/the-amia-healthcare-information.html.

26. Health Affairs paper by Williams C., et al. From the ONC: The Strategy for Advancing the Exchange of Health Information 31(3) 2012: 527-536.
27. Pak H, Hull S. Mobile health wallet as an enabler for patient engagement. *Healthcare Industry Perspective;* February 2013. Available at: www.Diversinet.com.
28. BlueButton+ Implementation Guide web site. Available at: http://bluebuttonplus.org.
29. Ricciardi L. Kicking off National Health IT Week: the Blue Button movement. *Health IT Buzz.* Available at: www.healthit.gov/buzz-blog/electronic-health-and-medical-records/blue-button-movement-kicking-national-health-week-consumer-engagement.
30. Blue Button REST API web site. Available at: http://blue-button.github.io/blue-button-plus-pull.
31. An open source CCDA parser for iOS applications web site. Available at: https://github.com/projectthreader/ios-health-data-standards.
32. Growth-tastic! web site. Available at: http://growth-pull.bluebuttonpl.us.
33. GitHub. Blue Button. Available at: https://github.com/blue-button/bluebutton.js/. + https://github.com/blue-button/bbClear.
34. C-CDA Scorecard. Available at: http://ccda-scorecard.smartplatforms.org.
35. Open Health Tools. Welcome to model-driven health tools. Available at: www.projects.openhealthtools.org/sf/projects/mdht.
36. S&I Framework Wiki. BlueButton+ Pilots. Available at: http://wiki.siframework.org/BlueButton+Plus+Pilots.
37. Mandel J. Getting data to patients: technology + policy. Smart. March 26, 2013. Available at: http://smartplatforms.org/author/jmandel/, Getting Data to Patients: Technology + Policy.
38. *Ibid.*
39. Telephone interview with Erin Poetter Siminerio, MPH, Policy Analyst, Office of Consumer eHealth, Office of the National Coordinator for Health Information Technology (ONC), U.S. Department of Health & Human Services; November 7, 2013.
40. Pak H, Hull S. Mobile health wallet as an enabler for patient engagement. *Healthcare Industry Perspective;* February 2013. Available at: www.Diversinet.com.
41. Boicey C. 2020: a look forward. HIMSS blog. Available at: http://blog.himss.org/2013/10/15/2020-a-look-forward.
42. Health 2.0. Blue Button Co-Design Challenge. Available at: www.health2con.com/devchallenge/blue-button-co-design-challenge/#background.
43. D+collab. The Patient Record. Available at: http://healthdesignchallenge.com.
44. Wong A. ONC announces winners of BlueButton+ Challenge. *Health IT Buzz.* September 16, 2013. Available at: www.healthit.gov/buzz-blog/health-innovation/onc-announces-winners-blue-button-challenge.
45. Datuit blog. What we learned during the blue button plus challenge. Available at: www.datuit.com/blog/entry/what_we_learned_during_the_blue_button_plus_challenge.
46. Kish L. Developing new patient engagement drugs. HL7. Available at: www.hl7standards.com/blog/2013/10/10/new-patient-engagement-drugs/#comments.
47. Nazi K. BlueButton+ implementation: a key investment. Veterans and Consumers Health Informatics Office, Office of Informatics and Analytics, Veterans Health Administration, U.S. Department of Veterans Affairs; May 30, 2013.
48. Nazi KM. The personal health record paradox: health care professionals' perspectives and the information ecology of personal health record systems in organizational and clinical settings. *J Med Internet Res;*2013;15(4):e70;doi:10.2196/jmir.2443.
49. Chilmark Research. Smashing myths & assumptions: PHR for urban diabetes care. Available at: www.chilmarkresearch.com/2010/11/12/smashing-myths-assumptions-phr-for-urban-diabetes-care.

50. NoMoreClipboard.com. Jubilee community health uses mobile PHR to improve diabetes outcomes for rural, uninsured patients. Available at: www.nomoreclipboard.com/news-and-events/171-jubilee.html.

51. Get Real Health. Case studies. Available at: www.getrealhealth.com/case-studies/medstar-health.

52. Caraballo C. Leveraging gaming and connected devices in patient engagement. HIMSS.org. Available at: www.himss.org/ResourceLibrary/ResourceDetail.aspx?ItemNumber=17876&src=sm.

53. NoMoreClipboard.com NMC case study. Available at: www.nomoreclipboard.com/wiki/images/9/95/NMC_Case_Study_COPE.pdf.

54. Telephone interview with Jeff Donnell, President, No More Clipboards, October 8, 2013.

55. National Association for Trusted Exchange. Available at: www.nate-trust.org.

56. Patientslikeme.com. Patientslikeme contributes free open-source parser to Blue Button initiative. Available at: www.patientslikeme.com/press/20120123/37-patientslikeme-contributes-free-opensource-parser-to-blue-button-initiative.

57. hData. Available at: www.projecthdata.org.

58. S&I Framework wiki. RHEx. Available at: http://wiki.siframework.org/RHEx.

59. hReader. Web site. Available at: http://hreader.org.

60. Mosquera M. VA enhances Blue Button features. *Government Health IT.* Available at: www.govhealthit.com/news/va-enhances-blue-button-features. January 23, 2012.

61. Humetrix. iBlue Button. Available at: www.humetrix.com/ibb.html.

62. Blue Button Trust Bundles. [web site]. Available at: https://secure.bluebuttontrust.org.

63. Humetrix. Humetrix ICE Blue Button wins the public vote for best app and second place award overall in the Blue Button co-design challenge. Available at: www.ibluebutton.com/pr-2013-icebluebutton-wins. September 13, 3013.

64. Health IT.gov. U.S. Department of Health & Human Services. The Blue Button pledge. Available at: www.healthit.gov/patients-families/pledge-about.

65. ANI. ANI initiatives and supported programs. Available at:www.allianceni.org/programs.asp.

66. S&I Framework wiki. Current 2012 S&I Framework Initiatives. Available at: http://wiki.siframework.org/S%26I+Framework+Initiatives.

67. National eHealth Collaborative. The Patient Engagement Framework. Available at: www.nationalhealth.org/patient-engagement-framework.

68. National eHealth Collaborative. Consumer eHealth Readiness Tool. Available at: www.nationalehealth.org/cert.

69. National eHealth Collaborative. The patient experience framework: using health IT to bring patients and providers closer together. [press release]. Available at: www.nationalehealth.org/blog/patient-experience-framework-using-health-it-bring-patients-and-providers-closer-together.

70. Kish L. The blockbuster drug of the century: an engaged patient. HL7 Standards. Available at: www.hl7standards.com/blog/2012/08/28/drug-of-the-century. August, 2012.

71. Doherty WJ, Mendenhall TJ. Citizen health care: a model for engaging patients, families, and communities as coproducers of health. *Families, Systems, & Health;* 2006;24(3):25163. Available at: www.drbilldoherty.org/pdf/Citizen_Health_Care.pdf.

Part II
The Drivers of Innovation

Chapter 8

The Drivers of mHealth Innovation

By David Metcalf, PhD

The nexus of mHealth's great potential and unique features with the enduring principles of innovation management is ripe for further exploration. Many of the tenants of this cross-section are found in the case studies throughout this book. Understanding some of the unique attributes and current trends in mHealth and applying these to a model for evaluating the effectiveness and worthiness of a particular innovation will lead to deeper understanding of the promises and pitfalls that mobile technology — and many other digital innovations hold for health.

BENEFITS AND FEATURES OF MOBILE DEVICES

mHealth is not defined by devices or their capabilities, but they do drive behavior and usage patterns that we can exploit to achieve health outcomes. The affordances of mobile devices carry great potential. Continuous connectivity, remote access, ease of use, lower learning curves, messaging, advanced sensors (cameras, accelerometers, GPS) and location awareness are just a few of the well-known characteristics that inform our daily use. Other important aspects include connectivity to devices and peripherals (including medical devices, fitness equipment, remote knowledge bases, enterprise systems and cloud-based resources). This connectivity supersedes apps, messaging and other capabilities contained directly on the device. The mobile device becomes a small window to the world and a gateway to the Internet of things that are emerging to connect to the new intelligence being imbued in devices as common as a refrigerator, fitness equipment and stethoscopes, or even advanced imaging systems and surgical robots. Fundamental changes are upon us and we are intuitively experiencing the effects in our daily lives inside and outside healthcare environments. As much as we are enthusiastic about the possibilities these affordances and trends open up, we must also mitigate issues of security, privacy, small screens and keyboards, accessibility, battery life and connectivity speeds. The potential to solve these problems drives as many innovations in mobile technology and mHealth as the brilliant capabilities.

ECONOMIES OF SCALE

One of the greatest aspects of mobile devices is their prolific growth and spread across the globe. On recent trips to Africa and some of the poorest countries in the Caribbean and Latin America, the spread and impact on people's lives even in developing countries was obvious. It is no wonder that with 6.5 billion devices in use — almost one per person, if it weren't for those of us who have multiple devices (you know who you are). How and why did this happen?

Cost Structures and Global Access

While the rest of the world outside of the United States does not have subsidized phones, there are incentives from various carriers and intense competition in many markets that keep prices low. In many countries, feature phones cost $30 and are the standard, with a small percentage able to afford smartphones. Cost of services can be reasonable for basic services like text messaging and mobile money applications. On a recent trip to Haiti, one of the carriers had a promotion, "Pay for three text messages, get 20 free." Text messaging costs and "banking of messages" encourages use and spill-over to other voice and data services. Call-me-back messages and other helpful universal data services can also be leveraged for health notifications. Keeping costs low and focusing on basic distribution using the simplest means possible is often effective.[1-3]

App Ecosystems

Another trend that has emerged and grown substantially is the model of apps — smaller software applications with fewer features, but easy-to-use interfaces to do a few things very well. From health information to tracking apps, health games and access to electronic medical records (EMR) or other clinical systems — apps have come a long way. App stores have emerged as a powerful model for economic stimulus and easier distribution and update of software. The Apple Appstore, Google Play and Amazon Appstore for Android, and GetJar are all examples. Having so many app stores has created some schisms in the marketplace and a sort of "format" and distributor war. This, plus the tight controls on some app ecosystems, does serve to limit the functionality available on certain platforms. Robust functions and complex processes can also be limited in the app ecosystem which may create a mismatch for some complex healthcare processes. Many successful mHealth programs include an app. Understanding how to navigate the app ecosystem, develop a sustainable business model, scale solutions for broad distribution across the various platforms, and determine where an app fits into the current marketplace can make or break a company or initiative.

Superapps

One possible solution to the dilemma of app size and limited function is to create suites of apps, or health kits made up of various apps that are loosely or tightly linked together. Something as simple as a folder to organize all of a certain type of app into a cohesive unit around a patient, condition or workflow could be a solution. A more sophisticated solution is to use superapps that can link various apps and media to each other. Superapps can integrate a capability across multiple apps (like speech recognition spanning several apps) or aggregate several apps' functionality under one umbrella app (like a portal framework). Either strategy can be used to build a robust linkage of capability across multiple apps.

Messaging for Health
Another form of connective tissue between apps is messaging. Whether using e-mail, text messages, instant messages or other forms of secure messaging like SDM (secure direct messaging), mobile access to messages can be the glue that links apps, capabilities, tasks and people to each other. Furthermore, it is often possible to educate, inform or even change behaviors and attitudes through lowest common denominator technologies that are used as gentle reminders, tips or links to media, systems or processes. Throughout the case studies in this book you will see advanced examples that use messaging for clinical applications, public health campaigns and education.

Hardware and Peripherals
Another trend we identified in our first book, *mHealth: From Smartphones to Smart Systems*,[4] was the evolution of hardware and peripherals. The actual devices themselves are advancing at a rapid rate. Other form factors are starting to emerge that go beyond the phone itself. From glasses to watches to shoe pods and many special-purpose, durable medical devices and home medical devices, the phone is quickly becoming a hub to unify data and specific health functions from a variety of sources. For both patients and providers, smartphones are transcending simple communication devices and simple app launchers. The model for connecting to complex, cloud-based systems and creating a link to Ashton's *Internet of Things* (1999), with the growing fleet of connected devices is creating a whole mHealth ecosystem.

Putting It All Together
Why is mHealth seen as so powerful and full of potential? The natural synergy of the entire mHealth ecosystem of smartphones, apps, messaging, easy access to media, superapps, connectivity to enterprise systems, peripherals and the Internet of Things coming together provides a multipurpose capability that goes beyond a simple handheld device. Through the cases, you'll see there is early evidence of the scalability and sustainability of mHealth and the ability to fulfill the Triple Aim of better care, faster and cheaper. We must also temper this with the ongoing challenges of security, global dissemination, durability and costs that are addressed in many of the cases.

Meeting Business and Health Goals
Beyond technical innovation, there are also process, business and health innovations that can be just as effective in promoting health. You will see myriad examples of novel business models and advanced processes that could be answers to a major concern over the sustainability and scalability of mHealth. Fig. 8-1, from *Business Insights*, adds clarity to the connections between key drivers.

Where Are We on the Innovation Curve?
With all of the promise and some issues that must still be addressed, it is easy to understand why mHealth may be high on the hype cycle, or even on the downward slope of a first of two innovation humps. Broken promises, unsustainable business

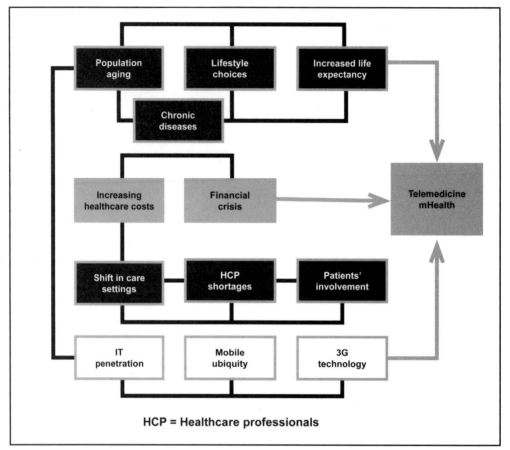

Fig. 8-1: Connections to Key Drivers.
(Source: Business Insights; Feb. 2011. Used with permission.)

models and a host of pilots that failed to scale or produce the expected clinical results have diminished some of the hopes and dreams of entrepreneurs and early advocates. We remain bullish, but have tempered this with a desire to share some of the failures or shortfalls of early projects so we can all learn from them, advance the state of the industry and fulfill some of the promises and dreams of mHealth (although probably not all of them).

Evaluating mHealth Innovation

Following models like Rogers *Diffusion of Innovation*[5] we can assess the effectiveness and outcomes of the various stages of mHealth and define a plan at a macro, societal level, as well as methods for determining the criteria for success with any given project or new product. Throughout the chapters you will see examples of methods for evaluating the outcomes, cutting through the hype and leading further down the road to mHealth projects and an entire mHealth ecosystem. These are the drivers of mHealth innovation.

REFERENCES

1. Dixon-Fyle S, Gandhi S, Pellathy T, Spatharou A. Changing patient behavior: The next frontier in healthcare value. *Health International.* 2012; *12*: 64-73. Available at: www.mckinsey.com/~/media/McKinsey/dotcom/client_service/Healthcare%20Systems%20and%20Services/Health%20International/Issue%2012%20PDFs/HI12_64-73%20PatientBehavior_R8.ashx.

2. Schwartz SM, Ireland C, Strecher V, Nakao D, Wang C, Juarez D. The economic value of a wellness and disease prevention program. *Population Health Management.* 2010; *13*(6): 309-317.

3. Shapiro JR, Koro T, Doran N, Thompson S, Sallis JF, Calfas K, Patrick K. Text4Diet: A randomized controlled study using text messaging for weight loss behaviors. *Preventive Medicine.* 2012; *55*(5): 412–417. doi:10.1016/j.ypmed.2012.08.011.

4. Metcalf D, Krohn R (Eds.). *mHealth: From Smartphones to Smart Systems.* Chicago: HIMSS Books. (2012).

5. Rogers E. *Diffusion of Innovation.* Boston: Free Press. (1999).

Chapter 9

Mobile Games for Health

By Brian Mayrsohn, MS, and Georges E. Khalil, MPH

"Over the next generation or two, ever larger numbers of people, hundreds of millions of people, will become immersed in virtual worlds and online games," wrote economist Edward Castroniova in *Exodus to the Virtual World*.[1] "The exodus of these people from the real world, from normal daily life, will create a change in social climate that makes global warming look like a tempest in a teacup," he continued. While this may seem a bit extreme to those unfamiliar with games, the numbers speak for themselves.

Gamers are everywhere, numbering more than 180 million people in the United States, 100 million in Europe and 200 million in China.[2] World-renowned game designer and best-selling author Jane McGonigal emphatically describes in her book *Reality Is Broken* that "reality doesn't motivate us effectively," and that in the real world our maximum potential is rarely achieved.[2] She argues that a major reason why people turn to games is to feel a "sense of being fully alive, focused, and engaged in every moment."[2] Games have been around for thousands of years, but never before have they been so pervasive within our culture. This is especially true considering how portable they have become. Mobile devices allow today's citizens to carry their game consoles everywhere, thus enabling them to casually sneak in short puzzles, races and mini-games whenever possible. As a result, avid gamers nearly eliminate mental downtime in their lives.[2] The original catalyst of this phenomenon was Nintendo, which introduced the Game Boy in 1989. Nintendo released a newer portable gaming console called DS, and Sony the PSP, in late 2004.[3] Subsequently, Apple introduced the iPhone in 2007 and a new cheap and scalable marketplace for games was born. When Apple first launched the iPhone in 2007, third-party applications (apps) were not permitted on the device, though there was a clear demand for it. Soon after its release, developers managed to "jailbreak" the iPhone. Since then, mobile apps have exploded. Today, the Apple App Store alone has more than 1 million apps for sale, including 100,000 games, forever changing the entire gaming industry.[4]

MOBILE GAMING: A BRIEF HISTORY

Smartphone stores opened a new marketplace for game developers to create games at more affordable costs. Emeric Thoa, CEO and Creative Director at The Gamer Bakers, estimates that most games developed on the Sony PlayStation Portable (PSP) range in development cost from $500,000 to $5 million.[5] In contrast, the games in smartphone stores cost anywhere from $50,000 to $300,000 (small to large indie mobile games) and from $500,000 to $1 million for big licensed app games.[5]

As of January 2014, Apple and Android's App stores combined boast more than 2 million apps, including 225,000 games,[4,6] whereas all Sony mobile devices plus DS have 2,354 combined (1,062 from PSP and 1,292 from Nintendo);[7,8] that is nearly 100 times more games! Fortunately, unlike these mobile relics, apps can be stored by the hundreds. No more clunky game carrying cases packed with cartridges. Some of the newer devices use memory sticks.

A noteworthy accomplishment for the gaming app industry occurred in November of 2011, when combined revenues for gaming apps on the Android and Apple iOS platforms outperformed the combined revenues of Sony's PSP and Nintendo's DS. (Fig. 9-1). This report from a mobile apps analytics company, Flurry, painted a very interesting story.[9] In the words of Dr. Bonnie Feldman, health games expert and entrepreneur, "The age of the smartphone and tablet as primary gaming devices is now upon us."

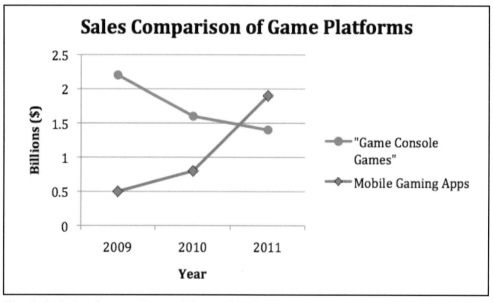

Fig. 9-1: Sales Comparison of Game Platforms.

MOBILE STATISTICS AT A GLANCE

In 2011, the Pew Internet & American Life Project reported that 80 percent of Internet users have looked up health-related information online.[10] Already, 18 percent of Internet users go online to look for others with similar health concerns, and studies show that people with chronic diseases are even more likely to participate.[11] Approximately 45 percent of Americans are already using smartphones and 26 percent of U.S.-represented respondents said they used iPods or other MP3 devices for sports-related exercise or fitness.[12] With 19 percent of smartphone users purchasing at least one health app from a sea of over 97,000 health apps, the mHealth marketplace is poised to hit $26 billion globally by 2017.[13] With such popularity and an abundance of sensors and affordable wearable technology, adopting health apps and games into one's daily life could not be easier. As sensor technology integrated with blue tooth and other data transmission processes on mobile phones becomes more advanced, self-reporting can be replaced with pathophysiological data, social context, activity level, and behavior patterns.[14] By harnessing the Internet's technological powers and social attraction, coupled with fun and engaging technologies, Internet-based games and game apps have the broad potential to increase physical activity and improve lifestyle choices.

GAMES FOR HEALTH

There are plenty of activities more fun than monitoring one's health. Most people would not put those words in the same sentence. What if doctors prescribed games to patients in an effort to captivate their imaginations and motivate them to engage in their health, or better yet, demystify medical jargon and reduce anxiety? Children's Hospital of St. Louis Missouri, currently uses mHealth games on iPads to relieve stress children experience prior to entering the operating room.[15] Thus far, clinical evidence has demonstrated games' tremendous potential to promote healthy behaviors and improve outcomes in areas including addiction, healthy eating, physical activity, smoking cessation, cancer treatment adherences, asthma self-management, and teeth-brushing technique.[16-21]

Traditional health interventions face many obstacles to dissemination, including low scalability, required manpower and resources. Internet video games may prove to be a cost-effective and efficacious alternative. "Video games offer a potential channel by embedding change procedures such as goal setting, modeling and skill development activities into a personally meaningful, entertaining and immersive game environment."[20] Furthermore, video games promote learning and social interaction, create an environment that enables users to see the effects of their actions and decisions, and encourage creative problem solving and understanding by encouraging systems thinking when helping the player see the "big picture."[22, 23] Additionally, once a game finishes production, it can then be scaled at a relatively low cost, especially when compared to traditional person-to-person interventions.

Over the past decade, Internet-mediated interventions that focus on physical activity[24-30] and diet[16,24,28,31,32] have become more prevalent. Games such as *Diab*[33] and *Zamzee*,[34] among other mobile and motion-controlled games,[25,35] have shown to have a statistically significant impact on anthropometric and physiological measures, as well as other health behaviors.

APPLICATION OF BEHAVIORAL CHANGE THEORY TO GAMES

While games apply different combinations of game mechanics, the most promising health games will likely be rooted in behavioral theory and applied psychological interventions.[36] The most researched game elements match constructs from several widely-used health behavior theories, including Social Cognitive Theory (SCT),[37] Self-Determination Theory (SDT), Transportation Theory (TT)[38] and Elaboration Likelihood Model (ELM).[36] Furthermore, these theories have been successfully used for decades in various types of interventions and experiments.[38-40]

In the context of games for health, cognitive-based theories such as SCT, SDT and ELM have allowed gaming researchers and designers to craft health messages that can be introduced in the game. For instance, research on narrative-based games have repeatedly applied SCT.[41,42] This theory argues that learning occurs through observational modeling; that is, through watching other people act in a particular situation and modeling behavior after exposure. In particular, SCT has allowed researchers to explicate narrative effects by investigating social modeling of virtual gaming characters and inspecting messages mentioned by the characters in the game. SCT as well as other cognitive theories have only inspected outcomes of exposure to health messages and have not been able to shed light on gaming characteristics that may explain such outcomes.

On the other hand, the study of interactive media effects reveals concepts that explicate well the success of games for health. For instance, experiential learning is a concept that highlights gaming characteristics that drive learning.[43] Experiential learning is an outcome of play that stimulates learning through experience. Activities in the game that bring about experiential learning provide an experience that is rich in exploration and that fosters curiosity. Players explore the virtual environment by taking actions. Ultimately, they begin to learn from the consequences of their actions. Such a learning method uncovers a diversity of outcomes that stem from healthy and unhealthy behaviors inside the game. Designers can simulate cause and effect relationships from behavior to health effects, in order to bring about experiential learning. As a result, games for health may arouse curiosity, which in turn encourages exploration and information discovery.[44,45]

Players do not only learn from the virtual environment that they explore, but they also begin to transfer the lessons from game play to the real world. Players tend to become immersed in the game world, which boosts perceived presence, leading to psychological and physiological outcomes.[46] As a result of spatial presence and experiential play, players begin to imitate virtual behavior when they encounter similar situations in the real world.[44,47,48] By linking the virtual experience to a real-world environment, players are able to shift their behaviors toward the desired healthy actions that are encouraged by the game.

In addition to experiential learning, transportation is key when the game is based upon a narrative. In the context of gaming, narrative is designed to be interactive. It is crucial to differentiate between traditional storylines (e.g., television dramas) and interactive narratives in games. While television dramas involve *watching* characters who find themselves in diverse situations and face multiple consequences, interactive narratives involve *becoming* characters that find themselves in situations and face consequences. As a result of narrative participation, gamers begin to pay more attention to the game's content, become emotionally involved in the game, and feel as if they are present inside the gaming environment. Such effects allow story immersion, which has been found to facilitate health promotion.[41]

GAME ELEMENTS MAKE LIFE FUN

Applying game elements in non-game environments to motivate users has proved highly effective at influencing behavior. Airlines and hotels use frequent flier miles and rewards in their loyalty programs to provide positive reinforcement and promote a certain level of competition. Businesses today have "gamified" marketing (banner ads of crosshairs shooting a target), sales (reward programs), customer engagement (games on company web sites), HR (internal gamified systems to track employees' lifecycles), productivity enhancement (levels and badges), and crowdsourcing data (experience points, rewards, competition and cooperation). Companies are finally moving into the healthcare space by taking advantage of the same principles that drive behavior change for a different purpose: to make people lead healthier lives. In 2008, Nike, the world's largest manufacturer of footwear and apparel, launched Nike+, a web site and app that syncs with smart phones to reward users upon completion of fitness milestones. These are examples of gamification, which is defined as "the use of video game elements in non-gaming systems to improve user experience and user engagement."[49]

GetHealth, a startup from Ireland that went through the Startup Health Academy accelerator in NYC, focuses on gamifying (verb for gamification) employee wellness. Their system is built on three pillars: Move, Munch and Mind. Their proprietary calibration system quantifies each activity an employee can choose from, and computes an equivalent value that allows friends with varying skill and exercise level to compete on an equal playing field (scorecards). GetHealth tailors messages to suit the needs of the individual in the form of "motivation" push messages that remind participants to "walk for 10 minutes" or "Eat five fruits and veggies today!" (quests) based on the original goals chosen by the employee in the beginning of the intervention (goal setting).

Healthcare and medical centers, too, see the symbiotic relationship in partnering with healthcare accelerators and startups. The centers provide a test-population for different games and products, and in turn the private sector demonstrates that the medical facility fosters innovation and bring leading-edge care directly at the bedside. Gecko Health Innovations, a startup supported by the Healthbox business accelerator since 2012, teamed up with a group of psychiatrists from Boston Children's Hospital to validate their gamified asthma medication adherence platform. GeckoCap, their first product, is a small, fun "smart cap" that fastens snugly atop an asthma inhaler to track medication adherence. It sends usage information to its cloud platform and displays the data in a gamified solution using points, rewards and goal-setting to drive medication compliance. According to Yechiel Engelhard, MD, MBA, MHA, Founder and CEO of Gecko Health Innovations, the firsthand connections between clinicians and their patients provided invaluable insight into asthma patients' needs, and helped determine how to increase the use of something kids inherently dislike.

More than just hospitals have joined the innovation efforts too. The range of potential partners is vast — from insurance carriers like Florida Blue and to smaller privately owned clinics like Metro Physical & Aquatic Therapy. The collaborative relationships between the startup community and healthcare organizations with built-in patient populations produces a mutual benefit that may ultimately improve the quality of care while also lowering costs.

THE ADVANTAGES OF MOBILE TECHNOLOGY FOR GAMING

Mobile games offer several advantages over their traditional counterparts. Not only do they offer availability, opportunities[50] and frequency[18] for interactive approaches,[30] but they also reach individuals through the diffusion of tailored information and messages.[51] In the context of public health, reaching the target population is paramount to achieving better outcomes. Media-based programs usually are able to reach a wide number of users, which facilitates the diffusion of information. For instance, with a wide reach of patients, physicians can save time and reduce unnecessary face-to-face communication with patients. As a result, patient-provider communication may become as easy as a click of a button. In particular, a survey of patients has shown that most prefer to have direct communication with their providers through their mobile phones, instead of simply using non-social applications.[58]

In the context of mHealth, reach is important for the mass diffusion of information and social interaction between players.[52] For instance, evidence-based research has shown that frequent text messaging of health information to mobile phone users can improve medication adherence.[53-55] Ultimately, mHealth programs can be successful tools in connecting patients to their providers for continuous support. The use of mHealth applications will allow the masses to gain access to behavioral interventions and online health services. Games for health present users with the opportunity to enjoy learning and be persuaded toward a healthy lifestyle through play. As a result, the diffusion of knowledge becomes a diffusion of enjoyment,[56] experience[57] and emotions.[20]

STRATEGIES FOR DEVELOPING A SUCCESSFUL GAME FOR HEALTH

Games for health are no longer a small industry. The medical community has begun adopting this health strategy as exemplified by the increasing number of conferences and the advent of a new medical journal:

- Games for Health: Exploring the intersection of video games + health
- Serious Games Summit
- The Power of Play: Innovations in Getting Active Summit 2011
- Games for Health in Europe
- A new medical journal *Games for Health: Research, Development and Clinical Applications*
- Games for Change Festival

In an interview with Patrick Haig, Vice President of Customer Success at MobileDevHQ, he explained that "building a health game in a very noisy ecosystem is very tough." He emphasized the importance of "conducting a competitive analysis to identify (a) whether something similar is already being done; and (b) who is in the space." This is important for more than just assessing the size of the market or the number of potential users, because market research can double as product development. By determining a competitor's success, a health game's popularity can help the designer formulate a strategy by either tapping into the existing user base or figuring out another market that is amendable to their game offering. Additionally, this guides game developers to successful game design strategies, meaning the most fun and engaging game elements can be recycled from these games.

HopeLab pursued this route for their redesign of *Remission-1*. Using Kongregate.com, a community that provides games for its members to play and rate, Hopelab easily navigated through hundreds of mobile game apps and chose six with excellent reviews and the game elements they were looking for. The HopeLab team chose mini-games that could lend themselves to killing cancer in the body. They then overlaid their cancer fighting messages and developed an equally successful, if not more efficacious version of their first game, both of which are featured in a case study following this section. As for the purchased mini-games, the original code and logic was left intact and new artwork helped "re-skin" the game. According to Austin Harley, the project lead, the "reskinning" procedure kept the cost of each of the six under $10,000. Harley highlighted "reskinning" as a cost effective alternative to developing a game from scratch, and it's Hopelab's belief that this can be a successful reproducible model that others can follow.

The popularity and success of games for health has caught the attention of the business community as well. "As we look toward the convergence of games and healthcare," Dr. Bill Crounse, Senior Director of Worldwide Health at Microsoft, told *MobiHealthNews* in an interview, "within our gaming unit, as we look at intake from around the world, we see more inquires in health and health-related industries than any other sector out there." Independent games and entertainment company Six to Start, entered the games for health space when they launched *Zombies, Run!* (see Chapter 11), but because they lacked Hopelab's funding, they followed a much different route.

Six to Start tapped into crowdfunding as a way to raise their development costs using a Kickstarter (a crowdfunding web site) campaign. The company sought $12,000 from public funds, but far surpassed their goal with $72,627 raised from 3,464 backers in October 2011. Adrian Hon, the company's CEO was able to launch the game with its core features intact with a minimal contribution of personal funds. As of January 2014, the game achieved 750,000 downloads. This is the second mHealth game that will be explored in greater detail in the subsequent sections.

The success of *Zombies, Run!* demonstrated that once a game hits broad acceptance, the research dollars follow. The American Heart Association has awarded the University of Texas Medical Branch with a grant to investigate the feasibility of using the game as part of a behavioral intervention. Hopefully this study will demonstrate the game's utility to extend beyond the general population, but also to augment health professionals' armamentarium in treating diabetes, obesity, hypertension and other lifestyle-related diseases. While the designers of the game admittedly were not trying to create a behavior intervention, the game mechanics and narrative techniques they used are quite similar to techniques used in health promotion interventions. Whether a private company or research institute develops a game, one aspect remains clear: both sides agree that key game elements are necessary to make fun games. Six to Start's methodology of creating a fun game validated by the masses assures the researchers that the game undergoing scientific research is proven to at least be fun, which is arguably the hardest element to create.

Here are two health games with two completely different development models, yet equally both successful in their own right. Their commonalities are their broad applicability that brings enjoyment to gamers and non-gamers alike. Applying games to healthcare is not a trend or fad. It is a rapidly growing and extremely collaborative field, and as technology continues to develop, so will the capabilities of the games. By creating games that augment our healthcare providers' treatment plans, we can empower patients by enhancing their learning through experiential and interactive approaches that ultimately drives behavior change. In doing so, people can live healthier and more fulfilled lives.

REFERENCES

1. Castronova E. *Exodus to the Virtual World: How Online Fun Is Changing Reality*. Palgrave Macmillan; 2007. http://books.google.com/books?id=iGoROxHt9pkC.
2. McGonigal J. *Reality Is Broken: Why Games Make Us Better and How They Can Change the World*. New York, NY; The Penguin Group; 2011.
3. UP1 Staff. PSP Japanese Launch IMpressions. 2004. www.1up.com/news/psp-japanese-launch-impressions.
4. Apple Inc. No Title. 2013. www.apple.com/ipod-touch/from-the-app-store.
5. Thoa E. Email Correspondance. (2013).
6. AppBrain. Android Statistics: Top Categories. www.appbrain.com/stats/android-market-app-categories.
7. Nintendo of America Inc. Nintendo Games. 2013. www.nintendo.com/games/gameGuide?system=ds&purchase=retail.
8. Sony Computer Entertainment America LLC. Play Station: Browse Games. (2013). http://us.playstation.com/ps-products/BrowseGames?console=ps3&beginsWith=Any.
9. Feldman B. *Mobile social and fun games for health*. http://mobihealthnews.com; 2011.
10. Fox S. The % of internet users who have looked online for information about... *Pew Research Center*. 2011. www.pewinternet.org/Reports/2011/HealthTopics/Part-4.aspx.
11. Fox S. Peer-to-Peer health care. *Pew Research Center* (2011). www.pewinternet.org/Reports/2011/P2PHealthcare.aspx.
12. NPD Group. Digital Fitness Devices Consumer Behavior Report. (2012). www.npd.com/latest-reports/digital-fitness-devices-consumer-behavior-report.
13. Research2guidance. *Mobile Health Market Report 2013-2017. The commercialization of mHealth Apps* **3,** (2013).
14. Pharow P, Blobel B, Ruotsalainen P, Petersen F, Hovsto A. Portable Devices, Sensors and Networks: Wireless Personalized eHealth Services. in *MIE* 1012–1016; (2009).
15. Chung BK.,Trtile BC in Oldenburg J, Chase D, Christensen, K, Trtile B., eds. *Engage! Transforming Healthcare Through Digital Patient Engagement.* 87–98. HIMSS Books; 2013.
16. Baranowski T, Baranowski J, Thompson D. Video Game Play, Child Diet, and Physical Activity Behavior Change. *American Journal of Preventive Medicine*; 2012; 40, 33–38.
17. Murphy EC. et al. Effects of an exercise intervention using Dance Dance Revolution on endothelial function and other risk factors in overweight children. *International Journal of Pediatric Obesity*. 2009; 4, 205–214.
18. Riley, W. T. *et al.* Health behavior models in the age of mobile interventions: are our theories up to the last? *Transl Behav Med* 1, 53–71 (2011).

19. Kato PM, Cole SW, Bradlyn AS, Pollock BH. A video game improves behavioral outcomes in adolescents and young adults with cancer: a randomized trial. *Pediatrics.* 2008; 122, e305–17.

20. Baranowski T, Buday R, Thompson DI, Baranowski J. Playing for real: video games and stories for health-related behavior change. *American Journal of Preventive Medicine.* 2008; 34, 74–82.

21. Jacobson D. BrushOff. (2013). at http://gamesthatwork.com/brushoff/#!

22. Wideman HH, et al. Unpacking the potential of educational gaming: A new tool for gaming research. *Simulation & Gaming.* 2007; 38, 10–30.

23. Gee JP. Learning by design: Games as learning machines. *Interactive Educational Multimedia.* 2004; 15–23.

24. Norman GJ, et al. A review of eHealth interventions for physical activity and dietary behavior change. *American Journal of Preventive Medicine.* 2007; 33, 336–345.

25. Staiano AE, Abraham A, Calvert SL. The Wii Club: Gaming for Weight Loss in Overweight and Obese Youth. *Games for Health Journal.* 2012; 1, 377–380.

26. Errickson SP, Maloney AE, Thorpe D, Giuliani C, Rosenberg AM. "Dance Dance Revolution" Used by 7- and 8-Year-Olds to Boost Physical Activity: Is Coaching Necessary for Adherence to an Exercise Prescription? *Games for Health Journal.* 2012; 1, 45–50.

27. Maloney AE, Stempel A, Wood ME, Patraitis C, Beaudoin C. Can Dance Exergames Boost Physical Activity as a School-Based Intervention? *Games for Health Journal.* 2012; 1, 416–421.

28. Buday R, Lu AS, Baranowski J. Design of Video Games for Children's Diet and Physical Activity Behavior Change. *International Journal of Computer Science in Sport.* 2009; 9, 3–17.

29. Foster C, et al. Interventions for promoting physical activity (Review). 1–3 (2013). doi:10.1002/14651858.CD003180.pub2.Copyright

30. Davies CA, Spence JC, Vandelanotte C, Caperchione CM, Mummery WK. Meta-analysis of internet-delivered interventions to increase physical activity levels. *The International Journal of Behavioral Nutrition and Physical Activity.* 2012; 9, 52.

31. Peng W. Design and evaluation of a computer game to promote a healthy diet for young adults. *Health Communication.* 2009; 24, 115–27 (2009).

32. Schneider KL, et al. Acceptability of an Online Health Videogame to Improve Diet and Physical Activity in Elementary School Students: "Fitter Critters."*Games for Health Journal.* 2012; 1, 262–268 (2012).

33. Thompson D, Baranowski T, Buday R, Baranowski J, Thompson V, Jago RG. Serious Video Games for Health How Behavioral Science Guided Simul Gaming. *Simul Gaming.* 2010; 41, 587–606.

34. Cole S. (UCLA), Hopelab, the R. J. F. New Research Shows Zamzee Increases Physical Activity by Almost 60%. (2012). http://blog.zamzee.com/2012/09/26/new-research-shows-zamzee-increases-physical-activity-by-almost-60.

35. Maddison R. et al. Effects of active video games on body composition: a randomized controlled trial. *The American Journal of Clinical Nutrition* 2011; 94, 156–163.

36. Michie S, Prestwich A. Are interventions theory-based? Development of a theory coding scheme. *Health psychology: Official journal of the Division of Health Psychology, American Psychological Association.* 2010; 29, 1–8.

37. Bandura A. *Social Foundations of Thought and Action: A Cognitive Social Theory.* Englewood Cliffs, New York; Pretince Hall; 1986.

38. Green MC, Brock TC. The role of transportation in the persuasiveness of public narratives. *Journal of Personality and Social Psychology.* 2000; 79, 701.

39. Ryan RM, Deci EL. Self-determination theory and the facilitation of intrinsic motivation, social development, and well-being. *American Psychologist.* 2000; 55, 68.

40. Bandura A. Influence of models' reinforcement contingencies on the acquisition of imitative responses. *Journal of Personality and Social Psychology.* 1965; 1, 589.

41. Lu, AS, Thompson D, Baranowski J, Buday R., Baranowski T. Story Immersion in a Health Videogame for Childhood Obesity Prevention. *Games for Health Journal*. 2012; 1, 37–44.
42. Bandura A, McClelland DC. Social learning theory. (1977).
43. Dewey J. *Experience and Education*. Free Press; 1938.
44. Wang H, Singhal A. In Ritterfield U, Cody MJ, Vorderer P, eds. *Serious Games: Mechanisms and Effects*. 271–292. New York, NY; Routledge; 2009.
45. Fox J, Bailenson JN. Virtual self-modeling: The effects of vicarious reinforcement and identification on exercise behaviors. *Media Psychology* 2009; 12, 1–25.
46. Wong WL, Shen C, Nocera L, et al. Serious video game effectiveness. Paper presented at: Proceedings of the international conference on Advances in Computer Entertainment Technology, 2007.
47. Fox J, Bailenson J, Binney J. Virtual Experiences, Physical Behaviors: The Effect of Presence on Imitation of an Eating Avatar. *Presence: Teleoperators and Virtual Environments* 2009; 18, 294–303..
48. Klimmt C. in Ritterfield U, Cody, MJ, Vorderer P, eds. *Serious Games: Mechanisms and Effects*, 248–270. New York, NY;Routledge; 2009.
49. Deterding S, Sicart M, Nacke L, O'Hara K, Dixon D. Gamification. using game-design elements in non-gaming contexts. Proceedings of the 2011 Annual Conference Extended Abstracts on Human Factors in Computing Systems - CHI EA '11 2425 (2011). doi:10.1145/1979742.1979575.
50. Nigg CR. Technology's influence on physical activity and exercise science: the present and the future. *Psychology of Sport and Exercise*. 2003; 4, 57–65.
51. Atkinson NL, Gold RS. The promise and challenge of eHealth interventions. *American Journal of Health Behavior*. 2002; 26, 494–503.
52. Luxton DD, McCann RA, Bush NE. Mishkind MC, Reger GM mHealth for mental health: Integrating smartphone technology in behavioral healthcare. *Professional Psychology: Research and Practice*. 2011; 42, 505.
53. Lester RT *et al*. Effects of a mobile phone short message service on antiretroviral treatment adherence in Kenya (WelTel Kenya1): a randomised trial. *The Lancet*. 2010; 376, 1838–1845.
54. Mills EJ, *et al*. Adherence to antiretroviral therapy in sub-Saharan Africa and North America. *JAMA*. 2006; 296, 679–690.
55. Rosen S, Fox MP, Gill CJ. Patient retention in antiretroviral therapy programs in sub-Saharan Africa: a systematic review. *PLoS Medicine*. 2007; 4, e298.
56. Vorderer P, Hartmann T, Klimmt C. Explaining the enjoyment of playing video games: the role of competition. in Proceedings of the Second International Conference on Entertainment Computing. 1–9 (Carnegie Mellon University, 2003).
57. Khalil GE. When Losing Means Winning: The Impact of Conflict in a Digital Game on Young Adults' Intentions to Get Protected from Cancer. *Games for Health Journal*. 2012; 1, 279–286.
58. Oldenburg J, Chase D, Christensen KT, Tritle B. *Engage! Transforming Healthcare Through Digital Patient Engagement*. Chicago: HIMSS Books; 2013.

CHAPTER 10

A Research-Driven Computer and Mobile Game for Health: A Case Study

By Georges E. Khalil, MPH; Brian Mayrsohn, MS; and David Metcalf, PhD

ABSTRACT

Mobile devices have become powerful tools for the diffusion of applications that can promote health in a broad and diverse network of users. In 2012, there were 694.8 million shipments of smartphones worldwide — a number that is expected to double by 2016.[1] With such a vast availability, mobile health (mHealth) programs begin to broaden their functions including clinical decision making, data collection for healthcare professionals,[2] health behavior change[3] and disease management for patients.[4]

Not only do mHealth systems offer state-of-the-art approaches to the diffusion of health promotion and disease prevention efforts, but they also take advantage of strategies that drive enjoyment, engagement and motivation. "People rarely succeed unless they have fun in what they are doing," explains Dale Carnegie, the famous author of *How to Stop Worrying and Start Living.* Indeed, when people want to succeed in reaching a healthy lifestyle, they need to have fun along the way. One example of a fun-driven mHealth strategy is the use of games for health. In an interview with BBC news, Cory de Gara, a patient with leukemia explained, "When you play games you don't even notice that you're sick. That's why I play. And it's fun of course."[5] Games are becoming important tools for modifying behaviors related to a variety of health topics such as cancer prevention,[6] medication adherence,[7,8] physical activity[9] and healthy dieting.[10]

In particular, the present chapter will discuss Re-Mission™ (www.re-mission.net), a cancer-related shooter game that was designed, pre-tested and disseminated by HopeLab (Redwood City, CA). First, we will present some background information about the game, as well as its developers' principles in health game design. Then, we will investigate the theoretical framework of the game and its success based on the findings of several research studies. Finally, we will discuss the transition of Re-Mission from being a stationary computer-based game to becoming an mHealth application.

SUMMARY DESCRIPTION OF RE-MISSION

Re-Mission is a third-person shooter game released in 2006 for adolescents and young adults who have cancer. The game was designed to improve medication adherence. In Re-Mission, players can control an avatar (a nanorobot character) called Roxxi, and go on missions inside the virtual bodies of cancer patients to destroy cancer cells, battle bacterial infections and manage cancer treatment side effects. As part of the game, players fight enemy cells by using weapons armed with common treatments such as chemotherapy, radiation and antibiotics.[7] The player is first presented with a narrative-based animation introducing the game's storyline. Dr. West, a virtual doctor in the game, has designed Roxxi, a nanorobot that can be injected in cancer patients' bodies to fight cancer cells. After injection, Roxxi meets her fellow hologram that acts as a guide through the human body and assists in navigation and cancer battles. The player controls Roxxi in the patient's body, and fights cancer cells using several weapons such as the "chemoblaster," "radiation guns" and "antibiotic rockets." Over the course of 20 levels, the player explores each patient's history and current diagnosis, ultimately gaining medical knowledge.

Design, Challenges and Opportunities

HopeLab is a non-profit organization that works to make use of technology for better physical and psychological health among youth. HopeLab faced many challenges creating Re-Mission, but one of the most crucial was to create a balance between enjoyment and health education. In essence, Re-Mission could not be purely fun without health impact, or purely educational without any fun. To overcome such a challenge, HopeLab built Re-Mission based on the organization's objectives. During the design process, HopeLab determined the health outcomes to be attained (increase in knowledge and improved medication adherence), established the main mediators based on theoretical frameworks (motivation and self-efficacy), and then translated such frameworks into gaming mechanics (helping a virtual patient fight cancer). In addition, HopeLab included the most important ingredient for success: they amplified the "fun factor."

By applying a participatory approach, HopeLab brought together game designers, health behavior scientists and cancer researchers during the design and development of Re-Mission. However, one challenge of such an approach was the ability to create a collaborative atmosphere during design. At different times, game designers, health behavior practitioners and biologists expressed conflicting opinions concerning best practices. For instance, in their overview of HopeLab's strategy in the design of Re-Mission, Tate, Haritatos and Cole describe how game designers strongly believe in the role of dramatic design and exaggeration for game appeal, while health professionals insist on scientific accuracy of health-related information.[11] In order to alleviate potential conflicts (e.g., dramatization versus accuracy), teens and young adults with cancer took part of the design process, and ensured the game answered their concerns and replicated their everyday struggles, while maintaining its core entertaining features.[12]

HopeLab focused on a theory-driven approach and consciously embedded cancer-related educational information in the creation, production and processing of the game to achieve health behavior changes among young cancer patients.[13] It is beneficial to outline theoretical processes that may be responsible for Re-Mission's success.

Theoretical Bases of Re-Mission
Re-Mission design was based on three main theories: the self-regulation model of health and illness,[14-16] social cognitive theory[17] and learning theory.[18] In addition to such theories, several conceptual aspects of game play may explain behavior change through Re-Mission. During game play, players find themselves in an immersive environment that elicits psychological, physiological and behavioral responses.[19] By feeling present in the gaming environment, players tend to imitate virtual behavior by experiencing it in reality.[20] Experiential play is also responsible for the transfer of perception from the virtual to the actual world.[21,22] In fact, players may embody certain characters (e.g., Roxxi) and explore different scenarios in the game (fighting cancer cells with different medications). Such exploration fosters the experience of gaming consequences. Digital games like Re-Mission involve becoming or controlling characters that find themselves in diverse situations and face consequences. Such experiential play ultimately drives motivation and empowers cancer patients to adhere to their medication.[7,8]

RE-MISSION FOR MEDICATION ADHERENCE

After design and development, Re-Mission was evaluated through different research studies.[7,8] The main study included 375 cancer patients who were randomized to either play Re-Mission or a control game. Psychological outcomes such as knowledge and self-efficacy were considered, as well as objective behavioral measures of medication adherence (e.g., blood assays). The findings of the trial showed that knowledge about cancer increased significantly more in the Re-Mission group when compared to the control group. While similar findings were obtained for self-efficacy, such a concept was not found to mediate the relationship between Re-Mission play and medication adherence. Blood assay measures also showed higher increase in medication adherence for Re-Mission players than for the control game players. Unexpectedly, this study on Re-Mission has found that neither self-efficacy nor knowledge explain the increase in medication adherence. As a result of such findings, researchers at HopeLab became intrigued in the mechanisms by which Re-Mission can bring about behavior change.

RE-MISSION FOR PRIMARY PREVENTION

While Re-Mission was designed to promote medication adherence among patients, recent research has re-appropriated its gaming function by investigating its ability to help healthy young adults change their perceptions concerning cancer risk and begin to seek cancer-related information.[6] During a laboratory experiment, healthy young adults who played Re-Mission at high conflict (i.e., high level of obstacles and challenges in the game) presented an increase in perceived cancer risk when compared to players at low conflict. An interesting finding from a study demonstrated that the more players perceived virtual cancer cells in the game to be threatening, the more they experienced an increase in perceived cancer risk.[6] This study suggests that by virtually experiencing the consequences of cancer cell behavior (e.g., cancer cell multiplication and attack of tissues), healthy players of Re-Mission began to understand the severity of cancer, and were more likely to feel susceptible to cancer. The presentation of threatening cancer cells may prove useful during the design of future games that aim to facilitate cancer risk perception among healthy youths.

MOVING TOWARD A MOBILE GAME FOR HEALTH

As a result of the successes achieved with Re-Mission, systematic reviews of the game play experience have been conducted to understand strategies and maximize its impact among patients. Several in-depth interviews were conducted with more than 120 Re-Mission adolescent players.[11] As a result, HopeLab explains the idea of fighting cancer cells empowered patients as they played. For instance, one patient mentioned that "it feels like you have control over your own destiny."[11] Also, patients report a sense of "revenge" when fighting cancer, which explains their feeling of empowerment as a result of victory against it.

In Re-Mission, players tend to use serious weaponry that rarely changes, and its effect on cancer cells tends to be redundant, creating a routine in game play. As a result, cancer patients begin to express a sense of boredom due to such monotony in the game. When asked how they would like to fight cancer cells, cancer patients began to express a variety of methods that are unrealistic, but humorous and creative. Some wished they could set cancer cells on fire, and others preferred to blow up cancer cells or unleash monsters that can eat the cells. With such creative minds, cancer patients made it clear that Re-Mission needed to be fun and challenging at the same time. The fun experience is ultimately crucial to cancer patients' motivation to adhere to medication.

The challenge of fighting cancer cells followed by victory allows the expression of positive affect toward the game. A research study by Cole, Yoo and Knutson[23] shows that Re-Mission play is able to activate regions of the brain that are responsible for reward (i.e., the mesolimbic neural circuit). As a result of the challenge of fighting cancer cells followed by the feeling of reward, players begin to form a positive attitude toward the game, and ultimately toward medication. In addition to such results, it was found that the activation of the left parahippocampal cortex was associated with players' attitude toward chemotherapy. These findings suggest that Re-Mission's success lies in its challenges and reward-stimulation.

As a result, HopeLab has taken a step toward the development of a new version called Re-Mission 2. Re-Mission 2 consists of a series of six mini-games available online: Nanobot's Revenge, Leukemia, Nano Dropbot, Stem Cell Defender, Feeding Frenzy and Special Ops. Each game presents players with a simplified version of the human body to fight cancer cells using a variety of weapons and super powers, such as chemotherapy, antibiotics and the body's immune system. Considering their simplified design and straightforward mechanics, all mini-games of Re-Mission 2 are perfect examples of games for mHealth. In particular, Nanobot's Revenge has been recently introduced as an mHealth application for iOS and Android. In this mini-game, players control a powerful microscopic robot that can blast cancer cells belonging to the "cancerous forces of the Nuclear Tytant." Players get the opportunity to blow up cells, burn them, eat them and even make them dizzy to death. This diversity in the means of fighting cancer stems from cancer patients' imagination when asked how they would imagine themselves fighting cancer.

As part of Re-Mission 2, HopeLab applies a "stealth-health" strategy during which designers sneak in health information to promote taking medications without the patient having to sit through a lecture. Camouflaged information is ultimately able to automatically promote medication adherence. For instance, players of Re-Mission 2 defend the body by using Prednisoldiers, a drug many cancer patients take. Through Re-Mission 2, patients get to re-conceptualize the purpose of chemotherapy. Instead of being viewed as a dreaded obligation that affects their body, medication was rebranded to become a powerful weapon to fight cancer.

Austin Harley, manager of research, design and production of Re-Mission 2, made sure that Re-Mission 2 involved games that are simple and genuinely entertaining. Re-Mission 2's simplicity allows players with all levels of gaming skills to appreciate the battle against cancer cells to attain a state of enjoyment and motivation. The diversity of games in Re-Mission 2 also allows pediatric cancer patients to play the games that are most appealing to them, while still attaining the same outcomes.

In addition to diversity and simplicity, Re-Mission 2's mobility through the phone app allows access to play during cases of emergency. On their smartphones, patients are able to access the game at any time or place. Patients may be at the hospital, at home, or in the car, and still benefit from game play to fight their distress, express their anger against cancer, feel empowered against the disease, and become motivated to adhere to their medication. mHealth is also expected to better serve the patients with game play at the points in time that they need it most. Re-Mission's provision of a motivation boost for medication adherence and empowerment against cancer can now occur at the point-of-care, in the clinic or at home.

LESSONS LEARNED

With several mHealth products available in the market, gaming has become of interest to many mHealth designers and researchers. In particular, Re-Mission is a digital game for health that has proved successful at many levels, and has formed an example of how games can evolve from being stationary (i.e., computer-based) to becoming mobile.

The first lesson of this case study is the importance of design methodology. Re-Mission's design was based on a scientifically driven method that emphasized interdisciplinary collaboration among game designers, game researchers, medical scientists and young patients. Such a collaboration allowed the comingling between medical, persuasive and appealing features of Re-Mission.

A second lesson is the importance of evaluation, which allows for the promotion of a credible evidence-based health program. As a result of a successful design, Re-Mission was scientifically evaluated. Findings from control trials showed that the game increases medication adherence among young patients and boosts their self-efficacy. Re-Mission did not stop its miracles with young patients, but also reached healthy young adults by allowing them to understand the risks of cancer and seek cancer information.

The third lesson of this case study emphasizes the importance of program updates and advancements through formative research. In fact, further research involving interviews with young players has included several important aspects, such as mobility, simplicity and creativity in cancer fights. All positive outcomes of Re-Mission that have been found after evaluation have allowed designers and researchers to move the game toward a more accessible version. With Re-Mission 2, one game became a series of mini-games that gave patients the opportunity to fight cancer cells using a variety of methods. With a wide selection of weaponry and ways to kill cells, patients become empowered to adhere to their medication. Finally, the game's update allowed designers and researchers to produce a version of the game that fills important gaps. Re-Mission 2's undemanding, easy-to-use system allows patients to play the game regardless of their gaming skills. Also, the simplicity of the design allowed the game to become accessible via smartphones, turning it into a successful mHealth application. By applying such a strategy for the design of mHealth games, designers may become able to produce several versions of one game, reaching out to a variety of mHealth consumers.

REFERENCES

1. Canalys. Mobile device market to reach 2.6 billion units by 2016. 2013. Available at: www.canalys.com/newsroom/mobile-device-market-reach-26-billion-units-2016. Accessed August 24, 2013.
2. Blaya JA, Fraser HS, Holt B. E-health technologies show promise in developing countries. *Health Affairs.* 2010;29(2):244-251.
3. Gurman TA, Rubin SE, Roess AA. Effectiveness of mHealth behavior change communication interventions in developing countries: a systematic review of the literature. *Journal of Health Communication.* 2012;17(sup1):82-104.
4. Cole-Lewis H, Kershaw T. Text messaging as a tool for behavior change in disease prevention and management. *Epidemiologic Reviews.* 2010;32(1):56-69.
5. BBCNewsTechnology. The online games teaching children about their cancer. 2013; http://www.bbc.co.uk/news/technology-23942665. Accessed September 12, 2013.
6. Khalil GE. When Losing Means Winning: The Impact of Conflict in a Digital Game on Young Adults' Intentions to Get Protected from Cancer. *GAMES FOR HEALTH: Research, Development, and Clinical Applications.* 2012;1(4):279-286.
7. Beale IL, Kato PM, Marin-Bowling VM, Guthrie N, Cole SW. Improvement in cancer-related knowledge following use of a psychoeducational video game for adolescents and young adults with cancer. *Journal of Adolescent Health.* 2007;41(3):263-270.
8. Kato PM, Cole SW, Bradlyn AS, Pollock BH. A video game improves behavioral outcomes in adolescents and young adults with cancer: a randomized trial. *Pediatrics.* 2008;122(2):e305.
9. Baranowski T, Baranowski J, O'Connor T, Lu AS, Thompson D. Is enhanced physical activity possible using active videogames? *GAMES FOR HEALTH: Research, Development, and Clinical Applications.* 2012;1(3):228-232.
10. Schneider KL, Ferrara J, Lance B, et al. Acceptability of an Online Health Videogame to Improve Diet and Physical Activity in Elementary School Students:"Fitter Critters." *GAMES FOR HEALTH: Research, Development, and Clinical Applications.* 2012;1(4):262-268.
11. Tate R, Haritatos J, Cole S. HopeLab's approach to Re-Mission. 2009.

12. Wang H, Singhal A. Entertainment-education through digital games. *Serious Games: Mechanisms and Effects.* 2009:271.

13. Tate R, Haritatos J, Cole S. HopeLab's approach to Re-Mission. *International Journal of Learning.* 2009;1(1):29-35.

14. Cameron LD, Leventhal H. Vulnerability beliefs, symptom experiences, and the processing of health threat information: A Self-Regulatory Perspective. *Journal of Applied Social Psychology.* 1995;25(21):1859-1883.

15. Leventhal H, Leventhal EA, Contrada RJ. Self-regulation, health, and behavior: A perceptual-cognitive approach. *Psychology and Health.* 1998;13(4):717-733.

16. Leventhal H, Brissette I, Leventhal EA. The common-sense model of self-regulation of health and illness. *The Self-regulation of Health and Illness Behaviour.* 2003;1:42-65.

17. Bandura A, McClelland DC. *Social Learning Theory.* 1977.

18. Choi J-I, Hannafin M. Situated cognition and learning environments: Roles, structures, and implications for design. *Educational Technology Research and Development.* 1995;43(2):53-69.

19. Wong WL, Shen C, Nocera L, et al. Serious video game effectiveness. Paper presented at: Proceedings of the international conference on Advances in computer entertainment technology. 2007.

20. Fox J, Bailenson J, Binney J. Virtual experiences, physical behaviors: The effect of presence on imitation of an eating avatar. *Presence: Teleoperators and Virtual Environments.* 2009;18(4):294-303.

21. Klimmt C. Serious games and social change: Why they (should) work. *Serious games: Mechanisms and Effects.* 2009:248-270.

22. Wang H, Singhal A. Entertainment-education through digital games. *Serious games: Mechanisms and Effects. New York and London: Routledge.* 2009:271-292.

23. Cole SW, Yoo DJ, Knutson B. Interactivity and reward-related neural activation during a serious videogame. *PloS One.* 2012;7(3):e33909.

Chapter 11

Zombies, Run!: A Case Study

By Brian Mayrsohn, MS, and Elizabeth Lyons, PhD, MPH

ABSTRACT

Physical activity is associated with a host of positive health outcomes, including reduced risk of cardiovascular disease, several cancers and all-cause mortality.[1-3] Unfortunately, the average American adult is active for only 4 percent of their day,[4] and most do not meet physical activity recommendations. The National Health and Nutrition Examination Survey (NHANES) estimates that as many as 34 percent of Americans have metabolic syndrome, a compilation of risk factors that include high blood pressure, high "bad" and low "good" cholesterol, high blood fat levels and abdominal obesity.[5] Each of these risk factors can be lowered by regular exercise[6], however, even within otherwise highly effective behavioral weight-loss interventions, physical activity levels decrease sharply over time.[7] Innovative methods for encouraging physical activity are clearly required to increase motivation to begin and sustain an active lifestyle. It is difficult to find the time to engage in a monotonous and un-engaging activity, but something as important as maintaining a healthy and active lifestyle requires a commitment.

Your chopper crash lands and a sea of zombies surround you, providing ample motivation to run (for your life) while playing *Zombies, Run!*, an epic narrative adventure app available for iOS and Android mobile devices. Naomi Alderman, the game's head writer and co-creator with Six to Start, recalls that she had just joined a running group when the idea came to her. She asked the members why they had joined; some wanted to lose weight, others hoped to get fit, and one person exclaimed, "To escape the zombie apocalypse." In a keynote presentation at the 2013 Games for Health conference, Alderman and Six to Start CEO Adrian Hon summed up the purpose of the game: "Not everyone wants to run, but everybody wants to *want* to run, and that is the gap that we fill."[8]

For many, running is simply not a very exciting activity, but playing a game certainly is. If running were a metaphor for life, world-renowned game designer and best-selling author Jane McGonigal says that it "Just doesn't offer up as easily the carefully designed pleasures, the thrilling challenges, and the powerful social bonding afforded by virtual environments."[9] While *Zombies, Run!* is not the typical virtual environment one would associate with a fitness video game, it is a conduit for arguably the most important aspect of a game: fun. Fun and enjoyment of exercise-related games are associated with behavioral and physiological changes,[10] and this game appears to truly resonate with its users.

STORY-DRIVEN ADVENTURE

Zombies, Run! is a story-driven adventure game that plays like a hybrid of an audio book, self-monitoring app and video game. Users can run, jog, walk or stroll while listening to an epic zombie apocalypse story. The player character is gender and age neutral, referred to in the second person as "Runner 5." Individual missions, lasting 30 minutes or one hour, consist of snippets of pre-recorded audio "transmissions" from story characters directed toward Runner 5. Between the brief bits of dialogue and action users listen to their own music. At random intervals, a zombie chase may occur, and the runner hears, "Warning: Zombies [number] Meters." For one minute, the player must increase his or her speed by at least 20 percent to outrun the horde of zombies chasing after him or her. If the runner cannot outrun the zombies, some of the virtual goods picked up over the course of the mission are dropped to distract the zombie hoard. After each walk or run, players can view highly detailed feedback, and use their collected virtual goods to build up their home base using the *base builder* component of the mobile app. The home base reflects the runner's dedication to not only the game, but also his or her exercise past. The more you run, the more virtual goods picked up, the bigger the base. The state of the base affects which missions become available and can even influence story events.

Each time the player returns to the game, they resume the role of Runner 5 and go on death-defying missions to save their base from starvation and outside invaders. The player becomes the hero of his or her own story, and all it requires is a music playlist, an iPhone/Android device and headphones. This app offers more innovative features than the typically measured key metrics of performance (e.g., distance and time); for instance, it tracks and records extremely specific information such as speed per song and improvement over time. This novel combination of immersive storytelling and exercise self-monitoring has produced a loyal fan base and sales of over 750,000 downloads.

Fig. 11-2 shows a map of a zombie mission. Notice the *Zombies, Run!* symbol located just after mile marker two. The location corresponds to the graph below the map, which is highlighted at the 20-minute marker. Looking at the right-hand column, one can see that the mile marker corresponds to the dot on the "Take a Minute" song graph. My pace during that song was 2 percent higher than my average, compared to the "Lovelier Than You" song graph above it,

Fig. 11-1: Game Portion of the *Zombies, Run!* Hybrid App

where my pace was 8 percent less than my average. Using MapMyRun app, I quickly cross-referenced the topography of the corresponding terrain to the songs. I noticed that I was traveling uphill during the song in which my speed dropped by 8 percent, and downhill when my speed increased by 2 percent, and determined that the songs had a smaller effect on my pace than I originally thought. This is just one way to apply quantified self measurements to improve one's performance.

THE BEHAVIORAL SCIENCE BEHIND *ZOMBIES, RUN!*

Self-determination theory posits that, like many other activities, video game motivation is driven primarily by feelings of competence, autonomy and relatedness.[11] Indeed, multiple studies have found that among both activity-related and sedentary video games, increases in self-reported autonomy, competence and relatedness were associated with intrinsic (volitional) motivation, leading to more frequent and more intense play.[11-13] *Zombies, Run!* differs from many traditional video games in that its story is mostly non-interactive. The game portion of this hybrid app lies within the zombie chases and base builder mechanics (Fig. 11-2), while the story is relatively self-contained. Thus, the game offers relatively little autonomy when compared to other console-based or mobile video games. Its strengths likely lie in its impact on perceptions of competence and relatedness among players.

Zombies, Run! may influence feelings of competence via its extensive self-monitoring tools. Self-monitoring applications such as *Runkeeper* and *Map My Walk* thrive on mobile devices, and there is a growing evidence base demonstrating the effectiveness of self-monitoring via electronic devices (e.g., PDAs, smartphones, pedometers).[14-16] *Zombies, Run!* and its web interface, *Zombielink*, provide extensive and specific feedback on exercise frequency, duration and intensity. There is a mapping feature that allows users to relive past runs via a virtual trail featuring an interactive icon that moves along with an intensity that mirrors the runner's actual speed. Dis-

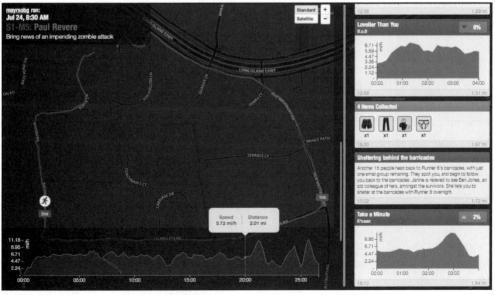

Fig. 11-2: Map of a Zombie Mission.

played on the side of the screen are the songs along with the times and distance run sandwiched between plot summaries of the radio transmissions. A green or red arrow, similar to a stock-market ticker, appears next to a percentage that compares the average pace of that workout to that song and conveniently informs the user of running speeds. By receiving real-time feedback, an individual can explicitly quantify improvements and achieve a sense of competence.

The game likely impacts feelings of relatedness via its immersive narrative and its social features. There is evidence that relationships with fictional characters in a narrative can provide a feeling of camaraderie and togetherness as part of the same social group.[17] Relationships with real-life friends and family are integrated into the game using the social features of *Zombielink*, the game's associated tracking web site. *Zombies, Run!* recently released a modified version of its web site and is currently beta testing a social element. Adam Bosworth, the CEO of the wellness program KEAS, asserted that "people are social and fundamentally like positive reinforcement" and therefore they can be agents for behavior change of others in their social community.[18] James Fowler and Dr. Nicholas Christakis agree with this sentiment, as noted in their book *Connected: The Surprising Power of Our Social Networks and How They Shape Our Lives*, where they suggest that social networks are extremely powerful vehicles that permeate joy or depression, and help maintain our health or spread obesity.[19] More importantly, a community can help us accomplish daring tasks that we otherwise may not achieve on our own. A study that analyzed the social components of Fitocracy, an online gamified fitness community, found that social factors can predict whether or not a user will continue using the app or recommend it to others. This relationship is further enhanced by the degree to which users interact with one another.[20]

The relatively low emphasis on autonomy may be less of an issue in this type of role-playing game than compared to others. For one, in a zombie apocalypse, the autonomy might end up killing you! Lack of autonomy for a soldier in a post-apocalyptic wasteland makes narrative sense. Additionally, autonomy could be dangerous in a running-centered game meant to be played in the real world. Adrian Hon noted, "You need to do what works for the real world; what worked on [traditional] game consoles doesn't necessarily work for mobile." The hardware used by the player is crucial because a traditional game console is stationary; meaning the player only has to avoid the dangers of the virtual world. Making decisions while jogging in real life might result in serious injury. Though the game lacks decision making while running, with the exception of choosing where to jog, it does provide players with many options regarding how the game will interact with them. The user determines how long the story plays, decides when to engage in side quests or to initiate "Zombie Chase Mode" or "Radio Mode," and chooses how to build the base.

Hon feels that when developing a game, "the important thing is creating a story that feels immersive, and in the case of *Zombies, Run!* it feels personal. You are physically out running in a game where you are the player." To really understand the game, I purchased the app and as I played the game I found myself reacting to the dialogue. I ducked when zombies were around and sped up as they approached; if people watched me they would definitely think I was crazy. In other words, the game's immersive narrative transported me into the storyline where I felt a part of the series of events that unfolded. According to theory, I was parasocially interacting with the characters, which in turn motivated me to maintain pace to evade the zombies and consequently exercise.[26] After reading fans' reactions to the game on social media, it is apparent they had similar experiences too. University of Texas Medical Branch is currently analyzing the game to determine whether this anecdotal evidence can be replicated in a more structured study. Positive results would have tremendous implications, because they would demonstrate the power a compelling story had on behavior change.

A Living Product

In this case, the design team centered the game on the concept of running and integrated an audio story in the background. As the player jogs, virtual items are randomly picked up at non-specific intervals. It has been suggested that unexpected positive feedback is likely one of the most effective in-game rewards.[21] Hon emphasized that each user is different, and therefore has varying levels of affinity for game mechanics. This concept is paramount when designing a game, because it is important to include enough game elements to engage a wide distribution of the population, but at the same time not overload them. Emotions vary from user to user, a concept Six to Start takes very seriously, so they do their best to empathize with the users to develop a game tailored to meet their needs.

Six to Start receives continuous feedback from users via blogs, Twitter and Facebook that allow the design team to continuously tweak the game which helps it evolve in real-time as it gains popularity. Hon emphasized the importance of listening to users; their comments have been included and ideas developed. Since the release of the game, its evolution has been anything but static. Hon refers to *Zombies, Run!* as a living product because of its evolving nature. He attributes much of the game's continued success to the fact that designers actively work to enhance gameplay based on user feedback such as GPX export and *RunKeeper* syncing.

Since the initial release date, designers have added 70 achievements, colloquially referred to as badges, to the game. Badges are representations of achievements and allow the game designer to recognize the player's achievement within the game. They are graphical, freeing designers to be artists to represent the vibe of the game. For the user, they represent accomplishments and demonstrate players' history by providing credentials that show the world their accomplishments.[22] More simply, people like to collect things and display them for friends to see.

In *Zombies, Run!* the badges were designed to entice players to navigate the different tools and functionalities of the web site, as well as to motivate them to run more frequently. For more avid *Zombie, Run!* fans, a hardcore category holds additional achievements with missing completion instructions. This forces users to figure out on their own just what is it that they need to do in order to unlock a specific achievement/badge (i.e., badge X is unlocked by running 1,000 km or collecting 500 supplies in a week). Some can be inferred from the title, but others require trial and error, incentivizing players to run faster than ever and to try different build combinations. Some achievements even reward poor game play: you can receive a rather dubious achievement for being caught by zombies a certain number of times! Interestingly, designers allowed achievements to be activated retroactively, giving some players achievements without actively seeking them. Our brains love surprises, something unexpected. This reward schema has no fixed schedule and is referred to by academics as "variable," and shown to be highly effective at driving effectance and empowerment, as well as health outcomes.[23,24]

Big Data
Zombies, Run! collects massive amounts of user data, including GPS-generated running distance, playlist songs, total and song-specific running speeds, most frequently-used game mechanics, and pace increases during zombie chases. To date, the data has been used in a multi-variant analysis assessing the speed increase in relation to beats per minute. Their conclusions were presented in a chart of the top 30 songs that have been shown to increase running speed. The "speed-up" from the first song and "slow-down" associated with the last song played in the playlist with respect to the start and finish to the run were among many variables taken into account in the statistical analysis.[25]

For now, Hon says they are not interested in selling the data, a reason being that their database pales in comparison to Runkeeper's. Of the 750,000 app purchases, 282,470 users have registered an online account and run the first mission. According to Hon, the game's stickiness (how likely a user is to return) is slightly better than comparable health apps. Using public data available from the *Zombielink* web site, it was noted that just over half (50.7 percent) of the users who ran the first mission opted not to complete the second mission. The user base continued to decline by an average of 15 percent between each mission until the 8th mission, where the numbers plateaued to approximately 26,000. This is the number of users that completed the first episode of the second season, which is just actually a few thousand higher than the last episode of the first season. This is about 10 percent of the initial user base.

Scalability
The app received its initial investment from a Kickstarter campaign (a crowdfunding web site) originally seeking merely $12,000, but ultimately raising $72,627 from 3,464 backers in October 2011. With additional personal funding from Hon, *Zombies, Run!* was launched in February 2012, with its core features intact. They built the game first (which sailed through the app store vetting process), followed by the statistics tracking web site. To date, the game has been purchased over 750,000 times at a price of $3.99-$7.99 per download. The app originally sold on the iPhone, Android and Windows operating systems, but recently Six to Start stopped updates for Windows phones due to lack of volume. Like any business, they tailor their product for the marketplace, which so far consists of English speakers. One of the shortcomings the company experienced was transitioning from Season 1 to Season 2. They revamped the entire app and altered the base-builder game element, which caused its users to push back. According to Hon, they would have been better served keeping the old base-builder. "It would have been more work, but also eased the changeover."

CONCLUSION

When Hon and Alderman set out to develop this game, they intended for all audiences to play it. Runner 5 has no gender and no running pace is ever set, therefore exercise enthusiasts of all levels can play without feeling as though their pace is inadequate. Therein lies a key strategy in the game's design, which ultimately contributed to its popularity: it is built for all shapes and sizes. Its broad acceptance and low user-startup budget makes it a perfect candidate as an adjunct to any exercise routine or standalone fitness app that can improve health among diverse populations. The prodigious success of this game is only the tip of the iceberg. Games for health as a sector within the gaming industry is in its infancy. *Zombies, Run!* has proved to be a popular model, but hopefully it can accomplish more than just sales. Ideally, the experiment currently underway at the University of Texas will provide insight into behavioral and health outcomes realized from the game, and if so, what mechanisms of behavior change were employed. The influence of self-monitoring tools, an immersive narrative, gameplay mechanics and interesting characters will be tested to better understand how and why the game may lead to increased exercise.

Enthusiasm across the Internet in the form of tweets, Tumblr tag activity, fan-art and fan-fiction indicate that something about this unique hybrid of audio adventure/narrative-driven videogame/exercise app has struck a nerve among many fans. Though its effectiveness for behavior change remains an empirical question, its sales and fan-base suggest that *Zombies, Run!* is a major success story for both narrative-driven and exercise-related mobile apps. Be honest with yourself, if you found yourself swarmed by zombies, you would have no choice but summon the stamina to run for your life!

REFERENCES

1. Sattelmair J, Pertman J, Ding EL, Kohl HW, Haskell W, Lee IM. Dose Response Between Physical Activity and Risk of Coronary Heart Disease A Meta-Analysis. *Circulation* 2011;124:789-U84.

2. Friedenreich CM, Neilson HK, Lynch BM. State of the epidemiological evidence on physical activity and cancer prevention. *European Journal of Cancer.* 2010;46:2593-604.

3. Woodcock J, Franco OH, Orsini N, Roberts I. Non-vigorous physical activity and all-cause mortality: systematic review and meta-analysis of cohort studies. *International Journal of Epidemiology.* 2011;40:121-38.

4. Spittaels H, Van Cauwenberghe E, Verbestel V, et al. Objectively measured sedentary time and physical activity time across the lifespan: a cross-sectional study in four age groups. *Int J Behav Nutr Phys Act.* 2012;9:149.

5. Mozumdar A, Liguori G. Persistent increase of prevalence of metabolic syndrome among U.S. adults: NHANES III to NHANES 1999-2006. *Diabetes Care* 2011;34:216-9.

6. Loprinzi PD, Lee H, Cardinal BJ. Dose Response Association between Physical Activity and Biological, Demographic, and Perceptions of Health Variables. *Obes Facts.* 2013;6:380-92.

7. Jeffery RW, Drewnowski A, Epstein LH, *et al.* Long-term maintenance of weight loss: current status. *Health Psychol.* 2000;19:5-16.

8. Alderman N, Hon A. How a Mobile Game (and Zombies!) Got 500,000 People Running for Their Lives! *Games for Health Conference.* Boston, MA: 2013.

9. McGonigal J. *Reality is broken: why games make up better and how they can change the world.* New York, NY; Penguin Books: 2011.

10. Mellecker R, Lyons EJ, Baranowski T. Disentangling Fun and Enjoyment in Exergames Using an Expanded Design, Play, Experience Framework: A Narrative Review. *Games for Health Journal: Research, Development, and Clinical Applications.* 2013;2:142-9.

11. Przybylski AK, Rigby CS, Ryan RM. A Motivational Model of Video Game Engagement. *Review of General Psychology.* 2010;14:154-66.

12. Ijsselsteijn WA, de Kort YAW, Westerink J, de Jager M. Virtual fitness: Stimulating exercise behavior through media technology. *Presence-Teleoperators and Virtual Environments.* 2006;15:688-98.

13. Lyons EJ, Tate DF, Ward DS, Ribisl KM, Bowling JM, Kalyanaraman S. Engagement, Enjoyment, and Energy Expenditure During Active Video Game Play. *Health Psychol.* 2013.

14. Conroy MB, Yang K, Elci OU, *et al.* Physical activity self-monitoring and weight loss: 6-month results of the SMART trial. *Med Sci Sports Exerc.* 2011;43:1568-74.

15. Kang M, Marshall SJ, Barreira TV, Lee JO. Effect of pedometer-based physical activity interventions: a meta-analysis. *Res Q Exerc Sport.* 2009;80:648-55.

16. Shuger SL, Barry VW, Sui X, *et al.* Electronic feedback in a diet- and physical activity-based lifestyle intervention for weight loss: a randomized controlled trial. *Int J Behav Nutr Phys Act.* 2011;8:41.

17. Gabriel S, Young AF. Becoming a Vampire Without Being Bitten: The Narrative Collective-Assimilation Hypothesis. *Psychological Science.* 2011;22:990-4.

18. Feldman B. Mobile Social and Fun Games for Health. 2011.

19. Christakis NA, Fowler JH. *Connected: The Surprising Power of Our Social Networks and How They Shape Our Lives.* New York, NY; Little, Brown and Company; 2009.

20. Hamari J, Koivisto J. Social motivations to use gamification: an empirical study of gamifying exercise. *The 21st European Conference on Information Systems.* Utrecht, Netherlands: 2013.

21. Rigby CS. Finding the right rewards to sustain player engagement. *GDC Austin.* Austin, TX: 2009.

22. Badges in Social Media: A Social Psychological Perspective. Proceedings of the CHI EA '11 Proceedings of the 2011 annual conference extended abstracts on human factors in *computing systems,* Vancouver, BC, Canada, May 7-12 2011. ACM.

23. Klimmt C, Hartmann T, Frey A. Effectance and control as determinants of video game enjoyment. *Cyberpsychology & Behavior.* 2007;10:845-7.

24. Khalil GE. Re-Mission: teasing out emotional gaming events responsible for cancer risk perception *Games for Health Europe.* Amsterdam, the Netherlands: 2013.

25. The Fastest Music in the World http://blog.zombiesrungame.com/post/35334103616/the-fastest-music-in-the-world. Accessed September 23, 2013.

26. Green MC, Brock TC. The role of transportation in the persuasiveness of public narratives. *Journal of Personality and Social Psychology.* 2000;79(5):701-721.

CHAPTER 12

Toshiba America Medical Systems: A Case Study

By Ross Gensler

ABSTRACT

Toshiba America Medical Systems (TAMS) has experienced notable success incorporating multiple wellness initiatives within its comprehensive "Health360" program. One such initiative, delivered by Sonic Boom Wellness since February 2011, has helped TAMS maintain a 62 percent active-employee-engagement rate (as of August 2013). Health360's ongoing success is attributable to the implementation of Sonic Boom Wellness, as well as the perseverance of the Benefits team at Toshiba.

THE COMPANY

Toshiba is a medical imaging technology company located in Orange County, CA, with a total of 1,250 benefits-eligible employees. Prior to Sonic Boom's implementation, healthcare costs had already been kept relatively low compared with market averages, and overall company culture and morale had been generally positive. This was a result of Toshiba's unique, forward-thinking wellness brand called Health360.

Implemented by TAMS' proactive benefits team, Health360 promotes overall awareness of health, fitness and personal wellbeing. The program is administered through a series of health-related activities throughout the year.

A shining example of Toshiba's unique approach to wellness is its "carnivalesque" health fairs, which are hosted each year in February. They are designed to educate employees and raise awareness around the company's healthcare and benefits options. They're successful because employees actually want to attend — and with features including a DJ, bounce houses, live exercise tutorials, and a variety of tasty-yet-healthy snack vendors on hand, it makes sense that employees make a point to show up.
The CEO even makes a special presentation to rally the troops, recognize significant employee accomplishments and provide a clear sense of support for those with an active desire to improve their health.

THE OPPORTUNITY

Although its medical-expenditure situation was seemingly better than most, Toshiba's administrative team believed it could do better. A strong foundation had been set, but Health360 needed something to boost employee engagement and improve the company's sense of culture. Enter Sonic Boom Wellness. In February 2011, the Sonic Boom program was integrated into Health360, and as a result of its revolutionary incentive-management system, quickly established itself as the nucleus of the comprehensive program.

Sonic Boom Components

Sonic Boom provides Toshiba employees with a variety of cutting-edge wellness tools, including web-based trackers, daily activities, team-based contests, social networking platforms and incentives. Though many different tools are available to Toshiba employees, the core initiative has largely been centered on Sonic Boom's two signature modules: Sonic Striding and the Wellness Incentive Management System (WIMS).

Sonic Striding

Sonic Striding seamlessly integrates a wireless activity tracker, manufactured by FitLinxx, with Sonic Boom's proprietary application programming interface software. FitLinxx's ActiPed, rebranded by Sonic Boom as the SonicPed, is a lightweight, waterproof tracking device that members wear on top of their feet. The SonicPed clips securely on the laces of a shoe; it can also be attached to other footwear (or bare feet) using Sonic Boom's one-size-fits-all elastic strap, which is known as a Boomer Band. The SonicPed can measure a bevy of metrics, including:

- Steps taken while walking or running.
- Speed and total distance traveled while walking or running.
- Length of time spent performing a variety of physical activities, including walking, running, cycling, running on an elliptical machine and swimming.
- Total calories burned while engaged in a variety of physical activities.

With built-in wireless technology, transmitting data to Sonic Boom's servers is as effortless as walking next to one of the many SonicPed receiver stations around Toshiba's workplace for a brief moment. Better still, TAMS subsidizes 90 percent of the cost of SonicPeds for employees, resulting in extremely high accessibility and a nonexistent price barrier to participation. Sonic Boom and FitLinxx focus on making daily engagement as simple as possible.

Data captured by the SonicPed is then seamlessly integrated with Sonic Boom's proprietary software, which provides an effective, personalized means through which members track their activity, compare stats to personal bests, compete with coworkers and more. The program also allows Toshiba to implement compelling contests and fun challenges across the entire population, breaking employees into any variety of teams they can imagine. Toshiba's recent "Summer Steppin'" contest, for example, required employees to achieve a daily average of 5,000 steps over the course of two weeks. Employees who succeeded were entered into a drawing for custom prizes. Without Sonic Boom's custom web-based software, this company-wide contest would have been difficult (if not impossible) to administer in a timely fashion. Contest results were tallied quickly, automatically, and with no unfair burden placed on Toshiba's benefits team.

WIMS

Sonic Boom's Wellness Incentive Management System (WIMS) is a sophisticated, flexible platform that integrates data with third-party vendors to deliver a one-stop shop for incentive administration. Using WIMS, Toshiba rewards employees for engaging in a variety of healthy activities, including biometric screenings, health assessments, dental exams and achieving long-term physical-activity goals. One of the rewards employed by Toshiba is a unique virtual currency known as Boomer Bucks, which integrates with the Sonic Boom program: 10,000 Boomer Bucks carry a cash value of $50, which can be spent in an online catalog of more than 3,000 items. Toshiba employees can earn Boomer Bucks by accruing points within the Sonic Boom system and reaching new levels in the program. For example, an employee can earn up to 50,000 Boomer Bucks per year for achieving healthy biometric ranges in areas such as blood pressure and triglycerides, completing two dental check-ups, one vision check-up, four tobacco-cessation coaching calls and completing 100 "Healthy Habit Days" throughout the year.

Implementation

Sonic Boom's innovative wellness tools are wasted if the workforce fails to "buy in" and participate in the program. Toshiba combats potential inactivity by employing a team of persistent program administrators who are staunch proponents of good health and wellness. Winners of multiple awards in 2013 (including Communicator, Hermes Creative, Employee Benefit News iCOMM and APEX), this team of sharp, attentive program admins is headed by Toshiba's director of benefits and HRIS, who won the 2013 Healthcare Consumerism Superstar Award for the Most Innovative Incentive Plan Design.

Evidenced by activities like the aforementioned health fair, Toshiba's program admins are extremely proactive. They maintain constant, consistent contact with the company's wellness ambassadors (dubbed "SuperChampions" by Sonic Boom), and regularly brainstorm to come up with compelling methods to maintain and promote the culture of wellness that they've worked to develop throughout the company.

RESULTS

Financial

The joint wellness effort by Sonic Boom and Toshiba has proven advantageous financially, with a steady decline in medical costs and year-over-year claims since February 2011. From 2012 to 2013 alone, medical expenditures decreased by 2.2 percent; by comparison, the year-over-year industry average is an increase of 10-20 percent. A trending decrease in health expenditures over the course of 2.5 years is a rare achievement and can be directly correlated to Sonic Boom, specifically its integration with FitLinxx technology and sophisticated incentive strategies that tie together all of Health360's key programming.

Cultural

Although Toshiba employees were already somewhat active and health-conscious (thanks to existing Health360 initiatives), Sonic Boom's implementation has bolstered the overall program. With the introduction of daily challenges and open recognition of employees' daily achievements, wellness has evolved from a dreaded chore to become a fun team-building activity. According to data gathered from the SonicPed, Toshiba employees have maintained an average of 5,570 steps a day since the program began in 2011; they also engage in an average of 97 minutes of daily activity. Compared to the overly sedentary average American, these are admirable statistics that give employees a sense of accomplishment and greatly increases morale and drive throughout the company. Team-based contests have also helped in building inter-office camaraderie, boosting communication between departments and even forging new friendships.

Wellness

Toshiba now boasts an active engagement rate of 62 percent among all eligible employees, which means that 62 percent of the eligible workforce regularly logs points in their personal Sonic Boom profiles. Because of its high engagement rate among employees, Toshiba's program was extended to spouses in August 2012, stretching the total number to 2,150 eligible members. Of those, 44 percent actively take part in Sonic Boom's wellness programs and activities.

Sonic Boom provides employees and their spouses with a comprehensive wellness portal with multiple activity-tracking options, but the high sustained engagement rate is in large part due to the implementation of Sonic Striding. The SonicPed provides a medium through which users can quantify exercise activity and view data that is clear and easy to interpret. It's also wireless and hassle-free, eliminating the need to plug anything in or self-report activity on a daily basis. Members simply wear their SonicPed and get on with the rest of their day. The TAMS' community is more inclined to follow through on the program because they can see progress in the form of concrete numbers. It is blatantly evident with Toshiba: among all Sonic Boom participants, 77 percent own a SonicPed, using it to routinely log activity data and participate in company-wide contests.

INDIVIDUAL SUCCESS SAMPLE

Pamela B. is one of many beneficiaries of Sonic Boom and the overall wellness program at TAMS. A hard worker with high blood pressure, Pamela took to Sonic Boom's program slowly, barely logging 1,000 steps per day with her SonicPed in early 2011. Determined to lose weight and improve her health, Pamela was fueled by creative incentives and made a personal commitment to change. She steadily increased her step count and made a series of minor nutritional changes, and then joined a gym in the fall to intensify her fitness regimen.

Two-and-a-half years later, Pamela has not only lost 23 percent of her total body mass, decreased her blood pressure from 140/110 to 120/75, and dropped four dress sizes, but she has managed to keep it all off for more than a year. She regularly participates in 5K and 10K events, and has been taken completely off of her cholesterol medication. She's no longer concerned about the rewards and incentives that TAMS and Sonic Boom provide; to Pamela, maintaining her newfound health is now the number-one objective. Without Sonic Boom to provide that catalyst, Pamela may not have been inspired to take the important first step that led to her drastic lifestyle improvement.

Moving Forward

To say that Sonic Boom's efforts have had a positive effect on Toshiba would be an understatement. As a company that's proactively promoting wellness and health-awareness programs, Toshiba is a stellar outlier, with additional potential to further improve its population's health. With a 62 percent active-engagement rate and a negative trend in medical costs over the past year, Toshiba is in a phenomenal position to continue the success and buck the traditionally sedentary lifestyle of the American tech industry. Additionally, with the implementation of Sonic Boom and FitLinxx's SonicPed technology, Toshiba is now equipped with quantifiable numbers with which to track its progress and make adjustments to programs as needed. This partnership between Sonic Boom and Toshiba is a clear example of how best to enhance existing health-awareness and advocacy programs in the corporate environment.

Part III
The Intersection of Mobile Health & Traditional Medicine

CHAPTER 13

mHealth and Traditional Medicine: Collaboration and Collision

By Rick Krohn, MA, MAS, and David Metcalf, PhD

The intersection of mobile and traditional medicine has created a huge question about how these vastly different approaches to care can play together — on the one hand traditional medicine — episodic, fragmented, provider-driven; and on the other mHealth — ubiquitous, "always on" and patient-centric. Will mHealth become absorbed by mainstream medicine to become another "tool in the toolbox?" Or will mHealth, by virtue of the explosion in global wireless technologies, coupled with the need for new solutions to healthcare's intractable issues — cost and quality — establish its own competing healthcare marketplace?

As we have argued here and in our previous HIMSS book, *mHealth: From Smartphones to Smart Systems*, it is our belief that mHealth is evolving into its own ecosystem, independent of and in contrast to mainstream medicine. mHealth is a complement to many existing healthcare processes, in the facility and practice, in the field and in the home. But mHealth possesses another dimension of value that exists beyond the boundaries of traditional health care delivery — it creates new stakeholder touchpoints, makes efficient use of resources, and extends the reach of healthcare entities. And most importantly, it recasts the provider-patient relationship by making the patient more engaged, more accountable, more knowledgeable, more invested in their own health. And those changing roles are establishing a new definition of healthcare delivery — one that emphasizes prevention rather than simply treatment.

Optimally, we could expect a smooth transition from the old model of healthcare to the new, with mHealth innovation acting as a lever. But the intersection of traditional medicine and mHealth is not a smooth one, and though there are clearly points of mutual benefit, there are obstacles as well. Those obstacles assume a variety of forms, and can be summed up in a word: complexity. And to this we can add another hurdle: industry disruption, which is depicted in Table 13-1.

Disruptive innovation is a term coined in 1997 by Harvard University Professor Clayton Christensen to describe how an existing market can be changed by introducing simplicity, convenience, accessibility and affordability where complication and high cost are the status quo. (See Fig. 13-1.) This definition neatly defines the intersection of mHealth and traditional medicine. Christensen's key idea: disruptive innovations are not breakthrough technologies that make good products better; rather they

Table 13-1: Industries Disrupted by New Technology.

Innovation	Disrupted Market
Automobiles	Rail roads
CDs, DVDs	Tapes
Downloadable Digital Media	CDs, DVDs
Digital Photography	Film Photography
Mini Computers	Mainframe Computers
Personal Computers	Mini Computers
Flat Panel TVs	CRT TVs
Robotic Factories	Assembly Line Factories
Jet Planes	Propeller Planes

are innovations that transform sectors to make products affordable and convenient, thereby making them available to a much larger population. A simple example: the computer industry, once dominated by large mainframes and affordable to the few, has subsequently been transformed in a linear progression by minis, by desktops, by laptops and now the phone — making information affordable and available to everyone. Fig. 13-1 describes this opportunity.

Disruptive innovation changes entire *markets,* and ultimately *displaces* a market and value chain, over an extended period. mHealth and its wellspring of industry innovation isn't just a disruptive force in healthcare — it's a *displacement* force that is reinventing healthcare delivery. And that market transition — from disruption to dis-

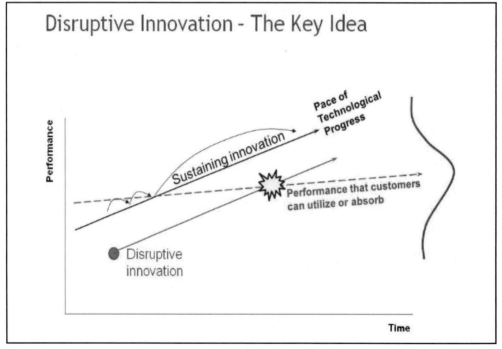

Fig. 13-1: The Innovator's Dilemma (Christensen, 1997).

placement — is accelerating. Unbound by the need to create products with huge commercial potential, mHealth innovators can introduce boutique solutions that address specific issues and are targeted to specific customers. As Fig. 13-2 describes, there is a market niche for innovative solutions which exists outside the current healthcare marketplace, where new entrants, with limited competition and limited resources, can thrive.

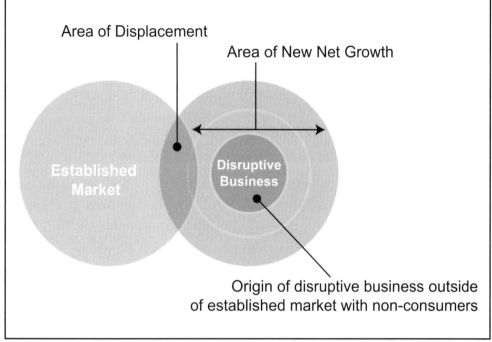

Fig. 13-2: Innovation Creates Its Own Market Niche.
(From the insight centre, 2012. Used with permission.)

mHealth is fertile ground for industry innovation — in concert with (disruptive) and in contrast to (displacement) mainstream, traditional healthcare. But to understand the push and pull that defines the intersection of mHealth and traditional medicine, it's important to recognize that this is a relationship with layers of complexity. There are multiple forces — people, processes, finance, technology and regulation — that influence the pathways and pace of mHealth innovation.

THE STAKEHOLDERS

It's generally accepted in the payer and provider communities that mHealth will become an integral component of healthcare delivery. Providers recognize that mHealth, as an adjunct to their existing workflows, can deliver value in areas such as patient compliance, care coordination and records management. Payers are finding opportunities to cut costs and engage their members in prevention via mHealth, and consumers, who have been the engine of mHealth's growth in the early years, continue to embrace self-care and engagement solutions. These indicators suggest that mHealth is becoming a component part of mainstream medicine.

But that outcome will hinge on behavior change among all the actors in the healthcare continuum. mHealth is disruptive, and on a macro level it must first overwhelm the cultural conservatism and aversion to technology that has been a feature of healthcare for decades. Change in healthcare is not only disruptive, it challenges a status quo that dates back decades. In the realm of technology, the electronic medical record (EMR) provides an archetype lesson. The EMR in some form has been trumpeted as a revolutionary tool in healthcare since 1985, and we still haven't achieved the tipping point of adoption. Several additional factors are creating a fissure between mHealth and traditional medicine. Not least among them is control.

Providers are concerned that mHealth will change the "balance of power" in healthcare, will make patients too independent, perhaps even divorcing themselves from mainstream medicine.

Patients want greater control and to make healthcare decisions based on convenience and cost — both brand identifiers of mHealth. And the patients (and in a larger context the healthcare consumer) that are emerging as the early adopters are those least served by existing healthcare services by issues of access, quality or cost.

Payers, drawn by the savings that can be captured in administration and preventive care, are gravitating toward a patient-centric market strategy, with mHealth as an organizing principle. mHealth offers the prospect of collateral benefits to payers, in terms of patient education and accountability, consumer preference, and personalized engagement. And in growing numbers, payers are reimbursing providers for delivering mHealth services (which are more cost-effective).

Entry, Sustainability and Scalability

mHealth has had some notable successes, most prominently in the global south where the opportunities to improve healthcare access and delivery are manifest. With fewer entrenched interests and a general lack of alternatives, mHealth is finding a smooth glide path toward acceptance. In the developed world, however, mHealth solutions aren't being introduced in a vacuum, and there are real hurdles to acceptance — healthcare systems with massive capital investments in wired infrastructure, a lack of a proven business model, marginal reimbursement and compliance issues make mHealth acceptance a more complex equation. Sustainability, particularly in immature, unproven markets is a genuine concern — and rapid innovation cycles in mHealth call into question the shelf life of these solutions. Even if they do work as advertised, will they scale? Just because a product is useful doesn't guarantee it will be embraced in large numbers, or that anyone will pay for it.

Business Rationality

One of the chief obstacles facing mHealth innovation is the complex arrangement of incentives that reinforce our current system. The prevailing model of healthcare reimbursement, despite years of foreshadowing of a shift from volume-to-value as the principal payment metric, remains fee for service. Put another way, providers get paid for producing services, regardless of outcomes. mHealth isn't particularly well-suited to this environment, because it removes to a large degree the freedom of providers to determine which services will be delivered and with what frequency. These services can range from routine office visits to diagnostic and chronic treatment — services that can be delivered remotely via mHealth, but at greatly reduced or no cost. In this scenario mHealth represents a threat, not an opportunity, to traditional medicine.

But as mHealth solutions evolve, the sheer volume and range of information that can be shared via mobile will make further inroads into traditional healthcare processes, with attendant consequences for reimbursement. A final consideration: an mHealth product will only be adopted if the customer sees an advantage in paying for it. Patients and consumers are price sensitive, and this sensitivity does not change with income. But as price points recede in the consumer space for devices and apps, that hurdle will subside.

Technology

For innovators, mHealth poses real challenges and barriers. Integration and interoperability are often cited as barriers to implementation of mHealth, particularly in larger organizations with many disparate systems. Rather than climb the "mountain of no's," one strategy of mHealth entrepreneurs has been to avoid interacting with huge, complex systems altogether. Another roadblock: both providers and payers list privacy and security as leading hurdles to greater adoption of mHealth, and many view the security of the mobile Internet with skepticism.

Regulation

Healthcare is a heavily regulated industry, and each new wrinkle in healthcare delivery opens the possibility of regulatory scrutiny. Technology has been a lightning rod of regulation, and mHealth is in the unenviable position of not only attempting to comply with existing industry regulations regarding technology, but to anticipate new regulations from agencies like the FDA, FCC and others that have yet to reveal themselves. And as an unintended consequence, providers are reluctant to invest in technologies whose regulatory future is uncertain.

Provider, and more particularly physician, resistance is likely to have a breaking effect on some aspects of mHealth. Thus, despite the new revenue opportunities offered, a significant number of providers are reluctant to surrender the control they have historically held in the provision of care. They are bound by the conflicting incentives and revenue drivers of traditional medicine. They are reluctant to interfere with existing workflows and systems, and are concerned about the difficulties associated with integration and interoperability. They continue to remain uncertain about the rock solidness of mHealth privacy, security and regulation.

With this obstacle in mind, the key to making disruptive innovation, or in the case of mHealth displacement innovation, work, is to make it a winner for everybody — an alignment of incentives. It's important to recognize that innovation challenges the status quo, that it steps on somebody's toes, and that somebody is going to have to pay for it. Stakeholders will pay for mHealth solutions if they detect real value and benefit from it *directly*. And here is where mHealth innovation shines — in its breathtaking application of imagination to healthcare problems.

From a product perspective, Price Waterhouse Cooper identifies six principles for innovators:

1. Interoperability — interoperable with sensors and other mobile/non-mobile devices to share vast amounts of data with other applications, such as EMRs and existing health plans.
2. Integration — integrated into existing activities and workflows of providers and patients to provide the support needed for new behaviors.
3. Intelligence — offer problem-solving ability to provide real-time, qualitative solutions based on existing data to realize productivity gains.
4. Socialization — act as a hub by sharing information across a broad community to provide support, coaching, recommendations and other forms of assistance.
5. Outcomes — provide a return on investment in terms of cost, access and quality of care based on healthcare objectives.
6. Engagement — enable patient involvement and the provision of ubiquitous and instant feedback in order to realize new behaviors and/or sustain desired performance.[1]

In sum, the organizing principle of mHealth innovation must be solutions — products and services, not technology. Those solutions must directly address a critical need, and establish a business model that generates sustainable revenues. Innovators must navigate a highly complex, culturally diverse group of stakeholders and appeal to each of them — according first to the problems these solutions can solve, but also to introduce solutions that create new revenue, increase access, improve quality, boost efficiencies and reduce costs. To some degree, the alignment of stakeholders and mHealth opportunities will grow as the industry's payment and delivery apparatus become more precarious — and that process is well underway.

REFERENCE

1. Emerging mHealth: Paths for Growth. PWC White Paper, 2012.

CHAPTER 14

Effective Engagement with Mobile Messaging: A Case Study

By Travis Good, MD, MBA, MS

ABSTRACT

As healthcare begins the course change from volume-based to value-based care, effective patient engagement is essential to help consumers self-manage disease. Effective patient engagement requires processes and tools to extend the reach of payers and providers, reaching consumers wherever they are and in ways they prefer to be reached. Mobile messaging, especially text messaging (SMS), is extremely effective at reaching people in real time. One additional benefit of SMS is that it is a highly effective means of reaching traditionally underserved populations. This chapter presents two case studies of one- and two-way SMS messaging for health literacy and patient reported data collection. As organizations look to scale consumer engagement strategies, simple messaging should be considered as an alternative to mobile apps.

INTRODUCTION

Incentives in U.S. healthcare are fundamentally changing. The dominant business model in healthcare has been payment for services delivered, or fee-for-service; do more to make more. As margins have been slashed over the years, health systems have been driven to provide more "care" to each patient in the form of more services for each patient. While most health systems today remain in this fee-for-service model by necessity, the fundamental shift to value-based care has begun. In fact, lots of systems are preparing for the time when they need to flip the switch and change the model of care, the model for which they've been built, and for which almost all operational decisions and tools have created.

Value-based care, in the most simplistic definition, is maximizing the quality of care while minimizing the cost to care for a patient.[1] Quality is inclusive of both health outcomes and patient satisfaction. Cost is the longitudinal cost to provide care to a patient over a period of time. Value-based care is not just about preventing readmissions, it's about preventing admissions. It's about delivering effective care in low-cost ways and in low-cost settings to prevent catastrophic, high-cost care in high-cost settings. In healthcare, that means keeping patients out of the hospital, ICU, OR and procedure suites as much as possible.

A large part of value-based care is patient engagement, especially digital patient engagement outside the traditional healthcare settings.[2] To effectively engage patients outside the four walls of the hospital or clinic, mobile is seen as a major component, and correctly so. Facebook has data that mobile users are twice as active, or engaged, as non-mobile users.[3] Facebook is not a bad model to learn from when it comes to engagement; it is a company built on the power of engaged users. Additionally, mobile text messaging, or SMS, is used by 74 percent of U.S. adults;[4] this is across all adults, not only young adults, where the use of SMS is considerably higher.

SMS has also been examined in marketing, and been found to have open rates of over 98 percent, compared to 22 percent open rates for e-mail. As opposed to e-mail, SMS messages do not sit in an inbox waiting for an open; the recipient typically sees the message almost immediately. This makes SMS as a method to engage patients very powerful.

The other interesting and potential power of SMS is helping to address disparities in access to care and services. Minority racial groups, both black and Latino, utilize SMS at higher adoption rates than the general population.[4] These minority groups have a higher burden of chronic disease. Additionally, lower socioeconomic groups often have a higher burden of chronic disease.[5] SMS, proportionally, has more potential to improve access to resource and improve the overall care of these groups.

The tools and repeatable processes needed to shift from fee-for-service to value-based care are still being discovered and tested. Certain systems, such as integrated delivery networks (IDN), are pioneering these tools and services, collecting the evidence needed to prove or disprove the value of different approaches and techniques. IDNs are uniquely placed to pioneer these services because many of them are already partially value-based in terms of business model. Other players in the health system, such as the Department of Health & Human Services (HHS) and private payers, are also incented to use messaging to deliver services with the hope of delivering better care at lower costs.

This case study presents the findings from two pilots. The first pilot was conducted at an integrated system, Denver Health[6], which built and assessed SMS as a means to effectively engage patients.[7] The second pilot was facilitated partially by HHS in a public-private partnership aimed at underserved pregnant women and new moms.[8]

STUDY 1: DENVER HEALTH SMS FOR DIABETIC SELF-MANAGEMENT

Denver Health, working with EMC Consulting and Microsoft Corp., built a patient relationship management (PRM) system to manage messaging activity. The goal of creating the PRM was to help patients with diabetes better self-manage their conditions between clinic visits. Patients were enrolled from a specific clinic. The majority of participants were over the age of 50 and predominately Latino.

To accomplish the objective of improving patient self-management between clinic visits, the PRM was used to develop specific rules around messaging. Study participants were sent regular messages prompting them to respond with glucose readings. Additionally, participants were sent appointment reminder and confirmation messages.

A sample SMS message used in the Denver Health pilot exchange follows:
- Glucose level request sent to patient by PRM: *Today is Wed, May 11. What is your fasting blood sugar today?*
- Well-formatted patient response: *185*
- PRM-generated response acknowledgement: *Denver Health received your message (185). Thank you!*

Of the 1,585 SMS messages sent as part of the pilot, 68 percent of messages received a response and close to 99 percent of those SMS responses were correctly formatted. Looking at sustained engagement, 79 percent of participants responded to SMS prompts more than 50 percent of the time.

The major limitation of the study was the size of it, with only 47 participants enrolled. Denver Health is expanding this pilot study significantly as part of an ongoing HHS Innovation Grant. This expansion includes new messages for things such as smoking cessation, diet tips, flu vaccinations and appointment reminders.

STUDY 2: TEXT4BABY AND ACCESS TO SERVICES

text4baby is a mobile messaging service to which new and expectant moms subscribe. The service is a public-private partnership, with technology provided by Voxiva Inc.[9] text4baby enrolls patients at health centers and targets underserved populations. These patients receive messages relevant to the stage of pregnancy and delivery.

The service delivers two types of SMS content for users:
1. Messages to educate users and facilitate more informed discussions for in-person encounters between patients and providers.
2. Messages about services for which users might be eligible.

A sample text4baby message follows:

• *Free msg: Have you visited a Dr. or midwife (CNM/CM)? If not, make an appointment now. Call your health plan. Or 800-311-2229 to connect to low-cost care.*

The text4baby is under active and ongoing assessment to determine its efficacy. Early data finds that the program is having success in meeting its mission with participants.
- 67 percent of participants discussed a text4baby message topic with their health provider.
- 40 percent of participants called a service they learned about in a text4baby message. This percentage moves up to 50 percent in uninsured populations.

text4baby is a model that has been used for other conditions and patient populations, including diabetes, child health and smoking cessation.[10]

IMPLICATIONS

SMS usage amongst U.S. adults has grown year after year. Increasingly businesses are using SMS for customer service and marketing. It's more highly regulated than e-mail, which is why there isn't as much SMS spam, but it's highly effective. Mobile touchpoints are great ways to stay top of mind, especially if those touchpoints can be personalized, contextualized and interactive.

As such, SMS holds phenomenal potential for patient engagement. In healthcare, patient engagement can be seen as a form of customer service and marketing; patient relationship management is just a unique term for customer relationship management. Patient engagement is essentially serving the healthcare needs of patients outside the four walls of the clinic and hospital, while also marketing, educating, and promoting healthy behavior and activity.

Today, many businesses utilize two-way SMS to conduct surveys and approve payments. In healthcare, these same services have been applied by organizations like Denver Health to collect patient-reported glucose readings. Denver Health has shown that older minority populations can be effectively targeted using SMS. If done simply, data collected from users as part of two-way SMS campaigns can be easily parsed and turned into structured, meaningful data.

Still other businesses offer SMS-based marketing promotions in the same way text4baby offers the promotion of healthy behavior. text4baby has shown the ability of SMS to inform and increase enrollment in health services, a key step in improving access and reducing cost.

The unique potential of SMS as a technology intervention for traditionally underserved populations cannot be understated. As payers and systems look to reduce the cost of care, targeting at-risk and overburdened populations will be a high priority. SMS is a great tool to engage these populations.

As health systems and payers look to prepare for the shift to value-based care, SMS serves as a key tool. Interestingly, despite being top-of-mind for most organizations and executives, no scaled examples exist for the use of SMS in effective patient engagement.

CHALLENGES AHEAD

Security and Privacy
SMS as a technology and conduit for messages cannot meet HIPAA requirements to carry protected health information (PHI). Today, organizations such as Denver Health that use SMS are de-individualizing the messages. This is still an area of interpretation by legal and compliance departments.

Interestingly, recent changes made to the HIPAA Security Rules enable organizations to allow patients to opt-in to unencrypted technologies. This can be interpreted to include SMS. This is a very new rule change, but one that may have far-reaching impact. It does not change the way that PHI needs to be treated by covered entities and business associates, other than allowing them use certain unencrypted channels to communicate with patients if patients opt-in to such unencrypted messages.

Scaling and Distribution
Enrollment is something that both Denver Health and text4baby have done through providers' promotion of services. text4baby works closely with health centers and markets through partners like HHS and Johnson & Johnson. Through these promotions, text4baby is able to capture patients at the point-of-care using things such as

QR codes and SMS links, both of which enable patients to be activated using mobile phones.

Despite the challenges around distribution, most of which can be resolved by integration of provider promoters, enrollment in SMS campaigns is many times easier than getting people to download a mobile app. All that is required is a mobile phone number, and of course, a documented willingness on the part of the patient to receive health-related SMS messages.

Denver Health faces challenges as additional clinical areas look to integrate SMS services. These services would ideally use the same PRM, opt-in and -out policies and procedures, security and message delivery platform. These are challenges moving from pilot to large-scale, organization-wide deployments. Best practices for opting into and out of health-related SMS services are not available, and will likely be driven at the organizational level.

One additional challenge with scaling is cost. Most message delivery services are priced based on the number of messages sent. In healthcare, these messaging services, based on the additional security requirements needed to handle storage and processing of PHI, are typically more expensive than services outside of healthcare. On a per-message basis, these higher costs can add up and make the decision to scale SMS a challenging one when it comes to ROI.

Workflow Implications

Broadly speaking, as healthcare shifts to see patient data as more than medical records, self-reported and ongoing monitoring data are becoming a large part of the definition of a patient. Data collected via two-way SMS in healthcare, as well as metrics around participation in SMS campaigns, will need to be integrated into systems that providers can use to help engage and care for patients in person.

In the case of Denver Health, triggers were created for glucose readings received that were either too high or too low — over 400 or less than 70, respectively. These triggers were sent to a care navigator assigned to the pilot, who dedicated 20 percent of her time to the pilot. This care navigator followed up on readings outside of a typical range.

Additionally, Denver Health has created reports that are viewable by providers for in-person consultations. The pilot was conducted at one clinic site, so provider education and buy-in were easier than if the model was scaled organization-wide.

Collecting additional data via SMS is great, and using that data to empower patients to make more informed decisions and improve self-management is very powerful. But, to effectively scale, provider buy-in is essential. And data collected directly from patients is not something most providers are accustomed to using, or for which they are compensated. Because of this, a large amount of effort is required to change workflows and achieve broad-based clinician buy-in.

WHAT'S NEXT?

As organizations continue to shift to value-based and accountable care models, services to reach and engage patients will grow, as will efforts to more widely distribute and quantify these services. Mobile apps alone are not the answer. Not everything requires a mobile app, especially transactional and proactive messaging. And some mobile apps benefit from integration of other messaging services such as SMS.

As organizations pilot and scale messaging services, more diverse mobile health offerings will emerge. It's very likely that in time a combination of mobile app, in-app messaging, PUSH, SMS, voice- and e-mail will be used to meet individual communication and usage preferences. Listening to users and offering flexibility in mobile health offerings to users will increase engagement metrics.

Despite its age in the market and limits in terms of security and multimedia, SMS continues to grow in adoption and usage, especially with business to consumer communications. As marketers outside of healthcare have learned, SMS may be an older technology compared to PUSH and mobile apps, but it is still the most effective in certain scenarios, especially user activation and engagement.

REFERENCES

1. Dartmouth-Hitchcock. What is value-based care? [web site]. Available at: www.dartmouth-hitchcock.org/about_dh/what_is_value_based_care.html.
2. http://marketplace.himss.org/OnlineStore/ProductDetail.aspx?ProductId=376977836
3. Facebook. Key facts [web page]. Available at: http://newsroom.fb.com/Key-Facts.
4. Duggan M. Cell Phone Activities 2012. Pew Internet & American Life Project. Available at: http://pewinternet.org/Reports/2013/Cell-Activities/Main-Findings.aspx.
5. California Department of Health. Burden Report Online. Available at: www.cdph.ca.gov/programs/Documents/BurdenReportOnline percent2004-04-13.pdf.
6. Denver Health. [web site]. Available at: www.denverhealth.org.
7. Fischer HH, Moore SL, Ginosar D, et al. Care by cell phone: text messaging for chronic disease management. º. 2012 Feb 1;18(2):e42-7.
8. Hoff A, Nunez-Alvarez A, Martinez KM, Maternal & newborn health: text4baby San Diego. Evaluation overview: October 2011-October 2012. Available at: www.csusm.edu/nlrc/documents/report_archives/Text4Baby_SanDiego_Evaluation_Overview.pdf.
9. text4baby. Who's Involved. [web page]. Available at: https://text4baby.org/index.php/about/partners.
10. Voxiva. Diabetes. [web page]. Available at: www.voxiva.com/index.php/products/diabetes.

CHAPTER 15

Mobile Prescription Therapy: A Case Study

By Malinda Peeples, MS, RN, CDE, and Anand K. Iyer, PhD, MBA

ABSTRACT

This chapter introduces a novel category of therapy that is born from the confluence of clinical, behavioral and data science innovation, and the ubiquitous access to and acceptance of mobile and Internet technology. Mobile prescription therapy (MPT) is a solution that holistically engages patients in the self-management of their disease in collaboration with their healthcare provider. MPT decentralizes, and in novel ways democratizes, the delivery of healthcare by empowering patients and providers through the use of wireless mobile devices, clinical and data science and the Internet. At its heart, MPT represents the convergence of mobile technology, clinical and behavioral science, and validated clinical outcomes to create a new-to-the-world healthcare solution that supports patients in their daily self-care, and provides their healthcare provider with additional data for decision making.

This chapter will first address the healthcare and economic challenges specifically associated with the management of type 2 diabetes and the rationale behind the need for mobile prescription therapy. It then presents the MPT solution components, primary features and value-enabling characteristics, and then summarizes the clinical and economic value propositions achieved. The chapter concludes with a glimpse into the future and illuminates the "vectors of value expansion" that MPT can unlock to achieve better health and better care in a cost-effective and scalable manner for all chronic diseases.

CHRONIC DISEASE: WHY MPT?

Chronic disease management is a challenge not only for the person with the disease, but also for the healthcare providers who are developing and guiding the treatment plan, the healthcare system, support and caregiver members and payers who provide the infrastructure for the care delivery.

In 2012, spending on chronic diseases in the United States represented 75 percent of the more than $2 trillion devoted to healthcare; such diseases were responsible for seven out of 10 deaths annually.[1] As recently as 2009, more than 86 million Americans had not had any healthcare insurance coverage during the previous two years[2]; millions more lack full healthcare coverage today.[3] The pharmaceutical industry laments the current state of medication adherence, which for many drugs quickly drops to below 30 percent in a matter of two to three refill periods for a given drug. And in disease management, the "high-attention" call-center-based services are tapping into every avenue to determine how to raise engagement rates from levels that currently sit below 15 percent.

Unfortunately, our traditional healthcare infrastructure, workforce numbers and tactics have not grown rapidly enough to accommodate the rapid rise in our chronic-disease patient population. One can argue that chronic-disease management, which has a large self-management component, should not be managed with traditional approaches. In fact, during the past decade, standardized approaches to chronic-disease management using tools such as the Chronic Care Model[4] have been rapidly evolving; increasing attention to and measurement for the patient's role have evolved as well.

That being said, there remain real barriers to managing chronic diseases that must be taken into consideration:

- **Chronic-disease management is incredibly burdensome for patients.** Management of many chronic diseases requires patients to monitor and track significant amounts of multi-variate data (e.g., medications, physical/psychological symptoms, metabolic measurement, activity and nutrition, etc.) asynchronously throughout any given day, and to recall the correct (and often complex) treatment pathways.
- **Patients have limited support outside of the clinical setting.** Our healthcare system (and others throughout the world) was designed to support acute care; they don't effectively support the needs of chronic-disease management. Patients forget much of their physicians' instructions within hours or days of leaving the clinic. In a dynamic world, patients need fingertip-access to relevant and timely education outside of their healthcare provider's office.
- **Healthcare providers don't get the data they need.** As a result of the undue burden on patients, healthcare providers often have limited, incomplete and/or inaccurate information to use as a basis for treatment modifications.
- **Office visits are too short and too infrequent.** Typically, primary care physicians or general practitioners have 10-15 minutes or less during an office visit to review charts, examine patients, analyze data and develop a treatment plan. Typical patients may only see their physicians two or three times a year.
- **Primary care physicians aren't always aware of the latest evidence-based guidelines.** As the gatekeepers to our healthcare system, primary care doctors see and treat the overwhelming majority of patients. In the current clinical paradigm, it is unrealistic to expect primary care physicians to know and treat according to the latest evidence-based guidelines for all chronic diseases.

While the role of patient self-management in chronic-disease outcomes has been clearly established during the past decade, the inclusion of this activity in quality reporting has not yet occurred. This omission is due primarily to the lack of well-defined and tested measures, the inherent challenges of self-reported data, and the technological ability to capture this data. Remote monitoring devices (e.g., blood pressure cuffs, weight scales and even blood glucose meters) have provided initial movement into this area, yet these devices have heretofore served primarily as data transfer devices to display patient data in an electronic medical record (EMR) for review and analysis by providers. Currently lacking with the remote monitoring, however, is insight or knowledge that can be gleaned through patients' self-reported data.

At the same time, we know that simply transmitting raw data from patients to physicians does not generate a positive ROI in the form of health or economic outcomes.[5] To date, the health and economic outcomes of effective management of chronic diseases have traditionally been driven and measured from the perspective of the healthcare system providers, as this was where the data was available for collection, aggregation and reporting. Initially, claims and administrative information provided the bulk of the data for reporting, and this informed the initial development of such national metrics as Healthcare Effectiveness and Data Information Set (HEDIS) and the National Committee for Quality Assurance (NCQA) quality measures. With the introduction of EMRs, electronic laboratory reporting and e-prescribing, the focus of these measures became more specific. For example, the diabetes care metric for glucose control has evolved from the percentage of the population having the hemoglobin HbA1c test done within a given timeframe to the percentage of the population having an HbA1c value greater or less than 9 percent.[6] However, as is well known today, healthcare providers are generally slow to adopt the use of EMRs for a variety of reasons, and among those were the cost and need to change their practice and workflow models. In 2009, the HITECH Act[7] incentivized electronic record adoption and promoted meaningful use of the records to impact quality of care. The Meaningful Use rules outline a staged approach to the implementation of interoperable records and increasing specificity of quality metrics and involvement of patient-centric care at each stage. As more providers adopt the electronic records and work to integrate quality reporting into their workflows, the expectation is that their ability to achieve national care metrics will be increasingly facilitated.

What is needed now is to transform patient data into meaningful and medically relevant information for patients — at the right place, at the right time, in the right format and with the right context. Mobile technologies help provide this missing fabric required to enable the transformation of data into actionable information and knowledge.

In 2012, cellular penetration in the United States crossed 100 percent of the population for the first time in history, topping 322 million subscribers,[8] an interesting statistic when compared with the 256 million passenger vehicles registered in the United States.[9] Monthly SMS volume has grown from a mere 5.8 billion messages in 2005 to more than 2 trillion in 2012.[10] There is an opportunity to leverage the cellular platform as a means of providing actionable healthcare information access to those who do not have access to traditional means of care. The United States has an unprecedented opportunity to leverage a lower-cost platform to connect patients and providers, to facilitate actionable care at the right time, in a manner that fits into the day-to-day lives of patients and the clinical workflow of providers. There is an opportunity to address the issues in a smart, novel and efficient manner.

The cellphone represents a technology platform that is available to the patient on a 24/7 basis with the capability of providing real-time messaging (alerts, reminders, feedback), geo-location services and other features, as well as being an ideal data-capture device. These technology capabilities have stimulated the development of more than 1 million health-related software applications for all the mobile phone operating systems (e.g., iPhone, Android, etc.). The applications range from health and wellness products to applications that are being specifically used to manage diseases. Some of the applications, depending on their actual and intended uses, will fall under the classification of "mobile medical application" and as such, will require review by the Food and Drug Administration (FDA).[11]

MPT: SOLUTION COMPONENTS

To overcome the challenges previously discussed, an MPT solution must exhibit several key characteristics:

- **Automation**: MPT must provide 24/7, real-time and longitudinal coaching for patients and decision support for healthcare providers to allow increased scalability and access to healthcare in the face of scarce provider resources.
- **Personalization:** The MPT must coach and provide feedback to patients based on the patient's personal profile and unique data inputs. That is, it must take into account their metabolic parameters, co-morbidity parameters and personal profile attributes in order to drive engagement that is tailored to them.
- **Contextualization:** Coaching must be relevant to an event that has just happened, is happening or that will likely happen. Therefore, the MPT must understand both temporal as well as situational context to increase the relevancy to and engagement by the patient.
- **Patient-level HCP decision support:** While healthcare providers today have access — through a plethora of media — to evidence-based guidelines, often times the guidelines may not apply to the patient in question. Therefore, the MPT should aspire to leverage evidence-based population guidelines that are tailored to the specifics of each patient's behavioral readiness, medical profile and personal data.

To satisfy these characteristics, the MPT should be comprised of at least three critical components, which are illustrated in Fig. 15-1.

1. **Virtual patient coach**: Software available on multiple operating systems and devices, that provides real-time, contextually-relevant, personalized, clinical and behavioral coaching for the management of a patient's chronic disease. This software is driven by both evidence-based guidelines and the healthcare providers' instructions and settings that are deemed appropriate for a patient (and hence, the prescribed nature of the solution).
2. **Automated Expert Analytics System**™: An intelligent, cloud-based, longitudinal algorithm engine that observes multi-variate patient behaviors over time and provides additional coaching to patients and suitably timed alerts to caregivers as necessary. This expert system is driven by a series of key patient indicators (KPI) and evidence-based rules that suggest either reinforcing or corrective actions that can be taken in response to an observed pattern. It pro-

vides longitudinal observation and feedback in many domains, including the management of medications, symptoms, metabolic data and lifestyle data to then power the virtual patient coach and clinical decision support.

3. **Clinical decision support**: A decision-making support tool for healthcare providers to help them optimize their patients' therapies, care plans and outcomes based on observations and patterns (e.g., with respect to testing behavior, medication administration, etc.). This decision support can also include an automated "smart" assessment that relies on evidence-based rules to identify gaps and facilitate recommendations for therapy plan adjustments to the healthcare provider so that they are not left to manage large amounts of data and manually perform the pattern recognition function in the limited time they have with patients.

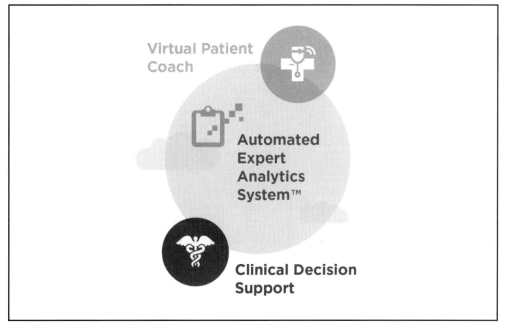

Fig. 15-1: MPT Solution Components.

APP vs MPT

A common question is, "What is the difference between a mobile application (app) and an MPT?" Of the million-plus mobile applications across such app stores as Apple and Google Play,[12] only a few can be categorized as MPT. Dr. Francis Collins, Director at the National Institutes of Health states "…we are also very concerned that as this technology comes forward so quickly, we need to be sure we're collecting the right evidence to show that these mHealth applications actually improve outcomes."[13] To demonstrate applicability for healthcare, the first condition an MPT must satisfy is to generate statistically valid results for health and economic outcomes. In addition, it must satisfy two additional conditions. First, MPT must meet the rules and regulations governing patient safety and repeatable, scalable and predictable quality systems (i.e., good manufacturing process). Second, to fit into clinical workflow and align with the treatment plan, MPT should be prescribed and controlled by a licensed healthcare provider. In studies, over two-thirds of patients indicated a preference to get their mobile health solution from their doctor.[14] Fig. 15-2 below summarizes these characteristics and hurdles that must be overcome for a solution to be considered an MPT.

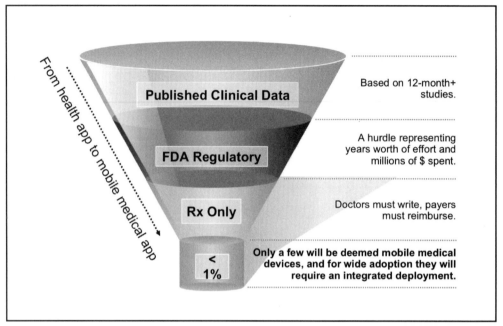

Fig. 15-2: Hurdles to Classify a Product as MPT.

MPT: VALUE PROPOSITION

The MPT value proposition for all healthcare stakeholders is multifaceted and must include the following benefits:

- Improved health outcomes: This is usually demonstrated as a statistically significant improvement in a key metabolic parameter (e.g., HbA1c for diabetes, cholesterol levels for hyperlipidemia, blood pressure for hypertension, etc.).
- Improved economic outcomes and ROI: Cost-savings should accrue due to multiple factors that can include reductions in acute-care costs (e.g., hospitalizations, emergency room visits, etc.), reduction in long-term care costs through improved health outcomes (e.g., reduced HbA1c), and the ensuing productivity uplifts that can be achieved (e.g., reduced absenteeism, increased presenteeism). The collective cost-savings must create a positive ROI and be achieved rapidly (e.g., in a six- to 12-month time frame).

MPT products must be systematically evaluated to demonstrate the value derived from their use. Even though this category of therapy is relatively new, the following data from clinical studies and costs-savings modeling of a diabetes MPT provides evidence that MPT impacts outcomes.

Improved Health Outcomes

The Mobile Diabetes Intervention Study (MDIS), a year-long, cluster-randomized, clinical trial (RCT) utilizing a diabetes MPT was conducted with 163 type 2 diabetes patients and their primary care physicians.[15] The primary outcome was the change in glycated hemoglobin levels (HbA1c) over a one-year treatment period. Patients in the intervention arm of the RCT received a diabetes MPT solution, and patients in the control group received standard care with their healthcare provider.

Using the diabetes MPT, patients entered diabetes self-care data (e.g., blood glucose values, carbohydrate intake, medications and other details) on a mobile phone and securely received automated, real-time educational, behavioral and motivational messages, with a further option to access their records and other helpful information via a web-based portal. The automated expert analytics system reviewed patient data and was able to supplement automated messages with additional advice and encouragement, with patients receiving an "action plan" every two and a half to three months.

The MDIS study results indicated the mean declines in HbA1c (the gold-standard measure for diabetes control) were 1.9 percent in intervention group and 0.7 percent in the control group (usual care alone), a difference of nearly 1.2 percent (P<.001). See Fig. 15-3.

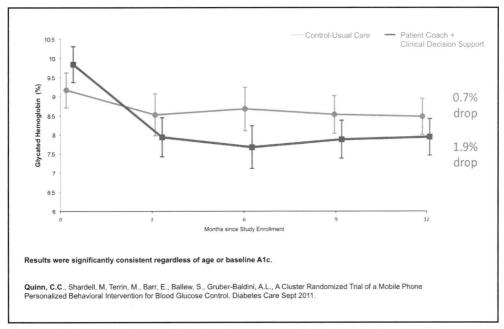

Fig. 15-3: Mean Decline in HbA1c, Control vs. MPT Patients.[16]

This diabetes MPT solution demonstrated meaningful health outcomes and prompted the following comment by Charlene C. Quinn, RN, PhD, University of Maryland School of Medicine, lead investigator of the study: "The results indicate that doctors and patients can engage more effectively using mobile health tools like the WellDoc system to enhance patients' diabetes care and their blood glucose."

These health outcomes also led Richard Bergenstal, MD, Executive Director of the International Diabetes Center at Park Nicollet and past president of the American Diabetes Association (ADA) to comment: "Finally, we have a good example of utilizing technology in the form of mobile diabetes coaching to help both patient and provider make the most effective lifestyle and management decisions."

IMPROVED ECONOMIC OUTCOMES AND ROI

To demonstrate the ROI of an MPT, a cost savings model was developed using data from the MDIS study. The model was developed in conjunction with Milliman, an actuarial firm, to estimate the direct and indirect savings associated with MPT. The estimated cost savings, as seen in Fig. 15-4, is based on improvement in A1C values over 12 months. Also, the cost savings are based on expected mitigation of complications associated with type 2 diabetes when patients improve and control A1C values. The estimated cost savings per user per month (PUPM) are as seen in Fig. 15-4.

Source	Description	Low PUPM Savings A1C>7%	High PUPM Savings Top 50% with A1C>7%
2012 Milliman Modeling of Market Scan, NHANES, & UKPDS – Direct Costs	7 UKPDS Complications Coded as Primary Diagnosis	$150	$250
ADA, NHIS, NHANES, INGENIX, MEPS, NIS, NAMCS, NHHCS – Direct Costs	Other Complications*	$90	$140
ADA, NHIS, NHANES, INGENIX, MEPS, NIS, NAMCS, NHHCS – Indirect Costs	Absenteeism, Productivity, & Unemployment	$150	$240
	TOTAL RANGE	$390	$630

*Other Complications includes codes beyond the 7 UKPDS complications and also those coded as secondary or tertiary complications (e.g. an diabetes infection captured as a regular infection)

Fig. 15-4: Estimated Cost Savings Associated with Using MPT.

Additional benefits of MPT on healthcare utilization were demonstrated in another one-year study with an urban, Medicaid population.[17] Patients using the diabetes MPT reduced their ER visits by 58 percent from the prior year and reduced hospitalization admissions by 100 percent. Additionally, they found the instant coaching feedback helpful and all agreed that the system improved their glucose testing behavior.

CONCLUSION

This chapter introduced the notion of MPT as a scalable, effective means of addressing many significant healthcare challenges for patients, providers and the system. To qualify as an MPT, a solution should be automated, personalized, contextually-relevant and be able to provide patient-level decision support to healthcare providers. Additionally, to qualify as being an MPT (vs. an app) the solution should have published outcomes, adhere to applicable regulations governing patient safety and good manufacturing process, and must fit into clinical workflow to facilitate adoption by patients and providers alike. The chapter provided clinical and economic evidence of a diabetes-related MPT to illuminate the tangible health and economic benefits that can accrue from an MPT solution.

Looking to the future, multiple "vectors of value expansion" are possible for MPT. These include, but are not limited to, the following:

- Disease continuum: Regardless of the disease, every patient who suffers from one or many chronic diseases must manage medications, metabolic measurement of some kind, lifestyle and symptoms. The rules and content will change. The platform will remain the same.
- Chronic care continuum: Whilst today much of the healthcare system is focused on acute care for chronic disease, MPT will allow movement further upstream in the chronic care continuum to include patients who are pre-disposed to a disease (e.g., due to family history, heredity of the disease, etc.) or even further upstream for prevention.
- Data continuum: In many ways, the value of the data collected from MPT will quite likely outweigh the value of the MPT itself! This data — which is both real-time and longitudinal and can be generated by a patient or an MPT system — can be mined and modeled in referential and inferential ways, that include the realm of predictive and adaptive modeling, as well as intelligent pattern recognition that gives new insights into things never before seen as it relates to drug therapies, disease parameters and patient behaviors.
- Technology continuum: The ever-growing realm of sensor data — such as that with activity and fitness, biometric sensors — that quietly capture important parameters for patients will dramatically help improve seamless engagement with multiple MPTs by patients. These solutions will be further accessible via multiple mobile Internet devices (MIDs), to ensure an enhanced seamless experience for the patient interacting with MPT through the device that is most convenient and available at any point in time.
- Personal continuum: As the data collected expands to include the realms of "mind, body, soul" — that is, psychosocial, metabolic and socio-cultural data — so will the value unlocked expand to provide more tailored, contextually relevant and culturally-adaptive feedback to patients.

MPT is at the dawn of a new outcomes-oriented era in healthcare delivery, where the innovation potential is boundless.

Disclaimer

The information contained in this document represents the current views of WellDoc on the issues discussed as of the date of publication. This document is for informational purposes only. WELLDOC MAKES NO WARRANTIES, EXPRESS, IMPLIED OR STATUTORY, AS TO THE INFORMATION IN THIS DOCUMENT.

Complying with all applicable copyright laws is the responsibility of the user. Without limiting the rights under copyright, no part of this document may be reproduced, stored in or introduced into a retrieval system, or transmitted in any form or by any means (electronic, mechanical, photocopying, recording, or otherwise), or for any purpose, without the express written permission of WellDoc.

WellDoc may have patents, patent applications, trademarks, copyrights, or other intellectual property rights covering the subject matter in this document. Except as expressly provided in any written license agreement from WellDoc, the furnishing of this document does not give you any license to these patents, trademarks, copyrights, or other intellectual property.

REFERENCES

1. The Center for Consumer Information & Insurance Oversight. Shining a Light on Health Insurance Rate Increases. Available at: www.healthcare.gov/news/factsheets/2011/05/grants05132011a.html. Accessed November 9, 2012.
2. Study: 86.7 million Americans uninsured over last two years. Available at: www.cnn.com/2009/HEALTH/03/04/uninsured.epidemic.obama. Posted March, 2009. Accessed September 7, 2013.
3. US Census Bureau. Health Status, Health Insurance, and Medical Services Utilization. Available at: www.census.gov/hhes/www/hlthins/data/utilization/tables.html. Posted May, 2013. Accessed September 7, 2013.
4. Wagner EH. Chronic Disease Management: What Will It Take to Improve Care for Chronic Illness? *Effective Clinical Practice.* 1998; 1:2-4.
5. McCall N, Cromwell J., Results of the Medicare Health Support disease-management pilot program. *N Engl J Med.* 2011 Nov 3;365(18):1704-12.
6. Cebul RD, Love TE, Jain AK, Hebert CJ. Electronic health records and quality of diabetes care. *N Engl J Med.* 2011 Sep 1;365(9):825-3.
7. Office of the National Coordinator for Health Information Technology. Health IT Rules & Regulations. Available at: www.healthit.gov/policy-researchers-implementers/health-it-rules-regulations. Accessed November 9, 2012.
8. CTIA. U.S. Wireless Quick Facts. Available at: www.ctia.org/advocacy/research/index.cfm/aid/10323. Accessed September 7, 2013.
9. U.S. Department of Transportation Federal Highway Administration. Office of Highway Policy Information. Our Nation's Highways: 2011. Available at: www.fhwa.dot.gov/policyinformation/pubs/hf/pl11028/. Accessed September 7, 2013.
10. CTIA. U.S. Wireless Quick Facts. Available at: www.ctia.org/advocacy/research/index.cfm/aid/10323. September 7, 2013.
11. U.S. Food and Drug Administration. Mobile Medical Applications. Available at: www.fda.gov/MedicalDevices/ProductsandMedicalProcedures/ConnectedHealth/MobileMedicalApplications/default.htm. Posted August, 2013. September 7, 2013.
12. IBM developerWorks. Developing mobile apps as medical devices: Understanding U.S. government regulations. Available at: www.ibm.com/developerworks/mobile/library/mo-fda-med-devices/. Posted April, 2013. Accessed September 10, 2013.

13. EHR Intelligence. NIH Director: mHealth needs to show results. Available at: http://ehrintelligence.com/2012/12/10/nih-director-mhealth-needs-to-show-results/. Posted December, 2012. Accessed September 10, 2013.

14. MobiHealthNews. Most patients want their doctors to prescribe apps. Available at: http://mobihealthnews.com/23418/most-patients-want-their-doctors-to-prescribe-apps/. Posted July, 2013. Accessed September 10, 2013.

15. Quinn CC, Shardell M, Terrin M., Barr E, Ballew S, Gruber-Baldini AL, A Cluster Randomized Trial of a Mobile Phone Personalized Behavioral Intervention for Blood Glucose Control. *Diabetes Care.* 2011 Sep;34(9):1934-42.

16. Quinn CC, Shardell M, Terrin M, Barr E, Ballew S, Gruber-Baldini AL, A Cluster Randomized Trial of a Mobile Phone Personalized Behavioral Intervention for Blood Glucose Control. *Diabetes Care.* 2011 Sep;34(9):1934-42.

17. Katz R, Mesfin T, Barr K. Lessons From a Community-Based mHealth Diabetes Self-Management Program: "It's Not Just About the Cell Phone." *Journal of Health Communications.* 2012; 17(Suppl 1): 67-72.

CHAPTER 16

Getting Smart About Wellness Data: An Analysis

By Randy L. Thomas, FHIMSS

A little more than 40 years ago, Texas Instruments introduced the first electronic hand-held calculator.[1] It could add, subtract, multiply and divide, retailed for $149.95, and was a proud status symbol among engineering students on college campuses (replacing the previously ubiquitous slide rule). Mobile phones were the provenance of fantasy on TV shows (e.g., "Get Smart" Max's shoe phone) and the very wealthy (e.g., car phones). Fast forward to 2013, when more than 55 percent of Americans[2] walk around with connectivity and computing power in their pockets, purses and backpacks that was unimaginable back then. Smartphones and tablets have dramatically altered our ability to connect to a vast array of information — and to each other — and are now a platform for a wide-ranging array of uses, including mobile health (mHealth).

Extending access to electronic medical records (EMR) outside of healthcare facilities and incorporating patient-generated health data (PGHD)[3] into the EMR are two goals of mHealth.[4] The next wave of healthcare transaction applications — following and related to the frenzy of MU-compliance seeking EMR implementations — will be mobile apps that engage both patients under active care and also well individuals in a defined-risk population not actively engaged in healthcare. EMRs are not the end; they are the beginning. Reaching out and interacting with people to keep them compliant with assigned regimens, understand their health status, and encourage healthy behavior will be the next frontier. This will further the de-centralization of healthcare as it becomes more personal and more mobile — and support the shift from focusing on healthcare delivery to improving overall health status.

The value of these mobile, personal apps will be two-fold. First, they will provide reminders and encouragement, track daily status and generally provide a tether between patients and their health providers. Second, as with EMRs, the data captured by these apps can be re-purposed to support ongoing analysis of what drives better outcomes and a healthier population. In addition to apps that help the acute and chronically ill recover from and manage their conditions, an entire new set of apps is already proliferating, focused on wellness (e.g., MapMyRide[5] and My Fitness Pal[6] are just two examples). With the perspective that the ultimate goal of integrated, accountable healthcare is improving the *health* of a population, leveraging the data collected via these types of apps will provide much-needed insight into what drives healthy behaviors and overall health status.

EMR implementations have vastly increased the amount of detailed, clinical data we have about how we treat patients. While EMRs support patient care at the point of delivery, they also generate a ton of useful data that can be repurposed to support performance measurement, outcomes analysis and ongoing performance improvement efforts.

The challenge with re-using data collected in EMRs (and other systems) is structure, standardization, and consistency. To be useful in analytics and measurement, data must be unambiguous (structured), represented according to a recognized vocabulary (standardized), and always the type of data planned for (consistent). To date, a set of standards is emerging to support the data captured in EMRs. The purpose of these standards is to ensure that data can be communicated consistently from provider to provider in support of integrated care.

As a point of reference, there are three types of standards that are "governed by the Standards & Operability (S&I) Framework of the Nationwide Health Information Network (S&I NwHIN)."[7]

- **Transport and security** mechanisms are employed to safely communicate health information over the Internet. The NwHIN portfolio is comprised of several transport and security measures including Certificate Discovery using the Lightweight Directory Access Protocol (LDAP) and Domain Name System (DNS) to ensure ultimate certificate discoverability and accessibility. Transport and security measures like these help to ensure that appropriate health information is transmitted between the intended certified parties.
- **Vocabulary and code sets** include documentation on common naming conventions, terminologies and identifiers for coding and classifying health-related data. For example, the NwHIN Portfolio identifies Logical Observation Identifiers Names and Codes (LOINC®) as a universal code system for laboratory and clinical observations, and SNOMED-CT (Systematized Nomenclature of Medicine — Clinical Terms) as a comprehensive clinical vocabulary.
- **The content structure** section of the NwHIN Portfolio includes implementation guidance to describe the content standards used for defining the structure for which health information is exchanged electronically, such as with care summaries and lab results.

Since the mainstream EMRs and other systems were originally created prior to any mandate that these standards be used, part of the current effort in EMR implementation is retrofitting them to the technology. Problem lists, allergies, lab tests and other types of data are often represented by proprietary code tables that are defined by individual organizations. With the adoption of vocabularies (e.g., SNOMED CT, LOINC) to standardize this type of data, healthcare organizations and vendors are cross-walking this proprietary data to the standard.

Data-standard adoption was not ubiquitous historically, because there were no drivers urging providers to all "speak the same language." The shift in healthcare delivery and reimbursement models from fee-for-service to fee-for-value is changing that. Integrated accountable care requires that data about patients flow securely and privately between providers. Re-casting healthcare data from a Tower of Babel to a common language, though, is not easy work. As an industry, we should endeavor to avoid the "messiness" of retrofitting standards to already deployed applications in the mHealth arena by establishing needed data standards *now* before mHealth is as ubiquitous as the smartphone. Mobile, personalized health engagement demands underlying standardization in transmission, vocabulary and content — not only to ensure that data can be fluid across the spectrum of healthcare providers to support the health status of an individual, but so that we can repurpose this data to support our growing understanding of what it means to promote and sustain health.

Genomic, proteomic and other "-omic" data combined with clinical data can help pinpoint risk and target interventions, but data about activity, diet, social interactions and other aspects of daily living will become critical inputs to our ability to improve the overall health of a population. This data is essential to creating a holistic view of health — including but not exclusively focusing on *care* delivery — and making the transition to from measuring clinical outcomes to measuring health status.

At the Institute for Healthcare Improvement (IHI) conference in 2010,[8] Cory Booker — then mayor of Newark, NJ — described how his administration realized that improving public safety did not exclusively rest within the efficiency and effectiveness of the public safety department (i.e., police, etc.). Associated agencies needed to look at the community infrastructure (could people safely walk to a park, a grocery store, school, church?), social support structures for families of incarcerated parents, services for re-introducing those recently released from prison back into the community, the prevalence of abandoned buildings, etc. Together with the department of public safety, this entire ecosystem worked to understand how to realize changes that would have a substantial impact on public safety outcomes. Following Mayor Booker's line of reasoning and applying it to healthcare, we will need to look beyond healthcare delivery systems to understand how we can improve overall health status. And we will need data — captured by healthy people in the course of day-to-day living — to support all that research.

In a recent *Health Affairs* blog, *A Framework for Accountable Care Measures*,[9] the authors argue that a new metrics framework is needed to measure the health of a population in support of the transition from fee-for-service to fee-for-value. "Current measures focus on process and clinical outcomes, as opposed to health status, and few are based on patient-reported data that would measure the overall care experience." They further emphasize that the metrics should *not* be based on data that is available. Instead, it should be based on data that is truly necessary to calculate a meaningful metric. The blog suggests that we'll need to capture data in novel ways — such as self-reported via mobile apps — to meet this objective. This perspective is certainly prescient — and it supports the assertion that standards to support this type of data (i.e., data about activities of daily living) should be a priority — *now*.

Without thoughtful consideration of what we may want to measure or study in the future concerning what sustains and improves the health of populations, we will unwittingly create a universe of apps that may provide good support to an individual (e.g., encouragement for achieving a weight-loss target) and may support a feedback loop between one patient and one provider (e.g., tracking compliance with recommended interventions such as medication regimens), but will not be able to support re-use of the data.

Technology is already being deployed to connect patients under active care with their providers. Studies have shown that patients like to be engaged in improving the accuracy of information contained in their EMR.[10] In the study of PGHD previously cited, information provided by patients is valued by providers, and readily contributed by patients and their families. But this data — allergies, medications, survey responses, comments or concerns — is either unstructured (e.g., comments) or the corresponding vocabulary is already accounted for in the inventory of standards in use (or planned) by EMRs. The applications involved in acquiring the data can be thought of as extensions of the EMRs.

Applications focused on wellness live outside the realm of EMRs. These apps are appealing because they offer positive reinforcement for diet and/or exercise choices. They provide this feedback by collecting data, but not the kind of data currently captured in EMRs.

Searching the Apple App Store using the word "wellness" returns 1,116 options;[11] "health and fitness" returns 334 options.[12] A quick scan of some common health-promoting apps, such as those mentioned above, identifies a number of similarities in the type of data they capture:

- Effort — speed, time, distance, calories burned
- Food logging — keeping track of what is eaten and calculating the number of calories and types of nutrients (such as fat and carbohydrates) consumed
- Personal progress tracking — charts showing weight loss progress, consistency of effort, changes in average speed
- Social network tie-ins — ability to post to Facebook, Twitter, or other social media during a daily work out or at milestone achieved

And some apps — such as the one associated with the Nike+ Fuel Band[13] — automatically collect data about effort (e.g., steps) from a wearable device and then log it. My Fitness Pal claims on its home page that millions of people have used the app to lose weight. While no mandate exists for the use of these various wellness-related apps, adoption — while not yet ubiquitous — is clearly on the rise. While there are apps offered by not-for-profit organizations (e.g., MyPlate from LiveStrong.com[14]), many of the apps are offered for free or at very modest prices. Since these organizations need revenue and ostensibly are also interested in generating a profit, there is the indication that a business model exists to support the companies offering these apps. And this business model does not even take into consideration the "greater good" they might contribute to the overall health status of the population, thereby (in theory) reducing overall healthcare costs.

Currently, no institutionalized, organized effort exists to encourage adoption of these wellness apps — in contrast to what we are now experiencing with the implementation of EMRs. As suggested at the start of this chapter, the next frontier of transaction-oriented technology in healthcare is likely to be driven by these wellness apps. And the data they generate, provided it is useable and accessible, will be invaluable in furthering our understanding of how to improve overall population health status.

We need to accelerate the identification and creation of standards that support this transition from a focus on improving healthcare delivery to improving overall health status. To fully realize the power of mHealth and tap into the power of mobile, personalized, decentralized support of healthy behavior, we need not only the apps but the data captured in and by these apps to re-purpose and use in population health research, analytics and measurement.

Establishing the data standards and access agreements will not be easy. Privacy and security considerations will be paramount, if history is any indication of future concerns. Agreement on data transmission and vocabulary standards will be needed from a diverse community of app developers that live outside the current circle of health-information technology vendors. And a substantial uptick in their business models will likely be required to convince these vendors to both participate and then adopt these future standards. (Organizations for at-risk population health outcomes may be interested in subsidizing either the development or the adoption of these standards-based apps.)

But the bottom line is this: if we are to be in a position to someday re-purpose the data collected in these apps to support population health analytics and measurement — and to support a virtuous circle of encouraging healthy behavior — the time to start tackling these difficult issues is now.

REFERENCES

1. Texas Instruments. TI-2500 Datamath calculator first TI consumer electronics product. Available at: www.ti.com/corp/docs/company/history/timeline/eps/1970/docs/72-ti2500_datamath_calc.htm. Accessed August 29, 2013.
2. Smith A. Smartphone Ownership 2013. Pew Internet & American Life Project. Available at: http://pewinternet.org/Reports/2013/Smartphone-Ownership-2013/Findings.aspx. Accessed August 29, 2013.
3. Patient-generated health data introduction and best practices. Report to the HIT Policy Committee Consumer Empowerment Workgroup by the Technical Expert Panel Convened by National eHealth Collaborative on behalf of the Office of the National Coordinator for Health Information Technology, July 18, 2013.
4. HRSA. What is mHealth? NIH consensus group definition. Available at: www.hrsa.gov/healthit/mhealth.html. Accessed August 13, 2013.
5. Map My Ride [homepage]. Available at: www.mapmyride.com. Accessed August 27, 2013.
6. My Fitness Pal [homepage]. Available at: www.myfitnesspal.com. Accessed August 27, 2013.
7. The Standards and Interoperability (S&I) Framework [homepage]. Available at: www.siframework.org/index.html. Accessed July 20,2013.
8. Institute for Healthcare Improvement [homepage]. Available at: www.ihi.org/offerings/Conferences/Forum2010/Pages/featuredspeakers.aspx. Accessed August 13, 2013.
9. Bankowitz R, Bechtel C, Corrigan J, DeVore SD, Fisher E, Nelson G. A Framework for Accountable Measures. Health Affairs Blog. Available at: http://healthaffairs.org/blog/2013/05/09/a-framework-for-accountable-care-measures/, Written May 9, 2013. Accessed August 13, 2013.
10. Dullabh P. Evaluating patient's role in providing feedback to improve the quality of information in the medical record. [PowerPoint presentation]. Consumer Empowerment Workgroup. July 18, 2013.
11. August 27, 2013, "wellness" typed into the search option on the Apple App Store.
12. August 27, 2013, "health and fitness" typed into the search option on the Apple App Store.
13. Nike+ FuelBand. [web site]. Available at: www.nike.com/cdp/fuelband/us/en_us. Accessed August 27, 2013.
14. Apple App Store. August 27, 2013, LIVESTRONG.COM—Calorie Tracker LITE.

CHAPTER 17

Home Monitoring After Liver Transplantation: A Case Study

By Giovan Battista Vizzini, MD, and Tommaso Piazza, PhD

ABSTRACT

Patients receiving an organ transplant need to maintain strict clinical follow-up, particularly in the immediate post-transplantation phase. This results in an increase in hospitalization or, alternatively, forces patients to travel frequently, and even great distances.

To address this problem ISMETT has adopted a home-monitoring system with the aims of speeding up hospital discharge of post-liver-transplant patients, enabling uninterrupted recovery at home and maintaining close contact with our medical teams. The technology used allows nurses and physicians to monitor and support transplant patients from the hospital, check their general condition, collect biometric data, manage their treatment, and, finally, offer face-to-face appointments via video conferencing.

In order to evaluate the new technology and the impact on patient care, ISMETT carried out a pilot study. All patients who received liver transplants at ISMETT and were discharged between July 15, 2011 and April 30, 2013, were included. The average hospital length of stay after transplantation of this group of patients was considerably lower when compared with a historical control of patients transplanted at ISMETT in an equivalent between 2009 and 2011 (19.8 vs. 25.4 days). There were also no urgent readmissions in the study population. In terms of economic benefit, the annual savings related to the reduction of the length of hospital stay (€396,000) was about nine times higher than the annual cost of home-monitoring.

INTRODUCTION

ISMETT (Istituto Mediterraneo per i Trapianti e Terapie ad Alta Specializzazione) was established in 1997 as a private-public partnership between the Region of Sicily and UPMC (University of Pittsburgh Medical Center). Situated in Palermo, Sicily, ISMETT is the only multi-organ (liver, heart, lung, kidney and pancreas) transplant center in southern Italy. It provides specialty surgical and non-surgical procedures to the entire regional population (approximately 5 million people). More than 1,400 patients have had organ transplants at ISMETT over the past 14 years.

Since opening, ISMETT has invested considerable efforts in the development of the electronic medical record (EMR) and of its IT systems, allowing it to no longer require paper documents for patient care. In September 2010, ISMETT was recognized as an HIMSS Stage 6 hospital. Of the 5,319 American hospitals studied by HIMSS only 7.3 percent operate at this level of computerization. In Europe, where the model was introduced in 2009, only 23 hospitals have been certified as Stage 6. In Italy, only two hospitals have reached Stage 6 of the HIMSS EMR Adoption Model.

In 2011, ISMETT implemented a new home monitoring system. The goal was to monitor the health status, for the first 90 days after the procedure, of ISMETT patients discharged after liver transplantation.

THE CHALLENGE

Liver transplantation is now considered the standard treatment for patients with end-stage liver disease. Patient survival after liver transplantation is extremely good (about 85 percent at one year, about 75 percent at five years) when compared with the natural history of the disease. However, a significant concern is early morbidity and mortality (first three to six months after surgery) due to the high incidence of severe complications, such as infections, rejection and drug toxicity. For these reasons, it is crucial to maintain a strict follow-up with the transplanted patient to identify early clinical and/or bio-humoral signs of complications.

The need to maintain strict clinical follow-up can result in a prolonged time of hospitalization or, alternatively, forcing patients (still in not optimal conditions) to travel frequently. Approximately one-third of patients transplanted by ISMETT from the start of its activities live in the Palermo area (about 1 million inhabitants), while two-thirds live in other areas of the Sicilian region or outside Sicily. The distances between Palermo and other Sicilian cities vary from 100 to more than 250 km, and the state of the road network and other communication routes is not optimal, creating a problem in maintaining a strict and continuous follow-up.

To address this problem, ISMETT designed a study using its telehealth technology with the aim of speeding up hospital discharge of post-liver-transplant patients, enabling uninterrupted recovery at home, and maintaining close contact with our medical teams. The technology used had the goal of allowing transplant coordinators and physicians to monitor and support transplanted patients from their homes, check their general condition, collect biometric data, manage their treatment, and, finally, offer face-to-face appointments via video conferencing. The challenge was to remotely manage patients who are not fully stable, have undergone an extremely invasive procedure, and are still suffering the effects of a prolonged disease.

SOLUTION IMPLEMENTATION

As defined by the American Telemedicine Association,[1] "Home Telehealth is a service that gives the clinician the ability to monitor and measure patient health data and information over geographical, social and cultural distances." The objective is to improve disease management and undertake "earlier and proactive interventions for positive outcomes."

The technology to be used is usually determined by clinical needs, health objectives and available resources. Remote monitoring technologies have the potential to improve clinical management of chronic diseases. There are currently several clinical conditions for which home monitoring is being used, and this approach has been found to produce benefits in a number of research trials.[2,3]

Home monitoring and remote monitoring systems are used for patients who have the following clinical conditions: asthma, diabetes, chronic obstructive pulmonary disease, chronic heart failure or mental health problems (anxiety and depression). There is little in the literature on the use of remote monitoring for non-chronic patients, and no experience has been reported on the monitoring of post-transplant patients.

Even if tele-home-care and remote monitoring are usually viewed as supplements to normal in-person care and not as substitutes, patients involved in this pilot used remote monitoring as the primary contact option between themselves and the ISMETT specialists. The patient was contacted daily by the transplant hepatologist, but the entire multidisciplinary physician team of ISMETT was involved in the project, and using the system the patient could receive indications for care from all the specialists.

To implement this new service, the ISMETT team had to find a partner with a significant presence in the region to provide the necessary technology to support patients in their homes.

This partner had to provide complete service, including:
1. Telemedicine equipment, including all the interfaced devices.
2. Equipment installation at the patient's home.
3. Equipment configuration to connect to the patient's Internet connection, or installation of a new Internet connection at the patient's home.
4. Training for the patient and family members.
5. Helpdesk service for technical issues.
6. Removal of equipment after the monitoring period.
7. Cleaning of equipment before the next installation.

Moreover, the technology partner had to provide a secure server that would allow the physician to visualize the patient parameters and the videoconferencing sessions with the patient. The required system would combine a home patient device with an online interface that is accessible on the Internet to properly authorized physicians. The web interface allowed physicians to monitor patients' health status and remotely manage care progress. The device installed at the patient's home had to be easy to use, even by people with no computer experience. Patient interaction with the system had to be supported by a touch screen.

Among the functions of the home monitoring system, those considered essential by the project team were:
- The possibility of delivering to the patient questionnaires prepared by the physicians to better evaluate the patient's progress.

- The possibility of displaying multimedia material concerning the patient's state of health prepared by the physician remotely and upgradeable via the web interface.
- The possibility of displaying a calendar of activities prepared by the physician.
- The possibility of displaying reminders via audio/visual aids to encourage the patient to follow treatment protocols.
- The possibility of having teleconferencing sessions between the patient and the referring physicians.
- The possibility of performing periodic measurements of the patient's vital signs, with automatic registration in the system.

Using the home monitoring device, patients have to be able to measure vital signs, answer health assessment questions and receive educational and motivational information. Once the session is completed, the results are made available to authorized healthcare professionals, who can use the latest recorded information to assess the state of the patient's health and, if necessary, modify the patient's care plan.

The selected system is able to connect to a variety of devices, both wired and wireless, and allows for monitoring and acquisition of measurements of the patient's parameters. The parameters that can be measured are blood pressure, blood glucose, pulse oximetry, spirometric data and weight.

All parameters can be part of a routine defined for the particular patient. In this case the system will alert the patient of the measure to be performed.

The home monitoring system installed at the patient's home is connected to a web-based service, with restricted access through encrypted connections. This web-based service allows physicians to configure the calendar of the patient and to define a series of questions to be transmitted to the terminal of the patient, or plan the "measurement sections" during which patient data are collected. All the patient's responses and collected data are stored in a central database and can be reviewed by the physician using a standard computer connected to the Internet.

One of the typical concerns in the home monitoring project is having a good Internet connection at the patient's home, which was critical for the success of the project. To allow the smooth flow of images during the video conferencing sessions, the Internet connection must have enough bandwidth and reduced latency. This meant that the service required of the commercial partner included a preliminary on-site visit to the patient's home in order to verify whether the patient had an Internet connection or whether it was possible to install an ADSL line. If these two options were not possible, the vendor had to provide a 3G modem for data transmission and support the connectivity costs.

To maintain data privacy, all the data transferred by the system had to be encrypted, and the connection between the telemedicine equipment and the server had to use encrypted VPN connections.

After a rigorous analysis of the available solutions on the Italian market, ISMETT decided to use the Guide, developed by Care Innovations. Care Innovations is a joint venture, formed in January 2011, between Intel Corporation and GE. Its mission is to create technology-based solutions that give people confidence to live independently, wherever they are. With the combined expertise of its parent companies — GE's in healthcare and Intel's in technology — Care Innovations developed a user-friendly tool that meets patient and physician needs. For healthcare professionals involved primarily in remote monitoring, Care Innovations offers the FDA-cleared and CE-cleared Intel-GE Care Innovations™ Guide, which allows seamless interaction with healthcare providers and home-based patients monitoring their health.

The system was delivered to the patient's home by Vivisol, the Italian distributor of the Care Innovations Guide, and a leading European company in the field of home care services with a significant presence in Sicily in terms of nursing and technical personnel available.

The system allows direct and visual contact between patients and physicians through a reliable system of video conferencing. It creates conditions similar to those of a hospital medical examination, with the advantage that the patient does not need to leave home. Through a special kit, the device allows for the periodic assessment of vital parameters, such as blood pressure, heart rate and blood oxygen concentration, and automatically enters the results into the system. The system includes an integrated camera, microphone and speakers for interactive videoconferences, offering face-to-face support during the patient-physician interaction. Clinicians and patients can take advantage of videoconferencing to discuss and evaluate the patient's condition, and patients have the opportunity to express their thoughts and voice any current concerns.

Using this telemedicine system, patients have access to a variety of multimedia educational content, including text, audio and video. Healthcare professionals can add content as part of a health session, and patients can access that content to help them gain a deeper understanding of their disease state, health status and care protocol.

Moreover, the physicians can design a personalized care path for each patient that defines which measurements have to be performed and how frequently, which assessment questionnaires have to be filled out, and what educational and motivational sections the patient has to study. The system empowers patients by giving them the means to actively manage their conditions, live as independently as possible, and engage them in their care path.

THE STUDY AND THE CLINICAL PROTOCOL

The pilot study described in this paper was funded as part of a project called Piano Sanitario Nazionale 2010 (Assistenza Domiciliare), sponsored by the Hospital Planning Service of the Region of Sicily's Department of Health.

All the adult patients living in Sicily or in Calabria who underwent liver transplantation at ISMETT and were discharged between July 15, 2011 and April 30, 2013, were included.

Staff involved was:
- At the patient's home:
  - Technician for the installment of the devices.
  - Nurse for patient education related to the use of the system.
- In Tele-Visit (tele-consult):
  - Physician (ISMETT-UPMC).
  - Transplant coordinator (ISMETT).
  - Others (e.g., physical therapist, psychologist).

The study population was monitored for a period of three months after discharge home, or until they stabilized. Patient parameters were monitored, and the physicians verified adherence to therapy (e.g., immunosuppression, other medications) and undertook videoconferences with the patients. The videoconferences were used to allow a post-transplant bio-humoral surveillance of the patient. ISMETT physicians called the patient daily using the home monitoring system in the first week after the procedure, three times a week in the first month, and once a week in the last two months. Based on the clinical parameters registered by the patient, the physician made additional calls depending on the clinical needs.

Associated expenses for this type of telemedicine usually include the one-time cost of acquiring and installing the necessary equipment, the on-going costs of telecommunication line charges associated with the clinical encounter, maintenance fees for the equipment, technical personnel necessary to operate the equipment, and administrative personnel to handle appointment scheduling.

In our study, most of the activities were outsourced to the technology partner, maintaining in-house only the activities strictly related to patient care. The vendor presented an all-inclusive per diem cost. The vendor provided the entire service at a daily fee of €7.50 per patient. The only additional cost was the one related to the ISMETT personnel involved in the remote consultation.

Results

Seventy-four consecutive adult patients who underwent liver transplantation at ISMETT and were discharged between July 15, 2011, and April 30, 2013, were included in the study. Sixty-six of these patients completed the follow-up period (three months). Because the entire liver transplanted population for our study period was included in the study, we used the liver transplanted patients discharged home in an equivalent period between July, 2009 and June, 2011 as a control group. As shown in Table 17-1, the average length-of-stay after transplantation in home-monitoring was 19.8 days, considerably lower when compared with the control group (25.4 days). No urgent re-admission was observed in the study group, compared with four urgent admissions (for an overall length of stay of 25 days) in the control group.

We can affirm that the introduction of this new monitoring system increased ISMETT physicians' confidence in discharging patients home because of the improved ability to monitor their progress without requiring any travel.

The questionnaires administered to the patients showed that the system was well-accepted and improved the patient experience in such a critical period as the first days after a liver transplant.

In term of economic benefit, the saving related to the reduction of the length of stay in hospital was €396,000, about nine times higher than the annual cost of home-monitoring (€44,550 for 66 patients followed for three months).

Table 17-1: Data Comparison Between Patients in the Study and Control Population.

	In Home-monitoring July 2011-April 2013	Historical controls July 2009-June 2011
Patients included	74	75
Patients in the analysis (> 3 months of follow-up)	66	75
Average length of stay (days)	19.8	25.4
Deaths during the three-month study period	0	1
Patients who needed urgent re-admission during the first three months after transplant	0	3
Overall number of urgent re-admissions during the first three months after transplant	0	4
Overall length of stay due to urgent re-admissions during the first three months after transplant (days)	0	25
Patient/family satisfaction rate (based on questionnaire administered)	98 percent	NA

CONCLUSION

It is believed that this increased intensity of disease monitoring and management will create improved patient health, with resulting reduction in acute and chronic complications, and that these will translate directly into decreased consumption of expensive emergency healthcare resources (emergency room visits and re-hospitalizations), and decreased long-term disease complications. This, in turn, should translate directly into decreased consumption of expensive medications, personnel, equipment and hospitalization days required to manage those long-term complications.[4,5] This pilot study demonstrates that the introduction of a home monitoring system to support the patient during the first three months after discharge can produce all these benefits.

The home monitoring system is an important solution, not only for early discharge from the hospital, but also for better day-to-day monitoring of transplant patients, which can be carried out more frequently, and without patients having to travel to the hospital for routine check-ups. This is particularly true in the first three months after a transplant, an extremely delicate moment from the clinical point of view, when patients need to be constantly connected with their healthcare team.

Telehealth monitoring is not only useful in reducing healthcare costs, but actually enables a two-way dialogue between patients and the healthcare staff (medical practitioners, transplant coordinators, therapists and psychologists), making patients feel better cared for and allowing them to ask for immediate support.

The results obtained in this study can be considered a "proof of concept": home-monitoring is a safe and effective solution not only in stable chronic patients, but also in unstable patients facing difficult issues in clinical and therapeutic management.

REFERENCES

1. Home Telehealth & Remote Monitoring SIG. Available at: www.americantelemed.org/get-involved/ata-member-groups/special-interest-groups/home-telehealth-remote-monitoring. Accessed September 10, 2013.

2. Kinsella A. Telehealth Opportunities for Home Care Patients. *Home Healthcare Nurse.* 2003; 21(10):661-665.

3. Paré G, Jaana M, and Sicotte C. Systematic Review of Home Telemonitoring for Chronic Diseases: The Evidence Base. *J Am Med Inform Assoc.* 2007; 14:269-277.

4. Hebert MA, Korabek B, Scott RE. Moving Research into Practice: A Decision Framework for Integrating Home Telehealth into Chronic Illness Care. *International Journal of Medical Informatics.* 2006; 75: 786-794.

5. Aoki N, Dunn K, Johnson-Throop KA, Turley JP. Outcomes and Methods in Telemedicine Evaluation. *Telemedicine Journal and e-Health.* 2003; 9 (4) 393-401.

Part IV
mHealth as a Business

Chapter 18

Managing mHealth Innovation

By Rick Krohn, MA, MAS, and David Metcalf, PhD

In previous chapters, we have seen how mHealth is being woven into the fabric of healthcare, and in the process has established its own ecosystem. We've examined mHealth as both a disruptive and displacement phenomenon, and how it is recasting the terms of care delivery. And we've seen how the principles of mHealth — patient-centered, value-based, connected and coordinated, on demand, integrated, and woven seamlessly into the professional and personal habits of the customer — are informing these solutions and constantly fueling the process of innovation.

mHealth has proved itself a rich palette for creative thinking about addressing healthcare's ills — access, affordability and quality — but it has also led to a free-for-all in terms of solutions development and deployment — too often with a single directive: "first to market." In mHealth, competitive advantage often has a brief shelf life, as evidenced by mHealth pioneers that have failed, including Zeo (sleep coach) and Vocel (medication adherence), both great concepts but early entrants that were revenue challenged or quickly overtaken by more advanced competitors. There have been innovative — even inventive — mHealth concepts that failed to translate into a salable product and solution, often for one of the following reasons:

Understanding of the industry. Healthcare is a highly complex, sometimes incoherent tangle of buyers and sellers, producers and users, made even more interesting by healthcare's unique financing and regulatory structure. mHealth innovators must understand that the industry has transactions — information, operational and financial transactions — that don't conform to common business practices. Legacy and enterprise information systems, third-party payment, and a cast of not necessarily friendly stakeholders with contradictory incentives are just a few of the challenges that can torpedo a genuinely useful, but ultimately unsalable mHealth solution. This is not the realm for gifted amateurs.

Understanding of the customer. Does your idea or solution address a specific problem? Is the problem in need of a new solution? Consumers have a sense of entitlement about healthcare, and will not pay much — if anything at all — for a solution that does not address an immediate need. Providers won't pay for solutions that don't generate a tangible benefit or that interfere with workflow, and payers have already supped deeply from the fountain of prevention and wellness. Consider the case of health apps: with 15,000 healthcare apps currently available, one must ask the obvious question — do we really need 15,001?

Understanding the user experience. According to HIMSS, usability may be defined as "the effectiveness, efficiency and satisfaction with which specific users can achieve a specific set of tasks in a particular environment." Does your solution complement or conflict with the daily activity flow of the user? In the case of clinical mHealth solutions, there must be a clinical voice in the development stage, not just as a reality check, but that also provides insight into the value that the solution delivers, the processes it may impact, and the obstacles it may encounter. And for the healthcare consumer, the hurdles are more of a retail nature. Is your solution convenient? Engaging? Connected? On demand? Cheap? Reliable?

Understanding the economics of healthcare innovation. In addition to the hurdles mentioned above, there are issues of funding — who will pay for development, and who will pay how much for your product or service? Investors, particularly institutional investors often expect a quick return, and innovation needs to appeal to the user, who may not be the same source as the payer. For instance, a health insurer's determination of value may differ from that of a patient. mHealth innovators must also be accountable for complying with industry rules regarding safety and privacy, offering "regulatable" mHealth solutions that perform as advertised, and introducing a cost effective alternative to existing products or services. Business model is also potential barrier, as a new technology solution may face resistance from providers or payers who view the solution as a competitive threat.

These qualifiers should inform — not mitigate — the creative flow of mHealth innovation. Disruption is never easy, displacement even more so, and healthcare is an industry notoriously resistant to change. That said, healthcare is an industry desperately in need of solutions that release its constituents from an antiquated model of episodic, reactive care delivery. So from a practical standpoint, and proceeding with foreknowledge of the hurdles looming ahead, what are the high-level strategic decisions that should define a road map for mHealth innovators? To create some context, Fig. 18-1 on page 161 describes the inputs to healthcare innovation using a simple provider-patient opportunity snapshot.

For the mHealth innovator, there is a hierarchy of conceptual issues that must be addressed. We'll start with some strategic considerations, and drill down to more tactical ones.

First, don't become distracted by technology as the wellspring of success at the expense of business principles. The benefits of innovation must be clearly recognizable to the customer, and that customer may be a single or multiple stakeholders. Remember, someone must be willing to pay for change, and innovation that fails to solve a problem, or deliver a tangible benefit, is facing an uphill battle towards adoption. And don't forget elementary sales principles like pricing, product, positioning and placement (more on this in Chapter 19).

Second, architect solutions with a bias towards value. Many entrants to the mHealth sweepstakes are coming from outside healthcare, and although this brings a wealth of new thinking to healthcare's challenges, it doesn't always translate into solutions that perform well within the mHealth ecosystem. Does the solution solve a problem efficiently and economically? Can the solution be integrated with existing systems? Does it favorably impact work flows? Does it produce actionable benefits? A domain expert — clinical, operational, financial or administrative — with deep

Chapter 18: Managing mHealth Innovation

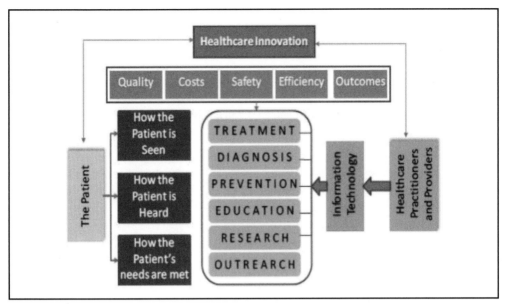

Fig. 18-1: Complexity and Ambiguity are Prominent Issues Confronting mHealth Innovators.[2]

industry experience can help avoid some of these pitfalls. Similarly, co-creating with the customer is a surefire way of keeping the solution relevant.

Third, the path of least resistance toward adoption may run through partnerships that create entre to healthcare stakeholders, deliver a larger impact and customer value. mHealth may be creating its own ecosystem, but that ecosystem doesn't exist independently of traditional healthcare. mHealth solutions will need to be integrated with existing healthcare infrastructures. Partners — technology partners, supply partners, and marketing partners — can provide much-needed horsepower to mHealth innovators, particularly to those with limited exposure to the industry.

And viewed from the perspective of the customer, there are an array of entirely different issues that must be addressed in crafting a solution strategy (Table 18-1).

Drilling down from the strategic level, it's important to manage innovation with a business sensibility. Now we must think in terms of the business value an mHealth solution delivers. As a point of departure, ask these questions to determine if the solution targets one or more of the following goals. Does it:
- Provide a better knowledge (or financial) transaction?
- Share knowledge among a wider circle of stakeholders?
- Promote provider/patient communication and/or integrating solutions and information?

Taken a step further, determine how the solution integrates with existing processes and information flows in such a way that makes it strategically aligned with the customer and commercially viable. Consider these factors when identifying and executing on an mHealth opportunity:

Customer: Identify the specific market segment for mHealth applications (consumer, employer, provider, pharma, device, payers, etc.). The customer might be one or multiple stakeholders, each with their own value drivers.

Mobility Strategy and Approach Impact	Questions to Address
Business/care goals and objectives	1. What are the key reasons for mobility (e.g., increase access, increase market share, introduce new business and care services, care and business process improvements, improve care provider and employee productivity, and others)? 2. What are the key business and care functions that are intended to be mobility-enabled? What are the target populations for mHealth — care providers, employees, patients, etc.? What are the stakeholder value propositions for using mobility? 3. Are there vendor partnerships in place in support of your business goals or for future business or care initiatives that would be impacted by mobility? 4. What regulatory and compliance requirements need to be addressed in the context of mobile applications? Is FDA approval needed for solutions that are considered medical devices or an extension of medical devices? Also, is care provided with the boundaries supported by state certification and reimbursement requirements? 5. Are care providers and employees already using mobile devices and for what tasks?
Technology	1. What type(s) of mobile devices and operating systems(s) do you intend to support? Will Bring Your Own Device (BYOD) be allowed? 2. What policies and procedures are in place to manage current mobile devices? This includes how they are provisioned, charge-back methods, software distribution, device refreshes, device tracking and troubleshooting. 3. How will you secure the devices and data stored on them in order to meet HIPAA privacy and security requirements? Will you require device segmentation to partition personal from organizational apps and data? In addition, will there be added device security? For example, if lost do you have the policies and technology in place for remote lock and wipe? 4. Is your organization planning to develop its own apps? If so, do you have or plan to purchase a Mobility Enterprise Application Platform (MEAP) tool? 5. Does your organization have an integration infrastructure for connecting with existing enterprise systems and applications? If not, how will integration be handled between mobile device-captured data and enterprise applications? Are there standards for data definitions, coded values and interfaces? 6. Describe the existing processes, if any, for the deployment and testing of mobile applications.
Operations and support	1. Describe the current IT environment supporting mobile devices and apps in your organization. 2. What skill sets are available for various aspects of mobile apps development, deployment, support and configuration? 3. What is the gap with planned mobility initiatives? What are your short- and long-term resource plans?

Table 18-1: Exploring New Product Strategy in Product Development.
(Source: Fran Turisco and Mike Garzone, Harnessing the Value of mHealth for your Organization, CSC, 2013. Used with permission.)

Pain points: Identify the current failure and pain points that mHealth solutions can more effectively address for the target market. But pressure-test your assumptions about the receptivity of a mobile solution among the target audience.

Workflow: Identify how mHealth could impact the efficiency and effectiveness of current processes, practices and work flow. Understand who benefits, and whose ox may be gored.

Vision: Create a vivid visualization of the mHealth solution and the characteristics of the offering that would create greater value. Communicate that vision effectively to investors, strategic partners, influencers and customers.

Value proposition: Create the value proposition that identifies, quantifies and measures the cost, convenience, confidence and compensation from outcome improvements from the mHealth solution.

Platform: Identify an existing platform, or the need to create a new platform, upon which the new mHealth solution should be launched, and the partners required for the platform components.

Business model: Create the business model that delivers the value proposition by leveraging existing or the development of new payment options.

Develop and launch: Develop and launch the mHealth offering for the target market through pilots, and then fully launch based upon realizing metrics and milestones of successful adoption.

Scale: Expand the solution feature set and business model to capture larger and adjacent markets.[1]

Managing innovation is a hands-on process. It proceeds from identifying and quantifying a market opportunity — with the key decision point — and asks the question, is the solution solving a problem, and does the problem need a new solution? It then moves into the strategy and product development phases according to two guiding principles — value and customer experience. Finally it enters the business development phase, including pilot testing, launch and market expansion. Each step of the process requires domain expertise, a clear vision of the solution's worth, the customer who will pay for it and the business strategy that will support its penetration of the market.

REFERENCES

1. "Healthcare Unwired: New Business Models Delivering Care Anywhere," Health Research Institute, Price Waterhouse Cooper, September 2010.
2. Omachonu VK, Einspruch NG. Innovation in healthcare delivery systems: a conceptual framework. *The Innovation Journal*; 2010; 51(1). Used with permission.

CHAPTER 19

The Business of mHealth

By Rick Krohn, MA, MAS, and David Metcalf, PhD

In the past three years, mHealth has had a wild ride from its beginnings with smartphone apps to its current deployments spanning the healthcare landscape. With tremendous speed and breathtaking innovation, mHealth has carved out its own space in health IT on a scale previously unseen in healthcare. It has proved its utility, from extending clinical reach to enabling new classes of care delivery (e.g., aging in place). But it has yet to achieve a business foundation that can sustain its growth.

Conceptually, as a class of solutions, mHealth makes economic sense in terms of resource efficiency, product affordability, scalability, demand generation, and other traditional business metrics. It is a tool to capture revenue streams (and avoid penalties) associated with MU, ACO, VBP, PCMH and the resurgence of risk contracting. It recasts the terms of clinical collaboration, and draws the consumer/patient into the process of care management. It has enormous market growth potential. Those sales propositions have attracted an army of software and product developers who are creating an ever-expanding array of mHealth solutions. But being disruptive doesn't guarantee business success, and the mHealth "gold rush" is generating a highly

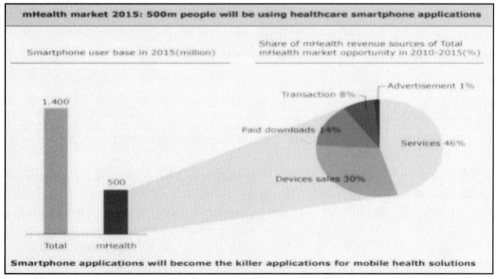

Fig. 19-1: Smartphone Applications will Become the Killer Applications for Mobile Health Solutions.

competitive — and crowded — marketplace. And that marketplace is exploding, as demonstrated by the smartphone app market (Fig. 19-1).

THE BUSINESS OF mHEALTH IS EVOLVING

Technical and product innovation have propelled the mHealth marketplace into an ever widening catalogue of solution sets, but great new solutions don't always translate into great new business. A good example of mHealth's shifting sands is the market for healthcare apps. It is now apparent in the wake of literally hundreds of thousands of health-related apps developed and more appearing daily, that consumers and patients are price-sensitive, and that selling apps isn't a sustainable business strategy. Solutions, not technology, are the key to success. And those solutions must be supported by business strategies that gain access to new customers, are aligned with larger industry trends like wellness and chronic care management, and are priced for mass consumption.

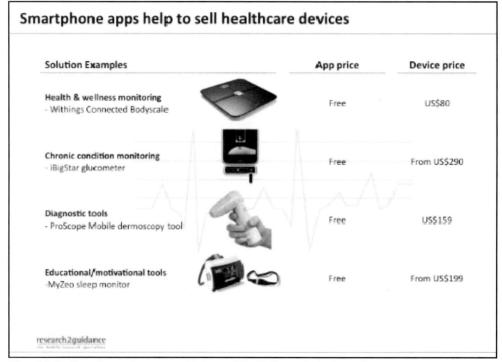

Fig. 19-2: Can Apps Increase Sales of Self-Care Solutions?

A growing trend within mHealth — adapting a successful sales strategy pioneered by the telecoms — is to give away the app and sell the device. As shown in Fig. 19-2, all manner of self-care solutions are being packaged with a free app that works with a proprietary device. And that device is increasingly multifunctional.

Employing a similar strategy, mHealth diagnostic tools are being targeted to providers who want more portable, easy-to-use devices, for dermatological evaluation, optometric tests, ultrasound and blood oxygen testing. Here again the roadmap is unclear with many unanswered questions. What is an FDA-regulated device? What are the liability concerns? Who determines the standard of care? mHealth innovators must tread carefully in evaluating the clinical and business hurdles that will impact the success of their solution.

What is clear is that the mHealth growth opportunity with legs is the value-added service. Mobile is fertile ground for customer outreach and commoditized services, and particularly in emerging markets, mHealth is demonstrating how filling the gap in healthcare access and cost can be extremely profitable. Mobile-enabled ask-a-doc, appointment setting, chronic-disease management, education and alerts, and in global south, even micro health insurance, can be offered via a simple feature phone and billed directly through the telecom. For a web-enabled customer, those services can be expanded to include security, storage, multimedia communication and care management. On the enterprise side, mobile can streamline wireless infrastructures, support multi-factor ID and integrate health IT with BYOD. It is a huge, still relatively untapped market.

REVENUE REFORM IS PIVOTAL

To date, the consumer has been the lifeblood of mHealth, buying all manner of apps, devices and services that are focused on self-care. That market dynamic is shifting, however, as mHealth innovators and entrepreneurs roll out mHealth solutions that bridge the gap between self-care and care coordination. Physician-facing apps, remote monitors and sensors, telehealth and social media are all emblematic of mHealth migrating to the provider space. The timing is opportune as the PCMH and ACO gain currency throughout the nation. Another signpost: payers are climbing aboard. In addition to the $25 copay for an office visit and $50 for emergency care, Blue Cross/Blue Shield of Florida now offers a new menu item — a $10 copay for an eVisit. This reduced cost and increased convenience will drive consumer behavior toward more efficient and cost effective care.

If mHealth is bending the cost curve, it must also be acknowledged that, at least for the present, mHealth has the capacity to reduce provider revenue. One of the chief obstacles facing mHealth innovation is the complex arrangement of incentives that reinforce our current system. The prevailing model of healthcare reimbursement remains fee for service: put another way, providers get paid for producing services, regardless of outcomes. mHealth isn't particularly well suited to this reimbursement environment, because it doesn't offer a richer source of revenue, may actually cause some revenue to disappear, and to a large degree, interferes with the freedom of providers to determine which services will be delivered and with what frequency.

That economic calculus is changing, as mHealth proves its worth. Payers are increasingly reimbursing providers for services like eVisits, and rewarding members for behavioral change and self-care via mobile tools. Healthcare facilities are imbedding mobile solutions into their operations, producing benefits in resource efficiency, patient engagement and satisfaction, clinical quality and cost savings. Providers are using mHealth tools to supplement staff resources, to manage patients more effectively, and to create brand preference. Governments are employing mHealth tools to promote population health, to increase access to underserved populations, and to address critical health issues. Finally, consumers and patients with chronic conditions are becoming increasingly accountable for their own health, and are willing to pay for mHealth tools that allow them to more effectively manage and maintain their health status.

There are a number of mHealth business models that are defining this market space, and they all conform to a core set of principles: patient-centric care, care-anywhere and pay for value. Here briefly are the three most common models:

Consumer Products and Services Model enables individuals to educate themselves about health issues, manage their health conditions, and share information with members of their care community — family, friends, clinicians and affinity groups. The consumer model does have limitations, however, because consumers have in some respects a sense of entitlement about healthcare (as part of their health insurance), and are unwilling to pay for additional products or services. What consumers *will* pay for is instant gratification. Instant results, instant feedback, instant communication.

Operational/Clinical Business Model enables providers, payers, employers, medical device and drug companies, as well as nontraditional healthcare organizations, to run their business operations better and more efficiently. These include transactions and services for customers, whether they are clinical in nature or related to the overall management of health.

Infrastructure Business Model connects, secures and speeds up mHealth services and information sharing. Key infrastructure markets include security, platform integration and interoperability.

For mHealth to succeed as an economic proposition, it's going to take a realignment of payment incentives tied to the shift from volume to value as the primary metric of reimbursement. It's going to require an alignment of incentives among healthcare's stakeholders, a clear value proposition and affordable solutions. But as mHealth solutions evolve, the sheer volume and range of information that can be shared via mobile will make further inroads into traditional healthcare processes, with attendant consequences for reimbursement. A final consideration: an mHealth product will only be adopted if the customer sees an advantage in paying for it. Patients and consumers are price sensitive, and this sensitivity does not change with income. But as price points recede in the consumer space for devices and apps, that hurdle will subside.

To be economically sustainable, mHealth solutions must conform to several principles aside from finance:

1. Interoperability to share data with mobile and non-mobile devices, with EMR, with legacy systems and plans.
2. Integration with existing provider workflows and patient lifestyles.
3. Intelligence — problem solving, intuitive, real-time answers.
4. Socialization — a trusted community of providers and peers.
5. Outcomes — clinical efficiency based on measurable objectives.
6. Engagement — putting the patient at the solid center.[1]

mHealth will only become economically rational when the calculus of healthcare includes a significant reliance on value-based revenue, a process reorientation towards patient-centered care, an integrated, standards-defined data sharing environment, and the creation of a true mHealth ecosystem. That ecosystem must meet the customer where they are — the hospital, the physician office, the workplace, the school, the home or anywhere in the community.

mFINANCE AND mHEALTH

The U.S. healthcare industry can be parsed into two principal activities: finance and delivery. Healthcare financing, which includes a spaghetti soup of payment sources including commercial payers, government, employers and the consumer, is complex, resource consumptive and wildly inefficient. As such, it is a rich vein of opportunity for technological innovation. Enter mFinance.

In keeping with the explosion of mobile services and products, mobile payments are becoming a natural extension of the mobile universe. It's a parallel trajectory — demand for mobile commodities and solutions are fueling the growth of mobile solutions. But there is another trend in play — the replacement of traditional payment mechanisms — founded on banking and credit systems — with a new mobile payment architecture that is entirely virtual. Mobile Financial Services (MFS) describes an electronic payment mechanism serviced through a mobile payment account, or mobile wallet. In healthcare, those payments can be of three varieties: services and supplies; administration; and the use of clinical data. But many transactions in healthcare aren't of the point-and-click variety. Health benefits generally require a linear process of approving, assigning and submitting charges for health related services. And there aren't many opportunities to buy ad hoc services at the doctor's office or hospital clinic, so how can the healthcare industry leverage MFS?

Taking healthcare transactions to the mobile space represents a huge revenue growth opportunity, but its adaptability to an industry that includes a patchwork of pricing and financial processing is problematic. To date, much of the activity in mHealth has been restricted to retail transactions, but MFS can be applied to collections, to purchasing insurance and to funding health savings accounts. Like the larger mHealth ecosystem, MFS is still in its opening stage. Like the larger mHealth ecosystem, MFS offers a huge opportunity for industry innovation.

There have been some early forays — with mixed results — into MFS. PayPal is an early success story, but other ventures like Google Wallet and Isis have suffered from unrealistic expectations. However, consumer uptake, particularly in the retail space, is on the rise. In healthcare, there are two hurdles to adoption. The lesser challenge is the consumer, who it is assumed, is willing to conduct healthcare transactions via mobile due to its convenience and with the same level of confidence that applies with any other industry. The larger challenge is in mobilizing the provider in a confusing payment environment.

WHO BENEFITS?

MFS has the potential to extend benefits to every stakeholder in the value chain. Consumers benefit by having the capability to pay for products and services when they need them, without fear of being denied due to a lack of insurance or readily available cash or equivalents. MFS can promote transactions among an underserved category of healthcare consumer — the poor, the rural and the under banked. These consumers often don't have access to traditional banking services, but do have financial resources. With an MFS wallet, they may also accrue health savings for anticipated expenditures. Providers benefit by increasing collections and accelerating cash flow. Payers benefit from exposure to an untapped product line (micro-insurance), from expedited remittances and payment of premiums. Finally, at a societal level MFS can have the effect of stabilizing poorer communities, in terms of improved population health, healthcare enterprise solvency and consumer asset protection.

A GLOBAL PERSPECTIVE

Looking beyond the United States, and focusing on developing nations, the likely trajectory of MFS becomes clearer. Around the world, more people have more access to a mobile phone than to clean water or the electrical grid. And among this same group, over 1 billion lack access to adequate healthcare. It's here that mFinance is catching fire.

Internationally, there's a natural bridge between the sea changes that are happening in both healthcare and finance due to mobile technology. There's both promise and challenge in the leap-frogging effect that is happening in developing nations as a result of mobile micro-payments juxtaposed with the increasing complexity of financial transactions for healthcare in the developed world. The desire to meet privacy, security, transactional integrity, cross coding and bank verification standards is an important set of requirements. Ease of use, transparency, and immediacy in healthcare billing could lead to incredible cost savings and the promise of improved access to care.

For example, in Kenya, mobile banking programs like M-PESA are having significant effects on access to healthcare and public health. M-PESA is not being used for direct medical payments, but allows for quick access to cash and the ability to pay transport costs to care facilities in emergencies.

These mobile payment for healthcare models in turn may affect other countries in Africa as they spur further innovations and development of competing solutions. We anticipate similar technologies coming to the United States and challenging traditional payment methods such as credit cards as well as transactional giants like PayPal and Intuit. Specialty finance providers in the healthcare space may also play a significant role. But before this happens, many issues must be addressed.

Standards and Interoperability
In the absence of standards, the same parochialism that has plagued established technologies like the EMR could translate to MFS. If MFS providers build independent systems the result will be costly, inefficient, and unable to scale.

Adoption
Like so many other aspects of mHealth, mFinance has yet to achieve a broad base of user adoption. Globally, MFS has reached the critical mass of commercial scale (1 million-plus users) in only one of ten deployments, and those deployments are concentrated in just a few countries (among them Kenya and the Philippines).

Revenue Model, Cost Structure and Sustainability

At a transactional level, revenue will accrue to the MFS provider. It remains to be determined how the payer, the provider and the consumer will be enticed to absorb these transactional costs to capture additional cash flow and productivity benefits.

Security

Data security, the never-ending challenge in healthcare, takes on an added dimension of complexity from mFinance. Identifiable patient data can be used to access enterprise billing systems and patient payment accounts to commit fraud and theft.

mFINANCE'S SUCCESS IN HEALTHCARE

There are some key factors that will determine, at least in the near term, the success of MFS in the healthcare space. First, mobile finance is not plug-and-play. The payee — the institutional billing department, the transactional vendor, the retailer, whoever — will need to implement the required infrastructure and ongoing services to support near field communication (NFC) or other mobile payment schemes. Mobile payments must co-exist with point of sale software, bank networks and plastic cards. The interplay of these systems is still largely conceptual.

Second, the consumer experience must be trusted and transparent. The process must be reassuring, convenient, reliable and secure. Mobile transactions must be bulletproof — security breaches are top of mind to everyone in healthcare. To drive adoption, consumers will need to be motivated to use a mobile payment alternative, either through promotions, discounts, loyalty programs or other means. To be sustainable, MFS must achieve a critical mass of both an installed base of merchants, and an installed base of customers.

Third, the mobile wallet or other MFS tool must be pre-installed on the mobile device, and its use must be accompanied by standards based, interoperable systems architecture.

Finally, mobile payment schemes must be ramped up quickly or both payer and payee will fail to recognize the value in switching from their current payment methodology. To the extent that mobile finance in healthcare can be integrated with mobile commerce in general — and mimic the mobile retail transaction — it will gain traction. But we are still a good distance from a unified mobile payment mechanism that is ubiquitous and safe.

Viewed strictly through an economic lens, mFinance demonstrates that healthcare can be affordable, accessible, efficient and utilitarian. It holds the promise of faster and more efficient financial administration, reduced A/R, lower operating costs and a wider customer base. And in a larger context mCommerce represents a huge opportunity in healthcare, by attacking some of the fundamental flaws — connectivity, communication and collaboration, service and product efficiency and accountability — that are deeply embedded in the industry.

For now, mFinance (and mHealth in general) is gaining its greatest adoption in developing nations, where it is less of a disruptive force, and where cultural resistance and regulatory oversight play less of a role. But looking ahead, globally mFinance will become part of a new model, consumer-centric healthcare, that will eclipse the tried and troubled model of episodic, insular care delivery.

REFERENCE

1. PriceWaterhouseCooper. Building mHealth Business Models that Work. PwC, 2013.

CHAPTER 20

Implications of a Mobile-to-Mobile Online Delivery Model: A Case Study

By William C. Thornbury, Jr., MD

ABSTRACT

Healthcare has a very serious distribution problem. Today's health system can diagnose more problems, and offer more treatments, to patients that live longer. The impending avalanche of expectant healthcare needs of the Baby Boomer generation tips the scale, such that health delivery and sustainability no longer become tenable within the construct of the present health system.[1]

Today, we largely seek care in the same manner that our grandparents did — in chronically congested medical offices. That is not going to continue. The market will find a solution; urgent/retail clinics and the tide of telehealth vendors that line the streets of healthcare are attempts toward this effort. There remains room, however, for further efficiency. There is the consumer peripheral device; there is mobility.

Today's culture has steadfastly moved into the digital age and has engendered e-commerce. In 2010, video rental giant Blockbuster recorded a profit of $160 million; the following year, having failed to appreciate the impact of the Internet economy, Blockbuster filed for bankruptcy.[11] Successful senior leadership will appreciate the cataclysmic change that the Internet economy — specifically, mobile-to-mobile platforms — will have on distribution services and the global healthcare markets.

MOBILE-TO-MOBILE, THE SECOND GENERATION OF TELEHEALTH

In healthcare, service is the commodity. Efficient distribution of service is directly related to economic viability and sustainability. Now, consider the case for mobility. The use of smartphones, tablets and other peripheral devices has become ubiquitous. Those not adept with this technology are either waning through attrition, or have become dedicated by proxy (children, caregivers or health workers). The "house call via smartphone" with one's own physician — considered the Holy Grail of mHealth — now exists in the marketplace.

Our team's consideration of the mobile model came through the search for a solution to provide access to care for our patients. We strongly believe that continuity of care and the medical home patient-physician relationship should be maintained. Also, a great many encounters simply do not require hands-on diagnostics skills. Mobility arose as the solution because we found it impractical and inefficient to conduct online care after-hours through a traditional computer.

After reviewing the literature for safety,[2] and the known experience of online care within the medical home model,[3] we felt comfortable applying it to our practice. We then engineered the encounter through a smartphone in such a way as to present the physician a complete HPI (history) and brief PMH (medical record), and deliver an exceptional care plan with information back to the patient in under four minutes (the time frame we deemed functional to engage the physician).

Once one begins to conduct care through a mobile model, it becomes immediately apparent that the door to a new generation of telehealth has been opened — one that is cheaper and more efficient. The model that we developed was efficient enough to engage our physicians. *Mobility allowed telemedicine to be conducted within the medical home* — yes, the same medical home demonstrated by every study conducted to lower costs and improve outcomes.[4-6] Mobility's efficiency would allow telehealth to become available to private physicians and health systems, alike. So efficient care, in fact, could be provided either during or after clinic hours without disrupting clinical flow or quality of life. Mobility provides telemedicine for the common man.

The last thought bears some examination. Let's assume that all telehealth works well for the patient, who benefits from increased access to care. However, healthcare providers are reticent to realize productivity and this acts as a major barrier to the benefit of maintaining the medical home relationship after clinic hours of operation. The business end of online care within the medical home is that, not only can minor acute care be provided online, but our study demonstrated that moderate acute care and stable chronic disease care — the latter representing 75 percent of the healthcare dollar — could be provided safely.

The 30-month study that we conducted with the academic cooperation of the University of Kentucky examined consecutive mobile online encounters with well-established patients in a rural healthcare setting. Our team found that 79 percent of care requests were submitted after-hours, though fewer than 5 percent occurred after 10 p.m. These patients, naive to online care, demonstrated that 97 percent of requests were appropriate. The first year was designated for minor acute care consistent with traditional online programs; however, the second year leveraged the advantage of the medical home relationship, adding some moderate acute problems and 20 percent stable chronic disease. The physician utilized a phone conversation to support the encounter 18 percent of the time, and the options for face-to-face video interaction with the patient was found to be unnecessary at any point during the study. The study area included five Appalachian counties as so designated by the federal government and encompassed about 15 percent of the state's geographic area. The average age was 41, with a distribution between 16 and 89 years of age. No safety issues were reported.[7]

Most importantly, we found that over the period of the study, the clinic's capacity improved 19 percent — more than an hour each day of added value. Further, the per-capita cost of care decreased 15 percent, which is critical for healthcare systems struggling on a 1 percent to 2 percent margin. And, not surprisingly, the surveyed patients frankly loved it. Rather than dividing patient and physician, the model seemed to facilitate the care relationship. *To restate: We provided care in less time, using fewer resources — and patients actually preferred it.*

THE EFFECT OF MOBILITY ON THE HEALTHCARE SYSTEM

Introducing *true mobility* for both patients and medial providers unleashes freedom that escalates throughout each aspect of the health continuum. It is one of the very rare times in healthcare when change actually improves every element of the system. Usually in business, someone's benefit is another's offsetting loss. Such is not the exact case with mobility, as its major benefit serves to liberate large quantities of waste previously hidden from view. In system change, removing waste is a much more powerful driver than penalizing one participant for the benefit of another. Walking through each principle in the system demonstrates mobility's cascading impact and disruption.

From the patients' point of view, they may receive care from their own healthcare provider anytime, anywhere. A mobile model saves them time, travel, work-related issues and is less disruptive to their daily life.

From the medical provider's perspective, it allows them to offer increased access to care during or after hours. It maintains care within the medical home model proven to yield the lowest costs and best outcomes. It lowers liability when contrasted to undocumented phone calls. And, e-commerce makes it possible to obtain compensation for the intellectual work and assumption of risk attributed to out-of-clinic encounters, in fact, rewarding those who save the healthcare system resources.

Medical practices benefit from increased productivity, celebrating the opportunity to add new patients and broaden provider panels, if desired. They may now offer same-day appointments or redistribute their time and talent to address high-acuity patients (proven to lower future healthcare expenses). Morale improves as efficiencies increase the quality of life for patients, providers and staff. Where electronic medical records (EMR) damper clinician efficiency, mobility enhances.

Enterprise hospital systems and ACOs (part risk-bearer, part healthcare provider) are winners as well. Mobility opens a new and permanent source of revenue: e-commerce. They realize increased productivity from outpatient clinics, both primary care and medical specialty. Critically, they bring primary care providers to the table, thus allowing the technology to be translated to other clinical areas, such as the ED and transitional care.

Employers visualize less absenteeism and presenteeism from increased access. Minor and moderate acute care, as well as routine chronic disease follow-up, becomes possible as the care relationship is maintained by the private health provider. Ultimately, lower acuity translates to stabilized insurance costs.

Third-party insurers see less acuity burden from a displacement of costs away from EDs, urgent clinics and in-person encounters. There is less testing (labs and imaging) and interventions (injections) than occur during onsite encounters. In addition, it obviously costs less to provide care outside the overhead-laden brick-and-mortar clinic. In fact, many carriers have recently resorted to providing their own secondary market of healthcare providers online (and outside the medical home model) to address this problem. However, it should be obvious that employing the medical workforce and patient-provider relationship already established is a much less costly and more effective alternative and, over time, much more likely to be sustainable.

Governmental entities also receive the core benefits they seek. Access to care is increased, especially after-hours. The mandate for lower cost of care is fulfilled. Mobile technology makes the medical workforce more efficient, and, if our specific model were extrapolated, it would theoretically meet the manpower needs of the economy. Lastly, mobility provides the virtual medical home that addresses care needs for disparate, at-risk, and isolated populations.

THE IMPLICATIONS OF mHEALTH

Mobility will come to allow healthcare systems economic benefit that they've not previously realized. Historically, hospital-based telemedicine, in all its forms, has been an economic sink. Market forces have initially pushed most telemedicine to third-party providers, a model enhanced by telemedicine companies directly marketing to industry andn patients. However, this current solution has been at the expense of continuity and the medical home relationship.

Consider the new model that mobility allows to occur: primary care providers conduct efficient and extended care with their patients online. The true workhorses of the medical system, primary care, allow healthcare systems to address readmission and emergency department losses. Studies currently demonstrate that after hospital discharge, a care coordinator can reduce readmissions by 25 percent. This immediately begs the question, how much savings might be incurred from an efficient online encounter from the physician most responsible for care of the discharged patient?

If a technology that costs pennies was offered to patients at risk for non-reimbursement in the emergency department, how much savings in uncompensated care, productivity and resource reassignment might be offset? Further, as a secondary benefit, such patients could be mobilized to primary care clinics — now more efficient through the mobile model which offer the capacity to accept them, minimizing the risk of a return ED visit for undiagnosed/uncontrolled chronic disease. Succinctly, a single provider that uses mobility in healthcare to displace one uncompensated readmission and one emergency department encounter will save a healthcare system about $10,000 annually. We estimate that direct and indirect clinic revenue may add another $32,000 per year per provider.

The power of true mobility in healthcare delivery might be condensed into a concept borrowed from Clayton Christensen's *The Innovator's Prescription*.[8] Discussing how a disruption within the least profitable part of an industry ultimately trickles up to affect the entire system, Dr. Christensen provided the example of the re-engineering of rebar in the steel industry. Once rebar became profitable, the whole industry ultimately changed. The healthcare executive might translate this to the ability of mobile online care to make Medicaid and Medicare profitable. This capacity changes the entire healthcare economy.

Mobility provides a second generation of telehealth that decisively increases engagement and productivity for both sides of the equation, patient and provider. Indeed, mobility fulfills technology's promise to make medical care more efficient and affordable. In one fell swoop, the mobile platform expands the medical home relationship, increasing the breadth of diagnoses available for care online; it lowers per-capita and global costs; and, unlike all previous telehealth models, increases healthcare professional productivity. Mobility fulfills the criteria of the goals of the Triple Aim.

ECONOMIC IMPACT OF mHEALTH

Some of mHealth's greatest advantages are inherent in the efficiency of the mobility model. The cost to care for patients online is simply less than the overhead of maintaining medical facilities. Furthermore, our experience demonstrated that in-office "no show" rates evaporated; patients don't miss appointments that they control. As we represented, nearly 80 percent of our acute cases occurred after-hours, which would have necessitated higher levels of acuity (and morbidity for delayed care).

Implementation costs for the mobile model are modest. There is no substantive change required in a clinician's application of care, and a healthcare system's IT infrastructure, likewise, requires little change. EMR integration is the only significant expense within the system, and that line item will diminish over time.

When the extrapolated findings of our study are applied to primary care in the United States, after-hours savings alone represented $9.4 billion annually by year two. Applied to the larger health system, we estimated a $28.8 billion annual savings for the 40 percent of outpatient care alone that could likely be mobilized online over time — greater than 1 percent of the total healthcare budget of the United States. Our finding, confirmed by a Deloitte Center for Health Solutions January 2013 independent study, estimated mHealth would save the U.S. healthcare industry $30.5 billion annually.[9] A supporting study prepared by PricewaterhouseCoopers in June of 2013 for the GSMA (global telecom community) postulated that the European Union could save nearly €100 billion in spending, increase GDP another €93 billion, and care for 24.5 million more lives with the same medical workforce.[10] Lastly, we did not consider in our estimates the savings in lost time, work, resources and transportation that are invoked by amending the care volume online.

In essence, a new delivery model that will permanently save hundreds of billions of dollars annually to the economy can be instituted for pennies on the healthcare dollar. For the first time, mobility has the intention of bending the mythical healthcare cost-curve downward. The healthcare system, like the culture it serves, is transitioning from the model of Blockbuster to that of Netflix.

RECIPROCAL BENEFITS OF MOBILITY

Consider the visual image of a bread truck. It travels back and forth between the factory and the customer. In healthcare, so does the medical record. The patient provides a history, which is forwarded to the provider where it is evaluated, then returned to the patient with instructions. It is a work product that serves the purpose of documenting the encounter for information, communication, reimbursement and legal protection.

Now, what might also travel aboard such a bread truck? Perhaps information from medical peripherals of the patient to the provider? Vital sign measurements, results from self- or home-lab testing, and symptom diaries are among such information — be it via the patient, caregiver or home health staff. Further, consider what the clinician may wish to forward back to the patient — complete instructions for care, a vignette, web site/app links, or other resources simply not possible to provide during the limited time of an office encounter.

Healthcare systems may benefit by staking a claim on the most valuable real estate in their marketplace, the hand-held peripheral device. In essence, mobility offers them a walkie-talkie directly to their customer. Databases can be engineered to forward health maintenance reminders to the patient's peripheral device — and how much future morbidity and cost might this reduce? By knowledge of a patient's specific health conditions, individualized updates on such issues could be sent from time to time, just like news reminders that are delivered throughout the day to the smartphone — all of this from a healthcare system that cares for them, informs them and markets to them. And, at the end of each of these communiqués, might there also be a patient-specific message promoting a resource or opportunity of the health system.

Lastly, Pharma may have an interest in the information gleaned from mobile encounters. The clinician forwarding a treatment plan for common influenza is, in fact, at the time and point of care. How effective might a coupon for a specific pharmaceutical or OTC pain reliever attached to the treatment plan be? How might such information (Big Data) be valued for use in future contacts with the healthcare provider? Mobility encompasses information *and* communication — a powerful combination not to be taken lightly.

CONCLUSION

It is clear that mHealth technology is a disruptive innovation whose time has arrived. A new and more sustainable model of healthcare delivery that is emerging to drive non-emergent care into the virtual space. It is ideal for the majority of medical care scenarios where providers serve as analysts, advisors, and educators. The culture that embraces e-commerce will likewise champion online healthcare — and reward those institutions that offer it to the market quickly and successfully. Online care from an individual's own caregiver is simply more personal and less disruptive to the hectic pace of life. For hundreds of years, people had to physically go to where healthcare was dispensed to receive treatment. Today, mobility offers a mechanism to provide much of this care on demand to the consumer with ease and convenience.

Mobility allows health systems to provide *individualized* care and *individualized* marketing just in time for a patient's need, a bond not easily broken. Health systems and their patients will build stronger symbiotic relationships. Once a community comes to depend upon a reliable healthcare partner, it may be very difficult to displace this bond.

Mobility presents the real possibility that a previously less-than-competitive healthcare institution may contend using different rules — and on a new battlefield:

e-commerce. Because such competitors no longer play by traditional rules, rivals may be blinded to the silent shrinkage that occurs when the market walks quietly across ZIP code lines to reward an alternative service. Their product will be an alternative delivered at a lower cost, more conveniently, and more intimately than traditional care. Competitors can do this with a relatively modest investment, utilizing technology that has been established for nearly a decade. Indeed, the risk-to-reward ratio is quite low; therefore, such "low-hanging fruit" is unlikely to go unnoticed by the market for very long.

Mobility and mHealth will permanently change the paradigm of healthcare delivery. The model not only supports the medical home and meets the goals of the Triple Aim, it becomes a competitive necessity in the marketplace — a marketplace already ingrained in a culture that fluently conducts e-commerce through peripherals. Mobility is the driver that will change healthcare's direction from the path of volume-based wastes of today, to one of value-based solutions for tomorrow. Indeed, mobility's influence is likely to be so pervasive that it may be the underlying solution to how Accountable Care Organizations, state Medicaid programs and the Affordable Care Act become sustainable. Leadership that recognizes this megatrend will position its healthcare system for success in the immediate and foreseeable future.

REFERENCES

1. Reid PP, Compton WC, Grossman JH, et al. *Building a Better Delivery System: A New Engineering/Health Care Partnership.* National Academy of Engineering (U.S.) and Institute of Medicine (U.S.) Committee on Engineering and the Health Care System; Washington (DC). National Academies Press (U.S.). 2005.

2. Munger MA, et al. *Safety of prescribing PDE-5 inhibitors via e-medicine vs. traditional medicine.* Mayo Clin. Proceedings. Mayo Clinic. 2008. 83(8):890-6.

3. Adamson SC, Bachman JW. *Pilot study of providing online care in a primary care setting.* Mayo Clinic proceedings. Mayo Clinic. 2010. 85:704-10.

4. Starfield B, Leiyu S, Macinko J. Contribution of Primary Care to Health systems and Health. *Milbank Quarterly.* Sept 2005. Vol. 83, Issue 3, p 457-502.

5. Starfield B, et al. Co morbidity: Implications for the Importance of Primary Care in 'Case' Management. *Ann. Fam. Med.* 2005; 1.

6. The Commonwealth Fund Commission on a High Performance Health System, Confronting Costs: Stabilizing U.S. Health Spending While Moving Toward a High Performance Health Care System, The Commonwealth Fund, January 2013.

7. Thornbury WC. mHealth & 2nd Generation Telemedicine: Making the Medical Home Mobile to Provide Care for World Populations. *Global Telemedicine and eHealth Updates-Knowledge Resources*, 2013, Vol 7, p 58-60.

8. Christensen CM, Grossman JH, Hwang J. *The Innovator's Prescription: A Disruptive Solution for Health Care.* New York, NY. McGraw-Hill. 2009.

9. Greenspun H, Coughlin, S. *mHealth in an mWorld: How Mobile Technology is Transforming Healthcare*, Deloitte Center for Health Solutions. 2012.

10. PricewaterhouseCoopers, *Socio-economic impact of mHealth: An assessment report for the European Union.* Presented for the Global System for Mobile Communications Association; June 18, 2013.

11. Lee RS. Corporate reorganization as corporate reinvention: Borders and Blockbuster in Chapter 11. *Harvard Business Law Review Online*; 2011; (1):53-55.

CHAPTER 21

mHealth: Helping Doctors Treat the Underinsured: A Case Study

By Joshua L. Conrad, PharmD

ABSTRACT

To overcome the challenges of limited resources and an increasing patient load, free medical clinics are utilizing mobile solutions to practice more efficiently and decrease costs. Providers at the Volunteers in Medicine (VIM) clinic in Stuart, Florida, and St. Clare Health Mission in Monroe County, Wisconsin, are embracing mobile devices and popular mobile health (mHealth) applications to help make quicker and more informed care decisions and to manage medication expenditures.

At the VIM clinic there is a lack of specialty expertise. Mobile medical applications help fill the void by giving providers information about unfamiliar diseases and medications. The use of mobile tools, such as Epocrates' drug interaction checker, assists providers in avoiding untoward effects and preventing costly emergency department visits.

Managing medication costs is also critical for underinsured patients. By using information on alternative treatments and lower cost generic medication options from mobile medical references, St. Clare Health Mission has increased the number of prescriptions filled while dramatically cutting costs. In 2012, St. Clare Health Mission providers wrote 1,000 more prescriptions than the previous year but reduced total medication costs by $11,000.

These case studies discuss the challenges volunteer providers at the VIM clinic and St. Clare Health Mission face, and explore how mHealth tools empower them to improve overall quality and efficiency of care.

VOLUNTEERS IN MEDICINE — STUART, FL

Volunteers in Medicine (VIM) is a national non-profit organization that provides sustainable, free primary healthcare for the uninsured in local communities. As of September 2013, there were nearly 100 VIM clinics across the United States.[1] The VIM clinic in Stuart, Florida, handles nearly 1,000 patient visits per month. Many of these patients have not received healthcare for a significant time and have a number of medical conditions upon initial presentation to the clinic.

Like most non-profit clinics serving the uninsured, operating costs at the VIM must be kept to a minimum to remain viable long-term. Resources are at a premium, and not all exam rooms have computers with Internet access or are stocked with hard-copy medical references. The VIM clinic in Stuart also has a lack of specialty expertise. Their clinicians are frequently challenged with caring for patients with multiple medical conditions, some of which would more commonly be managed by specialists under other circumstances.

Through a corporate philanthropy program, clinicians at the VIM clinic have access to Epocrates' premium mobile medical application free of charge. This mHealth application includes extensive drug and disease references, a drug interaction checker, and several other point-of-care clinical tools. Betty Tsarnas, an advanced registered nurse practitioner and clinical director of the VIM clinic in Stuart, uses the mHealth application to minimize the time she spends performing necessary point-of-care reference checking. She can do these tasks in the exam room on her mobile tablet device while engaging with the patient, rather than having to leave the exam room to go to a central computer station or reference library. Like many clinicians, she prefers a tablet device because she can visualize more information on a single screen, often as much as can be viewed on a computer monitor. Ms. Tsarnas' time-saving experience using mobile medical references is not unusual. In a recent survey of physicians, nearly half reported saving 20 minutes or more daily using Epocrates' mobile medical applications.[2] That extra time can translate into more time spent with each patient or more patients cared for.

Most of the evidence that supports the impact of mobile medical references on efficiency, cost-effectiveness and clinical outcomes are from survey data that reflect users' beliefs about these aspects. There has been a notable lack of studies on these aspects conducted in actual clinical settings. Though it is clear that clinicians believe that mobile medical references improve efficiency, cost-effectiveness and clinical outcomes, this is an area in which more confirmatory clinical research would be helpful. Prgomet and colleagues conducted a systematic review of the literature on the topic of mobile technology impact, published in 2009.[5] They identified 13 studies demonstrating positive impacts of mobile technology on a number of these factors. None of the studies, however, were conducted specifically on mobile medical references, and the authors agree that there is still need for more research on the healthcare outcome impact of mobile technology.

In addition to the time-saving element, having access to a mobile library of diseases that are not routinely managed by primary care providers can be invaluable to effective patient care in the setting of the VIM clinic. Through mHealth applications, Ms. Tsarnas is able to quickly refresh herself on conditions that she less frequently manages. She can also check dosing, adverse effects and interactions for medications with which she is less familiar. She feels that access to all this information at the point of care has helped her avoid medication errors and adverse drug events (ADE), and prevented more costly emergency room visits. And she is not alone. More than half of physicians surveyed estimate that they avoid at least one ADE per week using Epocrates' mobile medical applications.[2] Minimizing ADEs is an important and attainable component to reducing overall healthcare costs. According to the Centers for Disease Control and Prevention, ADEs are responsible for more than 700,000 emergency department visits and nearly 120,000 hospital admissions annually.[3] Costs associated with such acute care can be financially devastating for uninsured patients who are struggling just to make ends meet.

Mobile medical references are not simply for use in the clinic setting, where they can be a time-saving substitute for more traditional computer-based and hard-copy references and tools. They may be the only viable option in certain care settings. Kathi Harvey, a family nurse practitioner who works for the National Disaster Medical System and volunteers at VIM, was one of numerous healthcare providers who were deployed in the aftermath of Hurricane Sandy in 2012. With no power and extremely limited resources, access to a mobile medical application was, as she put it, "a godsend." Mobile tools, such as a pill identifier, which allows determination of a drug by its shape, color and markings, helped her and others on the team care for victims efficiently and effectively.

ST. CLARE HEALTH MISSION — MONROE COUNTY, WI

St. Clare Health Mission is a clinic that provides free healthcare, prescription medications and other treatments for persons who live in Monroe County, Wisconsin, and have no insurance or other financial means to pay for their care. The clinic is supported by and draws its volunteer staff from local medical clinics, hospitals and residents.

Like the VIM, resources are extremely limited and St. Clare Health Mission clinicians must see patients with multiple medical conditions that are not in their normal scope of practice. In addition, because St. Clare Health Mission has its own pharmacy and dispenses medications to patients on-site free of charge, the clinic must absorb most of the cost of the drugs prescribed for patients there. Keeping drug costs low is critical to the sustainability of the clinic.

Through the same corporate philanthropy program used by VIM, providers at the St. Clare Health Mission clinic have free access to Epocrates' premium mobile medical application. The clinic has a number of mobile devices that are shared by the staff and they access the application during and between patient encounters. The clinicians commonly use the mHealth application to perform drug dose and interaction checking and to assist them in educating patients on their medications and diagnoses. Dr. Emma Ledbetter, a retired emergency medicine physician and medical director of the St. Clare Health Mission clinic, finds that reading the descriptions and treatment options for her patients' conditions directly to them from her mobile device improves patient care. She also feels that showing patients images of their dermatologic conditions on a mobile device is extremely helpful during the patient encounter. Such interactions can increase the confidence patients have in their caregivers and, in the latter case, help overcome language barriers.

When new patients who are taking previously prescribed medications seek treatment at St. Clare Health Mission the providers also use the mHealth application to find feasible alternatives that are stocked by the clinic's pharmacy, as well as a suitable equivalent dose. If a patient requires a type of medication not carried by their pharmacy, the provider can use the mHealth application to find low cost prescription options that can be filled elsewhere, increasing accessibility and the probability of ongoing adherence. All of this can be done on the mobile device in the exam room, while in discussion with the patient. By using mobile medical applications to aid in managing medication expenditures, St. Clare Health Mission drug costs were reduced in 2012 by about $11,000 from the previous year, despite the fact that they filled 4,100 prescriptions in 2012, 1,000 more than in 2011.

FUTURE TRENDS

The cases of the VIM and St. Clare Health Mission clinics illustrate how the use of mHealth applications in the care of underinsured patients can increase productivity and efficiency, improve patient care, and decrease ADEs and drug costs. Looking to the future, it is likely that mobile device use among healthcare providers will continue to rise. Smartphone use in a professional capacity has increased amongst healthcare providers from 78 percent in 2012 to 86 percent in 2013, and is expected to increase to 94 percent in 2014, while mobile tablet use in this capacity increased from 35 percent in 2012 to 53 percent in 2013, with an expected increase to 85 percent in 2014.[4] The largest increases, however, are expected in those healthcare providers classified as "digital omnivores," who routinely use a computer, smartphone and mobile tablet for professional purposes. Digital omnivores accounted for 28 percent of the healthcare provider population in 2012, a proportion that increased to 47 percent in 2013 and is expected to reach 82 percent in 2014.[4]

Though the trends in mobile technology adoption are apparent, what is less clear is what the role of free and low-cost medical clinics that serve those individuals who cannot afford healthcare will be in the era of the Affordable Care Act. Dr. Ledbetter speculates, "While the Affordable Care Act reforms that went into effect at the start of 2014 are expanding healthcare coverage to many more Americans, there is an ongoing need for providing care and medications for low-income people who still cannot afford doctor's visits and medications. St. Clare Health Mission will continue to fulfill this need, and Epocrates will continue to be an essential tool that helps us provide quality, low-cost medical care for our patients."

REFERENCES

1. Volunteers in Medicine. VIM Clinic Directory Web site. http://volunteersinmedicine.org/vim-clinics. Accessed September 12, 2013.

2. Epocrates, Inc., an athenahealth company. 2012 Specialty Survey [Microsoft PowerPoint]. www.epocrates.com/oldsite/2012SpecialtySurveys/2012_Specialty_Survey_External.zip. Published November 2012. Accessed September 12, 2013.

3. Centers for Disease Control and Prevention. Medication Safety Program. Adults and Older Adult Adverse Drug Events web page. www.cdc.gov/MedicationSafety/Adult_AdverseDrugEvents.html. Updated October 2, 2012. Accessed September 12, 2013.

4. Epocrates, Inc., an athenahealth company. Epocrates 2013 Mobile Trends Report: Maximizing Multi-Screen Engagement Among Clinicians. www.epocrates.com/oldsite/statistics/2013%20Epocrates%20Mobile%20Trends%20Report_FINAL.pdf. Published 2013. Accessed September 12, 2013.

5. Prgomet M, Georgiou A, Westbrook JA. The impact of mobile handheld technology on hospital physicians' work practices and patient care: a systematic review. *J Am Med Inform Assoc.* 2009;16:792-801.

Part V
Standards, Security & Policy

CHAPTER 22

Mobile Health IT Standards

By Keith Boone

Within this book there are many varieties of mobile health. To usefully talk about IT standards for mobile health, it is useful to have a definition that provides a useful distinction. A difference that does not matter, well, it simply doesn't matter.

In *mHealth Solution: What is mHealth*, John Moehrke identifies various classifications of mobility with respect to mHealth, which I paraphrase below:
1. Data are mobile.
2. Data access devices are mobile.
3. Authorization enables data mobility.
4. Sensors (data capture devices) are mobile.
5. Consent to access is mobile.
6. Healthcare devices are moved.
7. Data about mobility is created or accessed.

For this section, I will focus on cases one through four. The remaining three kinds of mobility do not add value to this discussion. We will also further constrain what it means to be mobile because that again provides distinguishing characteristics. A mobile device for the purpose of discussion in this chapter is:
1. Personally, locally or wirelessly network connected some part of the time.
2. Easily carried.
3. Operable one or no-handed.

Narrowing the space this way produces some interesting constraints and limitations: power, bandwidth, memory, CPU capability, and input/output capabilities may all be limited. These also create some interesting constraints on the IT standards that might be supported and investigated in this chapter.

At the high end of the spectrum are tablets and smartphones. Some tablets barely qualify on the easily carried and operable one-handed fronts. These devices are as powerful as the desktop computers we used a decade ago. At the low end are small-footprint embedded devices, some of which hobbyists can now purchase and program for less than $100 with various sensors.

TYPES OF NETWORKS

The Continua Health Alliance (Continua) is a membership organization focused on the use of standards in healthcare devices designed for home use. Many of the devices

in this space fit within the classification described above. Continua describes four categories of networks used for communication between home health devices.
- PAN – Personal Area Network (sometimes referred to elsewhere as Body Area Network)
- LAN – Local Area Network (elsewhere referred to as WLAN when it supports Wireless connections)
- WAN – Wide Area Network (your connection to your ISP or cable modem is a WAN device)
- HRN – Health Reporting Network

From the Continua perspective, PAN also includes wired (USB® connected) devices. The Health Reporting Network (HRN) classification deserves some explanation. This is a network end-point at a healthcare provider organization designed to receive healthcare data; as it uses generally applicable health IT standards, it will not be further discussed in this chapter.

COMMUNICATION PATTERNS

Communications involving mobile devices fall into one of a few patterns:
- Peer-to-peer
- Client-server
- Server-mediated

Peer-to-peer communications is where multiple mobile devices communicate with each other using the same communications standards. This kind of connection shows up in Bluetooth connection between your headset and your cellphone.

The client-server pattern is one in which a server operating with a great deal more capability provides services to a usually less-capable mobile device. This is a common pattern used with devices that have fairly simple interfaces, e.g., activity monitors, scales, etc., which then communicate to a personal computer. The personal computer can then act as client to another server to support upload of data yet again. In this pattern of communication, the networking technology often changes between hops. My activity monitor connects to my laptop or phone via Bluetooth®. It is then uploaded to a server via the digital cellular network, or my LAN to WAN connection (a cable modem).

Another pattern is a server-mediated pattern, in which mobile devices communicate with each other mediated through a centralized server. Think Twitter, Instagram or FaceBook, although not always with a web site in the middle. Cellphone communication is also server-mediated.

SHARING DEVICE CAPABILITIES

Due to limited capabilities in the mobile component, mobile health applications often share capabilities of different devices to support the user applications. For example, the keyboard and mouse of your personal computer help to control the activity monitor sitting in your pocket. The touch screen on your smartphone could become the display and input device to manipulate health data captured by some other sensor.

The mobile component of the health application is a key component and feature of an entire system, made up of several communicating parts.

The communication between these systems is mediated by networking and storage device standards and application-level standards.

Standards at the Network Layer and Below

Networking constraints for mobile devices depend upon the system requirements for connectivity. Does the system need intermittent connectivity or data storage? When the system needs connectivity, is it in short or long bursts of data? What is the latency from senescence (sleeping) to a fully active connection?

Size and mobility constraints lead to concerns about the use of power. If you have ever turned Wi-Fi® off on your phone to conserve power, or watched your phone battery deplete itself as it repeatedly searched for a signal, you understand that some communications methods are power hungry, but they also provide plenty of bandwidth, enough to support audio and in some cases video.

Connectivity constraints lead to reliance on an unfamiliar network stack for those having been accustomed to building traditional computer software. Communications standards include Near Field Communication (NFC),[1] Body Area or Personal Area Networks (BAN or PAN) such as Bluetooth or ZigBee®, Short Message Service (SMS), Wireless LAN (WLAN) such as Wi-Fi, and various digital cellular communications (GSM, EDGE, 3G, 4G/LTE) for networking services.

Other devices rely on portable storage media using Secure Data (SD®) memory cards (e.g., a C-PAP), or Universal Serial Bus (USB®) connections (e.g., a glucometer) instead of wireless connections. Interfaces to devices using these standards most often appear as a file system.

Available but not commonly used are the IrDA® standards for infrared data communications. While IR devices and IrDA compliant communications were commonly available in smartphones and PDAs prior to 2000, they have declined greatly since the ascent of Bluetooth and Wi-Fi communications. Infrared relies on line of sight and can be readily blocked by people, coffee cups and other solid objects.

Developers of mobile devices have to trade between latency, data volume, power and communication range requirements. Table 22-1 illustrates the range of variation available.

The standards described for communication are largely developed by the communication or storage equipment manufacturers and major users of those devices. The standards cover a wide range of requirements and are updated every few years to support additional capabilities (e.g., lower power consumption, greater bandwidth and lower latency).

Google® Glass is an example of a mobile device that is designed to share its specialized input/output capabilities with other devices. It communicates with the user's cellphone to provide additional computing and networking capabilities.

Table 22-1: Networking/Storage Tradeoffs.

Communications	Latency	Bandwidth	Range	Power
NFC	100ms	100 Kbps – 400 Kbps	20 cm <	L
IrDA®	10 ms	115 Kbps – 4 Mbps	1 m	L
ZigBee®	30ms	250 Kbps	100 m	L
Bluetooth®	3 s	700 Kbps – 24 Mbps	10 m – 100 m	M
Wi-Fi®	3 s	144 Mbps	100 m	H
SMS	N/A	160 character / message	35 km	M
Digital Cellular	N/A	500 Kbps – 10 Mbps	35 km	VH
USB®	1 ms	1500 Kbps – 480 Mbps	Wired	M
SD®	N/A	2 MBps – 10 MBps*	Wired	M

* bps = bits per second. Bps = bytes per second. 8 bps = 1 Bps.

STANDARDS ABOVE THE NETWORK LAYER

Security and Privacy

Access to data being communicated from a mobile health device represents both a safety and a privacy concern. Most communication or storage described previously provide some encryption and access control capabilities, however, additional standards may also be applied. Many mobile devices are already uniquely identified, but that does not equate to identification of the user of that device.

The ITU-T X.509 standard for digital certificates supports identification of mobile equipment, people and organizations. Installing such a certificate on a mobile device enables the device or its user to be identified, and supports a mechanism by which access to the network resources can be controlled. Thus, in a healthcare environment, Wi-Fi networks can be secured and yet still enable mobile device access. Another growing trend alongside mobile health is the notion of bring your own device or BYOD, where these same standards can also be applied.

Digital certificates are also a critical component in Transport Layer Security (TLS), which serves to authenticate communicating end-points, and encrypt communications. While Triple-DES had previously been the most popular choice for encryption, the Advanced Encryption Standard (AES) is now the most commonly used standard.

Syntax

Simple mobile devices need support for just a few basic operations: read this chunk of data, write that chunk of data, and perform some command and control stuff (e.g., flush device data capture buffers). Few devices using PAN standards (in the upper half of Table 22-1) apply any sort of standard syntax to their data.

More complex devices will use one of a few standards describing the syntax of the communications. For most wireless devices, simpler is better. Traditional network syntaxes for machine-to-machine exchange include Advanced Syntax Notation 1 (ASN.1) (e.g., used for DNS), Hypertext Markup Language (HTML), Extensible

Markup Language (XML) and JavaScript Object Notation (JSON). XML has been the dominant standard for syntax for system-to-system communication, but JSON is rapidly gaining traction. I doubt you will find much in the way of ASN.1 being used to communicate mobile health data.

For machine-to-machine interchange, the choice between XML and JSON is simply a matter of preference, as they are equally capable. JSON and XML can be readily transformed back and forth, although there are some special issues that have to be addressed with special characters and rules in each. While XML parsing and manipulation capabilities are available for every development environment, JSON parsing and manipulation capabilities are built-in or nearly so in most of them.

When presentation to humans becomes a part of the communication, HTML 5, CSS and ECMAScript (commonly known as JavaScript) are also important standards in the mobile space. HTML 5 is especially relevant as it has better support for the variety found in mobile displays, and also supports image, audio and video data exchange using widely available standards. Many mobile applications rely heavily on HTML 5, as it provides a layer of device independence in the application, hiding variations between different mobile device operating systems.

Application Layer Standards

What is the most common application protocol used today? If you said Hypertext Transport Protocol (HTTP) you would be wrong. If you said e-mail or Simple Mail Transport Protocol (SMTP), you would be right. Worldwide, we send more e-mail a day than we view web pages on average. Having made that statement, it is much more likely that a mobile device will use HTTP rather than SMTP to communicate with other systems because communication using HTTP is much more dynamic and has a lower latency than e-mail exchange.[2]

At the application layer, there are three schools of thought on standard ways to exchange information. Only one of these is widely used in mobile applications. Traditional applications use the Simple Object Access Protocol (SOAP), with interfaces described in the Web Services Description Language, and objects represented using an XML Schema. Some applications skip the SOAP part and just exchange XML messages in an ad hoc way. And others use something called the Representational State Transfer paradigm (REST), which is not quite a standard but deserves some discussion.

REST is considered by many[3] to be a competitor to SOAP. The SOAP vs. REST debate went on for some time in the enterprise, with no real determined outcome, even today. But mobile devices changed the nature of the battle. SOAP, WSDL and XML Schema require software tools and libraries that are not as widely available on the mobile platform. Some very excellent open-source projects supported these standards in enterprise computing. But they did not survive the transition to mobile operating systems and platforms as well.

The tools still exist in the native development environments for mobile platforms, but they are not as mature, or well supported, or as easy to debug. Also, while those tools are supported in the native hardware platform, one could argue that the truly native platform for many mobile devices is the web: using HTML 5, CSS and

ECMAScript. SOAP, WDSL and XML Schema are not nearly as well supported in that environment.

REST is not a standard. It is more of an architectural style; I would go so far as to call it a manifesto. Key principles of the REST style are reuse of HTTP methods (PUT, GET, POST, DELETE) to support the basic Create, Read, Update and Delete operations (CRUD) on resources. A resource is something that is identified by a URL. A programming style developed that was consistent with REST is known as Asynchronous JavaScript and XML (AJAX). Programming using AJAX enabled application developers using native browser capabilities to use the XMLHttpRequest standard interface to dynamically request content using AJAX and JavaScript. The resulting XML was then transformed into HTML, which was dynamically inserted into the page. If you have ever seen a table or list of items expand dynamically when you scrolled to the end of it, you have probably seen AJAX in action. While some AJAX interactions used SOAP, most just used XML without any SOAP wrappers or complexity.

Early developers using AJAX realized that you could exchange not just XML, but also text, and more specifically text containing JavaScript code, which could dynamically update the screen. Of course dynamic code injection is a red flag to security experts, and that notion was almost killed, except that it made life very easy for developers. A better way to support similar capabilities was to define a safer set of operations, using only data declarations in JavaScript. These could not be used to inject malicious code into an application. Thus was JavaScript Object Notation (JSON) born. It became an Internet Engineering Task Force informational publication[4] RFC-4627 in 2006, and the mime type application/JSON was thereby created.

Within a RESTful framework and approach, other standards emerged to support user authentication and authorization. Authentication is the process by which a proof of identity is provided. The OpenID specification was created to enable web-based applications to work with a user-owned and third-party mediated identity credential (a login or user name). Another specification, OAuth was created to support user authorization, the process of granting access to a resource to another entity. If you use a smartphone and an application that accesses an online service like Twitter or Facebook, you have used OAuth. Recently the IETF released OAuth 2.0, which is in some ways more capable than the original OAuth, but also less well defined because it is a framework for authorization, rather than a single way to accomplish authorization.

EMERGING HEALTHCARE STANDARDS FOR MOBILE DEVICES

Over the past few years, many standards development organizations have been working toward a set of healthcare-specific standards supporting mobile access to data.

Mobile Access to Health Documents

In 2011, Integrating the Healthcare Enterprise (IHE) began development of a profile of existing standards called Mobile Access to Health Documents (MHD), which is currently in the trial implementation stage. This specification used a JSON representation for metadata, RESTful protocols and metadata describing patient documents already defined in the IHE Cross Enterprise Sharing of Documents (XDS) to create a simple way for mobile devices to access and create health data in a document format. The documents themselves could be exchanged in any standard format, but the most commonly expected formats would use standards like the Health Level Seven (HL7) Clinical Document Architecture Release 2.0 (CDA®), and would be based on other HL7 or IHE implementation guides on CDA, including the HL7 Continuity of Care Document (CCD®) or the more recently developed HL7 IHE/Health Story Consolidation Guide Release 1.1 (C-CDA).

The current draft is expected to be updated to use the HL7 Fast Healthcare Interoperability Resources (FHIR®) specification.

Automate the Blue Button Interface and BlueButton+
In 2012, the Office of the National Coordinator for Health IT (ONC) started a project in its Standards & Interoperability Framework (S&I) to develop a protocol to support patient mediated automated download or access to health records. This project was originally named the Automate the Blue Button Interface (ABBI), and has since been renamed to BlueButton+. The original Blue Button specification was developed by the U.S. Veterans Health Administration and based on a Markle Foundation specification. It enabled veterans to download their data as a text document. The newer specifications being developed by the ONC in the S&I Framework BlueButton+ project serve a similar purpose but with several additions.

1. The format of the downloadable content is based on nationally selected standards, including the HL7 CCD® and C-CDA specifications. Other formats can also be downloaded.
2. Users can authorize applications to access their data using OAuth 2.0.
3. The API used to enable downloading is based on the HL7 FHIR specifications from HL7.

At the time of writing this chapter, the BlueButton+ specifications have been published and are about to enter pilot testing.

FAST HEALTHCARE INTEROPERABILITY RESOURCES

In 2011, one of the members of HL7 spent several months developing a proposal for HL7 he initially called Resources for Health in response to an HL7 initiative to take a fresh look at itself and its offerings. Grahame Grieve offered this specification to HL7 contingent on it being freely available during and after the initial development process. HL7 agreed and adopted the work item, and that has now become what we now call FHIR® within HL7.

The specification is designed around the web, is RESTful, supports HTTP and defines a small number (presently 49) of well-defined information resources for Clinical, Administrative and Infrastructure resources which can be represented in both XML and JSON. Clinical resources include specifications for things like problems, medications and allergies, but also resources for medical devices and studies and observations. Administrative resources include people, places, things and workflows (e.g., orders) that must interact together. Infrastructure resources include basic utilities like lists, but also security resources like provenance and security events, resources supporting data exchange, and conformance testing.

A number of other organizations also have converged on FHIR in their use of standards. As described earlier, IHE is moving toward use of FHIR in the MHD profile, and BlueButton+ has adopted an early version of it. Digital Imaging and Communication in Medicine (DICOM) is also playing[5] with FHIR to support the next generation of digital imaging standards.

FHIR is not yet a standard, nor at the time of this writing even a standard in draft. It is expected by the time of this publication to be a draft standard from HL7. Already there are three reference implementations of FHIR, one in Java, another in .Net and a third in Groovy and Java.

PRIOR EFFORTS

FHIR would not be where it was today if it had not built upon existing efforts in HL7. Many of the resources defined in FHIR started with models developed from the HL7 CCD specification. RESTful patterns established in FHIR were well informed by the HL7 and OMG **hData** project. IHE's MHD efforts paralleled and later converged with FHIR, resulting in DocumentReference resources supporting compatibility with IHE's XDS family of specifications, developed and starting almost a decade ago (2005). And those specifications were informed by other specifications that had started development nearly a decade before that.

RESOURCES

- 3G *http://en.wikipedia.org/wiki/3G*.
- 4G *http://en.wikipedia.org/wiki/4G*.
- Bluetooth *www.bluetooth.com*.
- CDA *www.hl7.org/implement/standards/product_brief.cfm?product_id=7*.
- Continua Health Alliance *www.continuaalliance.org*.
- FHIR *www.hl7.org/fhir*.
- HL7 *www.hl7.org*.
- IHE *www.ihe.net*.
- MHD *http://wiki.ihe.net/index.php?title=MHD*.
- MHD *www.ihe.net/uploadedFiles/Documents/ITI/IHE_ITI_Suppl_MHD.pdf*.
- NFC *http://en.wikipedia.org/wiki/NFC*.
- SD *www.sdcard.org*.
- USB *www.usb.com*.
- USB *www.beyondlogic.org/usbnutshell/usb4.shtml*.
- XDS *www.ihe.net/Technical_Frameworks/#IT*.
- ZigBee How does ZigBee compare with other wireless standards? Software Technologies Group last retrieved at *www.stg.com/wireless/ZigBee_comp.html*.
- ZigBee *http://en.wikipedia.org/wiki/ZigBee*.
- ZigBee *http://zigbee.org*.

FOOTNOTES

1. Also variously known as ISO/IEC 18092 or ECMA-340 or NFCIP-1, and/or ISO/IEC 21481 or ECMA-352 or NFCIP-2.
2. Some readers may recall the days when e-mail sometimes took a day or two to be sent and received. Others may wish it wasn't yesterday.
3. Including this author.
4. Not a standard, but rather something for people to learn about. Few people really care about that distinction. If it starts with RFC, most believe it is a standard even though they REALLY SHOULD NOT (see RFC 6919).
5. There are a number of puns about FHIR, usually pronounced fire, but also fear and vier (German for four, a joke on HL7 Version 3 and FHIR).

Chapter 23

Mobile Security

By Jeffrey L. Brandt, BSCS, GC-BMI

There is an abundance of dialog available on the subject of mobile security. In this chapter, I hope to provide some meaningful insight into the latest technologies, along with strategic (plans and procedures) and tactical (things you can buy) ways to protect and secure your organization's systems. In addition, I have provided some "deeper dives" and information on mobile device management (MDM).

There have been numerous advancements in the understanding of security in mobile devices; however, with the accelerated rate of new devices and technologies being introduced to the market, CIOs and their staff are challenged to stay abreast. Devices like Glass, Google's new wearable computer, have the potential to be "always on," recording what caregivers, patients and visitors observe in real-time, introducing a entire new set of privacy, security and disclosure issues.

The consequences of the lack of security, policies and procedures can lead to extensive liability exposure, such as Office of Civil Rights (OCR) fines and reputational damage. Healthcare organizations have no choice but to remain diligent in securing their ePHI in their facilities and beyond.

The Security Rule defines technical safeguards in §164.304 as "the technology and the policy and procedures for its use that protect electronic protected health information and control access to it."[1] One of the most important aspects of privacy and security protection is an organization's policy, procedures and training, although I do not plan to cover this topic in depth; I will refer you to the mHIMSS Roadmap, which covers the security framework.[2]

NEW TECHNOLOGY

There are many innovations, products and companies that can assist organizations in achieving their tactical security objectives. One innovation is the concept of a memory "container," a logical, separated area that safeguards an organization's data, including PHI on a user's device. Containers separate PHI from the user's personal data, such as pictures, apps, e-mail and text messages.[3] Another innovation, which I was fortunate to see in a pre-release demo, is the use of a Virtual Machine (VM) to isolate BYOD data from the user's personal data. A VM is a logical container housing its own OS and accessible memory. An MDM controls the VM and the apps residing in the VM container within the device. In the event that the phone is compromised or removed from service, the MDM can remove the VM from the phone, leaving no trace of organizational data, including PHI on the device, without affecting the user's personal data or device operation. This is a huge advancement in information protection and BYOD management. This demo product is scheduled to be released in the near future.

Big data has the potential to save lives and reduce healthcare costs; however, it also may expose additional patient and employee privacy concerns. A study by iMedica predicts that 1.8 million people worldwide will be remotely monitored by 2017.[4] Policies and procedures must be developed to monitor the use, protection and sharing of this data. The FDA released their Draft Guidance of Management of Cyber Security in Medical Devices (510k) on June 14, 2013.

SMARTPHONE MEDICAL DEVICES

Smartphones and their apps are becoming the "human hub" for personal digital health data. That is, the common connected human data aggregation device. There are thousands of healthcare apps on the market today, however, only a few of those apps are connected. Without connecting to the EHR or fitting into the workflow of the caregiver, they provide little overall value.

AliveCor's ECG app and iPhone hardware recently received its FDA 510k,[5] making the iPhone itself a significant component of the medical device, rather than just a tool or accessory. Most smartphone medical apps available today only transmit and display patient data, requiring a lower classification, Medical Device Data System (MDDS) Class 1.[6]

Many believe that smartphones incur numerous new issues of security. Smartphones are essentially mini, mobile, connected computers, similar to laptops with many of the same vulnerabilities. As with laptops, smartphones have operating systems, memory and Bluetooth Wi-Fi connected capabilities. The vulnerabilities are somewhat the same, where loss, concealment and access to networks are the biggest threats. Most of the same precautions organizations take with laptops should be extended to smartphones.

APPS

Privacy Rights Clearinghouse (PRC) studied 43 popular health apps. Nearly 72 percent of the apps presented as medium to high risk with regard to personal privacy. According to the PRC, free apps were the most likely to collect and sell personal data.[7] Common sense should be enough to realize that it's rare to get something for free; normally there is a catch. Companies cannot exist on a "for free" business model. Organizations and healthcare providers must perform their due diligence when selecting smartphone apps for their patients and providers.

It is a known issue that caregivers use non-HIPAA compliant phone apps such as camera/photo and text messaging to store and share PHI. This practice exposes the caregiver and their organization to liabilities, regulatory sanctions and fines. Oregon Health Science University Medical School was sanctioned in July 2013; doctors were using Google Drive apps for storing PHI. Google Drive may be secure for personal use, but it is not HIPAA compliant. Organizations may want to consider monitoring the app that resides on the provider's phone, as well as provide an approved app "white list" from which their employees can select. App monitoring can be facilitated via MDM software. Another thing to note about remote storage solutions such as Google Drive, is that it can be accessed via a webapp through the browser on the phone without having a mobile app installed. The term "app" is overused, however it is prudent to understand the difference, as well as educate your users. The obligation of securing PHI within an app or webapp is viewed the same.

My rule of thumb for using a clinical healthcare app/web app that houses PHI: If the vendor is not willing to sign a Business Associates Agreement (BAA/BA) with a Covered Entity (CE) or a Vendor of a CE, the app is most likely not HIPAA compliant.

REGULATORY

The Omnibus ruling went into effect September 23, 2013, and calls for all vendors of CE to have BAAs in place. Vendors that supply products and services to a CE must also have their vendors sign BAs. That is, if a CE wishes to purchase a software solution, such as Cloud storage, the vendor of that solution must also sign the CE's BA. If the Cloud storage company contracts out some of their solution, they must have a BA in place with that contracted company. The law was enacted to help protect the patients, providers and organizations by providing a chain of responsibility.

DEVICE MANAGEMENT & ORGANIZATIONAL READINESS

The wireless mobile medical device market is predicted to explode in size. NERAC predicts that the remote monitoring market alone will reach $5.1 billion by 2013 and that greater than 160 million Americans will be remotely monitored and treated by 2020.[8] My health insurance payer, Anthem Blue Cross, recently provided an option to access a doctor via telemedicine rather than utilizing face-to-face visits.

Health IT must take appropriate steps now to be prepared for the onslaught of devices entering the health domain. Leaders must have strategic and tactical plans in place to manage these devices, as well as the processes to update existing plans as new devices are introduced to the market.

The variety and quantity of wireless devices has quickly expanded over the past few years. Some examples at the time of the writing of this book are cellphones, pads, tablets, phablets, bio-sensors, wearable computers (Google Glass), connected watches and supporting RF (radio frequencies) (e.g., Medical Area Body Networks (MBANs), RFID devices, Near Field Communication (NFC), Bluetooth, Bluetooth-2 and Wi-Fi). We should also consider the magnitude of data these devices will produce, interference they may cause and the associated security issues.

Though we look to technical solutions to provide security, the formulation of internal policies, procedures, education and training is the first line of defense and provide the overall framework of protection.

Technical solutions play an integral part in supporting the organization's security policies and procedures. Specialty trained staff add to the cost of supporting these solutions and must be a part of the organization's security budget.

PROTECTING YOUR ORGANIZATION

Numerous high-capacity devices (CPU and memory) are being introduced every month, further escalating security concerns. These mobile devices empower organizations to extend their networks to almost anywhere. This reach introduces additional exposure and responsibility to protect your networks beyond the physical walls. There is also growing pressure to support BYOD on your networks, thus increasing the challenge of control in the extended virtual environment. This section provides guidelines to assist with protecting your organization, as well as reducing liability both now and in the future.

Risk Management

To summarize risk management, it is the action of managing risk through understanding the threat, identification, containment and control. Risk management is formally defined and documented in the ISO 3100 family of standards. The *National Institute of Standards and Technology* (NIST) provides a framework, as illustrated in Fig. 23-1:

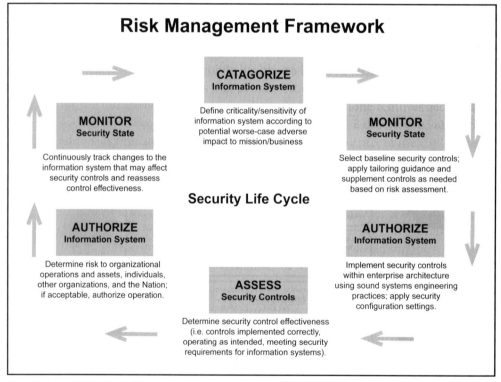

Fig. 23-1: NIST Risk Management Framework[9]
(Source: National Institute of Standards and Technology. Used with permission.)

Risk Assessment

A risk assessment encompasses much more than a set of rules and guidelines. It is the actual effort of performing the process that provides a true assessment, explains John Moehrke, Principle Engineer at GE. Moehrke's blog provides an excellent overview of risk assessments.[10]

A formal risk assessment may be one of the most valuable tools to adopt for protecting your organization. The assessment should be performed first as part of your strategic plan. (See Fig. 23-2).

There is a lot of information available on the Internet about this subject, so I will not duplicate the effort in this chapter. The GAO provides very good fundamental information on their web site.[11]

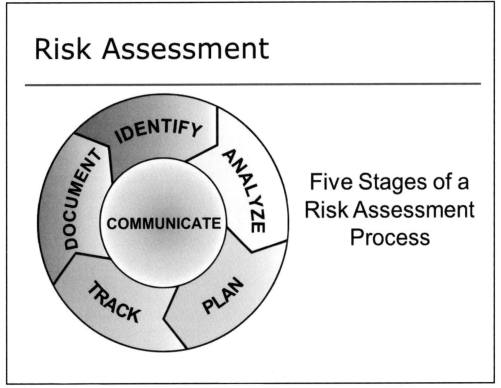

Fig. 23-2: HL7™ Risk Assessment.[2]

DISCOVERING MOBILE DEVICES WITHIN YOUR ORGANIZATION

Knowing who or what is on your network is a necessary component of protecting your organization. Commercial products like Cisco's Identity Services Engine (ISE) offers self-registration to eliminate the need for employees or guests having to interact directly with an IT member to gain network access. These types of systems can also provide required audit functionality.

Detection
Wireless Intrusion/Detection and Prevention (WIDS/WIPS) radio frequency monitoring devices "listen" for unauthorized attempts to infiltrate a system. Once intrusion is detected and identified (e.g., Man-in-the-Middle), preventions and countermeasures can be launched to halt the threats.[12] Commercial WIDS/WIPS monitoring systems are available.

Protection Software Solutions

There are numerous commercial solutions on the market today to help to protect devices and organizations. The following examples should be considered as part of your overall security strategy:

- Anti-malware
- Anti-virus
- Remote wiping — data removal
- Disk encryption
- Geo-location
- Device inventory

Resource Monitoring

Resources monitoring, such as bandwidth utilization, will provide a window into your RF (wireless) network. Bottlenecks, unauthorized use and attacks can be pre-empted with monitoring. Organizations should consider viewing bandwidth as a cost center commodity. As part of your plan, you may want to track usage and precedence, that is, the prioritizing of employees and guests considering their access needs, bandwidth and priority. Pre-emption methodology may also need to be considered depending on your facilities mandate. Consider developing policies governing these issues and facilitate for both hardware and software.

Authentication

Authentication is the process utilized to identify the user or device that is requesting access to your network. User authentication is when you attempt to validate the person that is trying to access your network. Device authentication is the act of identifying the device that is attempting to access your network. Cellphones have multiple IDs, including the phone number that uniquely identifies the hardware; however, these IDs can be compromised.[13] Strong authentication utilizes combinations of both the user and device authentication.[14] There are numerous authentication schemes, from simple pattern recognition to biometrics. Management must analyze which solution is best for their organization and make it part of its policies and procedures.

The following is a list of commonly used (not extensive) authentication strategies:

- UserID and password
- Certificate
- Digital ID
- Tokens
- Software on Device Authentication (SODA)
- Two-factor
- Bio-metric
- Proximity
- Three-legged, e.g., OAuth

Physical Security

Most data breaches are facilitated by what I like to call "SneakerTheft," that is, unsecured devices with patients' PHI just walking out the door. Massachusetts Eye and Ear Associates were recently fined the maximum, $1.5 million, by the HHS Office of Civil

Rights following the theft of an unencrypted laptop in 2010. Again, policies, procedures and training are the best defense to combat this type of breach. A risk assessment should have established a simple requirement for disk encryption or remote disk wiping that would have prevented this exposure of e-PHI and $1.5 million in fines.

MOBILE RF TAG DEVICES

Radio Frequency Identification (RFID)

Radio Frequency Identification tags have the potential to address many authentication issues in healthcare. RFID chips provide a short-range (<40 feet, passive, backscatter) ID signature that may effectively operate outside of the line-of-sight and without an internal battery. The second style, know as active tags, utilizes internal batteries to provide longer range of up to 300 feet and may have up to 65KB of memory.[15] Healthcare currently uses this technology primarily as an electronic inventory control tag (e.g., positive ID of a patient, drug, equipment and tissue samples). Yet there is the potential for additional uses related to benefits in patient care (e.g., remote patient temperature monitoring). There has also been research on the subcutaneous use of RFID to identify patients, including babies. This use-case has already run into roadblocks of opposition.

A main concern of using RFID is security and privacy. If used incorrectly or for the wrong application, there are associated risks. Active RFID tags can be read from up to 100 meters. Hawrylak, et al. wrote that threats include the interception, interruption, modification, as well as the fabrication of RFID signals. They also mentioned that the "major barriers to adoption include technological limitations, interference concerns, prohibitive costs, lack of global standards and privacy concerns."[16]

Near-Field Communication

NFC-enabled (Near-Field Communication, ISO 18092) smartphones and credit cards have introduced NFC to the mainstream via mobile payments. NFC, unlike RFID, is for very close proximity (~ 5-10cm) applications, hence reducing privacy and security exposure issues. NFC devices equipped with Secure Element (SEC) chips (NFCIP-1)[17] facilitate secure communication between them. For example, the new payment option where no swipe of the credit card is necessary to charge, simply a wave of the card or smartphone near the receiver; this technology was first introduced at gas stations and coffee shops. NFC could provide numerous time- and cost-saving opportunities in healthcare. Bio-sensors may communicate via NFC-initiated ad hoc networks, providing enhanced security for transporting data and reducing the opportunity for interference.

As with most technologies, there are drawbacks and as with RFID, security and privacy are also a concern of NFC. Some of the known threats are as follows:
- Eavesdropping (less than RFID because of proximity)
- Interference data corruption
- Intentional data modification
- Data insertion
- Man-in-the-Middle attacks
- Unauthorized use

Haselsteiner & Breitfuss noted in their paper that there are easy solutions for these security issues; it has been mentioned here to make the reader aware of these problems.[18]

The take-away here is to ensure that your organization's NFC devices and solutions used as a HIPAA-covered solution are NFC-SEC equipped.

Smartphones

Smartphones such as Android (available from some manufactures), iPhone (equipped with third-party hardware) and others utilize both NFC and RFID, along with their standard communication of voice, data and geo-location. NFC-enabled smartphones have the ability to collect NFC and RFID data via apps that then forward the information via the phone's data connection. By adding a NFC/RFID tag to a phone, the phone itself can be identified and tracked.

The following is a list of cellphone threats, provided by NIST.[19]
- Their size and portability.
- Their available wireless interfaces and associated services.
- Loss, theft or disposal.
- Unauthorized access.
- Malware.
- Spam.
- Electronic eavesdropping.
- Electronic tracking.
- Cloning.
- Server-resident data.

There is a new sector of smartphone apps that are being marketed to providers as clinical mobile solutions. These apps provide technology at the point-of-care that was not possible until recently.

The caveat is that anyone with little or even no programming knowledge and no healthcare experience can build and distribute so-called healthcare apps. To date, there is little governance of these apps. The FDA and FCC have started to take on the responsibility of regulating apps, however, they have little demonstrable influence or enforcement capabilities to date. Basically, it is the "Wild West" out there, where almost anything goes. According to Research2Guidance, there were more than 40,000 health and fitness apps on the market in 2012.[20] Let's say that most of these "health" apps have the best-intended efficacy and goodwill. The question is, how do you protect your organization against rogue, unsecure or malicious apps? Organizations such as HIMSS, HL7, IHE, ONC, HHS, private groups such as Continua Health Alliance, and for-profit companies like Happtique, are publishing documents to help standardize and regulate app security.

Securing a smartphone app takes the knowledge of a skilled software engineer who's given the appropriate requirements and resources to make sure that the data on the phone and the transmission of the data is secure. Apps that are not designed correctly may unknowingly expose PHI. Unsecure databases and cache memory on smartphones can be compromised. Developers that utilize Secure Digital (SD) to store data expose PHI to multiple vulnerabilities unless proper precautions are taken.

Apps utilized in your organization should be approved before an employee is permitted to download. Corporations may want to consider utilizing a "white list" of permitted apps for employees (i.e., a list of approved apps). Android phones have the facility to download apps from any server. This capability has pros and cons, and each app should be risk assessed. Healthcare facilities could host a site that offers approved apps for employee downloads. A must-have policy is that employees should never download an app from a non-approved site. Non-official and unknown site downloads is one of the easiest ways to infiltrate your network via a Trojan Horse. Companies such as Happtique, the maker of boutique app stores for healthcare facilities, help organizations distribute approved apps.

BYOD

Bring Your Own Devices (BYOD) may be a new acronym, however, it is not a new concept. Workers have been bringing their laptops and MP3 music devices to work and accessing corporate networks for many years. The significant difference today is the number of devices that have the capability to access the network, the high capacity of storage on hand-held devices, and the ability to rapidly copy data. It is not uncommon for workers to carry multiple devices that have the ability to access networks, e.g., a physician may have a BYOD iPad (PadTab), and a laptop and one, maybe two, smartphones (one corp. owned, one personal BYOD). In addition, that physician may also have an electronic stethoscope, spectrometer, thermometer and blood pressure cuff, all with the ability to access a wireless network. Some devices are company provided and some are employee purchased. This results in the need for additional infrastructure to manage and support the additional bandwidth and IP endpoints. These commodities utilize real budget dollars, so we must take these costs into consideration and manage them as resources.

There is also guest BYOD, consisting of visiting providers, temporary employees, contractors, or now more than ever, patients and their families. They all expect access to the Internet via your network. This leads to even more resource management and you are now compelled to allow non-trusted users to access your network.

Management of these devices and additional users is a challenge to health IT departments. Many of your IT staff may be deficient in needed skills and will need additional training or staff augmentation. We must remember that only a few years ago, a majority of health IT work consisted of supporting wired desktop PCs and telecommunication systems. We will revisit this discussion later in the chapter.

Additional traffic can put a strain on the network infrastructure (e.g., streaming video music, pictures). Organizations may want to consider limiting the number of devices that can have access to the network at a given time or limit the available bandwidth allocated for guests.

If your organization does not have a plan and budget for BYOD, it is time to start. The following is a list of items to consider:

Access and Authorization:
- **Who.** Who to allow on the network.

- **What.** Which devices to allow on the network. This will be a moving target as new devices are introduced. What apps will have access to the network — this will also become an ongoing task.
- **Where.** What is the boundary and reaching arm of remote networks, e.g., can providers reach the network from remote sites on their own devices? How powerful is the Wi-Fi signal and how far away from the building can it be accessed?
- **When.** Consider time of day usage-per-user profile, e.g., HR Department has access from 9 a.m.-6 p.m. only.
- **How Many.** Connections have real costs associated with them, such as support and bandwidth. Organizations need a plan to limit the number of guest users on their networks and permitted usage, e.g., streaming music, video, etc.

Part of your policies on BYOD are the "terms and conditions" (T&C) of use. Users should acknowledge these legal agreements when accessing the network. T&C must be tailored to fit each organization. Policies must strike a compromise among users, guests and the organization's health IT security. Roger Baker, VA CIO states, "There are a variety of things that 95 percent of the population will say 'that doesn't bother me at all,' and 5 percent will say, 'No, you're not going to do that with my device,' that clear communication is necessary to keep everyone in the loop on expectations."[21]

Mitigating Risk (Defense)

"Information security typically suffers due to a lack of serious commitment by an organization," states author Eric Hansen.[22] Hansen is referring to organizational guidelines and agreements for governing security in your organization, a structured proactive approach to security.

Mitigation of risk is the act of reducing risk, which helps provide security. In the process of reducing or avoiding risk, we must be cognizant that we do not impede staff in performing their duties. Though there is always a trade-off between productivity and security, with planning, an organization can implement precautionary policies and enforcements while striving to create balance.

Pennock and Haimes of the Center for Risk Management of Engineering Systems state that three key questions can be posed for risk mitigation[23]:
- What can be done and what options are available?
- What are the tradeoffs in terms of all costs, benefits and risks among the available options?
- What are the impacts of current decisions on future options?

Policies

This chapter is about security, but I cannot emphasize enough that corporate policies and procedures are the best forms of defense to protect your organization, employees and patients. The next is the use of defensive software and the deployment of Mobile Device Management (MDM) for both company owned devices and BYOD.

Some of the policies that should be considered are the following:
- Employees and guest access and policies.
- Policies presented to guests each time they get access along with an e-signature T&C.
- Restrict access of "jailbroke" or rooted phone to the network.

- Downloading of MDM to all devices that access the network.
- All phones must have remote wiping software installed.
- Electronic inventory of devices.
- Encrypt all HIPAA-covered data stored on device and during transmission.
- Password policies.
- Secure Wi-Fi.
- Only use smartphone apps that are known to be secure if PHI or other valuable data is stored or transmitted on them.
- Utilize a "white list" for apps.
- Protect devices from Malware and viruses .
- Require passcodes.
- Blacklist passwords (http://dazzlepod.com/rootkit).
- Efficient termination procedures.
- Budget.
- Training.
- Consider allowing only approved apps to be downloaded to corporate-owned devices.

Testing

You really don't know if your organization or devices are secure and compliant until you test, test and re-test. Jonathan Hassell, a security consultant, wrote that wireless networks are a "Virtual Port" into your network and that the boundary is only limited by the signal strength of your wireless routers. That is, your network can be accessed from outside of your building and perimeter of physical control.[24]

Testing needs to be an integral part of any organization's security team's processes and strategy to protect. Acceptance testing should be part of all new software installation and upgrade procedures. Many times I've heard people in healthcare preaching that security is a must, but talking about it is one thing, and proving the SLA (Service Level Agreements) or testing to insure compliance is another. Vendors often flaunt their systems' security features at trade shows, in glossy brochures and with flashy presentations, but how do you know that what they tell you is true? The answer is only found through your own due diligence, acceptance test plans and actual testing. Make sure the level of security promised is in the SLA, then test to make sure it complies.

The National Institute of Standards and Technology (NIST) provides a list of security levels for evaluation and policies. Program Review for Information Security Management (PRISMA):

- IT Security Maturity Level 1: Policies.
- IT Security Maturity Level 2: Procedures.
- IT Security Maturity Level 3: Implementation.
- IT Security Maturity Level 4: Test.
- IT Security Maturity Level 5: Integration.

Penetration Testing

Penetration testing is a simulation of an attack on your network to exploit and locate vulnerabilities. It also provides a facility the opportunity to test internal staff on their ability to react to an attack. There are commercial companies that specialize in this type of testing, however, larger facilities may consider purchasing software to perform this testing in-house, or develop a separate testing team.

Incident Response

A security incident response is defined by Eric Sinclair, CISSP, "as the ability to detect and resolve problems that threaten people, process, technology and facilities."[25] If a breach does occur to a "covered entity" under HIPAA and you determine PHI is at risk, it is required by the HITECH Act that you report the incident.[26] A HIPAA Covered Entity should have an incident response plan in place so it can quickly provide protection for your organization and patients. Author Robin Ruefle recommends that organizations have a computer security incident response team (CSIRT) in place to coordinate and support a response in the event that an incident occurs. CSIRT are responsible for providing response, guidance and recovery for organizations.[27]

The following agencies provide information for building your incident response plan:
- NSA
- Department of Homeland Security
- NIST
- US-CERT

Tools to Protect Devices

There are numerous commercial and open-source tools available to protect e-PHI, sensitive data, devices and networks. This is only part of the equation when building a plan for protection. First and foremost you have to have management in place that understands security and the laws that protect patients' records. As part of your plan you must determine if you have the needed skills on staff or if you need to recruit outside of your organization. You may also consider a new position, CSO (Chief Security Officer), someone who is outside of your health IT organization. You must have trained staff that understands what you are trying to protect, and the skills to ensure that the tools to protect are being used correctly. Many health IT staff were installing and supporting desktop applications only a few years ago. Much has changed in that time period as health IT moves from the desktop world to enterprise and now to mobile. Support of these systems requires completely different skills. Determine if you have the skills in-house to support mobile in the enterprise. Your plan must survey and evaluate your staff's skills and determine if additional training or augmentation is needed. The DoD's Information Assurance Workforce Improvement Program is a good reference for skill level assessment, training and management of workforce providing Information Assurance.[28]

Following is a list of protective and defensive software technology:
- Mobile Device Management (MDM) technology.
- Mobile Application Management (MAM).
- Remote data wiping.
- Tracking software.
- Anti-virus.
- VPN.

There are also open-source projects that can help with your security needs, such as The Open Web Application Security Project (OWASP), a not-for-profit organization whose mission is to reduce security risk. Their web site is a good source for additional information on security.

Encryption

HHS specifies encryption and destruction as the technologies and methodologies that render PHI unusable, unreadable or indecipherable to unauthorized individuals.

HHS states that, "We emphasize that this guidance does nothing to modify a covered entity's responsibilities with respect to the HIPAA Security Rule, nor does it impose any new requirements on CEs to encrypt all protected health information. The Security Rule requires Covered Entities to safeguard electronic protected health information and permits Covered Entities to use any security measures that allow them to reasonably and appropriately implement all safeguard requirements."[29]

AES-256 encryption, the Federal Information Processing Standards (FIPS), is viewed as the strongest encryption available today. Even the strongest encryption does not mean that it cannot be broken; however, it does ensure an infiltrator will not have the computing power and time to break it. According to EE-times, a brute-force attack on an AES-128 key would take 1.01×10^{18}, or 1 billion years, to crack with the computer. Mohit Arora states in his article, "AES has never been cracked yet and is safe against any brute force attacks contrary to belief and arguments. However, the key size used for encryption should always be large enough that it could not be cracked by modern computers despite considerable advance in processor speeds based on Moore's Law."[30]

Utilizing AES with a key larger than 64 cannot be used in exported products from the United States. When evaluating products you may want to check what size key is being used.

Apple implemented a new key strategy for the iPhone encryption around AES. They burn (imprinted) the AES keys into the silicon (chip) so that developer can better protect app data. This is a great advancement that hopefully is open to being utilized by other manufactures.

Secure Socket Layer (SSL)

SSL is a point-to-point protocol to protect data during transmission or "in-flight" over the web. It is based on public and private key exchange. Note: this provides no security at the endpoints. That is, once the data is received, SSL provides no additional protection of the data. The data would then need to be encrypted before storing or "at-rest."

Tracking

Commercial tools are available to track the 3-Ws, "Who" "What" and "Where," a part of an authorization strategy for monitoring your system. Your risk assessment should include the 3-Ws. (e.g, restrict guests with smartphones in sensitive areas).

There are tools available for placing a virtual electronic fence around your facility. Guests must receive authorization before their phones will operate within the perimeter.

Physical Security

Physical security is another best practice to secure data and devices. Remember, PHI and devices do just walk out the door. This is where policies, procedures and common sense play an important role. Here is a non-extensive list of physical security best practices to consider:

- Password protect every device.
- Never leave a device unattended.
- Place your contact information on the phone.
- Utilize location software.
- Utilize physical locks and cables.
- Keep software up to date.
- Utilize surveillance.
- Devise a disposal protocol of retired devices.
- Consider utilizing an inventory tracking system.
- Cable lock laptops to desks.
- Take caution in public places, be aware of your surroundings and protect your device(s).

Identity Management

"The combination of trusted identity and complete audit trails is key to a multi-layered defense against privacy breeches," said John Halamka, MD.[31] In essence, the problem is that "on the Internet, nobody knows you're a dog," stated by Anonymous. How do we know who is using your assets if you cannot identify them? Most systems utilize userID and password to authenticate the user. However, passwords can be easily compromised if the users, systems, or policies and procedures do not manage them correctly. The DEA demands NIST Assurance Level 3 (High Confidence, cryptographic token and one-use passwords) for e-prescribing controlled substances.[32] There are commercial products available that provide identity management enterprise solutions.

Halamka also says that "A key component of enforcing security policy is ensuring the identity of those who use applications." Halamka also mentioned in his blog that his vote would be to achieve NIST Level 3.[33]

Policy Enforcement and Monitoring

Policies without monitoring or enforcement can lead to more risks than no policies at all. Employees and guests must understand the importance and priority of an organization's policies and the consequences for disobeying them. Organizations should develop well-thought-out policies and fair discipline for those who do not comply or are inconsistent in enforcement.

DHL Express' Karimi states, "We secure networks; however, in the average bin of the photocopying room there are many company secrets waiting to be picked up." So last but not least, be aware of the little stuff, the unlocked PC or the unaccountable thumb drive, that can expose your organization to a serious breach in security.

CONCLUSION

Security is based on a trust relationship with the users, vendors and endpoints. "*Trust is an essential element in the doctor-patient relationship,*" states Dr. Kevin Pho. It is also an essential element of the organization and employee relationship, a building block of the security plan.

For those of us responsible for guarding and ensuring patient trust, we must extend the responsibility of protecting patient PHI. Additionally, health IT should share the same personal responsibility as providers, ensuring that the enclave of patient trust remains secure.

The one takeaway I hope you get from this chapter: If a patient's PHI is compromised, you, your organization and the patient may experience irreparable damage. My suggestion is to focus on your policies and procedures as well as challenge your staff to share in the responsibility of protecting the patient's PHI.

REFERENCES

1. HHS. HHS Security Series Security Standards: Technical Safeguards. [On the Internet.] www.hhs.gov/ocr/privacy/hipaa/administrative/securityrule/techsafeguards.pdf. Accessed August 9, 2013.
2. mHIMSS.org mHIMSS Roadmap. [On the Internet] www.himss.org/ResourceLibrary/mHIMSS.aspx. Accessed August 15, 2013.
3. Messmer E. *Containerization is no BYOD panacea:Gartner.* Network World.
4. Mearian L. In-home health monitoring to leap six-fold by 2017. [On the Internet] Computer World www.computerworld.com/s/article/9236026/In_home_health_monitoring_to_leap_six_fold_by_2017. Accessed August 23, 2013.
5. FDA, 510k approval. [On the Internet] http://google2.fda.gov/search?requiredfields=-archive%3AYes&q=+AliveCor&client=FDAgov&lr=&proxystylesheet=FDAgov&output=xml_no_dtd&getfields=*&sort=date%3AD%3AL%3Ad1&entqr=3&entqrm=0&oe=UTF-8&ie=UTF-8&ud=1&site=FDAgov&btnG=Search. Accessed August 5, 2013.
6. FDA. Medical Device Data Systems > MDDS Rule. [On the Internet] www.fda.gov/MedicalDevices/ProductsandMedicalProcedures/GeneralHospitalDevicesandSupplies/MedicalDeviceDataSystems/ucm251897.htm. Accessed August 5, 2013.
7. Njie L, Craig M. Technical Analysis of the Data Practices and Privacy Risks of 43 Popular Mobile Health and Fitness Applications. [On the Internet] www.privacyrights.org/mobile-medical-apps-privacy-technologist-research-report.pdf. Accessed September 8, 2013.
8. NERAC. Wireless Medical Devices: Security Issues, Market Opportunities and Growth Trends. [On the Internet] www.nerac.com/nerac_insights.php?category=articles&id=181. Accessed August 25, 2013.
9. National Institute of Standards and Technology. Risk Management Framework. Computer Security Division. Information Technology. Accessed September 24, 2012.
10. Moehrke J. Healthcare Security/Privacy Blog. http://healthcaresecprivacy.blogspot.com/2012/03/how-to-apply-risk-assessment-to-get.html. Accessed September 18, 2013.
11. GAO. [Webpage]. www.gao.gov/special.pubs/ai00033.pdf. Accessed September 5, 2013.
12. Wikipedia. [Web page]. http://en.wikipedia.org/wiki/Wireless_intrusion_prevention_system. Accessed September 26, 2012.
13. TIA [Web page]. www.tiaonline.org/standards/numbering-resources/electronic-serial-numbers-esn-and-meid. Accessed September 27, 2012.

14. Intel Corp. *Network Access Control: User and Device Authentication.* 2005. [On the Internet] http://cache-www.intel.com/cd/00/00/26/07/260786_260786.pdf. Accessed September 27, 2012.

15. The Summary of RFID Standards. RFID Journal. [On the Internet] www.rfidjournal.com/article/view/1335/1. Accessed September 23, 2012.

16. Wamba, S. F. RFID-enabled healthcare: applications, issues and benefits, *Journal of Medical Systems*, 2011.

17. Standard ECMA-340 2nd addition. 12/04. [On the Internet] www.ecma-international.org/publications/standards/Ecma-340.htm. Accessed September 24, 2012.

18. Haselsteiner E, Breitfuss K. Security in Near Field Communication (NFC), Philips Semiconductors. [On the Internet] www.google.com/url?sa=t&rct=j&q=&esrc=s&source=web&cd=1&ved=0CCIQFjAA&url=http%3A%2F%2Fevents.iaik.tugraz.at%2FRFIDSec06%2FProgram%2Fpapers%2F002%2520%2520Security%2520in%2520NFC.pdf&ei=hek8UN_dOMqq8AGVs4GwCw&usg=AFQjCNHZReSQSfeAF_CEuyITPDLSf2ZRQ&sig2=QtfZH83k8FS6mczZO_EWxw. Accessed August 28, 2012.

19. Jansen W, Scarfone K. *Guidelines on Cell Phone and PDA Security*, NIST US Dept. of Commerce. Publication 800-124.

20. Cohn M, Hopkins researchers aim to uncover which mobile health applications work. *The Baltimore Sun.* [On the Internet] http://articles.baltimoresun.com/2012-03-14/health/bs-hs-mobile-health-apps-20120314_1_health-apps-mhealth-mobile-health. Accessed September 24, 2012.

21. Mosquera, M. VA moves to protect mobile devices for employees., HealthcareIT News. [On the Internet] www.healthcareitnews.com/news/va-moves-protect-mobile-devices-employees?topic=16,29,18,19. Accessed September 28, 2012.

22. Hansen E. Internal SLA (Service Level Agreements) for Information Security GSEC_Practical_version 1.2F, 2001. www.sans.org/reading_room/whitepapers/standards/internal-sla-service-level-agreements-information-security_548. Accessed August 28, 2012.

23. Pennock M, and Haimes Y. Principles and Guidelines for Project Risk Management. *Systems Engineering.* 2001;5(2), 89-108.

24. Hassell J. Wireless Attacks and Penetration Testing. *Semantic Communit.* Nov 2010; 02. [On the Internet] www.symantec.com/connect/articles/wireless-attacks-and-penetration-testing-part-1-3. Accessed September 23, 2012.

25. Sinclair E. Security Incident Response, United Governmental Services, LLC, [On the Internet] www.hipaacow.org/events/SecurityIncidentResponse.ppt. Accessed August 22, 2012.

26. *HITECH Breach Notification Interim Final Rule,* HHS. [On the Internet]. www.hhs.gov/ocr/privacy/hipaa/understanding/coveredentities/breachnotificationifr.html. Accessed August 2009.

27. Ruefle R. Defining Computer Security Incident Response Teams, Carnegie Mellon University. 2007-01-24; Revised 2008-08-20.

28. *Information Assurance Workforce Improvement Program.* DOD. December 19, 2005. Revised January 24, 2012. www.dtic.mil/whs/directives/corres/pdf/857001m.pdf. Accessed August 23, 2012.

29. *Breach Notification for Unsecured Protected Health Information,* Department of Health & Human Services. 45 CFR Parts 160 and 164 RIN 0991–AB56.

30. Arora M. How secure is AES against a brute force attack? May 7, 2012. www.eetimes.com/design/embedded-internet-design/4372428/How-secure-is-AES-against-brute-force-attacks-. Accessed August 29, 2012.

31. Halamka J. Life as a Healthcare CIO. [On the Internet] http://geekdoctor.blogspot.com/2009/12/strong-identity-management.html. Accessed September 23, 2012.

32. Dept. of Justice. Electronic prescription application requirements. 1311.120, [On the Internet] www.deadiversion.usdoj.gov/21cfr/cfr/1311/subpart_c100.htm. Accessed August 29, 2012.

33. Halamka J. Strong Identity Management. Written December 2, 2009. http://geekdoctor.blogspot.com/2009/12/strong-identity-management.html. Accessed August 29, 2012.

CHAPTER 24

Approaches to Policy: Organizational and Regulatory Perspectives in Mobile Health

By Thomas Martin and Robert Jarrin

U.S. policy and regulations surrounding the use of wireless innovative technologies in healthcare continues to lag behind the pace of innovation. This chapter presents two distinct approaches to policy and policy making. The first approach outlines major regulatory policy issues and trends at the time of writing. These trends are both regulatory and legislative in nature, and we discuss how they impact the role of mHealth in our national healthcare system. The second approach is to provide organizational-level solutions that aid, mitigate or outline industry trends among vendors and healthcare providers involved with mHealth technology. This organizational approach is intended to provide examples of approaches to compliance with the regulatory structure.

With a vast array of mobile solutions available for deployment and the increasing convergence of medicine with communications technologies, no one example can encompass all of the nuances of any specific approach or organization. Rather, the goal here is to aid and inform on the topic rather than dictate specific solutions or recommendations.

REGULATORY AND LEGISLATIVE ACTIVITIES IMPACTING mHEALTH

HIMSS Public Policy Principles

Starting in 2013, a number of public policy principles focused on the role of mobile technology were added to the existing HIMSS Public Policy Principles. These principles are Board-approved and provide a platform for the organization to assess its stance and alignment when newly proposed legislation is introduced. The Public Policy Principles were introduced by HIMSS and mHIMSS to provide a brief introduction of important issues and trends in the health information management industry. In this section the most current principles are stated with observed trends and supplemental information provided for the reader. The entire list of Public Policy Principles can be found on the HIMSS web site at www.himss.org.

Mobile Public Policy Principles from HIMSS

13.2: Integrate mobile technologies into the design and deployment of healthcare information technology systems to leverage current and future incentives associated with the Office of the National Coordinator's (ONC) Meaningful Use definition and the Centers for Medicare & Medicaid Service's Incentive Payments regulations.

Observed Trend

The recent Request for Comments from ONC for Meaningful Use Stage 3 alludes to the scalability of certified electronic health record (EHR) solutions, especially when engaging populations on a broad scale. It also offers a glimpse on how patients may be given the ability to submit self-generated health information to improve care of high-priority health conditions.

As Meaningful Use advances and requires more patient access to information, ubiquitous mobile services and devices are the best suited to make that a reality in Stage 3. However, closely aligning incentives with the use of mobile devices, including advancing the debate around privacy and security issues, remain key topics.

13.5: Monitor the regulatory environment for legislation and promulgation which affects mobile technology (mHealth) as well as the pace of innovation to ensure that it is not hindered, but rather encouraged; and **13.11:** Collaborate with stakeholders to work toward a unified regulatory approach in the field of mHealth.

At the time of this writing, disparate, limited and at times, competing efforts between Congress and federal agencies continue to shape the way mobile and digital health solutions will be implemented by the U.S. healthcare system. At the congressional level, legislation is focused largely on the removal of barriers to technology innovators by reforming the regulatory oversight of medical devices by the Food and Drug Administration (FDA) — both mobile and other forms of health IT software.

CONGRESSIONAL ACTIVITY INVOLVING mHEALTH

The 112th and 113th Congress have taken a keen interest in the field of mHealth. In a recent survey by GigaOM Pro, nearly 54 percent of the world's mobile developers are located in North America, with many firms located outside Silicon Valley. This powerful constituency has increasingly focused on the regulatory barriers facing innovative companies and the need for nimble policies that are flexible and can enable rapid technology cycles.

As a result, a number of bills have appeared in Congress, potentially impacting mobile health technology. The Healthcare Innovation and Marketplace Technologies (HIMTA) Act, introduced in two successive sessions, seeks to establish funding that creates a special Office of Wireless Health at the FDA to provide recommendations on mobile health application (app) issues.[1] The Application Privacy, Protection and Security (APPS) Act, introduced in the 113th Congress, seeks to strengthen mobile privacy protections for consumers. A major challenge to consider in the mobile world is the interconnectedness and ability for developers to post apps in various app markets from all over the world. Enforcement of privacy and security rules becomes a major concern.

State licensure and interstate practice of physicians continues to remain at the forefront of attempts to increase the use of telemedicine. Previous legislative efforts include the Telehealth Promotion Act. More recently, the TELEmedicine for MEDicare Act of 2013 was introduced, which seeks to reduce barriers to physicians practicing across states lines in areas where reciprocity, compacts or other agreements between state medical boards are absent. At a high level, legislators remain interested in addressing issues of access by leveraging remote and wireless technologies, while maintaining a fair and equitable set of licensing standards for providers. A major challenge remains — identifying areas of cost savings and rigorous, timely comparison of interventions.

At the state policy level, HIMSS released an in-depth assessment of various state legislative initiatives, the mHIMSS Roadmap. Using the framework laid out in the Roadmap, the document assessed state policy from a number of perspectives, including areas of reimbursement, the use of technology, and standards within the mHealth space. The document highlights the need to elevate issues of privacy and security to include HIPAA plus state regulations with a strong focus on coordination across all states to ensure consistency with the enactment of legislation.

SECTION 618 FDASIA WORKGROUP

The Food and Drug Administration Safety Innovation Act (FDASIA) was signed into law on July 9, 2012, and expanded the FDA's authorities by strengthening the agency's ability to safeguard and advance public health. Section 618 of the Act charged the Secretary of Health & Human Services (HHS) to act through the Commissioner of the FDA, in consultation with the Office of the National Coordinator for Health Information Technology (ONC) and the Chairman of the Federal Communications Commission (FCC) to publish a report by January 2014 that expresses "a proposed strategy and recommendations on an appropriate, risk-based regulatory framework pertaining to health information technology including mobile medical applications, that promotes innovation, protects patient safety, and avoids regulatory duplication." Section 618 also allowed the Secretary to convene a workgroup of external stakeholders to provide expert input on issues and concepts identified by FDA, ONC and the FCC to inform the development of the final report. This external workgroup presented its final report to ONC's Health IT Policy Committee on September 4, 2013. The report made various recommendations, particular to mHealth, including calling for the FDA to expedite guidance on health IT software, mobile medical apps and related matters. On September 23, 2013, the FDA issued its Final Mobile Medical Applications Guidance Document.

FDA MOBILE MEDICAL APPLICATIONS GUIDANCE DOCUMENT

The FDA released its final guidance regarding the Agency's current thinking on the topic of Mobile Medical Applications (MMA). It is important to note that the guidance published by FDA is solely focused on clarifying a specific issue, in this case, a subset of health apps to include regulated mobile medical apps and does not bind

FDA or the public. The MMA also does not discuss other forms of software currently under the regulatory purview of the FDA.

The guidance does not cover clinical decision support (CDS) software. The final guidance includes a thorough analysis of which mobile apps are regulated by providing high-level examples in Appendices A, B and C of the final document; those that are regulated but the Agency will chose to exercise "enforcement discretion;" the small subset of mobile medical apps that the Agency will enforce; and those apps that are not subject to regulation. This document is deregulatory in nature, allowing for innovation, and answers many of the initial questions faced by the mHealth apps industry. Additionally, the FDA created a web site and an e-mail address — mobilemedicalapps@fda.hhs.gov — for questions related to the MMA and coinciding with the release of the guidance to ensure flexibility in a rapidly changing technology space.

FCC'S mHEALTH EFFORTS

mHealth regulation entails numerous federal agencies. In July 2010, the FCC and FDA jointly agreed to a memorandum of understanding which seeks "To jointly ensure the safety of medical devices, promote investment in the mHealth space, and streamline regulatory efforts." In September 2012, the FCC released a set of findings and recommendations. Key areas of interest include interagency discussions around standardization of secure health messaging services between the FCC and the ONC. The findings of the taskforce also focus on the need to advance the National Broadband Plan, specifically Chapter 10 of the plan, which aims to provide increased access to information technology infrastructure. Furthermore, the document calls for FCC involvement in the creation of test beds associated with the allocation of Spectrum for medical needs. These areas include the use of Spectrum for the creation Medical Body Area Networks (MBAN), which promote innovative approaches to enable connected medical devices. The development of MBAN requires additional assessment after proof of concept, as the current state lends itself to proprietary interfaces that could inhibit interoperability.

HIPAA UPDATES AND THE BLUE BUTTON INITIATIVE

As of September 23, 2013, a number of updates to HIPAA occurred. A number of changes impact the use of mobile devices as an accessory for many providers, patients and caregivers working in or navigating a complex healthcare system. The first update to HIPAA that impacts users of mobile devices includes expansion of liability for Business Associates. More information on Business Associate agreements can be found at www.hhs.gov/ocr/privacy/hipaa/understanding/coveredentities/contractprov.html. Updates to HIPAA present major opportunities to develop a more robust engagement strategy for the conduct of research approved by Institutional Review Boards (IRB). The final rule reduces burden by streamlining individual's ability to authorize the use of their health information for research purposes. A Covered Entity may use or disclose protected health information without individual's authorizations for the creation of a research database, provided the Covered Entity obtains documentation that an IRB or privacy board has determined that the specified waiver criteria were satisfied.[2]

From an mHealth research perspective, many advantages exist to engaging in robust data collection via a mobile device. Numerous researchers and organizations highlight the need to expand the role of exploring mHealth interventions.[3,4] These updates to HIPAA could significantly impact the ability to enroll and conduct targeted research with potential additional impacts on the role of the mobile device.

Finally, changes to HIPAA include that patients may request a copy of healthcare records in electronic form if the information is already maintained in an electronic form. Healthcare providers must produce that copy within 30 days. It is important to note that the largest fines from the Office of Civil Rights (OCR) include instances of access by patients to their own health information.[5] While breaches of patient data from wireless devices remain high, OCR has placed increased emphasis on the right for patients to access information in a timely fashion and with these updates to HIPAA, the challenge becomes creating an environment that is mobile-friendly and interoperable.

An interesting trend to note with respect to supporting updates to HIPAA is the Blue Button initiative introduced by the Veterans Affairs Department and further advanced by the ONC. The initiative seeks to provide consumer access to EHRs. The ONC is conducting pilots to assess various models for patient engagement surrounding access to medical records. While not specifically created for mobile devices, Blue Button remains an interesting trend to watch with respect to impacts on development for mobile-enabled PHRs. Over the long term, Blue Button could provide inroads with respect to HIE, with consumers increasingly serving as the "hub" for movement of clinical data between providers. Blue Button is also discussed in Chapter 7.

ORGANIZATIONAL APPROACHES TOWARD IMPLEMENTING POLICY MEASURES

While federal policy impacts many levels, the implementation of organizational policy is unique, based on a company's business, size, circumstances, complexity, workforce and partnerships. This section provides insights on how organizations are approaching the use of mobile health from an organizational perspective, and current practices for implementation of policies, both organizational and regulatory focused. When appropriate, readers are directed to industry use cases that serve as examples of industry best-practice implementations or adherence to regulations.

Mobile Device Management and BYOD Policy

The Bring Your Own Device (BYOD) phenomenon continues to challenge organizations. While BYOD solutions may not work for every organization, Meneghetti provides eight steps for organizations undertaking such an effort.[6] A number of these topics are worth exploring. Traditionally, BYOD is formed by three main pillars that include a software application for the management of devices, a written policy outlining the use of devices and an agreement the end user must sign. More simply, access, documentation and accountability comprise important steps for organizations to adhere to when crafting mobile device usage policies. The standardization of device registration and setting boundaries are best accomplished via organizational policies. As highlighted by Meneghetti, federal policy impacts a number of decisions regarding adoption of a BYOD policy. She adds that the standardization and setting of boundaries is best accomplished at the location of the provisioning of technology and that the source of information access is a key tenant to address. A number of examples exist to provide context for approaches to the standardization of devices within a care setting in the following three major areas.

Access. A mobile focused or added to an existing acceptable use policy is a good first step. Many acceptable-use policies cover mobile technologies. In some instances, clearly defining the role of mobile devices within an organization's guiding documents on the use of technology aids in addressing organizational "buy in."

Documentation. A major step in undertaking BYOD policy from an organizational perspective is to create documentation of devices. A number of examples of end-user written agreements exist. Written documentation for BYOD policies should include information on:
- Devices and support provided.
- Reimbursement policies, if applicable.
- Security, password settings, backups and remote wiping of data.

A number of BYOD documents are widely available. Links to examples can be found at www.himss.org/mobilehealthit.

Accountability. Some specifics to note when undertaking a healthcare-specific deployment of BYOD strategies includes assessing for HIPAA compliance with vendors should PHI data be present or potentially available. With respect to enterprise apps placed on devices, two levels of security are desirable. This includes potential integration with Active Directories, and use of Personal Identification Numbers to launch or access mobile apps. Finally, a robust mobile device management (MDM) platform provides a final or last ditch effort for accountability. For some time, MDM platforms could only perform total remote wipes. This often served as a major disincentive to participate in BYOD programs. Increasingly, MDM platforms provide targeted wipe capabilities where only select work related areas of the device are targeted. Finally, periodic audits of devices provide an opportunity to assess compliance. Endpoint management software may prove useful to proactively identify users or discover executable files that may suggest that desktop devices are used to support mobile devices.

CONCLUSION

Technology continues to outpace the pace of policy, especially in the arena of mobile technologies in the healthcare sector. However, policy makers, both legislative and regulatory, have taken note. Current legislative efforts focus on increased privacy and security protections for consumers. The maturation and convergence of mHealth and telemedicine is only bolstered by attempts to increase patients' access to care. In addition, legislation is working to provide access for innovators to gain insights from federal agencies on regulatory efforts. From a regulatory perspective, work is underway by agencies to coordinate approaches to creating policy surrounding mHealth. The work of the FDASIA provides a framework for agencies to operate over the short- and long-term. In addition, final guidance from the FDA provides regulatory certainty for an industry in need of rules for the road. From an organizational perspective, written policies surrounding use is often a starting point for deploying mobile devices. However, with increased access comes increased accountability. As mobile technologies evolve, organizational policies must evolve in line. Items of interest for further consideration include the need to contemplate or create policies for remote monitoring solutions or elements of the patient-centered medical home (PCMH), as well as Accountable Care Organizations (ACO), many of which are only in the beginning stages of organizational and policy formation. Furthermore, consideration should be given to potential policy frameworks that further support or incent the proper use of tools to mitigate or reduce HIPAA violations. Currently, the policy framework of privacy and security enforcement by penalties, without incentives to adopt new technologies, places an undue burden on providers and organizations that should be examined further.

REFERENCES

1. Kim L, Patricia K, Robert J, Martin T. The mHIMSS Roadmap-Chapter 4. 2012. Available at: www.mhimss.org/sites/default/files/mHIMSS%20Roadmap-4.pdf. Accessed September 22, 2013.
2. Department of Health & Human Services. Does the HIPAA Privacy Rule permit the creation of a database for research purposes through an Institutional Review Board (IRB) or Privacy Board waiver of individual authorization? Available at: www.hhs.gov/hipaafaq/permitted/research/305.html. Accessed September 22, 2013.
3. Nilsen W. Advancing the Science of mHealth. *Journal of Health Communication*, 2012. 17(sup1): 5-10.
4. Atienza AA, Patrick K. Mobile health: the killer app for cyber infrastructure and consumer health. *American Journal of Preventive Medicine*. 2011; 40(5): 151-3.
5. Office of Civil Rights, 2011.
6. Meneghetti, A. Challenges and benefits in a mobile medical world: institutions should create a set of BYOD guidelines that foster mobile device usage. *Health Management Technology*. 2013; 34(2).

CHAPTER 25

Health App Certification: Frontline Lessons from the Self-Regulation Movement: An Analysis

By Corey Ackerman and Sandra C. Maliszewski, MSN, JD, MBA, with Travis Froehlich, Evan Harary, Leslie Isenegger, and Michelle Jacobs

ABSTRACT

The market for mobile health (mHealth) apps is growing fast and shows no signs of slowing down. There are tens of thousands of health apps available across multiple platforms, and the mHealth industry is expected to expand tenfold by 2017. While such growth is encouraging, there is a notable void: regulatory oversight — a stark contrast to the rest of the healthcare industry where, out of dedication to patient health and safety, all aspects are heavily regulated. Consequently, it stands to reason that if mHealth technology is to fully integrate into standard practice, it must clear a variety of regulatory hurdles. At present, anybody with a platform and basic programming skills can whip up an app and label it mHealth. As long as that remains the industry standard, healthcare organizations and clinicians will rightfully hesitate to fully adopt the technology into their toolkit for treatment and care management.

THE PROBLEM WITH mHEALTH APPS

By placing care management directly into the hands of patients, the potential for mHealth apps to improve patient health is clear. Apps that enable remote patient monitoring, enhance education or ensure medication compliance are just some of the ways in which mHealth can improve outcomes while reducing costs and supporting clinicians. But the impact that apps could have on healthcare delivery and chronic care management is limited by the level of mHealth adoption. To date, clinicians have been wary about incorporating health apps into routine medical practice, citing the overwhelming number of apps on the market and lack of assurance about the security or reliability of apps, generally.

On September 25, 2013, the Food and Drug Administration (FDA) released Final Guidance for mobile medical apps that provides oversight with respect to the safety and effectiveness of apps that constitute medical devices (mobile medical apps). To meet these criteria, apps must meet the definition of "device" in section 201(h) of the federal Food, Drug, and Cosmetic (FD&C) Act and (i) be used as "an accessory to a regulated medical device or (ii) transform a mobile platform into a regulated medical device."

Examples of mobile medical apps are products that, "transform a mobile platform into a regulated medical device," such as apps that use an attachment to measure blood glucose levels; "connect to an existing device type for purposes of controlling its operation, function, or energy source," such as those that control a blood-pressure cuff; or "display, transfer, store, or convert patient-specific medical device data from a connected device," such as those that connect to a beside monitor and transfer data for active patient monitoring.

However, many mHealth app categories do not qualify as mobile medical apps, and therefore fall outside the scope of FDA regulation. Apps that act as teaching aids or electronic medical records (EMR), automate managerial operations, or are used to log, record and track data related to maintaining general health and wellness would not come under FDA surveillance. Additionally, the FDA stated in the Final Guidance its intention to exercise enforcement discretion, which means that the FDA will not regulate some apps that may meet the definition of medical device because they pose a lower risk to the public. The guidelines, therefore, can be viewed as "deregulatory" in nature and should be a green light for continued mobile app innovation in the health and medical industry.

AN ANSWER TO THE PROBLEM OF REGULATORY CONCERNS

While the FDA Final Guidance may signal good news for app developers, it leaves the door open for the industry to create some form of self-regulation. mHealth thought leaders estimate that FDA regulation, as outlined by the Final Guidance, will apply to less than 20 percent of healthcare apps. The remaining 80 percent or more will remain entirely free of meaningful oversight. Anticipating this regulatory vacuum, Happtique, a patient-engagement solutions company, developed a health app certification process. The certification process was intended to provide a first step toward voluntary mHealth self-regulation by reviewing the large portion of healthcare apps left unattended by FDA regulation. Happtique modeled this program on existing third-party certification programs — such as The Joint Commission (TJC)—and like TJC, Happtique sought to improve mHealth care for patients and providers, in collaboration with other stakeholders, by evaluating apps and inspiring app developers to adopt certain standards as best practices.

To create the certification standards, Happtique convened a panel of healthcare experts with a wealth of relevant industry experience. The standards cover technical capacity and content, with the intention of establishing performance requirements for privacy, security, operability and content. To review health and medical apps, Happtique forged partnerships with an internationally recognized technology and informatics testing service, as well as recognized organizations that have the appropriate content expertise, such as the Association of American Medical Colleges (AAMC) and the Commission on Graduates of Foreign Nursing Schools (CGFNS International), the American College of Nurse-Midwives (ACNM) and the National Council on Strength and Fitness (NCSF), to name a few.

Happtique began development of a certification process with the goal of testing apps for credible content, safeguards for user data and appropriate functionality. Technical evaluation was subdivided into operability, privacy and security. The program's privacy standards follow the lead established by the Federal Trade Commission in "Protecting Consumer Privacy in an Era of Rapid Change: Recommendations for Businesses and Policymakers." Therefore, the app review included a test to confirm that the user is fully informed of the app's data usage policy and that the app is in compliance with relevant legislation. Reviews also addressed whether there is reasonable transparency for the user regarding the access of social networks and/or local resources (e.g., device address books, mobile/LAN networks). Finally, reviewers verified that measures to obtain consent (when appropriate) exist and are easily accessible.

Unique to this program, content was tested in a contextually sensitive manner by subject matter experts. And because healthcare apps range in type from cardiac monitors to electronic educational booklets, content assessments vary from one case to the next. However, in general, content standards are designed to ensure that the app is not misleadingly labeled, and that its functionality is based on credible information, such as accepted protocols, published guidelines, evidence-based practice, etc. Furthermore, the content standards dictate that apps explain any deviations in content from authoritative sources, and that the apps make readily available references to original sources used. Apps are tested to make certain that they are written in a manner that is appropriate for the intended audience.

INITIAL OBSERVATIONS

Our discussions with app developers have made one thing clear: to date, no one in the industry has their arms around what constitutes a "high quality" app or even how to determine if the health and medical recommendations within an app are credible. This void seems particularly perilous when you juxtapose healthcare — one of the most regulated industries in the country — with a market defined by an "all comers" approach and minimal startup requirements. The trust concerns created by the market's low barrier to entry are further exacerbated by the fact that much of mHealth is free. Software is free. Ad-supported apps are free. As one developer stated, "Where is the healthcare value in a market based on advertising and not science?" Therefore, creating some kind of objective vetting process seemed imperative for health apps to gain trust and widespread acceptance in the routine delivery of healthcare.

The Value of Certification
In a market as open as mHealth, it is not at all uncommon to encounter apps marketed as mHealth that make unsubstantiated claims, do not follow established medical guidelines and have not been clinically tested. So, in addition to improving credibility within the market and garnering increased accountability from developers for their products, certification provides an opportunity for all developers, including those new

to the healthcare industry, to become versed in the required industry standards and terminology. With a foundation in current federal regulations and a subject matter expert review process, Happtique, in earnest, attempted to provide some of that necessary guidance through the 2013 launch of the Health App Certification Program.

Happtique hoped that the establishment of a widely respected set of technical and content standards would raise awareness to patient and provider concerns, motivating developers to adopt and enforce mHealth industry standards. Ideally, such standards will raise the quality of apps, and healthcare providers will grow to trust apps, leading to increased mHealth integration in healthcare.

Healthcare standards have typically been developed in response to the desire to encourage positive patient practices, improve the quality of medical care and enhance reimbursement. Accordingly, Happtique designed its Standards and Performance Requirements to complement the objectives of key federal agencies — namely, the FDA, Federal Communications Commission, Federal Trade Commission and the Office of the National Coordinator for Health Information Technology — that are involved in the regulation of mHealth applications.

Certification is also a means of demonstrating self-regulation and adherence to applicable codes of conduct, as well as validating and distinguishing the efforts of people who have invested time and energy to implement best practices. App developers hold a powerful but precarious place in the healthcare industry. Using apps as direct conduits, app developers are not only empowering consumers, but empowering patients with the ability to better manage their healthcare directly from a mobile device. By building solutions for consumers, patients and providers at an astounding rate, app developers are forcing the healthcare industry to take a hard look at how mobile technology can impact patient-centered care.

But no matter how many healthcare apps are being downloaded, healthcare professionals won't consider adding apps as viable care management solutions for their patients until these apps are perceived as providing credible content, safeguarding user data and functioning as described, particularly with the healthcare industry's stringent regulatory environment. While mHealth offers a significant opportunity for healthcare providers and organizations to improve patient care and outcomes while reducing costs, the necessary oversight to make this a reality is not yet in place.

A FIRST STEP TOWARD INDUSTRY STANDARDS

The fastest way to bridge that gap — and instill confidence in consumers, patients and healthcare professionals — is for app developers to consider incorporating the following points when developing their apps.

Privacy & Security
In the general mobile space, app developers already need to be aware of the current regulatory environment.
- The Children's Online Privacy Protection Act (COPPA) is a federal law governing web sites/online services designed for children, or a web site geared to a general audience that could collect information from someone under the age of 13. There are new rules that spell out what a web site operator must include in a

privacy policy, when and how to seek verifiable consent from a parent and what responsibilities an operator has to protect children's privacy and safety online (e.g., the app does not knowingly collect personal information for children under 13, use that information to notify the child [or parent/legal guardian] that he or she cannot use your site; and app publishers must delete any information associated with underage users on their own servers or take other reasonable measures to delete the information). For apps that fall under COPPA, failure to comply with this law can result in law enforcement actions. The link to the Children's Privacy section at the Federal Trade Commission is www.business.ftc.gov/privacy-and-security/childrens-privacy.

- The U.S. National Telecommunications and Information Administration introduced its voluntary Mobile App Code of Conduct for Privacy, which addresses the need for app developers to provide users with short-form notices about what data an app collects and who it will be shared with. It is available at www.ntia.doc.gov/files/ntia/publications/july_25_code_draft.pdf.
- California's Online Privacy Protection Act requires web sites and services, including mobile apps that collect personal information, to have a privacy policy conspicuously placed that advises consumers about what information is being collected and how it will be used. In January 2013, the California Attorney General's Office issued its mobile app privacy practice guidelines. "Privacy on the Go: Recommendations for the Mobile Ecosystem" is an excellent resource that can help app developers focus on privacy practices early in the app development process. It is available at http://oag.ca.gov/sites/all/files/pdfs/privacy/privacy_on_the_go.pdf.

For developers looking to create an app for the mHealth space, the app must be compliant with data privacy laws relating to both the mobile and healthcare industries. Apps that share health-related data with Covered Entities (healthcare providers, health plans and healthcare services) are subject to HIPAA and HITECH Act rules. What a developer might consider an advanced feature — such as patient data flowing directly to the user's healthcare provider — could be easy to create from a development standpoint, but fail to comply with best practices when it comes to protecting patient data.

Not sure if an app needs to be HIPAA/HITECH compliant? There are a variety of resources available. The Office of the National Coordinator for Health Information Technology's subsection on Mobile Device Privacy and Security provides guidance on HIPAA compliance and mobile devices (www.healthit.gov/providers-professionals/your-mobile-device-and-health-information-privacy-and-security). Additional guidance addressing the need for increased transparency and control over the collection and use of data on mobile devices within the mobile advertising ecosystem has recently been published. The Network Advertising Initiative just released its self-regulatory program 2013 Mobile Application Code. Similarly, the Digital Advertising Alliance announced new guidance for advertisers. The Mobile Marketing Association also released guidelines for a model privacy policy in 2012.

Privacy Policy

The regulatory environment for the general mobile and/or healthcare space requires that app developers be vigilant about private information staying private and secure. But a recent study conducted by the Privacy Rights Clearinghouse (July 2013) indicated that 26 percent of free health-related apps and 40 percent of paid health-related apps did not have a privacy policy. Furthermore, of those that had a privacy policy, only 43 percent of free health-related apps and 25 percent of paid health-related apps provided a link from the app to a privacy policy on the developer's web site.

The privacy policy should address the app publisher's policy on how the app collects, stores and releases any personal information. The privacy policy should inform users about what specific information is collected and whether such information is kept confidential, shared with third parties or sold to other firms or enterprises. Specifically, the privacy policy should address the following areas:

- Does the app collect or use traffic data, such as IP addresses, domain servers, types of computers accessing the site, types of web browsers used to access the site, referring sources that may have sent the user to the app publisher's site, etc.?
- Does the app collect personal and/or sensitive information, such as contact data (specify), demographic data (specify), communications, etc.? If yes, why is this information collected (e.g., to access certain areas of the site, access additional functionality within the app)?
- Does the app collect other data through the use of interactive and installed tools? If yes, provide examples of the types of data collected and why it is collected.
- Does the app use cookies? If yes, how does the app publisher use them and can the user block/delete them?
- In the area of confidentiality and security, does the app publisher keep personal/sensitive information private? How? Are there any exceptions (e.g., to comply with court orders/other legal processes, to enforce terms of the app's usage, responding to claims)? Does the app publisher share this information with third parties? As it relates to the security of user's personal/sensitive information, does the app publisher follow generally accepted industry standards when transmitting, collecting, saving (i.e., during transmission and at rest) this type of information? Does the app publisher encrypt sensitive information and how? What does the app publisher do if there has been a breach of privacy/security safeguards? How is the user notified?
- Concerning lost/stolen user information, how does the user notify the app publisher that their data has been lost/stolen/used without permission? What does the app publisher do about it?
- Does the app publisher have links to other web sites? If yes, for what purposes?
- How does the app publisher handle updates/changes to your privacy policy? How is the user notified (e.g., posted on your site, a link is provided to the modified policy; the user is notified via the app, through the Apple Store)? Does the policy state when it was last updated?
- Who can the user contact for any comments, concerns or questions about the app publisher's privacy policy?

- How does the user access the privacy policy (e.g., in an "About" section, via a hyperlink to the company's/developer's web site)? How does the user consent to the terms of this policy (e.g., usage of the app as acceptance of the terms of the policy)?
- If the app content contains real patient videos or images, have releases/consents been obtained from those individuals for including these types of images within the app? Are facial features or identifying details removed such that only the area of interest is visible?

Data Ownership & Advertising

Mobile users were up in arms during the summer of 2012 when reports emerged that despite Apple's policy of rejecting apps that collect or transmit users' personal data without their permission, popular apps like Yelp, Gowalla, Hipster and Foodspotting were accessing users' address book of contacts without requesting access from the user. Similarly, the way that data was being used was often reckless — transmitting users' address books over unencrypted connections. Kevin Mahaffey, Chief Technology Officer of Lookout, a global technology security company, warned, "What separates malicious use from legitimate use is the element of surprise. If a user is surprised, that's a problem."

App developers need to address the issues of data ownership and advertising within the app, either as a part of the privacy policy or as a separate policy. App developers should specifically consider addressing the following:

- Do you use the user's personal/sensitive information? If yes, how is it used and do you use de-identified personal information? Why do you use the user's personal/sensitive information?
- Do you share the user's information? If yes, what categories of information are used and why?
- Do you allow advertisements within the app or via links to other sites? Do you contact users concerning your company, products and/or services? If yes, can the user opt-out of receiving these commercial messages from advertisers/marketers either within the app or when receiving an initial commercial message? How do you secure against viruses and the like?
- Does the user have any control over the personal/sensitive information s/he has provided as a registered user? If yes, to what extent can they control that information?
- As it relates to the storage of traffic data/posting, how long is this information stored and why? Can the user modify/delete it? If yes, how (e.g., can users delete the information through the app, or send the app publisher a request via a support e-mail link/comment box)?
- Do you use web site analytics? If yes, why and what do they do?

These issues are only some of the things that should be addressed and made available to users so that, as Mr. Mahaffey says, there are no surprises.

Proper Sourcing of Content

According to a 2012 report *mHealth in an mWorld*, published by Deloitte, "Health information (primarily oriented toward personal health, wellness, fitness and information on health services) is the fastest-growing content category for U.S. mobile users." But where is all of this content coming from? Throughout the app-development process, app developers should keep track of where the app's content is coming from — whether it's text, images or formulas — and how the content is displayed. Such information includes originally authored books, videos, articles or any other published information. In some cases, it may include originally authored materials or workbooks by university faculty members, like those typically sold in university bookstores. Specific citations should be provided, as well as links to access the information.

LESSONS LEARNED: CHALLENGES WITH CERTIFICATION

While the mHealth industry is supportive of self-regulation, exactly how to devise and implement a standardized review process is complicated at best. Finding the balance between the "Wild West" of healthcare innovation and patient/provider safety will be a challenge, with much still to be learned. Certainly, self-regulation offers important opportunities for mHealth stakeholders and app developers to minimize risks to consumers and build public trust while complementing existing regulations with supplemental rules in areas with absence of government oversight.

With this in mind, Happtique enlisted its review partners to certify an inaugural class of apps in Fall 2013. During this process, Happtique provided administrative guidance to participating developers (how to use the app submission portals, etc.) while the actual review was performed by third-party experts. To make this program as objective and impartial as possible, all reviewers were made to disclose any conflicts with the submitted apps as a requirement of reviewer participation. This inaugural certification process included 18 apps submitted by 10 different developers. Through this first-of-its-kind process, Happtique — and the mHealth industry — learned a number of critical lessons about app evaluation.

In terms of certification program logistics, participating developers provided meaningful feedback, much of which centered around the idea that apps are as different as the patients they intend to help. Therefore, it is unrealistic to think one set of standards will be universally applicable to health and medical apps. Participating developers suggested supporting different types of documentation (i.e., allowing for process flexibility to better accommodate different types of apps). For example, some developers will license functionality or content from other vendors, and therefore won't be able to provide the same types of content documentation as developers that create their own content. Other apps do not collect any information about the user, and therefore do not present the same types of privacy security risks as apps that log personal health information.

One of the bigger lessons learned arose from public feedback regarding a lack of clarity in the language included in one of the technical standards and inconsistencies with how the standard was being tested. In response, Happtique has undertaken a review of the testing methodologies in relation to the standards, as well as the standards themselves to ensure that expectations in the standards are stated clearly, and that the testing methodologies appropriately and precisely evaluate the performance requirements. Notably, this feedback demonstrated a critical issue: when it comes to rapidly-evolving technology, certification or any type of self-regulatory effort must be an iterative goal rather than an outcome at a point-in-time.

THE FUTURE OF SELF-REGULATION

Happtique developed its certification process to bring a basic level of due diligence to the mHealth market based on standards that resonate with the healthcare industry. So what have these lessons taught Happtique and the industry at large about the future of self-regulation? First, self-regulation is important and appealing to mHealth users and stakeholders alike. While Happtique's certification process has received its share of criticism, an equal if not larger number of providers, developers and regulatory experts have echoed the importance of creating some form of transparency and quality control in the health app marketplace.

Second, in the absence of one universally recognized authority (i.e., The Joint Commission or Better Business Bureau) or clinical trials, the mHealth industry needs to invest in creating more resources to help users evaluate and select health and medical apps. Download metrics, subjective reviews, recommendations from well-regarded experts–such as medical schools and specialty societies–and, ultimately, physician-prescribed apps all serve as resources to help patients determine whether an app is appropriate for their particular health goals and concerns. Since existing resources skew toward subjective reviews, the industry would clearly benefit from some type of objective certification or evaluation process.

Perhaps the most important takeaway from Happtique's certification pursuits is that to be effective, self-regulation needs to be an industry-led, industry-managed endeavor. Health app self-regulation needs to involve many stakeholders, including those representing consumers and the public interest, who all agree to monitor compliance and provide remediation mechanisms. Given how quickly the mHealth marketplace is evolving, any certification system needs to be an ongoing process in which stakeholders strive to adopt and maintain best practices for what constitutes high-quality, effective apps. To this end, Happtique is reaching out to mHealth stakeholders to gather additional support for true industry-led self-regulation in the mobile health marketplace.

The future of mHealth is full of potential — potential that will only be realized when developers and other stakeholders start to think about how to achieve clinical integration of apps. The development and adoption of industry standards are critical steps to a day when doctors and patients can confidently use apps knowing that they have been protected by an objective vetting process. Through its health app certification process, Happtique has begun to forge this path for the mHealth industry.

CHAPTER 26

Evaluating the Quality of mHealth Apps: A Case Study

By Muhammad Nauman, MD, MS

ABSTRACT

The expansion of mobile devices leads to an exponential increase in the number of mobile health applications. These applications have the ability to transform patient care and can greatly improve the overall efficiency of the healthcare system. However, many first-generation mobile health applications don't have the clinical functionality, patient-centeredness or smart designs at their core. The purpose of this case study is to analyze current mobile health applications and to identify their clinical functionality and limitations. It also aims to serve as a consumer guide to help patients understand the usability and flexibility of these apps and how these apps give them control of their health and be an integral part of their ambulatory management. This chapter also looks at mobile health devices and fitness gadgets that can work in conjunction with mobile health applications and their expanding and interesting role in the future healthcare environment.

The emergence of the app store gives an opportunity to anyone in the world to come up with a mobile application. The Apple App Store has recently celebrated its 50 billionth download after only five years of existence.[1] The emergence of the Android platform just increases that opportunity without the regulations of the Apple Store. Google Play, the flagship app store for Android, now boasts to have around 1million available apps and a similar number of downloads.[2]

The number of mobile health applications constitutes only a fraction of all the available apps and can be useful in the prevention and management of health problems. There are approximately 50,000 mobile health applications currently available and the market of these apps is expected to be worth around $26 billion by 2017.[3] This rapid explosion of mHealth apps makes it imperative to understand their popularity not only on the frequency of downloads, but also on the basis of clinical usefulness and effectiveness. The Mobile Health Applications 2012 study done by Verasoni provides deep insight into current worldwide trend of mobile health applications. The study showed that by looking into the top 150 health apps downloaded in the Apple and Android platforms, weight loss and fitness apps far outweigh other health applications.[4] This can be due to the fact that these apps are often used by younger people who are better connected and are focused on their health and fitness.

These apps can be used individually to improve fitness and achieve weight management, but the use of fitness gadgets like Nike Fuel Band, Fitbit Flex and UP Jaw Bone with these apps can also help users to track their daily activities and achieve their fitness goals. This information can be shared with friends and family members that could help users to get encouragement to stick to their goals and connect with other people online who are trying to achieve similar goals and have similar problems that can be shared.

There is no single method available to classify these apps on the basis of their clinical usefulness and functionality. The growing number of mHealth apps make it imperative to have a classification system for these apps not only on the basis of downloads, but on the basis of their functionality and usefulness for patients. The numbers of apps available to diagnose and treat disease conditions are increasing in frequency and are estimated to grow exponentially in the near future. This chapter aims to provide a reference guide for classification of mHealth apps on the basis of functionality to make it easier for both physicians and patients to use them accordingly. It would also look into different health and fitness gadgets available in the market place that can work with different mHealth apps and can be useful in providing continuous information regarding patients' health status. This can help give patients control of their health and can help in their ambulatory management by sharing this information with their providers that can be stored in their EHR, if needed. (See Appendix A on page 339 for functional comparisons of mHealth apps.)

BACKGROUND

There are different ways mHealth apps are classified by different organizations. This chapter will try to identify some of these methods and how they are used to classify these apps.

1. Happtique[5]: Happtique Health App Certification Program (HACP) is designed to help healthcare providers and consumers to identify health and fitness apps that can deliver quality content safely and easily. HACP focuses on four key areas that can help evaluate apps against a set of standards and associated performance requirements. The four key areas are

- i.) Operability (OP1-OP9): There are nine operability standards to meet interoperability requirements between different devices.
- ii.) Privacy (P1-P6): The six privacy standards would help users understand their rights and how their information is accessed, collected and used by third parties.
- iii.) Security (S1-S7): The seven security standards demand that the app publisher comply with best practices related to secure user health information.
- iv.) Content (C1-C11): There are 11 content standards that seek to classify everything from content source to its truthfulness and accuracy.

2. HealthTap[6]: A mobile health platform that connects about 40,000 doctors rolled out AppRx to help consumers discover the most recommended apps by their doctors. AppRx will empower individuals to find reliable doctor-recommended apps across nearly three dozen health and wellness categories. Dr. David Wyatt, an Atlanta-based family physician, explained that with more than 600 different diabetes apps, 231 different children's health apps and 100 period-tracker apps, it is extremely difficult to assess the quality of health apps only on the basis of user reviews. He explained that he and his colleagues objectively and professionally rate the quality, reliability and helpfulness of the best apps on all platforms so that people have the ease of mind that these apps are recommended by doctors.

Ron Gutman, HealthTap Founder and CEO, stated that everyone can learn about best mHealth apps recommended by doctors and that can result in improved health and well-being. He also added that helping patients choose the right apps would result in huge savings in healthcare delivery. AppRx divides apps into 31 categories and you can choose between both iOS and Android apps. It can also search any particular app by using the AppSearch option. Once the chosen category is selected, it would show all the apps belonging to this category, whether the app is from iOS or Android platform, free or paid, and recommendations and comments from doctors.

3. AppAppeal[7]: This web site reviews 3,473 free web apps in 181 categories based on worldwide popularity. It shows the top 69 health and fitness apps that are classified into health, medical and sports. There are 29 free apps under the health category and WebMD came on the top on the basis of worldwide popularity.

4. TIME Magazine[8]: TIME's Mobile Tech Special Issue examines five great health apps that should be downloaded by their readers that can help them to eat right, exercise, schedule doctor appointments and even get enough sleep. Their five recommended apps are:
- Runkeeper
- Fooducate
- Sleep Cycle
- Lose It
- Zoc Doc

5. Greatist[9]: This web site provides health, fitness and happiness tips for their 100,000+ members to make life better. They have developed their list of 64 best health and fitness apps for 2013. They classified these apps not only on the basis of downloads, but on the basis of uniqueness, growth, innovation, user-friendliness and reliability. Most of them are free and they divide these apps into different categories:
- Fitness and Strength
- Tracking and Analytics
- Food and Nutrition
- Relaxation and Meditation
- Overall Wellness
- Running and Cardio
- Social Good and Innovation
- Interval and Circuit Training

- Science and Medical
- Yoga and Flexibility
- Weight Management

METHODOLOGY

There are several methods that can be used to classify mHealth apps. These apps can be divided into different categories on the basis of their functionality and also on their usage by age and gender. Another way to classify these apps is by the management of disease. There are five parameters that are proposed in this chapter that could be used to classify different mHealth apps and can make it easier for patients and physicians to prescribe and use these apps efficiently.

Risk

There can be several risks associated with the use of these apps. The risks can be associated with the manual entry if the data is wrongfully entered by someone other than the user or it may have been entered under a different person or category. There can be risk associated with automatic entry because of inability of the app or fitness gadgets to correctly map or measure the right amount of distance or calories associated with the specific food. These miscalculations can have serious ramifications if the patient is depending on this information to determine the right amount of medication to be administered. The risk has been divided into five categories starting from maximum risk that could result in severe disability or death, to no risk at all when the app doesn't necessarily have the features that could result in harmful consequences.

Risk Score:
0=Maximum risk; 1=Severe risk; 2=Moderate risk; 3=Minimal risk; 4=No risk

Usability

The usability of the app is the ability of the user to correctly use these apps without any significant technical knowledge. These apps have huge databases associated with them that can be very helpful for users to enter their information automatically rather than enter data manually. This is a very useful characteristic in case of information that is not readily available as in the case of food nutrients where it could be difficult to determine the percentage of each ingredient. It would also reduce the inaccuracies of manual data entry and make the apps more user friendly and increase compliance of the users.

Usability Score:
0=Extremely hard to use; 1=Very hard; 2=Hard; 3=Easy; 4=Can be used by anyone

Value

Most of the time value is defined as the amount of money spent on a product related to the result it produces. In this chapter this definition is not used because it could have resulted in the elimination of number of apps that have been used in this study. Instead, value of the app has been determined by its characteristics that can add value to users' lives although the app could be free of cost. The app could also be valuable if the user's time is well spent and the app's features help them to achieve their goals.

Value Score:
0=Not valuable; 1=Rarely valuable; 2= Mostly valuable; 3=Extremely valuable; 4=Always valuable

Reliability

Reliability is the ability of a person or system to perform and maintain its functions in routine circumstances. These apps can be extremely reliable when they perform their functions consistently without crashing in the process. The reliability can be increased dramatically if these apps have inherent functions that could result in automatic data entry. The apps that collect independent third-party information can also be very reliable because they are not under the influence of the app maker or manufacturer of the product.

Reliability Score:
0=Unreliable; 1=Rarely reliable; 2= Mostly reliable; 3=Extremely reliable; 4=Always reliable

Effectiveness

The effectiveness of these apps can be determined by their ability to help users manage and achieve their goals effectively. There are apps available for the management of weight loss, as well as for the management of diseases like diabetes, hypertension and cardiac problems. These apps can play an integral part in the ambulatory management of these conditions by giving patients the ability to access their information on a daily basis and share it with their providers. There can be a possible information overload because of the availability of too much data; and sometimes the important information can be masked if the apps are not effectively managed.

Effectiveness Score:
0=Non-effective; 1=Rarely effective; 2= Mostly effective; 3=Extremely effective; 4=Always effective

(See also Table 26-1 on page 240; Table 26-2 on page 242; and Table 26-3 on page 244.)

HEALTH & FITNESS APPS

Free-Standing Apps

LOSE IT[10]:

Risk: The risk associated with this app is minimal. The only thing that cannot be accounted for is the caloric and nutrient information of home-cooked meals and certain ethnic foods. *Score=3*

Usability: This app is user-friendly because of its large food database and easy-to-understand graphs and barcode tools. *Score=4*

Value: The free app has great features that make it valuable. However, the premium features are expensive. *Score=4*

Reliabilty: The app is reliable and there are very rare instances when data need to be entered manually. *Score=4*

Effectiveness: This can be a very effective tool in weight loss because of its comprehensive features and connectivity with friends and family for motivation. The premium version provides even better features to improve overall health. *Score=4*

Fooducate[11]:

Risk: There is no inherent risk in using this app. The availability of barcode scanning with the largest available UPC inventory decreases the risk associated with manual entry. *Score=4*

Usability: The app is easy to use and provides food grades and points to manage carbohydrate intake which is easy to understand. *Score=4*

Value: The app is available for free for both iOS and Android platforms. *Score=4*

Reliability: The app is reliable to use because it gets information from independent resources and not from the manufacturers that made these products. *Score=4*

Effectiveness: This is an effective app for weight loss as well as educating users about alternative food resources that are available. *Score=4*

ARGUS[12]:

Risk: The app can deactivate after a while and needs to be activated before it can record your data again. That could result in missing data or erroneous data entry. *Score=2*

Usability: The app is user friendly and has features that can automatically log most daily activities, thus minimizing the possibility of any manual entry. *Score=3*

Value: This is a free app and a lot of helpful features make it valuable to users. It can count your steps without the need for expensive sensors. *Score=4*

Reliability: The app still has some issues regarding the correct distance and steps taken, and they can also be miscalculated if the app is deactivated during the day. *Score=2*

Effectiveness: This can be a very effective app for tracking daily life activities because it can work seamlessly with other apps and devices to provide an overall picture of one's health. Yet it does go into hibernating mode, which can reduce its effectiveness. *Score=3*

FITNESS APPS ASSOCIATED WITH WRIST BANDS

Nike+FuelBand[13]:

Risk: The device cannot measure distance for specific runs, so people who train regularly have a risk of erroneous measurement. The wristband is a little big for small-sized people and can get caught in shirt sleeve. *Score=3*

Usability: It is easy to use and can be synced with the Nike Fuel Band app, as well as Nike+ web site. It has a screen to keep you posted with your numbers and gives you an instant idea of your daily activity. *Score=4*

Value: The device costs $149. There are certain free apps that when used together can perform similar functions. *Score=2*

Reliability: The device is a wristband with two accelerometers to measure users' activity. There can be decreased reliability when doing exercises that don't involve hand movements. *Score=2*

Effectiveness: The Nike Fuel measurement is a proprietary measurement of activity. It is sometimes unclear what Nike Fuel points really mean for overall health. *Score=2*

FitBit Flex[14]:

Risk: There is no apparent risk associated with this app or the associated FitBitZip device. *Score=4*

Usability: The device can sync wirelessly with the app so there is no difficulty in setting up the account or entering data from daily physical activity. *Score=4*

Value: The device costs $99.95. It has better value than Nike Fuel Band, but there are free apps that have similar functions. *Score=2*

Reliability: This is a reliable app because it collects information directly from the device and there is no need for any manual entry. *Score=4*

Effectiveness: This app can be an effective tool for improving physical activity and weight loss because of its connectivity with friends and family and other similar apps. *Score=4*

JawBone UP[15]:

Risk: The original Jawbone UP leaked, broke and didn't accurately record daily activities. The new version of wristlet is far better than the original and doesn't have these issues. *Score=3*

Usability: The rubber-made, water-resistant Jawbone UP can be worn in the shower or during swimming and is extremely comfortable. *Score=4*

Value: The Jawbone UP costs $129.99. It is one of the most expensive wristlets available on the market, but has no Bluetooth connectivity, making it less desirable than its counterparts. *Score=2*

Reliability: The device is far more reliable than the original model. *Score=3*

Effectiveness: The Jawbone UP can be an effective tool for monitoring daily activities and managing effective sleep cycle. It is extremely valuable in helping users develop new and better habits and exercise routines. *Score=4*

Table 26-1: Total App Score Comparison for Different Mobile Health & Fitness Apps.

App	LOSE IT	Fooducate	ARGUS	Nike+ Fuel Band	FitBit Flex	Jawbone UP
Risk	3	4	2	3	4	3
Usability	4	4	3	4	4	4
Value	4	4	4	2	2	2
Reliability	4	4	2	2	4	3
Effectiveness	4	4	3	2	4	4
Total App Score	19	20	14	13	18	16

DIABETES MANAGEMENT APPS

Free Standing Diabetes Management Apps

Diabetes Tracker[16]:

Risk: There is always risk for data breach and data inaccuracies in any application when the data is entered manually. *Score=3*

Usability: This app is easy to use and has features like bar coding and photo food service, which make it extremely useful to find the right food. *Score=4*

Value: The app costs $9.99. There are different apps that are free and perform almost same functions. The cost, however, is not prohibitive. *Score=2*

Reliability: The app is fairly reliable, but with each app that involves manual data entry, there is always a chance for error. *Score=3*

Effectiveness: This can be a very effective app for management of diabetes because it includes weight management, exercise regimen and medications, as well as insulin dosage. *Score=4*

Glucose Buddy[17]:

Risk: The apps don't have a food database, and therefore cannot give the amount of carbohydrates consumed by the patient and can miss glucose peaks. *Score=2*

Usability: This app is easy to use and provides features like graphs and logs to help patients understand their blood sugar measurements. *Score=4*

Value: The app costs $6.99 and includes BP and WT as well as two-way sync. The app is still valuable if we use other apps for carbohydrate consumption, BP and weight measurements and calorie count. *Score=2*

Reliability: The app is fairly reliable, blood glucose data is helpful and log entry is not difficult. The log data sometimes cannot be e-mailed. *Score=3*

Effectiveness: This is an effective app to manage diabetes because of the functions it provides. GB forum provides user platform for dicussions with other patients. *Score=4*

Wave Sense Diabetes Manager[18]:

Risk: This app doesn't provide a food database, therefore patients cannot enter the correct amount of food or calories associated with its intake. *Score=2*

Usability: Wave Sense is easy to use and users can record blood glucose levels, carbohydrate consumption and insulin data all in one place. *Score=4*

Value: The app is available for free and has great functions without intrusive advertisements. *Score=4*

Reliability: This app can help patients track their glucose for up to 90 days so they can achieve reliable information and their long term goals. *Score=3*

Effectiveness: Wave Sense can be a very effective tool for managing diabetes because of its features like graphs, logbook, color-coded results and video library that can help patient, understand different perspectives, regarding their problems. *Score=4*

Diabetes Management Apps Associated with Glucometers

iBG Diabetes Manager[19]:

Risk: This system should be used by a single user and can result in transmission of infectious disease if used by others. *Score=3*

Usability: iBG Star is not extremely hard to use, but it requires a certain skill level. It cannot remain attached continuously to the iPhone and needs to be kept within certain temperature limits. *Score=2*

Value: The device costs $74.99 and 50 strips cost $64.99. To connect with iPhone 5, it needs Apple Lightening to 30-pin Adapter which costs an additional $29.99. This price makes it far more expensive than regular glucometers. This could change if covered by major insurance companies. *Score=2*

Reliability: There are no indications that this device has any reliability issues associated with it and it behaves similar to other glucometers. *Score=3*

Effectiveness: The app could be a very effective tool to manage diabetes when it syncs with the glucometer and could improve patient outcomes. *Score=3*

Glooko Logbook[20]:

Risk: There doesn't seem to be a definite risk associated with the procedure but there is a certain risk associated with data transferred from different glucometers. *Score=1*

Usability: This logbook can be successfully used with 19 different glucometers and thus makes it extremely usable. *Score=3*

Value: The sync cable is $39.95. This would relieve the user from having to manually enter his or her glucose readings. *Score=3*

Reliability: The use of different glucometers makes it a reliable tool for blood glucose measurement in different patient populations. *Score=3*

Effectiveness: It can be an effective logbook for diabetes management because it reduces the risk of errors associated with manual entry and entries that can be missed because of forgetfulness. *Score=3*

Table 26-2: Total App Scores Comparison for Diabetes Management Apps.

App	Diabetes Tracker	Glucose Buddy	Diabetes Manager	iBG Diabetes Manager	Glooko Logbook
Risk	3	2	2	3	1
Usability	4	4	4	2	3
Value	2	2	4	2	3
Reliability	3	3	3	3	3
Effectiveness	4	4	4	3	3
Total App Score	16	15	17	13	13

BLOOD PRESSURE MANAGEMENT APPS:

Free Standing Blood Pressure Measurement Apps

Blood Pressure Monitor — Family Lite[21]:

Risk: The risks associated with this app involve manual entry and irregular readings that could result in medication dosage errors. *Score=1*

Usability: The app is user-friendly and has a variety of functions to import and export data that can be extremely useful. *Score=4*

Value: The app is available for free and can be extremely valuable because of its multiple features and statistical options. *Score=4*

Reliability: There are some reliability issues associated with this app, especially the absence of graphical warning signs in some instances. *Score=2*

Effectiveness: It can be an effective tool in the management of blood pressure because of its built-in reminder, flexible e-mail options, as well as medication correlation. *Score=4*

Heartwise Blood Pressure Tracker[22]:

Risk: The risk associated with the app would be associated with manual data entry. *Score=1*

Usability: It is a user-friendly app and has an easy-to-use interface that makes things easy to understand for the average consumer. *Score=4*

Value: This app costs $0.99. There are similar apps available that are free of charge and provide similar functions. *Score=3*

Reliability: The app is fairly reliable but if it has issues, customer support is almost non-existent. *Score=2*

Effectiveness: It can be an effective tool in the management of weight loss and blood pressure control because of its multiple features. *Score=4*

Health Tracker Pro[23]:

Risk: The risk associated with this app are the typical risks of manual data entry because it deals with a lot of different matrices. *Score=1*

Usability: There are some issues associated with entering the time, date of the event and weight entries and have them saved properly. Score =3

Value: The app costs $3.99. All of these functions can be found in free apps but not together and so patients would have to download multiple free apps. *Score=4*

Reliability: The app is a reliable tool for patients with multiple problems who may be seeing different physicians and want to keep their data in one place. *Score=4*

Effectiveness: It can be an effective tool for managing multiple health problems. *Score=4*

Blood Pressure Management Apps Connected to Devices

Withings Health Mate App[24]:

Risk: The risk associated with this app includes the fact that data can come from multiple devices and different apps that can be mixed up or inconsistent at times. *Score=1*

Usability: The app is easy to use and the "wing" model can help users focus on the aspect of their health that is not yet completed. *Score=4*

Value: This app is valuable because it provides different features that combined can provide a complete picture of users' health. *Score=4*

Reliability: This app is reliable in blood pressure measurement with Withings blood pressure monitor and weight measurement with Withings scale. *Score=3*

Effectiveness: This app can be an effective tool in the management of weight and blood pressure management. *Score=4*

iHealth Mobile App[25]:

Risk: There are risks associated with this app because it works with myriad devices, and some of them may not be able to perform consistently. *Score=1*

Usability: The app is easy to use and one can measure different things manually if the devices are not available to the users. *Score=4*

Value: It can be a valuable app because it measures everything from blood pressure to body weight to body fat. It is expensive when used with all the available devices. *Score=2*

Reliability: The iHealth monitor Wireless Blood Pressure Monitor is FDA-approved and also has CE certification. It is also approved by European Society of Hypertension. *Score=4*

Effectiveness: It can be an effective app for the management of different problems because of its integrated design with multiple devices. *Score=4*

Table 26-3: Total App Score Comparison for Blood Pressure Apps.

App	Family Lite	Heart Wise	Health Tracker Pro	Withings	iHealth
Risk	1	1	1	1	1
Usability	4	4	3	4	4
Value	4	3	4	4	2
Reliability	2	2	4	3	4
Effectiveness	4	4	4	4	4
Total App Score	15	14	16	16	15

CONCLUSION

This chapter provides a glimpse at the future of healthcare and how it can be transformed by the use of new technologies. Mobile health applications can change the way medicine is practiced today by providing continuous daily monitoring of patients that can serve as a role model of ambulatory management. The providers can look into that information at the time of patient encounter that can help them make correct decisions for their patients.

There are challenges associated with these applications that need to be resolved before they can be a part of mainstream medical diagnosis and management. Most of the popular mainstream apps are associated with health and fitness and there is no way to know that these apps are used by people who are already fitness enthusiasts or new users looking to get in shape. There is blood pressure and blood glucose measurement apps that can help patients track their progress by recording these numbers, but don't provide the ability to measure them directly. We are still measuring blood sugar the old-fashioned way, by pricking patient bodies rather than trying to find a way to measure it directly, like blood oxygen levels.

The chapter also compares mobile health applications and mobile health devices that work in conjunction with mobile health apps. These devices have the ability to continuously monitor users' activities, but there is a long way for them to have the necessary accuracy and effectiveness to be a central part of patient management. These devices can be used to measure blood pressure and blood glucose readings, but they are more expensive than their regular counterparts and there are no definite studies about their reliability although some of them have been tested through randomized control trials and proved to be consistent.

Mobile health applications have immense potential to change healthcare by providing information regarding patients' overall health in a continuous manner. However, because of the ever-increasing number of these apps it is extremely difficult for providers as well as patients to make sense of what apps are good for them. This paper evaluated some of the most popular apps that are available by providing and adapting a methodology that would make it easier for people to understand the usage and effectiveness of these apps in the management of different disorders. The methodology can also be applied to other apps that make it easier for consumers to understand and identify the apps that could fit their individual preference.

It is too soon to correctly predict the future role of mobile health applications in the healthcare environment. It is encouraging to see that providers are favorable to these apps and that some of them started to prescribe these apps. The huge number of these apps makes it impossible to select a few apps that could be best for any single person, and therefore the adherence and adaptation to these apps by the consumers should be directed by individual preference. The dependence of healthcare systems on insurance providers in the United States make it absolutely imperative that the apps that are expensive, as well as the devices that can help patients to achieve better management to their chronic disease should be covered under health insurance to make it mainstream and easily available to patients. These apps are in their infancy, and with any new technology more research and time is needed to correctly understand their impact in future healthcare environments.

REFERENCES

1. Apple. Apple's AppStore marks historic 50 billionth download. [press release]. May 16, 2013. Available at: www.apple.com/pr/library/2013/05/16Apples-App-Store-Marks-Historic-50-Billionth-Download.html. Accessed September 13, 2013.

2. Warren C. Google Play hits 1 million apps. *Mashable*. July 24, 2013. Available at: http://mashable.com/2013/07/24/google-play-1-million. Accessed August 11, 2013.

3. Jahns R. The market for mHealth app services will reach $26 billion by 2017. research2guidance. March 7, 2013. Available at: www.research2guidance.com/the-market-for-mhealth-app-services-will-reach-26-billion-by-2017. Accessed September 3, 2013.

4. Mobile health applications: 2012 Study. (n.d.) *Marketing & Public Relations Firm—Verasoni Worldwide*. Available at: http://verasoni.com/mobile-health-applications-2012-study. Accessed September 3, 2013.

5. App Certification | Happtique. (n.d.) Happtique. Available at: www.happtique.com/app-certification. Accessed September 3, 2013.

6. Ludwig S. News about tech, money and innovation. *VentureBeat*. May 30, 2013. Available at: http://venturebeat.com/2013/05/30/healthtap-apprx. Accessed July 11, 2013.

7. AppAppeal. Top 29 free health apps—1 to 29 based on popularity. Available at: www.appappeal.com/apps/health. Accessed September 3, 2013.

8. Sifferlin A. 5 great health apps you should download now. TIME.com. Available at: http://healthland.time.com/2012/08/16/5-great-health-apps-you-should-use-now. Accessed September 3, 2013.

9. Greatist. The 64 best health and fitness apps of 2013. March 27, 2013. Available at: http://greatist.com/health/best-health-fitness-apps. Accessed September 3, 2013.

10. Lose It! How it works. Available at: www.loseit.com/how-it-works. Accessed September 3, 2013.

11. Fooducate. Eat a bit better. Available at: www.fooducate.com. Accessed September 3, 2013.

12. Look M. Argus: an all-in-one health and fitness tracker. July 31, 2013. Available at: http://iphone.appstorm.net/reviews/lifestyle/argus-an-all-in-one-health-and-fitness-tracker. Accessed September 3, 2013.

13. Nike+FuelBand SE. [web site]. Available at: www.nike.com/us/en_us/c/nikeplus-fuelband Nike+FuelBand SE. Accessed October 15, 2013.

14. Fitbit® Flex™. [web site]. Available at: www.fitbit.com/flex. Accessed September 4, 2013.

15. UP system features. Jawbone. Available at: https://jawbone.com/up. Accessed October 11, 2013.

16. MyNetDiary Diabetes. [web site]. Available at: www.mynetdiary.com/diabetes-tracker-for-iPhone.html. Accessed September 4, 2013.

17. Glucose Buddy. [web site]. Available at: www.glucosebuddy.com/glucose_buddy_app. Accessed September 4, 2013.
18. Diabetes Center of Excellence. Top-rated diabetes apps. Available at: http://diabetes.ufl.edu/my-diabetes/diabetes-resources/diabetes-apps. Accessed September 4, 2013.
19. iBGStar. iBGStar Diabetes Manager Application. Available at: www.ibgstar.us/iphone-app.aspx. Accessed September 4, 2013.
20. Glooko. [web site]. Available at: www.glooko.com/solutions. Accessed September 4, 2013.
21. BPMonitor Lite. [web site]. Available at: www.taconicsys.com/app/bpmonitor-lite. Accessed December 11, 2013.
22. Aungst T. (July 9, 2012). Using HeartWise Blood Pressure Tracker as an ambulatory monitoring tool for patients requiring blood pressure management. iMedicalApps. Available at: www.imedicalapps.com/2012/07/heartwise-blood-pressure-app-patients. Accessed September 4, 2013.
23. Health Tracker PRO. [web site]. Available at: www.xlabz.com/MobileProducts/iphone/healthtrackerpro. Accessed September 4, 2013.
24. Withings. Health Mate App—Introduction. Available at: www.withings.com/en/app/healthmate. Accessed September 4, 2013.
25. iHealth MyVitals Mobile Application. [web site]. Available at: www.ihealthlabs.com/ihealth_myvitals_app.htm. Accessed September 4, 2013.

Part VI
Global Perspectives

CHAPTER 27

mHealth — A Global Perspective

By Rick Krohn, MA, MAS, and David Metcalf, PhD

Necessity is the mother of invention, and this vividly illustrates the explosion of mobile health (mHealth) in the developing world. Emerging markets are the trailblazers in mHealth adoption and innovation, among both patients and providers, because mHealth leverages tools and solutions that are cheap, scalable and most importantly, effective.

The need for innovative healthcare solutions is immediate: developing countries experience disease incidence and health epidemics that are largely unknown in the developed world. In these countries, healthcare infrastructure and clinicians are fewer, overburdened, underfunded and unevenly distributed (Fig. 27-1). It gets worse. OECD countries on average spend 10 percent of GDP on healthcare. In contrast, developing countries only spend around 5 percent of their GDP for health. Add to this the inefficiency, lack of national health priorities, and general inertia found in many

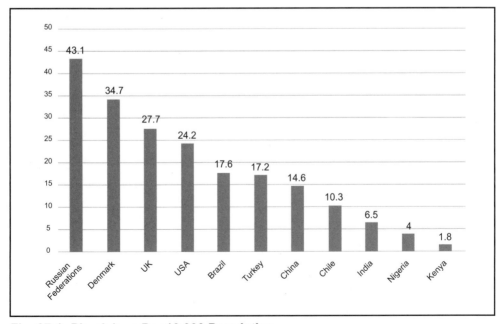

Fig. 27-1: Physicians Per 10,000 Population.

(Source: WHO, World Health Statistics 2013. Used with permission.)

government agencies in these countries, and the opportunity for healthcare crises — malnutrition, disease and epidemics — not only looms, but occurs regularly.

One of the most intriguing opportunities to fast-track an mHealth ecosystem exists in these emerging markets, where the infrastructure to support a fixed wired healthcare industry simply doesn't exist. Of the estimated 6 billion+ mobile devices in use around the world, 64 percent are in the hands of people living in emerging market economies. Although the level of mobile technologies has not yet reached the sophistication of advanced nations, in developing economies mHealth offers a far more cost effective and achievable alternative to establish an integrated, collaborative healthcare finance and delivery ecosystem.

Into this gaping void, mHealth solutions are being developed and deployed at a breakneck pace to address the spectrum of healthcare issues, from education and prevention to disease state management. mHealth fills a huge demand for access to healthcare, even if only the most basic kind, in remote regions and among underserved populations. It is a brilliant convergence of form and function: in these markets, mHealth leverages retail tools and technologies that breach geography, cost and access as barriers to care, those tools being mainly mobile phones and mobile networks. Viewed in their entirety, emerging markets provide a window into mHealth's potential to impact access and outcomes, and to move the needle from episodic to continuity of care.

It's been widely reported that mobile health is a leapfrog technology, providing a platform for the care of populations that possess established mobile networks but a weak healthcare infrastructure. Conceptually, a simple cellphone removes access and distance as barriers to both routine and chronic care. Fig. 27-2 describes a simple SMS tool that addresses prenatal health for women in Bangladesh.

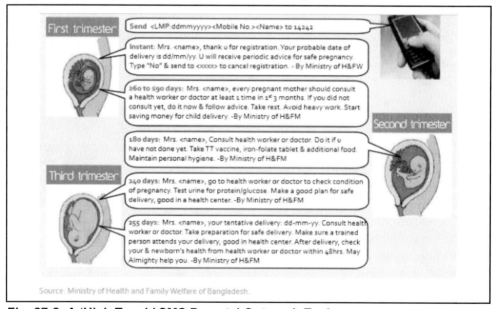

Fig. 27-2: A 'High Touch' SMS Prenatal Outreach Tool.

The impact on population health can be wide-ranging – consumer self-care, institutional and field resource management, decision support, education and prevention, mobile finance, and telemedicine — the template for innovation is ever-expanding. But the opportunities to affect change via mHealth are closely tied to local economic, environmental and social systems. In these markets mHealth innovation often happens at the periphery, where specific local problems define specific local, and thus more sustainable solutions. Here are just a few examples (See also Fig. 27-3):

India: Apollo Hospitals Group has launched a countrywide ask-a-doc service that allows rural citizens to speak to a clinician, 24 hours a day, via a call center. The service also serves as a population health monitoring tool and has the potential to reach 70 million people.

Brazil: Ambulances around the country can send cardiograms to the telemedicine unit of a specialist hospital in San Paulo, and within five minutes, receive a diagnosis to guide emergency treatment.

Ghana: A drug service, mPedigree, allows patients to SMS a coded number on the packaging of their medication to verify that the product is legitimate (drug counterfeiting is a huge problem in emerging markets).

Tanzania: Mobile operator TIGO has launched a health insurance product covering baseline services that is payable via a weekly phone charge. The coverage includes visits and overnight hospital stays.

Kenya: From anti-malaria campaigns to HIV awareness, billboards with text message campaigns associated with them abound. Payment service m-Pesa offers an innovative way to securely and quickly transfer money by USSD (Unstructured Supplementary Service Data) or IVR (Interactive Voice Response), and it is commonly used as payment in the healthcare industry. Services like m-Pesa are used for payment of all types of services including healthcare with 42 percent of the population making at least one transaction per day.

Global South: MAMA (Mobile Alliance for Maternal Action), a non-profit, offers free educational messaging for maternal and child health, targeted to specific health issues, in more than 50 countries.

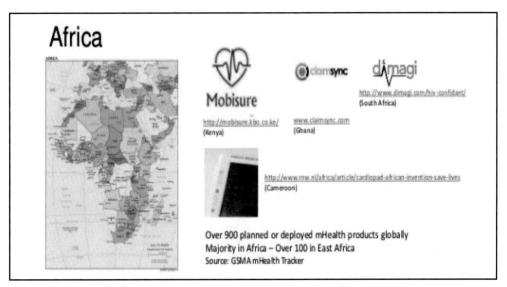

Fig. 27-3: A Snapshot of Global mHealth Initiatives in Play.

These examples merely scratch the surface. In Asia, the Middle East, Central and South America, there are hundreds of pilots, programs and products currently in play.

Beyond the technologies that enable a mobile society, there are also many process and business innovations in play. In emerging markets, microfinance is bolstering seedling economic activity and providing opportunities for hard-working individuals to buy durable goods that they can resell, or stock farms and small businesses. People are even paying for education in business, health and other careers through innovative programs like Kiva's student loan program with Strathmore University. It is amazing to see the leapfrog effect of these solutions in action — countries with less economic means than most of Europe or North America are able to innovate and leverage these new technologies quickly, efficiently and effectively.

Opportunities to improve outcomes for the underserved, poor, rural and minority populations, aren't restricted to emerging markets; they are staring at us right here at home. Though the examples above of mHealth's impact in the developing world don't directly translate to the domestic healthcare landscape, we can "reverse engineer" mobile healthcare successes elsewhere in the world to boost outcomes for our most vulnerable populations and weave these proven technology solutions into our domestic mHealth ecosystem. A mobile healthcare strategy will prove particularly effective in addressing the unmet needs among underserved minority populations, and that premise holds true for Native American and rural populations as well. At a baseline level, mHealth will become both an adjunct for, and a substitute to, the office visit by providing culturally appropriate health information, medication reminders, lifestyle advice and bilateral doctor-patient communication. In more advanced applications, mHealth solutions will serve as the conduit for patient treatments via remote patient management tools, self care and telemedicine.

There is also a unique collaborative phenomenon occurring in mHealth — a cross-pollination effect taking place in developed/developing markets. For example, Euro telco Telefónica created a geo-fence service (which triggers an alarm if the user strays from a defined area) for the UK. This same service is being marketed as a personal security tool in Latin America (where, sadly, kidnapping has become a growth industry). The opposite also holds true: we are again "reverse engineering" mobile healthcare successes elsewhere in the world to boost outcomes for our most vulnerable populations here in Global North, and weaving these proven technology solutions into our domestic mHealth ecosystems. Proven solutions like mobile messaging, field staff management and eVisits are proving to be just as effective in rural America as they are in Africa.

There are of course hurdles, and mHealth in emerging markets is facing some headwinds. Scalability is a common issue in countries where alignment between the owners of mHealth (often an NGO or private enterprise) and the government lack alignment or a shared urgency. At the operations level, there are issues of broken supply chain, under-trained health workers and unequal access to transportation.

From a strategy standpoint, GSMA has identified four key barriers that must be addressed for mHealth to reach its potential in emerging markets:

1. Fragmentation of service delivery.
2. Lack of scale across the full reach of mobile networks.
3. Limited replication.

4. Misalignment of stakeholders.

Those aren't minor obstacles, and it's going to take time for mHealth to reach its fullest expression in emerging markets. But right now, there are lessons we can learn from observing international trends in action. The ability to innovate based on essential health needs and services with lower-end technologies can provide us with models that can both scale to large audiences in developing countries and meet or exceed some of the cost constraint expectations in North America and Europe. Perhaps as initiatives in Africa, Southeast Asia and other regions define how to meet healthcare needs at lower costs using mobile technology, we can bring these technology, process and cost innovations back to developed markets and achieve the Triple Aim of better, faster and cheaper healthcare. The global opportunity: leveraging these mHealth innovations could lead us to a reorientation of the industry from healthcare to healthy living.

CHAPTER 28

Using Mobile Technology to Educate and Empower Low-Income Mothers and Families: A Case Study

By Joanne Peter, MBChB, MPhil

ABSTRACT

The Mobile Alliance for Maternal Action (MAMA) is a public-private partnership that supports programs delivering vital health information through mobile phones to mothers in low-resource settings. MAMA has launched country-wide programs in Bangladesh, South Africa and India, and released free, evidence-based mobile messages on pregnancy, child care, infant feeding, prevention of mother-to-child transmission of HIV, and post-partum family planning for organizations around the world to adapt and use in their own programs.

MAMA messages currently reach 600,000 mothers and families, and are used by more than 235 organizations in almost 60 countries. In a sample of MAMA Bangladesh subscribers, 63 percent reported attending four antenatal visits vs. a national average of 32 percent, and 83 percent reported exclusive breastfeeding for six months vs. a national average of 64 percent. Case studies of programs using the MAMA messages illustrate emerging best practices around close government engagement, highly localized content and using messages to drive demand for life-saving commodities. Barriers to successful implementation include lack of technology know-how within traditionally health-focused organizations, lack of follow-on funding and failure to establish commercial relationships with mobile operators.

MAMA is notable as a mobile health (mHealth) program achieving global reach through a diverse community of organizations; an example of a successful public-private partnership; and a platform for generating and sharing evidence on successful behavior change communication via mobile phones. As the network of implementing organizations grows, we will have an invaluable asset: a global platform that millions of women living in poverty trust to speak to them on important issues — from immunization to family planning and beyond.

PROBLEM/CHALLENGE

*"...more than 60 percent of all under-five child deaths can be avoided with proven, low-cost preventive care and treatment. Preventive care includes: continuous breast-feeding, vaccination, adequate nutrition and, in Africa, the use of insecticide-treated bed nets. ... **Families and communities need to know how best to bring up their children healthily and deal with sickness when it occurs**."*

— World Health Organization

Many of the simple health interventions that have been proven to reduce maternal and child deaths begin within the household. Their adoption requires the knowledge and willing participation of the mother, and other household and community decision makers. Programs aiming to reduce preventable deaths must include a focus on health education, promotion of healthy household behaviors and generating demand for preventive health services.

Several communication modalities — including TV, radio, billboards, print materials and face-to-face instruction via community agents — have been regularly employed for these purposes, but mobile technology offers significant advantages over these other approaches in terms of reach, cost, targeting and engagement. Mobile phone-based health messages are portable, accessible, discrete and can be saved or shared. They can provide information, offer support, dispel myths, highlight warning signs and connect pregnant women and new mothers with local health services. Messages can be targeted to a woman's stage of pregnancy or the age of her child so that the information reflects exactly what she is experiencing at a particular time. This helps to build an emotional connection with the mother and a sense of trust, making it more likely that she will be receptive to messages that encourage changes in behavior. A mobile messaging program accompanies each mother on her journey of learning and discovery, and acts as a step-by-step guide to a healthy pregnancy and healthy baby.

Real-world experience with mobile messaging for maternal, newborn and child health is showing excellent levels of user acceptability, with some promising suggestions of health impact. For example, 95 percent of users who responded to a survey (n=34,392) on the text4baby program in the United States said they would refer text4baby to a friend and rated the helpfulness of the service at 7.8 out of 10. Additionally, 74 percent reported that text4baby messages informed them of medical warning signs they did not know.[1]

A database of registered users can strengthen all other maternal and child health programs, because additional information and services can be layered on top, e.g. mass immunization campaigns, emergency outbreak notifications, reminders of health services, or vouchers for bed nets or nutritional supplements. Data collected from users can be used to target or refine other services.

BACKGROUND

MAMA — founded by the U.S. Agency for International Development, Johnson & Johnson, mHealth Alliance, United Nations Foundation and BabyCenter — is an innovative public-private partnership that engages a global community to deliver vital health information to new and expectant mothers and their families through the use of mobile technology. MAMA directly supports country programs in Bangladesh and South Africa, with India scheduled to begin in 2014. These programs support hundreds of thousands of women and families through their pregnancies and the first three years of parenting, and also serve as case studies to illustrate the diverse approaches required to establish a mobile health messaging program. See Appendix B on page 347 for Community Spotlights.

MAMA BANGLADESH

The MAMA Bangladesh program is called *Aponjon* (meaning *'the dear one'* in Bangla). After a year of pilot testing, *Aponjon* was launched nationally in December 2012 by Bangladeshi social enterprise Dnet in partnership with the Government of Bangladesh Ministry of Health and Family Welfare. In the nine months since launch, it has grown to serve more than 150,000 mothers and families, trained more than 3,000 community agents and brand promoters to registered subscribers, and brokered partnerships with six mobile network operators, three large corporate partners, and the Government of Bangladesh.

Information is delivered twice weekly in one of two forms: SMS or short 60-second "mini-skit" voice messages, with local actors playing the roles of a doctor, pregnant woman, mother and mother-in-law. The characters enact scenarios in an entertaining and educational format. Dialogues range from the doctor explaining the importance of iron-rich food to reminding the pregnant character that it is time for her medical checkup.

Dnet generates multiple streams of revenue through low user fees, advertisements, corporate partnerships and a "Sponsor-a-Ma" campaign in the stores of Bangladesh's largest retailer.

Aponjon costs 2 taka (about $0.025 USD) per message, but the service is provided free-of-charge to the poorest 20 percent of subscribers. MAMA Bangladesh has also created a unique service specifically for husbands and other household members, which reinforces messages provided to the mother and encourages family involvement in healthy decision making around pregnancy, birth and infant care.

Evaluation and Results

During a first phone survey, 63 percent of subscribers reported attending at least four antenatal visits, compared to a national average of only 32 percent; 45 percent reported a facility-based delivery compared to a national average of 29 percent; and 83 percent reported exclusively breastfeeding for the first six months, compared to a national average of 64 percent. More than 90 percent of subscribers were satisfied with the *Aponjon* service. MAMA Bangladesh aims to reach two million mothers in its first three years.

MAMA SOUTH AFRICA

MAMA South Africa currently consists of a free SMS program offered through two inner-city clinics in Hillbrow, Johannesburg; a dynamic community portal at www.askmama.mobi; and a USSD-based interactive quiz service. MAMA South Africa aims to expand to include a portal on Mxit, a popular mobile social network in South Africa.

The SMS service provides two messages a week from a mother's fifth week of pregnancy until her baby is one year old. She can opt to receive additional information specifically designed for HIV-positive mothers. The mobisite includes stories from real mothers, polls, articles and life guides. By registering with her due date or her baby's birth date, a mother can ensure that she receives information targeted to her and her child. Vodacom has made askmama.mobi available free of charge to all Vodacom subscribers in South Africa, an estimated 25 million people. The mobisite received more than 80,000 unique visits in two weeks post-launch.

Through these services, MAMA South Africa provides information to promote earlier antenatal care, encourage exclusive breastfeeding and support HIV-positive mothers to prevent transmission to their babies.

Evaluation and Results

The MAMA South Africa program conducted detailed user testing over a period of two months with a group of 22 pregnant women and new mothers.

In the test group, 80 percent of mothers reported acquiring new knowledge on childcare, such as when to introduce solid foods, how to monitor developmental milestones and when to vaccinate. Pregnant mothers reported learning about the signs of labor, the importance of a facility-based delivery to reduce the risk of HIV transmission, warning signs of illness, improved nutrition and relief of the minor ailments of pregnancy.

All mothers shared the information within their community. Some used the messages to correct misinformation from family members, or to help them negotiate with a partner around issues such as the use of condoms while pregnant.

Almost 3,000 women have been enrolled in an evaluation to assess the health impact of the messaging, particularly around prevention of mother-to-child transmission of HIV. This evaluation includes a review of medical records to compare user-reported data with actual uptake of health services.

A GROWING MAMA COMMUNITY

The MAMA country programs generate lessons and practical experience that MAMA uses to inform the design of tools and resources to help other like-minded organizations accelerate the launch of their own systems, creating a multiplier effect. The first MAMA resource has been a set of free, adaptable mobile messages. The set contains core messages for pregnancy and the first three years of a child's life, plus messages on specific health topics like infant feeding, prevention of mother-to-child transmission of HIV and post-partum family planning.

The messages come in two formats: text messages designed to be sent three times a week, and voice messages designed to be sent once a week. They were developed by BabyCenter, in partnership with a team of experts in maternal, newborn and child health. They have been rigorously researched and reviewed to ensure that they reflect the latest international evidence and best practices. The adaptable messages, an example of which is below, serve as a guide to recommended topics, tone, and timing so that organizations can quickly create messages appropriate for new and expectant mothers in their local setting. MAMA also provides adaptation guidelines to further aid the localization process.

Sample message: *Trust your instincts. If you think your child is unwell, take her to the clinic. You know her better than anyone else, so trust yourself.*

Sample message: *Keep your child away from anyone who coughs and sneezes. Many illnesses are spread through coughs and sneezes, including pneumonia.*

In less than two years, more than 235 non-profits, social enterprises and governments in almost 60 countries around the world have joined the MAMA community by downloading and using the evidence-based, mobile-formatted MAMA messages. As depicted in Fig. 28-1, the messages currently reach 600,000 new and expectant mothers globally.

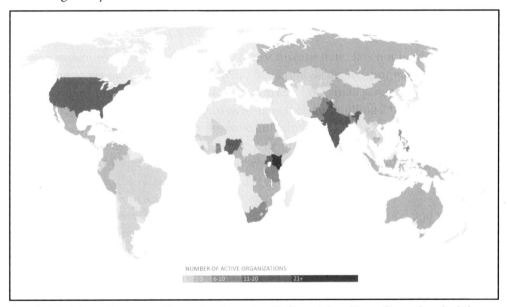

Fig. 28-1: More than 235 Organizations in 60 Countries Have Downloaded the MAMA Messages.

Members of the MAMA community have translated and adapted the MAMA mobile messages to suit the particular needs of their country and target audience. To date, the messages have been translated into twenty languages: Bangla, Zulu, Xhosa, Sotho, Afrikaans, Tetum, Swahili, Urdu, Sindhi, Filipino, Portuguese, Chinese, Pashto, Dari, Spanish, Luganda, Haitian Creole, Dagbanli, Chichewa and Chiyao.

Implementing a successful mobile messaging program requires more than just high quality content. Organizations must define a target audience, select a suitable technology platform for message delivery, perform user testing, obtain government and regulatory approvals, market to potential users, and establish systems for monitoring and evaluation. A survey of MAMA community members (n=57) asked organizations to describe their current stage of implementation. Just over half reported that they have begun a messaging program, or are poised to start once early content development, system design and user testing is complete. MAMA tools and resources aim to support these programs to transition from the initial start-up phase to live programs by reducing barriers to successful launch and scale-up.

To this end, the MAMA community convenes monthly for an interactive online learning session around a key implementation issue, such as translating and localizing content, selecting a technology platform, or negotiating with mobile network operators. Representatives of each organization interact through an online discussion forum and can participate in working groups on specific topics, such as monitoring and evaluation.

Already, new collaborations are beginning to form; representatives from Peru, the Dominican Republic, Venezuela and Colombia have recently joined forces to translate the MAMA messages into Spanish for use in Latin America.

COMING SOON: MAMA AFFILIATE PROGRAM

MAMA will soon launch a targeted capacity building program to cater for those organizations who wish to receive more individualized support as they launch mobile messaging programs. Following several in-depth stakeholder interviews, MAMA has identified a number of high priority areas where organizations would benefit from technical assistance beyond standardized guidelines and learning modules. These particularly pertain to technology platform selection and set-up, as well as associated negotiations with mobile network operators, aggregators and telecommunications regulators.

Starting with a comprehensive needs and capabilities assessment, MAMA will work with the Affiliate to build and execute against a mutually agreed implementation plan. A full-service capacity building program may include MAMA's support with translation and adaptation of MAMA's mobile content; selection of an appropriate technology platform and vendor; negotiation with relevant mobile network operator(s); government approvals (both health and telecommunications); and applications for funding.

Additional supplementary services could include guidance on best practices around customer outreach and acquisition, operational planning, and monitoring and evaluation.

MAMA is committed to the principles of local capacity building and partnership and will work with local country consortia, experienced technology developers, and other members of the mobile health ecosystem to help future MAMA Affiliates launch services that reach millions of mothers and their families with vital health information.

CONCLUSION

MAMA aspires to empower millions of low-income, at-risk mothers and families with relevant, culturally sensitive health information that is readily accessible through technology they already own. MAMA's approach to scale has been at two levels: through country programs with national reach; and through a targeted program of global learning that allows other implementing organizations to take advantage of lessons learned through the MAMA countries, practical resources such as the adaptable mobile messages and a collaborative learning community. There has been great demand for MAMA's mobile messages, with applications from more than 235 organizations in almost 60 countries. By supporting these organizations with the next steps in program implementation — from technology platform selection to operational planning and monitoring and evaluation — MAMA can decrease the barriers to successful program launch and scale, and serve as a platform for sharing evidence on the impact of mobile health messaging on maternal, newborn and child health.

Additional information on MAMA's work around the world can be found in Appendix B, "Mama Community Spolights."

REFERENCE

1. https://text4baby.org/index.php/about/data-and-evaluation.

CHAPTER 29

Using Mobile Phones to Provide Critical Family Planning Information in Africa: A Case Study

By Kelly L'Engle, PhD, MPH; Stacey Succop, MPH, PMP; and Heather Vahdat, MPH

ABSTRACT

In 2010, FHI 360, with support from the USAID PROGRESS project and in partnership with several in-country governmental and non-governmental entities, designed and launched Mobile for Reproductive Health, or m4RH, in Kenya and Tanzania. m4RH is a mobile phone, text-message-based, opt-in service that provides users with essential information about nine different short and long acting family planning (FP) methods. m4RH has helped fill a critical gap for women, men and young people of reproductive age who have limited access to accurate and comprehensive FP information. Three years after the launch, m4RH has been promoted by in-country partners in Kenya and Tanzania and has had more than 150,000 unique users access the system. Additionally, m4RH has been adapted to target youth in Rwanda to include information on puberty, pregnancy and sexual relationships, and HIV and STIs, in addition to the standard information about FP methods. With rigorous evaluation efforts underway, m4RH has already demonstrated its reach and feasibility, and thus its potential to improve reproductive health for millions around the globe.

PROBLEM/CHALLENGE/OPPORTUNITY

Reducing unmet need for family planning (FP) and increasing access to contraceptives are essential to achieving Millennium Development Goals (MDG) 4 and 5, goals which many developing countries are struggling to meet. Every day, approximately 800 women die from preventable causes related to pregnancy and childbirth. A notable 99 percent of these maternal deaths occur in developing countries,[1] where over 220 million women lack access to effective contraception and FP services.[2] Many women and children die unnecessarily from complications during pregnancy, childbirth and infancy, complications that could be reduced dramatically with increased use of modern FP.[3,4] Preventing unplanned pregnancies can eliminate 44 percent of maternal deaths.[5] In developing countries, spacing births at least 36 months apart would reduce deaths among children under five by approximately one-third.[6]

Yet, unmet need for FP remains high in many countries in Sub-Saharan Africa while contraceptive prevalence rates remain low. Despite considerable investments over several decades to increase access and demand for FP services, there were an estimated 80 million unintended pregnancies globally in 2012. Most unintended pregnancies (79 percent) occurred among sexually active women residing in developing countries who did not want to become pregnant, but were not using contraception.[2] Sub-Saharan Africa bears the highest percentage of unmet need for modern contraception at approximately 25 percent, and this has changed little since the mid-1990s.[7] In Tanzania and Kenya, family planning continues to be a critical public-health issue as nearly a quarter of women have an unmet need for FP, with unmet needs in rural areas approximately 7 percentage points higher than in urban areas in both countries. Current use of modern contraception by women remains relatively low at 23 percent in Tanzania and 28 percent in Kenya.[8,9]

Concerns about side-effects, coupled with widespread misconceptions, misinformation and rumors are top reasons that women and men report unwillingness to begin FP. If and when women begin using contraceptive methods, more than one-third discontinues use within the first 12 months, putting them at renewed risk for unwanted pregnancy. Therefore, accurate information about the benefits of FP and variety of available methods is critical to supporting FP uptake and continuation.

SOLUTION PROCESS

Mobile phones can help further FP efforts while increasing reach to the most vulnerable populations. With more than 85 percent of the world's inhabitants having mobile connectivity,[10] millions of women and their families — even the approximate 50 percent of people living in rural populations globally[11] — can benefit from information delivered through what has become a standard 21st century means of communication.

The widespread presence, reach, convenience and privacy of mobile phones present a major opportunity to reach a wider audience with health information outside of a clinical setting. During the past decade, mobile phone penetration has rapidly spread across Africa. Between 2000 and 2010, mobile phone subscriptions in Kenya increased by nearly 200 percent.[12] In 2010, nearly half of the population in Tanzania (20 million people) used mobile phones,[13] and mobile phone penetration is expected to increase by another 70 percent by 2015. Mobile phones are accessible to younger populations in Sub-Saharan Africa where subscriptions for people under 30 are expected to reach 108 million in 2012.[14] Use of SMS, which is available on every mobile phone and is often referred to as "text messaging," has increased dramatically on a global scale, with more than 200,000 text messages sent every second (2010).[15] Several factors make communicating via SMS appealing: text messages are an inexpensive (typically US$.01-.05/message), private, and efficient means of communicating.

Chapter 29: Using Mobile Phones to Provide Critical Family Planning Information in Africa: A Case Study

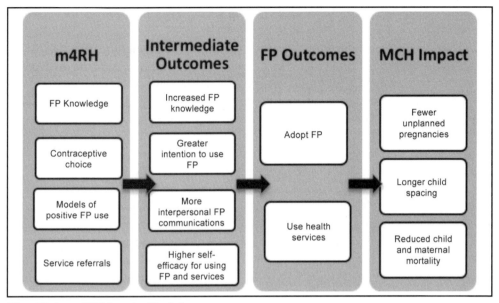

Fig. 29-1: m4RH Logic Model.

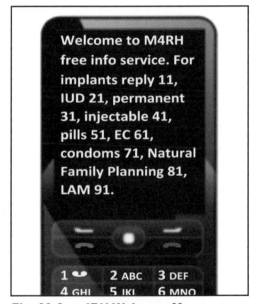

Fig. 29-2: m4RH Welcome Menu.

Mobile for Reproductive Health (m4RH), developed by FHI 360 with support from the USAID PROGRESS project and in partnership with several in-country governmental and non-governmental entities, is a mobile phone-based, automated, interactive and on-demand SMS that provides users with easily accessible, accurate, and confidential information about nine different short and long acting family planning (FP) methods. m4RH is a strategically designed system that leverages and integrates the latest scientific, information and communication technology, and behavioral change advances into a simple, powerful, and scalable solution. Fig. 29-1 shows the approach of m4RH: its content is designed to impact intermediate behavioral change outcomes to affect use of FP and health services, ultimately impacting key maternal and child health outcomes.

Accessing m4RH is simple — a user sends a keyword via SMS to a short-code telephone number (e.g., 15014) to receive selected FP content (Fig. 29-2). The user can access as much information as many times and whenever they want. In two to three message screens, m4RH presents essential facts about each contraception method (including implants, IUDs, permanent methods, injectable, oral contraceptives pills, emergency contraception, condoms, and natural methods) and addresses FP misconceptions and norms through narrative stories that model FP decision-making and use.

m4RH also provides a searchable database that allows users to locate nearby FP clinics via SMS.

Given the increasing ubiquity of mobile phones in the developing world, m4RH represents a simple, yet powerful means to put contraceptive information and decision-making directly into the hands of African men and women. It was designed to reach the general public and particularly people underserved by traditional methods of public health and family planning promotion. m4RH was designed to provide information via text message because the SMS protocol is available across all makes and models of mobile phones. Taking advantage of this universal aspect of mobile phone functionality ensures that the potential reach of the m4RH service is maximized. In addition, m4RH provides family planning information in a format that is novel and often surprising to users — and that helps to overcome many of the barriers to access. Typically, family planning information is provided in health facility settings or increasingly by community health workers, and rarely is information about the full range of contraceptive methods provided to clients. m4RH has revolutionized the notion of "choice" in provision of family planning information because any person can access standardized and essential information in simple language about every family planning method available. Through m4RH, potential barriers to use of family planning — including cost and logistic challenges associated with traveling to health facilities and stigma of certain population segments inquiring about or adopting family planning — are mitigated. This is particularly true for younger people but also for adults in need.

SOLUTION IMPLEMENTATION

FHI 360 conceptualized, developed and deployed m4RH (Fig. 29-3) as part of a research study aimed at determining the feasibility of providing FP information via text message, the reach of this communication channel, and suggested impact on FP use. It was piloted and evaluated in Kenya and Tanzania from 2010–2011 in collaboration with several partners including the Ministries of Health in both countries, Text to Change (TTC) as the technological partner, and numerous other health entities.

FHI 360 worked closely with a variety of organizations in Kenya and Tanzania, including Ministries of Health, service delivery partners, community-based organizations, and health communication and media partners, in addition to the technological partner. These stakeholders influenced and guided the development process by articulating the local family planning and reproductive health (FP/RH) priorities and needs, by providing technical expertise and contextual experience in FP/RH, by providing locally-relevant suggestions for effective promotion, and by linking m4RH to service delivery organizations. In turn, partners viewed promoting m4RH as a means to support national health and development goals and objectives, to reach their target audiences with health education, and to create demand for family planning and reproductive health services. Said one m4RH service delivery partner: "We were interested because we also provide family planning services and we have a network of facilities, so we found that m4RH will be valuable to our project, since we also want to network and inform people where our services are."

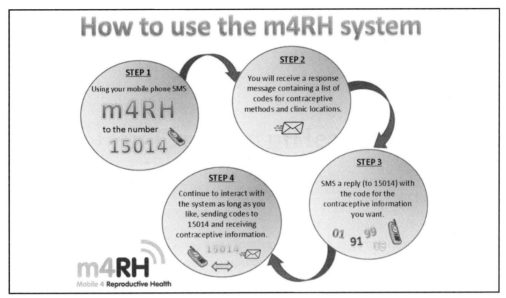

Fig. 29-3: The m4RH System.

With support from these partners and stakeholders, m4RH was developed based on best practices in health communications design, health behavior change theory and family planning research. The text messages about family planning available in the m4RH system were systematically developed using best practices for health communication by engaging the target audience, identifying their perceptions and specific needs related to contraception and creating targeted messages to meet those needs (Fig. 29-3). Messages, which conformed to the 160-character limit for texts, were based on WHO and country-specific family planning guidance, as well as literature about family planning uptake and continuation. They were tested with target users to determine the acceptability of providing family planning information via text message, the usability of the system interface (e.g., ability to understand how to navigate through the system) and comprehension of the messages. Results from the formative research led to important modifications to the system content and architecture. Final messages also were reviewed by global and in-country family planning experts, clinic partners, and Ministry of Health representatives.

The m4RH text messages (Fig. 29-4, page 268) address not only technical information about family planning methods (e.g., side-effects, duration of use) but also barriers and misperceptions about family planning. For example, the m4RH text messages state that family planning is for both married and single people, that family planning does not impair future fertility and that it is best if discussed with partners. The use of "role model stories" that model adoption and use while addressing barriers and misconceptions to family planning are an innovative approach to health promotion, especially considering that these stories are delivered in timed installments via SMS to the m4RH user.

During the pilot study, m4RH was largely promoted in clinics. Partners such as Marie Stopes in Tanzania and Kenya and Family Health Options of Kenya displayed m4RH posters in their facilities, offered flyers in their waiting rooms and asked their providers to notify clients of the service and distribute palm cards with the short-code. Over time, more partners began promoting m4RH in increasingly diverse ways. Partners including Pathfinder and the ROADS Project in Tanzania oriented their community health workers and peer educators to the service and provided them with palm cards for distribution to their target audiences. Both PSI in Kenya and JHU-CCP in Tanzania featured m4RH within larger mass media campaigns promoting family planning.

RESULTS

During the pilot period, users made a total of 4,813 contraceptive queries (2,870 unique users) to the m4RH system in Tanzania and 12,954 queries (4,817 unique users) to the Kenyan system. The most popular contraceptive method queried was natural family planning (21 percent in Tanzania; 22 percent in Kenya), followed by condoms (12 percent in Tanzania; 17 percent in Kenya). (Table 29-1).

> **m4RH INJECTION MESSAGE:**
> Injection in arm or hip, like Depo. Effective for 1-3 months. Get on time, return even if late. Irregular or no monthly bleeding not harmful. May gain weight. For married and singles. After stopping may take a few months to get pregnant. No infertility or pregnancy loss. Private.

> **m4RH CONDOM MESSAGE:**
> Male condoms are effective when used correctly every time. Only method to prevent HIV, STIs, and pregnancy. Use a new condom every time. Easy to find, inexpensive. Best if discussed with partner. Easily used with practice. For married and singles.

Fig. 29-4: Sample m4RH Messages.

Table 29-1: Number of Family Planning Methods Queried by m4RH Users During Pilot Period (by country).

	Kenya (12,954 queries) (Jan. 2010 – June 2011)	Tanzania (4,813 queries) (Sept. 2010 – June 2011)
Methods queried		
Natural family planning	2,851 (22%)	1,012 (21%)
Condoms	2,146 (17%)	585 (12%)
Implants	1,458 (11%)	560 (12%)
Injectables	1,409 (11%)	536 (11%)
IUCD	1,269 (10%)	457 (9%)
Oral contraceptive pills	1,426 (11%)	450 (9%)
Emergency contraception	1,350 (11%)	754 (16%)
Permanent methods	1,045 (8%)	459 (10%)

During the pilot period, m4RH users who accessed the system were sent four demographic and behavior change questions (in Swahili in Tanzania and English in Kenya) via SMS. The questions asked users about their gender, age, where they learned about m4RH, and how m4RH has affected their use of family planning. From this data collection effort, it became evident that m4RH was used by many men and young people.[26,27] In Tanzania, 56 percent of users were female and 44 percent were male, and 59 percent were 29 and younger. In Kenya, 61 percent of users were female and 39 percent were male, and 82 percent were 29 years and younger. In addition, the data suggested that m4RH has the potential to impact contraception and condom use behavior.

Since the pilot study, the m4RH system has garnered wide interest among partners, leading to system expansions such as development of more in-depth FP content as well as comprehensive sexual and reproductive health content, testing bilingual (Swahili-English) and multi-lingual systems (Kinyarwanda-English-French), and exploring different technological options, including a combined SMS-Unstructured Supplementary Service Data (USSD) protocol. In Tanzania, m4RH has been incorporated into a national family planning campaign that led to 50,000 people using m4RH in just three months. In Rwanda, the Ministry of Health requested that m4RH be adapted for young people by including information on contraception, HIV, other sexually transmitted infections, sex and pregnancy and puberty. In Kenya, Abt Associates, expanding on mHealth research and SMS data collection methods pioneered by FHI 360, conducted an independent evaluation of the impact of m4RH messages on FP adoption.

By the end of 2012, the m4RH system had received more than 400,000 queries (Table 29-2).

Table 29-2: Number of Queries by m4RH Users Through 2012 (by country).

	Kenya (52,338 queries)	Tanzania (351,493 queries)
Menus queried		
Main menu	12,739	109,075
Secondary menus	10,178	102,369
Methods queried		
Natural family planning	6,236	24,202
Condoms	3,772	19,241
Implants	2,770	11,624
Injectables	2,525	10,337
IUCD	2,437	9,583
Oral contraceptive pills	2,703	11,036
Emergency contraception	2,503	15,255
Permanent methods	1,847	12,628
Clinics queried	4,628	26,143

CONCLUSION

This mHealth solution is one of the first to provide comprehensive family planning information to citizens in sub-Saharan Africa. Other mobile phone programs in high-income countries have shown that providing sexual health information to youth is feasible and effective in promoting use of health services and healthy sexual behavior.[16,17] This project demonstrates that information about the full range of contraceptive methods can be feasibly delivered and accessed by women and men of reproductive age via mobile phone.

m4RH has reached several important demographic segments. Men represent a large portion of users, and they seemed to be investigating contraceptive methods for themselves as well as their female partners. Evidence shows that communication between couples and shared decision-making predict increased use of family planning,[18,19,20,21] and women are more likely to use contraceptives if men are involved in and supportive of the decision.[22,23] Mobile phones provide a new channel for reaching men and encouraging shared decision-making around contraceptives.

Adolescents and young adults are the heaviest users of m4RH. This is not surprising considering that young people tend to be frequent users of mobile phones and text messaging.[24] Condom information is a top choice for users ages 29 and younger, and in pilot study data collection mentions of condom use were the first or second most frequently cited family planning change among these younger age groups. Importantly, younger users also were interested in a variety of short- and long-acting methods. Some evidence suggests that when presented with the option to use long-acting methods, young people intending to use short-acting methods may accept the longer acting method instead.[25] Data from the m4RH project suggest that using mobile phones to reach adolescents and young adults with information about the range of contraceptive options may help to overcome barriers that limit their use of modern contraceptive methods, such as lack of knowledge, limited access and concerns about side effects.

Another interesting finding came from the users who were also community health workers (CHWs) and peer educators. Both of these groups reported that they promote m4RH and use it as a means to review information when counseling about family planning. They recommend m4RH to their clients, and their clients use m4RH to supplement what they learn from the CHW. The use of m4RH to support the work of peer educators and community health workers is an unintended positive outcome that demonstrates the applicability of this tool in multiple settings.

The m4RH pilot and partner expansions demonstrate the extraordinary reach and potential for large-scale and behavioral impact. Even people in very remote rural areas access FP information and service referrals using the m4RH system; after the pilot study was concluded, between April and September 2012, data from about 25,000 users in Tanzania documented that m4RH reaches into rural and urban areas, with users located in 127 out of 129 districts in Tanzania.

The innovative packaging of diverse information and behavior change components in a single technology is the first time that science and technology, service delivery and demand creation have been integrated into one systematically developed and tested family planning intervention. m4RH has revolutionized the concept of informed choice in the provision of FP because any person can access standardized, essential information in simple language about every method available. Comparable mechanisms for providing FP information and support include health provider counseling in clinical settings, community health and peer-educator counseling, community events, and use of other mass and small media channels. m4RH complements these traditional approaches, while offering numerous added benefits to overcome historical barriers to FP access and use such as cost and logistical challenges associated with traveling to health facilities; lack of staff trained in FP counseling; and stigma for certain population segments including youth or male partners inquiring about or adopting FP. Given the severe shortage of health workers and weak health infrastructure in most developing countries, these benefits of m4RH are especially noteworthy.

Disclaimer
Some of the data presented in this chapter have been published previously. [26, 27]

REFERENCES

1. World Health Organization. Maternal Mortality. *Fact Sheet No. 348* 2012. Available at: www.who.int/mediacentre/factsheets/fs348/en/. Accessed June 24, 2013.
2. Singh S, Darroch JE. Adding It Up: Costs and Benefits of Contraceptive Services. *Guttmacher Institute and UNFPA*. 2012.
3. Cleland J, Bernstein S, Ezeh A, Faundes A, Glasier A, Innis J. Family planning: the unfinished agenda. *The Lancet*. 2006;368(9549):1810-1827.
4. RamaRao S, Townsend J, Askew I. *Correlates of inter-birth intervals: implications of optimal birth spacing strategies in Mozambique*: Frontiers in Reproductive Health, Population Council; 2006.
5. Ahmed S, Li Q, Liu L, Tsui AO. Maternal deaths averted by contraceptive use: an analysis of 172 countries. *The Lancet*. 2012.
6. Rutstein SO. Effects of preceding birth intervals on neonatal, infant and under-five years mortality and nutritional status in developing countries: evidence from the demographic and health surveys. *International Journal of Gynaecology and Obstetrics*. 2005;89(1):S7.
7. Guttmacher Institute & International Planned Parenthood Federation (IPPF) (2010). Facts on satisfying the need for contraception in developing countries. In brief. *Washington, DC, Guttmacher Institute and IPPF*.
8. National Bureau of Statistics Tanzania. (2011). *Tanzania Demographic and Health Survey, 2010*. National Bureau of Statistics.
9. Kenya National Bureau of Statistics (Nairobi). (2010). *Kenya Demographic and Health Survey 2008-09*. Kenya National Bureau of Statistics.
10. UN News Service. Deputy UN Chief Calls for Urgent Action to Tackle Global Sanitation Crisis. 2013. Available at: www.un.org/apps/news/story.asp?NewsID=44452#.UcmiHKHD_ct. Accessed June 24, 2013.
11. The World Bank. Rural Population (% of Total Population), 2011. 2013. Available at: http://data.worldbank.org/indicator/SP.RUR.TOTL.ZS/countries. Accessed June 24, 2013.
12. (ITU) ITU. Key 2000-2011 country data: Mobile-cellular subscriptions. 2012.
13. CIA Factbook. Available at: www.cia.gov/library/publications/the-world-factbook/geos/tz.html. Accessed November 14, 2011.
14. Brown G. Young people, mobile phones and the rights of adolescents; African Mobile Observatory 2011: Driving economic and social development through mobile services: GSM Association; 2011.
15. The world in 2010 facts and figures: International Telecommunication Union; 2010.
16. Gold J, Aitken CK, Dixon HG, et al. A randomised controlled trial using mobile advertising to promote safer sex and sun safety to young people. *Health Educ Res*. 2011;26:782-94.

17. Gold J, Lim MS, Hocking JS, et al. Determining the impact of text messaging for sexual health promotion to young people. *Sex Transm Dis.* 2011;38:247-52.

18. Shattuck D, Kerner B, Gilles K, et al. Encouraging contraceptive uptake by motivating men to communicate about family planning: the Malawi Male Motivator project. *Am J Public Health.* 2011;101:1089-95.

19. Edwards SR. The role of men in contraceptive decision-making: current knowledge and future implications. *Fam Plann Perspect.* 1994;26:77-82.

20. Kimuna SR, Adamchak DJ. Gender relations: husband-wife fertility and family planning decisions in Kenya. *J Biosoc Sci.* 2001;33:13-23.

21. Sharan M, Valente T. Spousal communication and family planning adoption: effects of a radio drama serial in Nepal. *Int Fam Plan Perspect.* 2002;28:16-25.

22. Santelli JS, Kouzis AC, Hoover DR, et al. Stage of behavior change for condom use: the influence of partner type, relationship and pregnancy factors. *Fam Plann Perspect.* 1996;28:101-7.

23. Schuler S, Rottach E, Mukiri P. Gender Norms and Family Planning Decision Making in Tanzania: A Qualitative Study. Washington, D.C.: C-Change, 2009.

24. Brown G. Adolescence: An Age of Opportunity. The State of the World's Children. New York: United Nations Children Fund, 2011.

25. Hubacher D, Olawo A, Manduku C, et al. Factors associated with uptake of subdermal contraceptive implants in a young Kenyan population. *Contraception.* 2011;84:413-7.

26. L'Engle KL, Vahdat HL, Ndakidemi E, Lasway C, Zan T. Evaluating feasibility, reach and potential impact of a text message family planning information service in Tanzania. 2013; [in press].

27. Vahdat HL, L'Engle KL, Plourde KF, Magariz L, Olawo A. There are some questions you may not ask in a clinic: providing contraception information to young people in Kenya using *SMS. Intl J Gyno Ob.* [in press].

CHAPTER 30

Improving Lives Through Mobile Phones in Ghana: A Case Study

By Kimberly Green; Nana Fosua Clement; Siadeyo M.W. Torgbenu; Gladys Damalin; Samuel Benefour; and Samuel Wambugu, MPH

ABSTRACT

In Ghana, Africa, there are high rates of HIV infection in two populations: female sex workers (FSW), 11.1 percent: and men who have sex with men (MSM), 17.5 percent. Both groups are stigmatized and face discrimination in daily life because underlying gender norms and legal prohibitions against sex work and same-sex relationships. FSWs and MSM in Ghana experience significant barriers to social acceptance and access to services.

Given the high levels of discrimination experienced by these populations, an mHealth intervention was piloted in 2008; Text Me! Flash Me! Call Me! HelpLine. Individuals can SMS, "flash," or call nurse counselors seven days a week with health or psychological concerns. This service now reaches more than 3,500 people annually with anonymous HIV prevention, care and treatment and mental health support.

INTRODUCTION

In this case study, we describe the role of mHealth in reaching MSM, FSW and people living with HIV (PLHIV) with critical HIV information, counseling and referral to services. Text Me! Flash Me! Call Me! HelpLine provides anonymous counseling to highly stigmatized populations in Ghana. Government nurse counselors are trained to provide non-judgmental and empathetic support. We report on the methods used and key results in reaching hidden populations through mHealth. Based on these results, we argue that mHealth in Ghana is a very effective tool in providing anonymous support to highly marginalized populations who would otherwise have limited access to health information and services.

HIV, Stigma and Poor Access to Information and Services

In Ghana, there are high rates of HIV infection in two populations: female sex workers (FSWs), 11.1 percent; and men who have sex with men (MSM), 17.5 percent.[1,2] They are more than 10 times at greater risk of HIV infection than the general population.[3]

Both groups are stigmatized and face discrimination in daily life due to underlying gender norms and legal prohibitions against sex work and same-sex relationships. Sex workers often operate clandestinely to avoid police raids and arrest. They are the victims of rape and abuse by intimate partners, clients and police.[4] Stigma and hatred towards MSM is so formidable that those whose sexual preference becomes known are subject to harassment and violence. As a result, FSWs and MSM experience significant barriers to social acceptance and access to services.

Access to HIV prevention, care and treatment services also remains a challenge for PLHIV in Ghana. Busy public anti retroviral therapy (ART) clinics do not have the staff time to respond to the concerns of PLHIV. HIV-related stigma and discrimination remain high, particularly within rural communities. As a result, a substantial number of PLHIV die each year (11,655 in 2012) outside the reach of lifesaving treatment, often hidden at home or in prayer camps.[5]

Social media and Internet usage in Ghana is growing. More than 80 percent of the population has access to a mobile phone. At the end of 2012, active mobile-phone accounts stood at nearly 25 million, roughly the same as the population of Ghana.

FROM PILOT TO PROGRAM: mHEALTH SCALE-UP FROM 2008 TO 2013

In 2008, an assessment was conducted by the Strengthening HIV/AIDS Response Partnership (SHARP) project (funded by the U.S. Agency for International Development) to gauge the acceptability of mHealth in improving MSM access to HIV-related information and services. MSMs were overwhelmingly positive of this approach and identified friendly public healthcare sexually transmitted infection (STI) nurses as counselors for the initiative. The pilot involved five nurse counselors in Accra (the capital city) who were trained to provide non-judgmental information on condom use, negotiating safer sex, HIV risk assessment, HIV testing and counseling (HTC), STI prevention, symptoms and treatment, HIV care and antiretroviral therapy. Each nurse was equipped with a phone and a local SMS aggregator, SMS Ghana, was hired to connect those using SMS to nurses for free using the short code "HELP." Users could also "flash" (call and hang-up free of charge) and be called back by one of the nurse counselors within 24 hours.[6]

Also introduced as part of the "Text Me!" component were HIV-prevention messages sent to MSM and FSW who opted for the service. HelpLine was advertised through leaflets and word of mouth from peer educators and healthcare workers. The leaflet tagline was "To get more information about friendly services in your area, use your phone to send a short text and the name of your town to 1906. Worried that you may have gotten an infection from sex? Text STI. Need to know where to go for friendly HIV testing? Text VCT. Want to know about medicines and therapies for HIV-positive people? Text ART. Want to know where to buy condoms or lubricants? Text PROTECT. Need to talk to someone in private about your HIV and AIDS questions? Text PROTECT."

A number of job aids were developed to support the nurse counselors and to ensure quality control. These included a script, HIV service referral information, a HelpLine leaflet with phone numbers of the nurses on duty each day and short-code information, and data collection tools to track anonymous caller information.

During the first month of operation, 439 MSM used the service.[7,8] The top three reasons for people using SMS or calling were to learn more about HIV transmission, HIV disease signs and symptoms and HIV testing.[9] There was a substantial increase in HIV testing uptake the month following the launch of the campaign, from 13 the previous month to 76 after the launch.[10]

Given the initial success of the program, it was expanded to reach FSW in February 2009. Seven more nurses were hired in Accra to support this growth. SHARP ended in 2009 but when the follow-on project, SHARPER (Strengthening HIV/AIDS Response Partnerships with Evidence-Based Response) was awarded to FHI 360 Ghana in 2010, HelpLine was restarted. In 2011, HelpLine further expanded to include PLHIV, and five nurses in Kumasi (the second largest city in Ghana) were added to the program. The service was promoted by peer educators among PLHIV and their family members. In 2012, 20 additional nurses from across the country were recruited and trained to participate in HelpLine. Promotional materials were revised to reflect this change.

RESULTS

A mid-term evaluation, involving a random selection of 135 MSM callers, revealed important service utilization results from HelpLine: 47 percent of respondents said that they received HIV testing, whereas 77 percent said they intended to seek HIV testing and counseling. In addition, 87 percent of MSM callers stated they shared what they had learned from the nurse counselor with others, and 40 percent of those receiving an SMS text had forwarded it to someone else.[11,12]

During the scale-up phase of the HelpLine, there was a significant increase in the number of new and repeat users. From October 2012 to March 2013, a total of 2,398 callers were reached, representing 1,225 (51 percent) females and 1,173 (49 percent) males — the majority of them were PLHIV (1,275, 53 percent) and MSM (546, 23 percent). Out of the 2,398 callers, 1,356 (57 percent) were new and 1,042 (43 percent) were repeat callers. There was a 30-percent increase in the number of clients reached, compared to the previous six-month period (April – September 2012). This increase in patronage was influenced by the placement of additional HelpLine counselors as well as continuous quality assurance and promotion of the service.[13] A total of 7,022 individuals have spoken with a HelpLine counselor since 2011.

In terms of qualitative impact of HelpLine, MSM, FSW, PLHIV and healthcare workers have reported benefits ranging from improved condom use for HIV prevention to help with disclosing their HIV status to loved ones. Below are quotes from users of the HelpLine service.

Facilitating HIV Prevention

I had a lot of issues affecting my social and sexual life, especially condom use and lubricants, that I was not able to discuss with anybody, not even my partner...but the HelpLine counselor became a friend that I can trust. The HLCs have given my partner and I important information on STIs, condom use, healthy living.... and this has encouraged us to always use condoms and lubricants... very, very helpful. – PLHIV

In Africa, it is difficult to talk about condoms as a woman because of our culture. But when you talk to the HLCs, they are able to talk to you confidently about the benefits of condom use. So they empower us and we are able to discuss condom use with our partners. – PLHIV

So many of us [PLHIV] do not understand the benefits of ART and how to prevent our unborn children from becoming infected. My friend who is HIV positive became pregnant so she called a HLC. She was counseled and this has helped her to have a baby who is not positive. – PLHIV

Linking People to Health Services

In the past, we did not have any contacts to call when in need [sick]. But now we have contacts [HLC] we can call direct any time for the necessary arrangements to be made before we arrive at the hospital. Normally you go to the hospital where you wait the whole day but because of this model, what happens now is you go to the hospital and they give you quick service and you go home. – PLHIV

Through the HelpLine Counseling, you are assured and linked to friendly health workers who will treat you well. – PLHIV

Help with Disclosure of HIV Status

My friends said counseling received from some of the HLCs gave them enough confidence to be able to disclose their [HIV] status to their partners. – PLHIV

Helping People at Risk of Suicide

I want to thank [the HLC] very much for responding to my text message and for saving my life. I really wanted to kill myself but the HLC gave me hope through their good counseling. I now have reason to live, complete my education, work and take care of my single mother, who raised me. – PLHIV

People wanted to commit suicide because they are HIV positive. People wanted to commit suicide because they are not wanted in their homes because they are MSM. The services have helped a lot of people and have saved a lot of lives. – MSM

Confidentiality

The HelpLine is a good model that makes it easier to access health information. It helps in reducing stigma - you [HLC] do not see me [PLHIV], I do not see you.

Very confidential. A lot of us may have died in silence but the HelpLine has broken our silence and is giving us hope. – PLHIV

Most of my friends do not want to go to the health facilities because some peers have had experiences where health workers have disclosed their HIV status to others — it is not fair. So the HelpLine is more acceptable, people tend to really confide in the HLCs because it is strictly confidential — it is only their voice and the HLC's on phone. - MSM

Responsiveness to Callers

Commitment of the counselors — When they see your missed call, but cannot talk immediately, they will let you know...They are very patient and polite — please, I will return your call within an hour. They will keep to their promise and call you back — very important. - MSM

CONCLUSION

HelpLine counseling offers some of the most vulnerable people in Ghana the opportunity to receive confidential support, information and referral to services. It has reinforced HIV prevention, facilitated disclosure of HIV status and promoted uptake of HIV testing and counseling.

REFERENCES

1. Adams B, Wambugu S, Nagai H, Green K, Atuahene K, El-Adas A, Amenya R, Rahman Y. Evidenced-based data for HIV prevention interventions among key populations in Ghana. National HIV/AIDS Research Conference, Accra, Ghana, September 11–13, 2013.
2. Ghana AIDS Commission (GAC). Integrated Biological and Behaviorial Surveillance Survey and Population Size Estimation among Men who have Sex with Men in Ghana 2010 – 2011: Summary of Key Findings. Accra, Ghana: GAC, 2013.
3. National AIDS Control Programme (NACP). HIV Estimates 2012. Accra, Ghana: NACP, 2013.
4. Oye N. Study on human rights abuses of female sex workers by the Ghana police service. Accra, Ghana: Human Rights Advocacy Centre, 2011.
5. National AIDS Control Programme (NACP). HIV Estimates 2012. Accra, Ghana: NACP, 2013.
6. Text Me, Flash Me Helpline. 2009. http://www.comminit.com/content/text-me-flash-me-helpline.
7. *Ibid.*
8. Clemmons L. Reaching MSM in Ghana with HIV and AIDS Interventions, MARP Technical Working Group Meeting, Chenai, India, 2009. http://www.aidstar-one.com/sites/default/files/day_2-18_clemmons.pdf.
9. *Ibid.*
10. *Ibid.*

11. Clemmons L, Shillingi L. Special Report: ICT is Effective in Supporting Behavior Change Communication, Strengthening Peer Outreach and Facility-Based Services, and Increasing Service Uptake Among MSM and FSW, 2009. Available at: http://66.199.148.216/global/content/special-report-ict-effective-supporting-behavior-change-communication-strengthening-peer.

12. Impact Data - Text Me! Flash Me! Helpline. 2009. Available at: http://66.199.148.216/global/content/impact-data-text-me-flash-me-helpline.

13. FHI 360. SHARPER Semi-annual Report. May, 2013: Accra, Ghana, FHI 360, 2013.

CHAPTER 31

Brothers for Life's Mixed-Media Campaign Improves Voluntary Male Medical Circumcision Services in South Africa Using a Mobile Information Platform: A Case Study

By James BonTempo, MS, and Meredith Puleio DuBoff, MBA

ABSTRACT

The Brothers for Life campaign, launched in February 2012, sought to expand access to and demand for Voluntary Male Medical Circumcision (VMMC), a proven method to reduce the risk of HIV infection, across South Africa. By integrating a clinic locator and follow-up messaging service — accessible using basic mobile phones — into a large-scale, mixed-media social mobilization campaign, Brothers for Life was able to link the target population to services and facilitate healthy post-operative behaviors.

INTRODUCTION

Voluntary Medical Male Circumcision (VMMC) is a successful measure in the prevention of HIV transmission. Results from three randomized control trials in South Africa, Uganda and Kenya showed that male circumcision reduces the risk of HIV infection by up to 60 percent.[1] In response, the South African Department of Health (DOH) began a national effort to roll-out of free VMMC services in 2009. In addition to establishing national standards and guidelines, training health professionals to perform the VMMC procedure, and assuring the quality of services provided, the target population — 4.4 million males over the age of 15—had to be informed, motivated, and supported to seek out and utilize the services. The ambitious goal was to circumcise 80 percent of the target population, more than 3 million men.

PROBLEM/CHALLENGE/OPPORTUNITY

In support of the scale-up of the national VMMC plan, Brothers for Life, a national health communication campaign targeting HIV prevention and health improvement among men, was expanded to include a focus on creating demand for, and use of, VMMC services. Supported by a five-year U.S. Agency for International Development (USAID) award to the Johns Hopkins Bloomberg School of Public Health's Center for Communication Programs, and implemented locally by Johns Hopkins Health and Education in South Africa (JHHESA), the campaign uses a mixture of interpersonal communication, mass and social media, and grassroots advocacy to reach its audience. Since 2010, the campaign has been leveraging mobile phones to link men to VMMC services through a clinic locator, and provide post-operative messaging and support.

The campaign chose to utilize mobile phones to support their VMMC efforts for three primary reasons:

1. *Mobile phones and mobile service subscriptions are pervasive and accessible* in South Africa across all income levels and within the target age group. According to statistics released by the GSM Association in September 2013, 66 percent of the 52 million people in South Africa are unique mobile phone service subscribers.[2] In addition, more than 75 percent of people in low-income groups who are 15 years or older own a mobile phone.[3] Neither income level nor age severely limits mobile phone ownership among the target population.
2. *Mobile phones allow for privacy*, which is important when dealing with a culturally sensitive topic such as circumcision. It was understood that males would potentially seek VMMC services beyond their immediate location to avoid stigma in their communities, and the clinic locator service on the phone would allow them to do so with ease. In addition, given the high levels of phone ownership, post-operative follow-up messages can be delivered directly to the VMMC clients themselves, rather than through devices owned by family members or friends, ensuring privacy and confidentiality.
3. Complementing other outreach efforts with the mobile phone services would be a *cost effective* means to provide clients with timely, location-specific, and personalized information regarding VMMC services and follow-up actions.

SOLUTION PROCESS

To support the development and management of the mobile solution, JHHESA partnered with Cell Life, a local South African non-profit organization that provides technology-based solutions for the management of health in developing countries. JHHESA was already working with Cell Life on a monitoring and evaluation initiative, so the partnership grew organically to include meeting the needs of the VMMC campaign.

When the VMMC national effort was initiated, the clinics equipped to provide VMMC services were scattered across the country, and there was a need to inform men where they could find nearby facilities offering the procedure. JHHESA worked with the DOH, USAID and the Centers for Disease Control and Prevention to map the available services according to clinic GPS coordinates. With this information, Cell Life created a database of the location and service availability data that has, in turn, been updated over time to include 650 clinics.

To use the mobile clinic locator service, an individual sends an SMS to a designated number. In reply, the service sends a number that the person uses to access an Unstructured Supplementary Service Data (USSD) menu. The USSD connection creates a real-time, interactive session where the individual is able to choose if he wants to find an HIV counseling and testing clinic or a VMMC clinic from the menu options on his screen. Once the selection has been made, the system will generate the addresses of the three sites closest to the individual's location, triangulated using nearby cell towers.

The second component of the service is for clients after they undergo the VMMC procedure. At the clinic, they can work with a service provider to opt-in to an SMS-based service that sends them support messages for six weeks after the operation. The messages include reminders to attend follow-up visits and information about wound care and delaying sex until the wound heals. Message content was informed by testimonies from clients who underwent VMMC, to best understand clients' needs and issues after the operation; DOH clinic partners, to ensure that the messages were in accordance with clinical and national policy guidelines; and civil society service providers, such as The Centre for HIV and AIDS Prevention Studies (CHAPS), who provided input on post-operative care for the wound.

SOLUTION IMPLEMENTATION

Brothers for Life launched a multi-channel national campaign in February 2012 to amplify awareness of, and demand for, VMMC services. While thousands of men had already taken advantage of the government's free VMMC services since 2010, a concerted, large-scale, mixed-media campaign was needed to drive the VMMC numbers into the hundreds of thousands. The initiative included a television commercial, a 26-part radio talk show on 11 SABC radio stations, bi-monthly four-page *Daily Sun* features, outdoor media and commuter advertising, and social mobilization in communities and schools. The number for the clinic locator service was integrated into all promotional activities and materials, as shown in Fig. 31-1, and served as an additional call-to-action to facilitate getting men to clinics quickly and conveniently.

Fig. 31-1: Brothers for Life VMMC Campaign Promotional Material.

JHHESA made the decision early on not to implement a limited pilot of the clinic locator and post-operative messaging service based on the fact that private sector institutions were already successfully operating similar systems in South Africa. Instead, the service was launched immediately at scale, nationwide.

The Brothers for Life campaign relies on a host of partnerships for implementation, including Sonke Gender Justice Network, Cell Life, CHAPS, the Anova Health Institute, the South African National AIDS Council, the National Department of Health, and more than 100 other civil society partners. Partners have critical roles in strategy, broadcasting, media advocacy, capacity building, marketing/creative, research and community outreach.

RESULTS

The VMMC mobile information service is monitored through monthly reports on usage generated by Cell Life. From February to August 2012, results show that the clinic locator service consistently received an average of more than 6,000 queries per month. However, when the television commercial was not aired (August–October 2012), there was a corresponding drop in average SMS queries to below 4,000. In total, the clinic locater service yielded over 50,000 queries in the 2012 calendar year. Service delivery data show that VMMC uptake varies directly based on the extent to which the number for the clinic locator service is advertised.

The healthsites.org.za web site, which utilizes the same service locator database, gets an average of 19,000 hits a month with minimal marketing.

A more robust assessment of the post-operative service is needed. It is not known how many people that access the clinic service locator follow through with the procedure, or whether the post-operative messages increase follow-up appointment attendance or decrease adverse events due to improper wound care. These efforts have been delayed while an ethical research methodology that does not violate clients' privacy rights is developed.

From a purely technological perspective, the campaign's mobile information service has faced a number of challenges:

- *Data maintenance.* It is difficult to keep the locator service up-to-date given the increasing number of clinics offering VMMC services. There is often a delay before the data from additional sites are provided and the database is updated.
- *Location-based limitations.* The clinic database only has information for fixed, brick-and-mortar clinic sites, and cannot link individuals to mobile health services that provide services in more rural locations.
- *Triangulation with cell towers.* The clinic locator service relies on cellphone tower triangulation, which can be unreliable. If service at a nearby tower is down, a more distant tower is used for triangulation. As a result, the individual can receive clinic recommendations that may be 100 km away when the nearest clinic may actually be much closer.
- *System downtime.* The clinic locator service was down between January and February 2013, towards the end of the summer season. As a result, JHHESA staff members constantly monitor the system to ensure that it is functioning.

Despite the challenges faced, JHHESA has positive preliminary findings regarding user satisfaction from a qualitative evaluation of the VMMC campaign. For example, when asked about the mobile information service, one respondent replied, "I was happy with the service that was provided. I was satisfied and there was no judgment — it was up to standard." Another respondent explained how he shared information about the locator service with his friends and family and encouraged them to take advantage of the VMMC services, "Well I have shared it with my friends on Facebook, the guys I stay with and my uncircumcised little brother. I think he went to the clinic earlier this year because he said he would go while he was in Bryanston. I told him that it's safe."

CONCLUSION

The Brothers for Life campaign is an example of how demand-generation activities can be linked to health services by leveraging the utility and ubiquity of basic mobile phones. The clinic locator service allows men to take action immediately after hearing or seeing a campaign message to find out where and when they can undertake the VMMC procedure, while the follow-up messaging provides reinforcement of knowledge needed to ensure healthy post-operative behaviors and outcomes. While a more robust evaluation of the follow-up component is needed, the popular mobile information service serves as an important element of the VMMC social mobilization campaign, and demonstrates how a mobile service deployment can be an important component of a larger health communication and service delivery initiative.

REFERENCES

1. Randomized Controlled Trials and Related Studies. Clearinghouse on Male Circumcision for HIV Prevention. [On the Internet] Available at: www.malecircumcision.org/research/clinical_research.html. Accessed September 10, 2013.
2. Mobile phone subscription base in Nigeria, South Africa, others hits 781m in Q2. *The Guardian.* September 2, 2013. Available at: www.guardian.ngrguardiannews.com/business-news/131638-mobile-phone-subscription-base-in-nigeria-south-africa-others-hits-781m-in-q2. Accessed September 10, 2013.
3. Mobile phone usage in SA. Finweek. January 22, 2013. Available at: http://finweek.com/2013/01/22/mobile-phone-usage-in-sa/. Accessed September 10, 2013.

Part VII
The Future of mHealth

CHAPTER 32

Where Mobile Health Technologies Are Needed in Healthcare

By Steven R. Steinhubl, MD

Mobile health (mHealth) is a wide-ranging term most commonly used to describe the utilization of a wide variety of therapeutic interventions, from something as straightforward as text messaging appointment reminders, to novel, stand-alone diagnostic and monitoring tools that can identify health concerns in real-time, virtually anywhere in the world with access to a wireless network. The potential for mHealth to lead to the complete re-engineering of healthcare is limited by only two things: our imagination and, more immediately pressing, the need for direct evidence to guide its implementation.

The predictions for the future of mHealth are uniformly positive and optimistic. It has been estimated that mHealth will develop into a $26 billion market by 2017.[1] This optimistic outlook for the industry is partially due to the remarkable growth in wireless connectivity in general. In a world with slightly more than 7.1 billion people it is astonishing that at the end of 2012 there were 6.8 billion mobile subscriptions, with an estimated 3.2 billion unique mobile users.[2] In the United States. three out of five mobile subscribers own a smartphone — the equivalent of having an Internet-enabled computer in their pocket. Beyond this availability of mobile, personal computing power is the recognition of the need for innovative, transformational solutions to improve healthcare, but to also drive down its cost. Finally, there continues to be growing recognition of the need to move healthcare beyond population-based therapies toward greater individualization. Successfully accomplishing this requires a much better understanding of individual differences that can be made possible with an increasing array of wearable biosensors.

Despite the multiple forces driving the future success of mHealth, there are also major challenges to its incorporation into clinical practice. Perhaps the greatest challenge facing the rapid uptake of patient-empowering mobile technologies is the current payment structure in much of the healthcare system that reimburses sickness care but rarely incentives models of care that support wellness behaviors. Additionally, although providers are very supportive of technology in general and those that can improve patient care, concerns exist that the patient empowerment allowed by mHealth tools may further weaken the already hobbled doctor-patient relationship, leading to a breakdown in trust and, potentially, a negative impact on healing. Finally, as noted earlier, when mobile technology development and availability outstrips the evidence supporting its use, an environment is created that can harm its long term acceptance and uptake through the use of ineffective, or even worse, harmful mHealth solutions. For example there are greater than 40,000 healthcare-related apps available for download, but the FDA estimates it has reviewed only ~100 in total. This lack of oversight is worrisome and contributes to the increasingly high likelihood of useless and possibly even dangerous apps being downloaded by unsuspecting consumers.[3] The current mHealth environment is reminiscent of the unregulated pharmaceutical industry of a century ago with its plethora of cure-all elixirs and other unproven therapies. The lack of strong data supporting a benefit for the majority of currently available mHealth technologies can undermine the entire field if left unchecked.

While the data directly supporting the role of the vast majority of mHealth solutions are currently lacking, there are ample and compelling data which will be highlighted in what follows, of inefficiencies and challenges faced by both consumers and providers in the current healthcare system that can be effectively addressed via mHealth.

This overview is not an all-encompassing overview of the entire spectrum of mHealth technologies that will be available, but rather is designed to focus on some of the most critical healthcare needs of the non-hospitalized population. The plethora of primarily fitness-focused devices, or devices for hospitalized patients and the team caring for them will not be addressed, although there are tremendous advances being made in mobile technologies in both of these settings.

mHEALTH'S IMPACT ON THE MEDICAL CONSUMER

mHealth can benefit non-hospitalized individuals by both increasing their ability to accurately diagnose acute conditions at home, and improving the ease of monitoring, tracking and communicating important biometric data to simplify and improve the management of chronic conditions. There are already longstanding successful examples of mobile solutions for both of these situations: home pregnancy testing has been possible since the late 1970s with more than 20 million tests being used in the United States annually, and home glucose testing that has also been available for more than 40 years and proven to improve outcomes in insulin-dependent diabetic patients. Several mobile technologies are, or soon will be, available that will dramatically expand the potential to empower individuals to better manage more of their acute and chronic medical conditions.

Diagnosis and Management of Acute Conditions

During an average month, for every 1,000 men, women and children living in the United States, it is estimated that 800 experience some symptoms of acute conditions, 327 consider seeking medical care and 217 end up being seen in a physician's office.[4] Roughly 34 percent of all physician office visits are related to an acute condition, and up to a quarter of all patients presenting in an emergency room could be managed in the ambulatory care setting.[5,6] Some of the most common acute complaints for which individuals seek medical care are upper respiratory tract infections, otitis media and urinary tract infections.[7] Innovative mHealth devices have the potential to allow patients to bypass a physician or emergency room (ER) visit for these and a number of other acute complaints.

Viral respiratory tract infections, or "colds" are the most common acute illness in humans and the most common reason for an urgent office visit with an estimated total economic impact of $40 billion annually in the United States alone.[8] Because the diagnostic role of laboratory investigations and radiologic studies for viral infections is limited, individuals with upper respiratory tract infection symptoms are an ideal cohort for home diagnostics and triage. A thermometer-enabled smartphone that not only measures one's temperature but also tracks associated symptoms, allows users to send that information to a physician's office, and even connect people with their local digital community to see how many others in the schools or workplaces have similar symptoms, would likely provide the information and peace of mind necessary to determine whether further evaluation is needed. For individuals whom measuring temperature alone may not provide adequate information, innovative devices under development, such as the Scanadu Scout, provide all of the biometrics previously available only at a medical facility. This cookie-sized, wireless device is capable of measuring not only temperature, but peripheral oxygen saturation, pulse rate, blood pressure and several other parameters that can help accurately track the severity of one's illness and guide next steps. In the future, individuals will likely have the ability to diagnose the specific infectious etiology of their symptoms as smartphone-based point-of-care devices are developed.[9]

Recurrent ear infection is the most common acute complaint of children and leads to healthcare costs over $5 billion annually in the United States, not including lost work time by family caregivers.[10] In fact, for every 100 children utilizing a healthcare service because of their parent's suspicion for an acute ear infection, only 50 are actually determined to be ear infections.[11] By giving parents the ability to digitally image their child's tympanic membranes at home with a smartphone-based otoscope, the vast majority of office visits could potentially be prevented with remote image transmission and diagnosis.

Urinary tract infections (UTI) are the most common bacterial infections in adults. Accounting for roughly 7 million office visits, 1 million ER visits and 100,000 hospitalizations annually, UTIs are responsible for an estimated cost of $2 billion each year.[12] Women presenting with one or more symptoms of an acute UTI have a 50 percent chance of being clinically diagnosed with one after an office visit.[13] Several mobile devices are designed for at-home urinalysis with analytic, tracking and transmission capability, potentially eliminating the need for an office visit. While current devices are limited to testing for signs of infection, such as the presence of nitrates, future advances will likely allow for the detection of both the presence of infection and the exact pathogen via a mobile electrochemical biosensor.[14]

mHealth technology can play a role in informing patients and decreasing costs in a host of other settings. For example, nearly four million individuals visit the (ER) with a complaint of dizziness, with costs of $4 billion for the ER work-up alone.[15] Patients now have the ability to perform an electrocardiographic (ECG) rhythm strip just as simply as adding a case to their smartphone. This data can be recorded, transmitted and evaluated anytime, anywhere their symptoms strike. Automated rhythm detection algorithms will provide immediate diagnosis and feedback guiding next steps. In other cases, high risk individuals will be able to wear shirts or patches that continuously monitor and transmit their ECGs.

Management of Chronic Conditions

Over 90 percent of healthcare spending in the United States is limited to the 50 percent of individuals who have at least one chronic medical condition.[16] For the population over age 65, one-third have four or more chronic conditions, but account for 74 percent of the $300 billion Medicare spent in 2010.[17] Among adults, hypertension and diabetes are two of the most common chronic illnesses, whereas in children, asthma and diabetes are the most frequent. There are mHealth solutions for all of these, as well as many other chronic conditions.

One out of every three American adults has hypertension, with total costs in 2010 of over $93 billion, $47.5 billion in direct costs.[18] [19] Of the over one billion office visits that occur every year in the United States, nearly 40 million have a primary diagnosis of essential hypertension, making it the most commonly diagnosed condition for an office visit.[5] Despite the cost and time that goes into treating hypertension, and the fact that it accounts for half of the risk for heart attacks, and 75 percent of the risk for strokes, less than half of hypertensive individuals have their blood pressure under control.[19] Home monitoring is one method to improve blood pressure control and minimize the need for office visits. Supporting this are studies showing that home monitoring is associated with a small, albeit statistically significant improvement in blood pressure.[20] When home blood pressure monitoring is coupled with provider feedback and improved patient engagement, however, significantly greater blood pressure control can be achieved beyond home monitoring alone.[21] A new generation of home blood pressure cuffs can now wirelessly transmit individual readings or long-term trends to a provider, allowing for rapid feedback and limiting the need for an office visit to only times when critically necessary. In the next several years innovative devices that can monitor beat-to-beat blood pressure non-invasively during real-world activities will allow for even greater refinement of the diagnosis and treatment of hypertension.[22]

More than 25 million adults and children in the United States have diabetes — roughly 8 percent of the adult population — while an additional 79 million are pre-diabetic.[23] The total cost of diabetes in the United States for 2012 was $245 billion, with $176 billion in direct costs.[24] Not surprisingly, diabetes is also one of the most common primary diagnoses for an office visit, accounting for over 30 million visits a year.[5] Mobile transmission of glucose values and other pertinent parameters, coupled with personalized feedback, would substantially decrease the need for these visits. Not only would doing so increase patient convenience and decrease costs through substantially fewer office visits, this digital bi-directional communication could also significantly improve clinical outcomes. Self-monitoring alone is of limited benefit in non-insulin treated diabetics.[25] On the other hand, interventions that train patients in self-management and improve their communication channels with providers, can significantly improve outcomes and decrease costs.[26,27,28] A number of glucose monitors are already available that can transmit their data to a smartphone or tablet, and then onward to providers and family caregivers. The degree of clinical benefit associated with the heightened engagement this allows is just starting to be tested. Further advances in technology offer even greater promise, such as continuous glucose monitoring, allowing for the development of a smartphone-based artificial pancreas.[29]

Asthma affects more than 20 million children and adults, and is responsible for more than $37 billion in direct medical costs each year, plus an additional 25 million lost school and work days.[30] A novel mHealth technology, Asthmapolis, allows real-time feedback to the patient and their provider in regards to their level of asthma control. The device attaches to the top of an asthma patient's inhaler and passively collects the exact location and time the inhaler is used, and transmits that data wirelessly to a smartphone with the option to share the information with providers and family members. These types of data empower the patient by making them more aware of their triggers and true level of control. It also allows providers to monitor how well their asthma patients are doing and their compliance with inhaled medications. From a population health perspective, knowledge of geographic and time clustering use of inhalers in a community of asthma patients would potentially allow for the identification of environmental triggers. In one small study of 30 patients, use of this technology led to significant improvements in asthma control and daily symptoms.[31]

mHEALTH'S IMPACT ON HEALTHCARE PROVIDERS

If the incorporation of mHealth technologies into the healthcare ecosystem achieves its potential, leading to greater patient empowerment and digital connectivity and thereby enabling improved care with substantially less healthcare resource utilization, what are the ramifications for the healthcare provider? Not surprisingly, physicians have expressed concern regarding mHealth, and surveys find them to be much more hesitant and less enthusiastic about mHealth than are consumers.[32] Undoubtedly, the changing role of patients in their care management will definitely lead to changes in the role of the healthcare provider. But rather than damage the doctor-patient relationship, the incorporation of mHealth technologies will instead reinforce this relationship via a more activated and knowledgeable patient and a less time-pressured provider. In this process, physician satisfaction will increase and the projected shortage in healthcare providers will be eased.

Recent surveys suggest that physicians, in general, are unsatisfied with their careers.[33] Physicians rate the morale of over 80 percent of their colleagues as negative, and almost two-thirds would not recommend medicine as a career to younger individuals. This same survey of more than 13,500 physicians found that over 80 percent identified patient relationships to be the most satisfying aspect of their practice. Unfortunately, the current systems of care have evolved to minimize what providers find most satisfying, and at the same time make it virtually impossible to provide the kind of quality of care physicians desire and patients need.

Average face-to-face time of primary care providers with their patients during a visit is just over 10 minutes.[34] Given that limited time, and considering the average ambulatory patient has 15 risk factors and requires 24 guideline-recommended preventive services, it is not surprising that adults receive < 10 percent of their recommended preventative screening tests.[35,36] It has been estimated that it would take a primary care provider with an average-sized panel of 2,500 patients 7.4 hours a day to just provide preventive services.[37] Add to that another 3.5 hours a day for managing the top 10 chronic diseases when they are stable, or 10.6 if they are not, and a provider's day is already well overloaded without even taking into account acute problems (roughly one-third of all visits) and other activities like well-child visits.[38] It is no wonder providers are frustrated in a system that does not allow them to efficiently or successfully care for their patients. This trend is not expected to improve. Without dramatic changes to our current systems of care it is estimated that an additional 52,000 primary care physicians will be needed to meet the population's needs by 2025.[39]

As outlined earlier, mobile technologies create the ability to maximize patient health and minimize, or even eliminate, the need for office visits for the routine management of some of the most common acute and chronic issues. Preventive needs can be personalized and automated. Large cohorts of patients can be tracked passively for any abnormal or concerning readings, which can then be proactively addressed when needed; by text message, e-mail, phone call, and if significant enough, an office visit. In the future, when financial incentives are better aligned with the needs of patients, much of the current time demands on physicians will be eliminated due to greater patient self-management and shared care, practice features already associated with greater physician satisfaction.[40]

CONCLUSION

mHealth technologies have tremendous potential to transform nearly every aspect of medical care, and to do so while both improving outcomes and lowering costs. For patients, mHealth offers the promise of improved convenience, more active engagement in their care, and greater personalization. For healthcare providers, mHealth will allow an unloading of the demands on their time created by their unneeded involvement in algorithmic, precision medicine and instead allow them to refocus on the art of medicine as a diagnostician and educator.

mHealth is in the very earliest stages of implementation. The road will not be smooth and there is a tremendous amount of work to do to achieve its immense potential to transform healthcare. Most critical to driving this transformation is the need for real-world clinical trial evidence of the overall benefit of mHealth to the patient and the healthcare system.

Extraordinary advancements in technology over the last several decades have allowed for the possibility to completely re-engineer care, and there is no doubt that even grander technological innovations are to come. But technology alone is not enough to transform healthcare. The foundation of medical care has been and always will be the human relationship. Successful mHealth technologies will need to enhance and reinforce relationships; relationships between doctors and their patients, people and their family caregivers, and maybe most importantly, individuals and their own health. We can achieve this. It is now time to start proving it.

Disclosure

SRS — research support via Qualcomm Foundation.

REFERENCES

1. research2guidance. Mobile Health Market Report 2013-2017. 2013; http://www.research2guidance.com/shop/index.php/downloadable/download/sample/sample_id/262/. Accessed August 16, 2013.
2. Helgason CM, Bolin KM, Hoff JA, et al. Development of aspirin resistance in persons with previous ischemic stroke. *Stroke.* 1994;25:2331-2336.
3. Wolf JA, Moreau JF, Akilov O, et al. diagnostic inaccuracy of smartphone applications for melanoma detection. *JAMA Dermatology.* 2013;149(4):422-426.
4. Green LA, Fryer GE, Jr., Yawn BP, Lanier D, Dovey SM. The ecology of medical care revisited. *The New England Journal of Medicine.* Jun 28 2001;344(26):2021-2025.
5. National Ambulatory Medical Care Survey: 2010 Summary Tables. Available at: http://www.cdc.gov/nchs/data/ahcd/namcs_summary/2010_namcs_web_tables.pdf. Accessed August 16, 2013.
6. Weinick RM, Burns RM, Mehrotra A. Many emergency department visits could be managed at urgent care centers and retail clinics. *Health Affairs.* Sep 2010;29(9):1630-1636.
7. Mehrotra A, Wang MC, Lave JR, Adams JL, McGlynn EA. Retail clinics, primary care physicians, and emergency departments: a comparison of patients' visits. *Health Affairs.* Sep-Oct 2008;27(5):1272-1282.
8. Fendrick A, Monto AS, Nightengale B, Sarnes M. The economic burden of non–influenza-related viral respiratory tract infection in the United States. *Archives of Internal Medicine.* 2003;163(4):487-494.
9. Cao Q, Mahalanabis M, Chang J, et al. Microfluidic Chip for Molecular Amplification of Influenza A RNA in Human Respiratory Specimens. *PLoS ONE.* 2012;7(3):e33176.
10. Bondy J, Berman S, Glazner J, Lezotte D. Direct Expenditures Related to Otitis Media Diagnoses: Extrapolations From a Pediatric Medicaid Cohort. *Pediatrics.* June 1, 2000;105(6):e72.
11. Laine MK, Tähtinen PA, Ruuskanen O, Huovinen P, Ruohola A. Symptoms or Symptom-Based Scores Cannot Predict Acute Otitis Media at Otitis-Prone Age. *Pediatrics.* May 1, 2010;125(5):e1154-e1161.
12. Foxman B. Epidemiology of urinary tract infections: incidence, morbidity, and economic costs. *The American Journal of Medicine.* July 8, 2002;113(1, Supplement 1):5-13.
13. Bent S, Nallamothu BK, Simel DL, Fihn SD, Saint S. Does this woman have an acute uncomplicated urinary tract infection? *JAMA.* 2002;287(20):2701-2710.
14. Mohan R, Mach KE, Bercovici M, et al. Clinical validation of integrated nucleic acid and protein detection on an electrochemical biosensor array for urinary tract infection diagnosis. *PloS One.* 2011;6(10):e26846.
15. Saber Tehrani AS, Coughlan D, Hsieh YH, et al. Rising Annual Costs of Dizziness Presentations to U.S. Emergency Departments. *Academic Emergency Medicine.* 2013;20(7):689-696.
16. Machllin MS, Cohen JW, Beauregard K. Statistical Brief #203: Health Care Expenses for Adults with Chronic Conditions, 2005. In: *Quality AfHRa, ed. Medical Expenditure Panel Survey.* 2008.
17. Antiplatelet Trialists' Collaboration. Collaborative overview of randomised trials of antiplatelet therapy - I. Prevention of death, myocardial infarction, and stroke by prolonged antiplatelet therapy in various categories of patients. *Br Med J.* 1994;308:81-106.
18. Heidenreich PA, Trogdon JG, Khavjou OA, et al. Forecasting the future of cardiovascular disease in the United States: a policy statement from the American Heart Association. *Circulation.* Mar 1 2011;123(8):933-944.
19. Vital signs: prevalence, treatment, and control of hypertension--United States, 1999-2002 and 2005-2008. *MMWR. Morbidity and Mortality Weekly Report.* Feb 4, 2011;60(4):103-108.
20. Uhlig K, Patel K, Ip S, Kitsios GD, Balk EM. Self-Measured Blood Pressure Monitoring in the Management of HypertensionA Systematic Review and Meta-analysis. *Annals of Internal Medicine.* 2013;159(3):185-194.

21. Green BB, Cook AJ, Ralston JD, et al. Effectiveness of home blood pressure monitoring, web communication, and pharmacist care on hypertension control: A randomized controlled trial. *JAMA.* 2008;299(24):2857-2867.

22. Chung E, Chen G, Alexander B, Cannesson M. Non-invasive continuous blood pressure monitoring: a review of current applications. *Front. Med.* March 1, 2013;7(1):91-101.

23. Centers for Disease Control and Prevention. National diabetes fact sheet: national estimates and general information on diabetes and prediabetes in the United States, 2011. *U.S. Department of Health and Human Services, Centers for Disease Control and Prevention.* 2011.

24. American Diabetes A. Economic costs of diabetes in the U.S. in 2012. *Diabetes Care.* April 2013;36(4):1033-1046.

25. Clar C, Barnard K, Cummins E, Royle P, Waugh N. Self-monitoring of blood glucose in type 2 diabetes: systematic review. *Health Technology Assessment (Winchester, England).* March 2010;14(12):1-140.

26. Norris SL, Engelgau MM, Narayan KM. Effectiveness of self-management training in type 2 diabetes: a systematic review of randomized controlled trials. *Diabetes Care.* March 2001;24(3):561-587.

27. Aubert RE, Herman WH, Waters J, et al. Nurse case management to improve glycemic control in diabetic patients in a health maintenance organization. A randomized, controlled trial. *Annals of Internal Medicine.* October 15, 1998;129(8):605-612.

28. Sidorov J, Shull R, Tomcavage J, Girolami S, Lawton N, Harris R. Does Diabetes Disease Management Save Money and Improve Outcomes?: A report of simultaneous short-term savings and quality improvement associated with a health maintenance organization–sponsored disease management program among patients fulfilling health employer data and information set criteria. *Diabetes Care.* April 1, 2002;25(4):684-689.

29. Kovatchev BP, Renard E, Cobelli C, et al. Feasibility of Outpatient Fully Integrated Closed-Loop Control: First studies of wearable artificial pancreas. *Diabetes Care.* July 1, 2013;36(7):1851-1858.

30. Kamble S, Bharmal M. Incremental direct expenditure of treating asthma in the United States. *The Journal of Asthma: Official Journal of the Association for the Care of Asthma.* February 2009;46(1):73-80.

31. Van Sickle D, Magzamen S, Truelove S, Morrison T. Remote monitoring of inhaled bronchodilator use and weekly feedback about asthma management: an open-group, short-term pilot study of the impact on asthma control. *PloS One.* 2013;8(2):e55335.

32. PwC. Emerging mHealth: Paths for Growth. *A global research study about the opportunities and challenges of mobile health from the perspective of patients, payers and providers.*2013:1-40.

33. A survey of America's physicians: Practice patterns and perspectives. 2012; An Examination of the Professional Morale, Practice Patterns, Career Plans, and Healthcare Perspectives of Today's Physicians, Aggregated by Age, Gender, Primary Care/Specialists, and Practice Owners/Employees. Available at: http://www.physiciansfoundation.org/uploads/default/Physicians_Foundation_2012_Biennial_Survey.pdf. Accessed August 11, 2013.

34. Gottschalk A, Flocke SA. Time spent in face-to-face patient care and work outside the examination room. *Annals of Family Medicine.* November–December 2005;3(6):488-493.

35. Medder JD, Kahn NB, Jr., Susman JL. Risk factors and recommendations for 230 adult primary care patients, based on U.S. Preventive Services Task Force guidelines. *American Journal of Preventive Medicine.* May–June 1992;8(3):150-153.

36. Ruffin MT, Gorenflo DW, Woodman B. Predictors of screening for breast, cervical, colorectal, and prostatic cancer among community-based primary care practices. *The Journal of the American Board of Family Practice/American Board of Family Practice.* January–February 2000;13(1):1-10.

37. Yarnall KS, Pollak KI, Ostbye T, Krause KM, Michener JL. Primary care: is there enough time for prevention? *American Journal of Public Health.* April 2003;93(4):635-641.

38. Ostbye T, Yarnall KS, Krause KM, Pollak KI, Gradison M, Michener JL. Is there time for management of patients with chronic diseases in primary care? *Annals of Family Medicine.* May–June 2005;3(3):209-214.

39. Petterson SM, Liaw WR, Phillips RL, Rabin DL, Meyers DS, Bazemore AW. Projecting US Primary Care Physician Workforce Needs: 2010-2025. *The Annals of Family Medicine.* November 1, 2012;10(6):503-509.

40. Sinsky CA, Willard-Grace R, Schutzbank AM, Sinsky TA, Margolius D, Bodenheimer T. In Search of Joy in Practice: A Report of 23 High-Functioning Primary Care Practices. *The Annals of Family Medicine.* May 1, 2013;11(3):272-278.

CHAPTER 33

Next-Generation Solutions in mHealth
By David Metcalf, PhD

In an effort to begin our journey of examining the future, we start with a good view of the current state of emerging technologies, trends and ideas that hold promise and are shaping our world. This chapter is a potpourri of ideas, mini-case examples and technology descriptions that may point the way to the near-term future of mHealth.

Simplified Interfaces
A current trend that will affect mHealth is that most major platforms are simplifying user interfaces and restructuring the content layouts with layers. Windows 8 Mobile, Google's Android and Apple iOS 7 have all started using "flat" interface elements like content and app tiles that are larger and easier to select. Apple has dropped the iconic "skeumorphism" design (where everything looks like it is wrapped in a shiny transparent film) for a flatter looking iconography. The move to simplicity is also reducing the amount of choices present on screens and reorganizing content and apps into multiple layers, much like our familiar folder structures from the desktop that can help bring order to the chaos of too many apps available. This trend will continue to expand and create opportunities for improved usability in mHealth and connectivity to desktop computing systems because of common interface standards between mobile and computer interfaces.

Peripherals
Another major trend identified in our earlier book, we cite: "In addition to working in conjunction with upstream systems like EMRs, PHRs and LIS systems, mobile devices also complement downstream technologies, such as peripherals. Think of a mobile device as a central hub, radiating spokes in all directions. These spokes could be things like dictation systems, electronic pens, bar-code readers and scanners, blood-glucose meters with Wi-Fi access, Bluetooth security badges, ZigBee medical equipment tracking systems, electronic stethoscopes and advanced telemedicine and telerobotic systems that automate communication and the impact of a complete mobile solution linking a wide variety of components in a healthcare ecosystem."[1]

We anticipate the trend of peripherals expanding into the mHealth ecosystem to continue to increase as more complex devices like the Scanadu Scout "medical tricorder" continue to provide further opportunities for easy access to data for providers and patients.

Interconnectivity

Keith Boone provides a series of examples of standards and interoperability in Chapter 22. New developments in both formal and de facto industry standards will continue to propel us forward in the coming years. As certain protocols help promote success in mHealth, they will scale to meet the ongoing needs. Examples include Direct Secure Messaging (DSM) for mobile access to alerts between healthcare IT systems (EHRs, EMRs, LIS, etc.) and other hospital and physician practices.

Another standard that may hold future promise is HL7 and next generation interoperability frameworks. Using other web and mobile standards in conjunction can make complex integrations easier.

Peer2Peer connections through Wi-Fi Direct, iBeacon (Bluetooth 4) and Near-Field Communication (NFC) will also facilitate the type of sophisticated communication between peripherals described in the paragraphs above.

Other connectivity at the hardware level will come from both industry and defacto standards like 2Net from Qualcomm. Non-profit organizations like RFID in Healthcare and the Intelligent Health Association are paving the way for expanded testbeds that can demonstrate capabilities for the intelligent hospital of the future.

Another trend in interconnectivity is the loose connection between text messaging, e-mail, voice-mail, web and apps in an integrated suite of messaging operations. Examples can include public health campaigns across multiple devices and platforms. A recent example is the UCF Regional Extension Center's Million Hearts™ campaign (Fig. 33-1).

Fig. 33-1: Million Hearts™ Public Health Campaign.

The Mixed Emerging Technology Integration Lab (METIL) has partnered with the Regional Extension Center at the College of Medicine (REC-COM) to work with the Department of Health & Human Services (HHS), the Centers for Disease Control and Prevention (CDC), and Centers for Medicare & Medicaid Services (CMS) to prevent a million heart attacks and strokes in the form of a campaign known as Million Hearts™. Our responsibility was to provide a learning campaign using social media, mobile technology, e-mail, video and print media to aid the efforts of the Million Hearts initiative to educate the American public and healthcare providers how to prevent, manage and care for cardiovascular disease. A novel component of the Million Hearts Campaign is the use of visual search technology and augmented reality.

To best understand the potential of augmented reality (the combination of digital overlays on the world around us) a short case study on mHealth's connection to physical assets and the context of the real world may illustrate the potential for this technology.

CASE STUDY: COMBAT MEDIC

Another example of the crossroads between mHealth and mLearning is the Combat Medic Card Game (CMCG), mobile app, online game and most recently the Augmented Reality version of the cards that automatically launch an interactive video or animation of the medic procedures. The complete set of tools has been developed at UCF's Institute for Simulation and Training for Army Research Lab, STTC under Dr. Christine Allen. In the most basic, low-tech version of the learning modules, the cards help teach emergent combat medical procedures printed sequentially on an ordinary deck of playing cards. These cards are much like the cards used by warfighters to play, socialize and unwind while in the field. Extending this natural propensity of warfighters to play with cards, Combat Medic gives soldiers the opportunity to reinforce their knowledge of emergent medical procedures while relaxing, increasing the value of their time and of their attention (Fig. 33-2).

Fig. 33-2: Sample Card: Adhere Band.

To examine the effectiveness of the CMCG as a learning resource for novices to the Combat Medic and Combat LifeSaver (CLS) curriculum several studies have been performed.[2]

In one, the relative effectiveness of CMCG card and app modalities were compared. Overall results from this study suggest the CMCG to be an effective tool for learning, both in the card and app modalities when instructions are provided to engage with the CMCG following a flashcard-based study process. Perceived usability of the CMCG and reported engagement in the learning activity were also rated positively and did not differ between study conditions. Ratings of intuitiveness and usability also suggest the CMCG can be successfully used by a learner without the need for extensive training. This enhances the distributability of the CMCG because it can be implemented by a learner with little to no additional support needs. Augmented Reality adds an expanded didactic component to the training activity: applying a leading augmented reality mobile application, Aurasma, the Combat Medic Cards can be used to view 2-D and 3-D videos of one of the seven medical procedures.

Process
- A Medic scans a Combat Medic Card with Aurasma.
- A 2-D or 3-D link launches in an application called the Universal Connectivity Framework (UCF).

- A video (recorded procedure or animation) demonstrates the procedure.
- Videos can be paused, stopped or replayed to learn procedures.

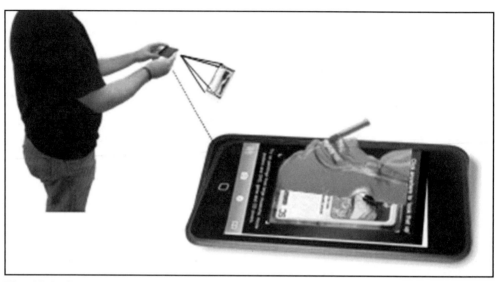

Fig. 33-3: Expanding the Possibilities Within mHealth.

Wearable

A natural extension beyond Augmented Reality is the integration of Wearable technologies. At FutureMed 2013, experts like Dr. Daniel Kraft were exploring the various wearable sensors worn on the wrist, as an adhesive patch and Google Glass for heads-up display. Here are a few comments from Kraft: "This technology can enable me to take certain measurements with me, some of which may not be just data from one sensor; it can be a lot of them integrated together. So far it's mostly on the health side, e.g., I can track my steps or my workout, but something like this Basis watch allows me to read my heart rate —my heart rate is 86, and I've done 9,000 steps today and burned 2,200 calories. And it even tells time!

So the interesting thing about that is it provides an opportunity to track my steps and my heart rate, but if I'm trying to treat a patient with a beta blocker and I want to see what their heart rate is throughout the day, it's much more realistic than having them come to the clinic to see what their heart rate is. So we go from quantified self to quantified health. And as a physician, I may literally prescribe you exercise. So I would say, 'David, you're really not doing well on your diet, I'm going to prescribe you to do 8,000 steps a day.' I'm going to get that data into my electronic medical record (EMR), and even if I never look at it, if I know I'm tracking my workout regimen, I might change my behavior and that can make a subtle difference over time."

With Google Glass, hints of a future iWatch from Apple, Samsung Galaxy Gear and a host of other sensors like the FitBit, Nike Fuel Band, Basis watch, Jawbone UP, the age of the body area network (BAN) is upon us. The trend of the quantified self for fitness, nutrition, sleep monitoring and future integration in healthcare monitoring will continue and expand (Fig. 33-3).

3-D

Another trend to watch is the integration of 3-D displays into healthcare. It is too soon to say whether consumer-grade gaming platforms like Oculus Rift will emerge as immersive, 3-D health tools, but there are hints of some early clinical evidence of the effective use of 3-D visualization for breast cancer screening at Emory and other applications.

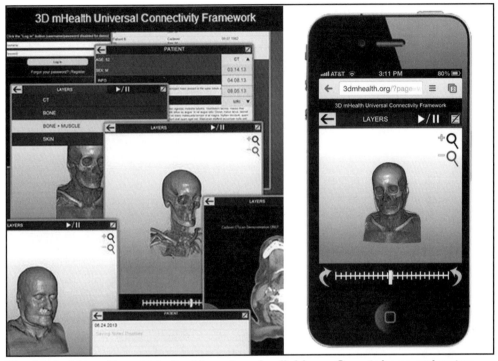

Fig. 33-4: A New Era of Medical Imaging, Available on Smartphone or Laptop.

Example of 3-D mHealth.org

The Universal Common Framework (UCF) 3-D mHealth Widget provides universal access to DICOM PACS data and advanced 3-D visualizations for practitioners, staff and patients to view and manipulate medical imaging. We have solved the problem of cross browser, device and app viewing of advanced 3-D data types by creating a widget "controllable window" to an advanced imaging server. Clinicians, staff and radiologists now have ready access without expensive custom medical visualization systems. Using the Open mHealth Initiative's framework, we have data interoperability and easier integration to multiple sensors and systems (Fig 33-4).

CASE STUDY: TELEHEALTH IN ACTION

Lake Nona Institute (Orlando's Medical City) has inspired a Well Home model for Ambient Health. The following is a summary of the practical, takeaway actions that have come out of the initial development.

This Intelligent Home seeks to accomplish a paradigm shift — putting home at the heart of personal and family wellness. It is a healthy reflection of those living with it. It integrates with daily life and assists in making healthy choices easy.

Inspired by innovations from Cisco, Florida Blue, GE, Johnson & Johnson, UCF, and the VA, among other current and future partners, we are reimagining health in the home.

We welcome you to follow the lives of the family in this Ashton Woods model home as they experience health without the hassles, exploring conveniences that inspire health, fitness and quality of life while saving time and money.

While examples in our living laboratory at Lake Nona Institute represent an advanced future, there are some simple things users can do in their homes.

Background

Many of the ideas presented in the Intelligent Home are simple, inexpensive and easy to implement in almost any home. Some quick suggestions follow the principles of NUDGE outlined below:

- Incentives: Motivate people.
- Understand: Help them understand impact of their choices.
- Defaults.
- Give feedback.
- Expect error ("look right" signs on UK streets).
- Structure complex choices.

Tips

1. Encourage healthy choices in the kitchen. Consider smaller plate sizes, portions measured out by the size of your fist, and the layout of your drawers, refrigerator and pantry to encourage easy access to healthier foods.
2. Make fitness equipment easily accessible and pervasive throughout the home; something as simple as a seven-minute routine, like that taught at the Human Performance Institute, can make all the difference.
3. Health can be fun! Challenge each other and consider health games, like some of those listed in the apps section, or create your own games that don't even require technology.

Apps and Web Sites

Here are some of the free or inexpensive apps and resources used throughout the home.

- Habit Heroes App (www.habitheroes.com)
- SuperNutrition (www.supernutritiongame.com) — UCF/J&J
- Huff & Puff asthma app — stories and games for kids (Apple App Store/Google Play)
- Zombies Run! exergame app (www.zombiesrungame.com)
- iFit/Nike+
- J&J Life Project
- Canyon Ranch
- Florida Blue App

- J&J Digital Health Coaches
- AllRecipes.com
- Jessica Seinfeld, Deceptively Delicious vegetable pureed sauces
- Truly Healthy Cookbook
- Pinterest Cookbook
- Nudge

Tools

A low-cost digital scale with Bluetooth can be used to track weight loss and many vital signs important to monitoring your health status. Get one that's Bluetooth enabled or has another connection to the internet to automatically track vitals on your mobile phone or electronic health record (EHR). It's easy to have a record for your healthcare provider when you need it.

Fitness bands or a workout mat may be all you need to do simple exercises that increase strength, flexibility, endurance, and cardio fitness.

An X-box One Kinect can be used to measure heart rate and report this back to you or your health provider automatically.

An instant heart rate app and a smart phone can also be used when you are on the go. Simply put your finger on the camera and get an accurate measure of how you're doing.

We hope these helpful tips will engage and inspire health innovations for you and your family. For more information, visit http://www.lnih.org.

Projects like the Intelligent Home in Lake Nona/Medical City can serve as a test-bed for mHealth technologies.

BIG DATA IN ACTION

IBM, Memorial Sloan Kettering and WellPoint pilot the Watson engine for differential diagnosis. We caught up with Marty Kohn recently and got an update on the latest developments.

Ever see the computer that beat the two Jeopardy champions on national TV? That's IBM Watson. Now think about applying this technology to medicine. Using natural language processing (your voice as input) along with clinical data, it is possible to run results and potential treatments against a multi-million page knowledge base and ask the computer's Artificial Intelligence to predict the best few options. A doctor can choose to use these as a secondary consult, of sorts, in making complex decisions. This may be what next generation mHealth CDSS (clinical decision support systems) look like.

IBM Watson is being used in truly transformative ways. Giving doctors access to an evidence-based second opinion in fields like oncology is as simple as providing case inputs and in a matter of seconds, getting a series of weighted treatment plans based on a differential diagnosis of the data.

Some studies have shown that as few as 20 percent of diagnoses are made based on clinical evidence. Watson holds the promise to change this. The system is being used and "trained" by WellPoint and Memorial Sloan Kettering and already shows great promise. This is one to watch closely. "We are just seeing the beginning of what might be possible with this advanced technology for diagnosis," said Dr. Kohn.

CONCLUSION

This potpourri of technologies, trends and recent projects may point to future trends in mHealth. The integration of other technologies with mobile is a thematic trend seen in many of the cases throughout this book. Next generation mHealth solutions may involve big data, 3-D, Cloud-based systems, telehealth, peripherals, augmented reality and other complementary innovations.

CHAPTER 34

Designing an Open, Collaborative Platform to Transform Productivity in an Era of Anywhere, Anytime Care: A Case Study

By Gautam Gulati, MD, MBA, MPH, and Will Comerford

ABSTRACT

Medical information has become available to practitioners like never before in history. In fact, the sheer quantity of information and its exponential growth presents the healthcare community with a new challenge: How do we cut through the clutter, filter out the noise, and provide individual clinicians with the precise information they need at the point of care to maximize the potential of each patient interaction and improve outcomes?

This chapter explores the case of Omnio, a next-generation mobile medical app, and how it was designed and built according to the principles of convergence: open architecture, interoperability and data responsiveness. These three principles are key in allowing it and others to scale to the availability and growth of new information, and to curate it effectively through a crisp and intuitive interface. This type of intelligent platform ultimately allows a practitioner to take advantage of all the latest evidence-based findings, the crowd-sourced opinions of the institutions and colleagues they trust, and the vast data sets emerging through electronic health records.

A customizable, convergent mobile app holds the promise of becoming the new digital black bag for medical professionals: an indispensible tool, curated with all their medical must-haves, and providing the confidence to be ready for any situation they encounter.

MAKING THE CASE

A physician is eating dinner at a restaurant with his family. A shrill electronic beep cuts through the subdued murmur of the dining room, and others look over in irritation as he checks the device on his belt. Unfazed, he gets up and makes his way toward the lobby. He finds a quarter in his pocket and uses the pay phone for a call to his answering service, scribbling a number on a cocktail napkin as he takes the message. Producing another quarter, he calls a colleague who has a question for him. It's a tough question — he thinks it over for a minute and gives a preliminary answer, but makes plans to look it up in a textbook when he gets back home.

The pager was an exciting advance in mobile medicine. For many doctors practicing today, using a pager and a pay phone were common practice a mere two decades ago.

But with technological changes coming at an ever-accelerating rate, today we find ourselves in a landscape of nearly universal adoption of smartphones, widespread use of tablets, and as the HIMSS 2012 technology survey pointed out, an ever-widening array of functions for these devices: recording data at the bedside, viewing patient data, reviewing guidelines, sharing educational information with patients and more.[1]

The challenges and goals of mobile medicine have evolved over the past decades. In the mid-1990s, when physicians carried a Casio, Palm or other "personal digital assistant"—and the Internet as we know it was only beginning to take shape — there was a need to make medical information more available. Skyscape was one company to jump at this challenge early on, converting traditional textbooks into digital format and making them available on multiple devices.

Users no longer had to hurry back to their bookshelves to read up on a rare patient presentation — for the first time, they could carry a library in their pocket. After offering several medical references on the Apple Newton in the mid-1990s, Skyscape expanded to multiple devices and 20 reference titles in 2001; by 2003, the number of titles exploded to 300; and by 2009 reached 600.

This growth in offerings paralleled an extraordinary growth in the availability of digital information over the same years:

- The publication of new medical data has rocketed upward, in large part driven by a major increase in clinical trials — growing from 5,644 registered trials in 2000 to 138,874 in 2012.[2,3]
- PubMed now offers 22 million records, and it grows at a rate of approximately one record per minute. This is fueled by a proliferation of open-source journals, such as *PLOS One*, which grew from 138 articles in 2006 to more than 23,000 articles last year.[4-6]
- In 2006, an "app" was something you ate before dinner. Now, there are tens of thousands of mHealth apps available, with a user base that is increasing 15 times faster than users of the Internet.[7,8]
- Although luminaries began talking about electronic health records (EHRs) in the early 1960s,[9] less than 20 percent of providers were using any kind of electronic system in 2003.[10] Legislation has fueled a mass migration of millions of medical professionals: adoption rates reached 48 percent in 2009, and 72 percent last year.[11]
- Up to 90 percent of physicians in a recent survey expressed interest in using secure social networks to learn from experts and peers.[12]

This boom of medical information has easily kept pace with the exponential growth curves that Ray Kurzweil predicted for data and computing power in general. Or as Google's Eric Schmidt put it: "There were five exabytes of information created between the dawn of civilization through 2003, but that much information is now created every two days, and the pace is increasing."[13]

Clearly, the problem we face today is no longer about having access to information: It is about making sense of the abundant information and using it effectively to improve efficiency and outcomes.

Skyscape has been in a unique position to observe the trends in how medical professionals have engaged with mobile medical information. In some sense, "less is more": individuals want less to choose from, less to navigate, less to think about. Rather than carrying a library in their pocket, they want a customized tool that takes all the abundance and complexity and makes it simple, fast, and intuitive.

Consider a few examples:

- Medical calculators are a great fit for mobile devices — and several app makers offer 300, 400 or even 500+ calculators to choose from. But most medical professionals who use mobile calculators need between one and five on a day-to-day basis.[14] The challenge now is not to grow the list of offerings to 1,000 calculators: It is to connect users to the right calculators. Could it be possible to immediately provide the few calculators a clinician needs — and then recommend and teach the workflow for a few additional calculators they are most likely to benefit from?
- Guidelines are available for every major disease state. It is not hard for a clinician to get guidelines, in some form, on a mobile device. But navigating a tiny index and scrolling through dozens of pages on a small screen could be more of a hassle than simply walking back to the office and pulling a book off the shelf. The challenge is to construct mobile guidelines so a user can find the answer he or she needs immediately. Could it be possible to get the right answer with a single tap — and then see how a newly published study might affect that guideline? Or see the related opinion of a respected colleague? Or even see how your past decisions in a similar area turned out?
- All major peer-reviewed journals have a strong online presence, and many have developed apps as well. But the sheer abundance makes keeping up a challenge, whether it's sorting through a stack of print journals, scrolling through long e-mails of indices or jumping to multiple apps. Could it be possible for clinicians to be a touch away from the studies in their favorite publications? Or from relevant studies in journals they don't usually read?

We realized that to take the next step in serving medical professionals, we had to begin to connect the dots for our users, pull together the pieces they are looking for, personalize their experience.

The information is there; what is needed is *convergence*.

SETTING THE STRATEGY

Let me explain.

Physician use of the black medical bag has a long history. Consider this quote: "All these [situations] require arrangements… so that you can have the tools, the equipment, the metallics and the rest of it [gauzes, compresses, bandages, drugs] already prepared. Because the shortage of these things creates embarrassment and causes harm."[15] This was written by Hippocrates nearly 2,500 years ago.

The ancient tradition of the black bag continued through the nineteenth and twentieth century, when a worn and well-stocked leather bag became a symbol of the profession, as beautifully illustrated in LIFE's 1948 photo essay, "Country Doctor."[16] W. Eugene Smith's photos show how the black leather bag accompanied a country physician every step of the way, preparing him for any situation and helping to mark him as a recognized and revered member of the community.

But at some point in the 1970s or 1980s, most physicians stopped carrying black bags. This wasn't just because of the disappearance of house calls, as most medical professionals remained highly mobile. A major factor in the black bag's disappearance was surely the hyperkinetic growth of medical information outlined above. If keeping a black bag was an act of personal curation, how could physicians of recent years possibly curate the resources needed to keep up with it all?

As Hippocrates went on to write about the black bag: "The most appropriate is the one which follows a methodic layout, because the physician cannot keep everything in mind."[15] The challenge of keeping "everything in mind" has never been more daunting, considering that the half-life of medical knowledge is estimated to be about five years. Fifty percent of what we believe is correct today may be proven obsolete in coming years.[17]

Yet mHealth technology is now bringing us full circle, enabling physicians to reunite with their carefully curated, indispensible, portable companion.

A traditional black bag may have carried a few key medications that a physician found most important: perhaps aspirin, epinephrine and theophylline. But with a massive expansion to our pharmacopeia, doctors began to simply write a prescription and let the patient figure out how to deal with today's complexities of cost and access to get it filled. Now, suddenly, mHealth is capable of tackling such a challenge: with a tap, a doctor can find the drug that's right for the patient that's also on their formulary, or perhaps direct them to the pharmacy with the lowest cash payment.

A traditional black bag might have carried one or two condensed references, such as the *Washington Manual*. Yet in recent times, with the amount of new information coming out every week, the idea of a few hundred printed pages having much to offer is no longer viable. Instead, stacks of journals reporting new studies pile up on the work desk, almost taunting the physician with how quickly the knowledge in their head is growing outdated. But now, with mHealth, all this new data can be tamed — automatically selected and curated for a user's specialty, then personally adjusted so that the most relevant new information is served.

This kind of intuitive simplicity for the user is only possible with convergence. In moving from the traditional mobile reference model of Skyscape to a new generation product, three central principles of convergence guided the design and development:

1. Open architecture is the essential framework that allows multiple content creators to play in the same sandbox and deliver the content that users need. Just as the structure and content of iTunes fueled the rise of the iPod, people need a flexible and open system designed to handle the healthcare information challenge.

As described above, the task of curation, given today's abundance of information, is more than a full-time job. If physicians set out to personally curate all the information they needed, they would no longer be physicians — they would be librarians. By making a platform open, curation becomes a group effort. Groups of people — especially when they have specialized knowledge as medical professionals do — can be extraordinarily efficient at sorting, sharing, and evaluating information. Leveraging the power of collaborative IQ lessens the burden for each individual, and produces more powerful results.

Within this personalized, mobile medical library, any individual can curate a set of resources. For example, an individualized home page can be assembled, with all of a user's most important tools. Additional pages can be curated and assembled for specific situations — perhaps a family practice physician might keep a page for pediatrics, a page for patient educational material, an evidence-based guideline page and more.

But what if a physician is new to using a tablet and isn't sure how to best curate a page? Or maybe, due to a shift in practice, is beginning to see more geriatric patients? Rather than spending precious time on curation, the physician can follow the page of a colleague with more experience in that area. Just as a physician may have once modeled the organization of a black bag based on what a senior partner carried, open architecture apps make it easy to follow and learn from trusted colleagues.

What's more, institutions and organizations can create and publish branded pages, allowing member physicians to follow and continuously learn from them, perhaps pulling the latest resource offered by their professional society into their own Home Page. The open architecture becomes an efficient system for dissemination and socialization of mobile tools and resources.

2. Interoperability and connectedness allow different platforms — scheduling, electronic records, clinical decision support tools — to speak to each other with the right application programming interfaces (APIs).

The information saturating the healthcare environment comes in many varieties: there are PDFs of new studies, web tools, blog posts, Tweets, not to mention electronic billing, scheduling and patient records.

The current digital workflow many clinicians face does not reward them for being early adopters. They may have an electronic record open, then switch to an Internet search for more disease background, then take out their smartphone to check an app about a drug, then close the app and hunt down another with additional formulary information. After they finally get all the information they need and complete the electronic record, it's time to switch again to their scheduling application to find out who they are about to see, and perhaps check several other digital tools to get ready.

A truly convergent platform needs to be built with the right plugs and outlets to connect to all these information sources, allowing for a simple, intuitive workflow that invites and encourages users to take advantage of available information. In a truly interoperable experience, the technology itself should disappear and become a natural extension of how the clinician treats their patients.

The app platform is structured in such a way that new sources of information — such as EHRs — can easily be plugged in, allowing the various sources of information to work together.

3. A data-responsive tool has the intelligence to adapt itself to the needs of each individual. This is possible through continual data analysis of usage and behavioral patterns, combined with direct user feedback and interactions.

If resources are simply integrated and aggregated, the central problem of information overload would not be solved. Given the abundance, complexity and types of information available, a sophisticated mechanism is needed to keep track of all the data and interpret it usefully, guided by user feedback and conversations about their needs.

Ultimately, the platform will apply its usage data to make recommendations to users to make them productive and efficient — and to achieve the best possible outcomes. With the proper data set-up, the possibilities for a data-powered suggestion engine are extraordinary:

- When you provide samples, first-fill adherence rates improve.
- When you share a one-minute disease education video with your patients, they are less likely to be re-hospitalized.

A responsive data-driven platform is the final key to effectively curate a medical professional's "black bag" tool in the big data era of healthcare.

To put this once again in historical perspective: Since the origin of the profession, physicians have carried personally curated kits as an aid in their care. For a brief period in the late twentieth century, this tradition was suspended — in part because the exponential increase in available information outpaced the ability to keep that information portable. But today's mHealth technology is once again allowing physicians to carry their personal tool collections. And these portable tools are enabling medical professionals to care for patients in unprecedented new ways.

DELIVERING WITH IMPACT

The vision for mobile apps is to use the principles of convergence to enable medical professionals to get the most out of the information now available. With proper execution of these principles, the sky is the limit — and medical professionals will once again be able to carry their black bag wherever they go, to be prepared for any patient they encounter, or for any unexpected twist or turn in how healthcare is delivered in the coming decades.

A day in the life of a medical professional is anything but routine, and the 21st century electronic black bag can provide key support every step of the way (Table 34-1).

But while a mobile medical app has the potential to bend the outcomes curve in a country like the United States — through incremental wins in how medical professionals make smarter judgments and engage their patients — even more dramatic outcomes may be possible by delivering mHealth to underserved regions of the world.

Table 34-1: mHealth Apps Transform the Way Medical Professionals Consume Information at Multiple Points through a Routine Day.

Medical Professional Need	Before Mobile Medical Apps	After Mobile Medical Apps
Finding time to keep up with advances in medical care and practice management	*Cluttered* • Sifting through stacks of journals. • Attending CME activities. • Curbside consults in physician lounges.	*Organized* • All a clinician's medical resources accessible from one location (journals, CME, drug and disease references, news sites, and more), with a customizable interface for individual workflows. • Peer-to-peer sharing of knowledge and resources.
Avoiding errors in diagnosis and treatment	*Memory-based* Clinicians rely on memory, which often becomes outdated as quickly as new information becomes available.	*Technology-enhanced* Access to a personal digital medical assistant which can: • Provide clinical decision support at the point of care, when and where you need it. • Keep track of updates, interactions, side effects, guidelines, formulary changes, and more, so the clinician doesn't have to.
Improving patient communication and adherence to care plans between acute care visits to achieve desired outcomes	*Patient drop-off* During an average seven-minute encounter with a clinician, patients remember only 20 percent of what they are told.	*Patient follow-up* • Clinicians create and prescribe customized care plans to ensure effective knowledge transfer, compliance, and adherence to agreed upon treatment plan. • Real-time monitoring of patient progress.
Reducing practice costs and optimizing reimbursement for the clinician	*Inefficient* Increasing complexities in coding, documentation, and communication tools result in inefficiencies and loss of revenue.	*Efficient* Consolidated, single access integration of productivity tools to ensure streamlined communication and efficient documentation to optimize practice and patient outcomes.
Minimizing interference of existing technologies within the workflow	*Fragmented* Jumping between multiple applications, devices, and operating systems to get answers slows down clinicians and creates frustration.	*Seamless* APIs allow for fluid integration designed to fit the workflow, keeping the clinician's focus where it needs to be: on improving patient health.

Health eVillages, a non-profit program founded by Kerry Kennedy and the Chairman of Physicians Interactive, the maker of Skyscape and Omnio, has the mission of providing state-of-the-art mHealth technology to medical professionals in the most challenging clinical environments around the world by training medical professionals to use new resources.

While mobile adoption has happened quickly in developing nations, practitioners continue to struggle with a dangerous dearth of basic health information. An electronic black bag can make an immediate and dramatic difference.

Okari, a nurse practitioner at a Health eVillages pilot site in Lwala, Kenya, was eager to get his hands on a device on his first day of training. The night before, his clinic had admitted a woman whose pregnancy was at high risk for prenatal asphyxia. With the device in hand, he could do more than worry: He promptly looked up "neonatal resuscitation" and reviewed a procedural summary and video.

The very next night, he checked on his patient just in time to help her deliver her baby. As he had feared, the baby was not breathing. Instead of trying to recall his medical training from years earlier, he acted decisively, with the procedure fresh in his mind. Okari resuscitated the baby. The next day, the mother was able to leave the clinic with her healthy baby boy.

Dramatic stories such as Okari's have quickly emerged, illustrating the potential for improved outcomes by arming frontline practitioners with the information they need. Through six pilot programs, clinicians have already avoided countless complications and improved outcomes through more than 50,000 patient interactions using Health eVillages devices and medical apps.[19]

But more than that, this technology has served to increase the confidence and authority of practitioners, and analysis of programs has begun to show a difference. In Kenya, community health workers trained to use Health eVillages devices have been working together with a Safe Babies program, designed to reduce infant mortality by encouraging expectant mothers to deliver at medical facilities. After a full year of Health eVillages involvement, the number of pregnant women giving birth at medical facilities increased from 47 percent to 92 percent.

There has never been a magic bullet — a secret panacea — in the history of medicine and health. And a black bag, whether leather or digital, is no exception. But today, a convergent digital resource can be a transformative tool — empowering medical professionals to master the daunting information challenge; helping to instill them with a level of confidence and authority that has always been important in the role of the healer; and allowing them to connect more powerfully with their patients, engaging them in their health and treatment plan, and leading them to better health outcomes.

REFERENCES

1. HIMSS. 2nd Annual HIMSS Mobile Technology Survey, sponsored by Qualcomm Life. Available at: www.mhimss.org/resource/2012-mhimss-mobile-technology-survey-results-himss-analytics Posted December, 2012. Last accessed September, 2013.

2. Druss BG, Marcus SC. Growth and decentralization of the medical literature: implications for evidence-based medicine. *J Med Libr Assoc.* 2005;93(4):499-501.

3. NIH. ClinicalTrials.gov trends, charts, and maps. [On the Internet] Available at: http://clinicaltrials.gov/ct2/resources/trends#RegisteredStudiesOverTime. Accessed September 2013.

4. NLM. Medline® citation counts by year of publication. [On the Internet] Available at: www.nlm.nih.gov/bsd/medline_cit_counts_yr_pub.html. Accessed September 2013.

5. Rod RJ, Sullivan DM. Trends in medical publishing: where the publishing industry is going. *Plas Recon Surg.* 2013;131(1):179-181.

6. Hoff K. PLOS One papers of 2012. [On the Internet] Available at: http://blogs.plos.org/everyone/2013/01/03/2012review/ Posted January 2013. Accessed September 2013.

7. Research2Guidance. The market for mHealth app services will reach $26 billion by 2017. [On the Internet] Available at: www.research2guidance.com/the-market-for-mhealth-app-services-will-reach-26-billion-by-2017 Posted March 2013. Accessed September 2013.

8. Research2Guidance. App user base is growing 15 times faster than stationary internet user base. What are the consequences? [On the Internet] Available at: www.research2guidance.com/app-user-base-is-growing-15-times-faster-than-stationary-internet-user-number-what-are-the-consequences Posted June 2013. Accessed September 2013.

9. Schenthal JE, Sweeney JW, Nettleton WJ Jr, Yoder RD. Clinical application of electronic data processing apparatus. III. System for processing of medical records. *JAMA.* 1963;186:101-105.

10. Gur-Arie M. 2011 EHR adoption rates. [On the Internet] Available at: http://thehealthcareblog.com/blog/2011/12/02/2011-ehr-adoption-rates Posted December 2011. Accessed September 2013.

11. CDC. NCHS data brief. [On the Internet] Available at: www.cdc.gov/nchs/data/databriefs/db111.htm Posted December 2012. Accessed September 2013.

12. Digital Media and Science. Rise of the digital doctor. [On the Internet] Available at: http://digitalmediaandscience.files.wordpress.com/2013/04/rise-of-the-digital-doctor_50291408875c3.jpg. Accessed September 2013.

13. Kirkpatrick M. Google CEO Schmidt: "People aren't ready for the technology revolution. [On the Internet] Available at: http://readwrite.com/2010/08/04/google_ceo_schmidt_people_arent_ready_for_the_tech Posted August 2010. Accessed September 2013.

14. Data on file. Skyscape survey of 106 HCPs.

15. Tsoucalas G, Kousoulis AA, Tsoucalas I, Androutsos G. The earliest mention of a black bag. *Scan J Prim Health Care.* 2011;29(4):196-197.

16. Smith WE. Country doctor. *LIFE.* September 20, 1948. [On the Internet] Available at: http://life.time.com/history/life-classic-eugene-smiths-country-doctor/#1. Accessed September 2013.

17. IBM Research. IBM Watson healthcare collaboration with Cleveland Clinic. [On the Internet]. Available at: www.research.ibm.com/articles/watson_medical_school.shtml. Accessed September 2013.

18. Macgregor AJ. Letter: half-life of medical knowledge. *Can Med Assoc.* 1975;112(10):1165-1166.

19. Health eVillages. Health eVillages raises $58,000 for global mHealth program. Available at: www.healthevillages.org/health-evillages-raises-58000-for-global-mhealth-program. Accessed January 2014.

CHAPTER 35

Innovation Cure for mHealth Barriers

By Douglas Goldstein and Gregg Masters, MPH

The drive for information technology adoption in healthcare started in earnest in the 1980s via an army of variably competent managed care organizations, their supportive management service organizations (MSO) and physician practice management companies (PPMC). Then in the late 1990s the "strategic mantra" driven largely by the managed care meltdown and subsequent provider risk pushback became "eHealth." Risk or no risk, challenges enabling electronic healthcare through the web were taking the healthcare world by storm. Today, the cry is for "mHealth" or mobile health through the ubiquitous mobile phone, tablets or other Internet connected devices. Today one primary channel for mHealth is the smartphone. With 1 billion smartphones worldwide, and approximately 50 percent of Americans using one, they are a primary channel for mHealth. In reality the mobile smartphone or tablet today is not really smart — it doesn't think per se, but it's a powerful, small computer that travels with us wherever we go. And it delivers a whole new dimension of life management and entertainment through apps and the mobilization of services. In the end "eHealth" and "mHealth" are a tapestry of options to connect and support choices that impact our "health." The big difference is that the mobile phone is always with us and is in essence a potential "life" management tool that can support fitness, health and healthcare 24/7, anywhere and anytime a person has their device(s) on.

Just as in the first digital Web age, the mobile digital age of the 2010s has numerous barriers slowing the functionality, scope and speed of adoption — not of the devices, but of specific functionality as it relates to fitness, health and healthcare. This essay describes 10 barriers affecting the spread of enhanced functionality, utility and effectiveness of mobile devices, technologies and solutions that support better health. We fondly call these "mBarriers." The narrative also outlines an "Innovate Now" approach and its five key strategies to attack these mBarriers with an increasing array of mobile services designed to support improved fitness, health and healthcare.

Today, mHealth just doesn't mean mobile phones; it includes tablets, iPads, wearable sensors built into clothing or worn somewhere on the body. Tomorrow's sensors may include implantable and nanosensors in our bodies and environment. mHealth also includes a vast array of passive sensing devices built into the environment ranging from automobiles that tell us our weight today, to talking appliances and a vast array of other sensors in the world of M2M (machine-to-machine) sensing and communication. Some people refer to this as the "Internet of Everything" because of the inter-connectedness of people and objects in our environment.

Today we live in the "experience" economy and the Internet mobile device is a continuous connection that can facilitate a positive experience. The mobile device is rapidly becoming a vital channel and connection to support the health, happiness and positive healing healthcare experience of the people we serve. We truly are in a unique position to take the rapid adoption of mobile technologies by the people we serve and their loved ones to transform health products and services. When successfully integrated into lifestyle choices, these tools support realization of the Triple Aim of improved population health, lower per capital costs and increased patient satisfaction.

Despite all the buzz about "mHealth," at the beginning and end of each day we can't lose sight that it's about a very personalized version of what constitutes individual health, happiness and productivity. Nonetheless, there are challenges ranging from systemic inertia and legacy infrastructure to regulations, the dominant disease care payment system and history that form barriers to mHealth adoption or "mBarriers."

The buzz about eHealth vs. mHealth might change but many of the same barriers that we encountered in the eHealth era are still plaguing us in the era of "mobile everything." The following list labels each mBarrier in health and provides an "Innovate Now" attitude designed to shape solutions being developed in the United States and globally. Now let's dive to the top 10 mBarriers to mHealth adoption and then we'll explore the "Innovate Now" cure in more depth.

EVERY mBARRIER IN HEALTH PRESENTS OPPORTUNITIES

What would life be without problems and challenges? Boring! mBarriers create numerous opportunities for leaders and innovators in the public, private and educational sectors to create new solutions that build bridges, break down silos and accelerate collaborative systems that address vital individual, family and societal needs. Today mHealth technologies and ecosystem solutions are the "chassis" of tomorrow's proactive, preventive health system.

Following are the 10 mBarriers that are slowing the adoption of mobile, digital health technologies by all the participants and stakeholders in the health and healthcare ecosystem today. They are coincident to the rapid adoption of technology including smartphones, tablets, M2M and an exploding family of sensors by users and professionals in their everyday personal and professional lives. Together the mBarriers encompass the spectrum of

- Infrastructure — across the nation, regions and into every health organization.
- Incentives that support disease care, not pro-active healthcare (cost/value proposition).
- Integration — into lifestyle, medical practice or enterprise workflow.

App-itis
mBarrier: Over a decade ago the web was flooded with a wave of sites that were limited in their ability to deliver transactions, services and meet other recognized and unrecognized needs. Then and now, the world of mobile Internet connected devices is changing how people navigate their lives, entertain themselves and manage their

health. In this mobile Internet wave of health and medical innovation, there are too many apps that are point solutions disconnected from a person's doctor, hospital or health plan.

Tens of thousands of health, fitness and medical apps have been created, but how many of them are based on evidence and good data? How many are sticky and deliver continuous engagement? How many of them are connected and deliver true service? Today it's a small percentage, but it will grow as mainstream health leaders get their infrastructure digitized and mobilized and translate this foundation into mobile services and products.

Innovate Now Direction — Deliver better, smarter, more convenient service anywhere, anytime. The good news is that we are coming out of the mobile "hype phase" of the Gartner cycle where the vast majority of health and medical apps were disconnected from the services that people needed to do on the go. Part of the innovation fix can be found in the rise of the Happtique, SocialWellth and the other app rating services and curators that will help guide both the consumer and healthcare professional in making good decisions about the app services that enhance their lives.

Another factor is the increasing robustness of the service components in apps from leaders such as Walgreens. Walgreens mobile app service enables anywhere prescription refills, transactions and other services today. Tomorrow you will be able to make medical appointments, talk to a pharmacist and much more.

Fitness apps can be effective as standalone, but to truly improve the health of persons with chronic condition care they must be integrated into the vital sign monitoring of a care team. Health app services from doctors and health organizations need to be about service. They need to enable seamless appointment scheduling, prescription refills and access to the right knowledge when needed. They also must integrate and present in a useful way longitudinal medical records — providing virtual, live access to real and avatar doctors and nurses 24/7, and enabling other transactions that support the management of a person's health and medical care. In our view, it's not about apps, it's about the service and the problem to solve, either perceived by the patient or end user. mService is the cure for app-itis.

Data is Jailed

mBarrier: Data silos in the public and private sectors still exist, but the walls are coming down, albeit slowly. Fitness, health and medical data remain separated by organizations, formats and proprietary business interests from rational though arguably short-sighted executives seeking to protect near-term business advantage. Health data interoperability and smooth, seamless data exchange is not yet a mainstream market demand or reality. Many first mover enterprises adopting mobile health apps or platforms stand alone in an otherwise disconnected ecosystem of healthcare providers.

However, there is also progress to report, albeit unevenly distributed by local market considerations including delivery system characteristics, risk tolerance, and the specific terms of payer contracts. Healthcare organizations, particularly those working under or toward global budgets, value-based pricing, or capitation vs. production incentives, are leveraging cloud technologies to created unified data warehouses. Regional, state and national information exchanges have gotten off the ground, organized governance structures, and moved into operations, exchanging key health and medical data that can improve the efficiency and cost effectiveness of patient care.

Innovate Now Direction — Get on Board. Take the Blue Button Pledge and Support It. Data liquidity is a dream today, but is tomorrow's reality! Leadership in the liberation of health data has come from key federal government agencies. Personalized health data is the oxygen of this emerging patient-centric healthcare ecosystem and the symbol has become Blue Button.

The concept of a "Button" that represents data liquidity and access evolved out of a Markle Foundation public/private work group in early 2010. The concept of a "Blue Button" health data download function gained rapid acceptance by leadership at HHS, VA and DoD. In the fall of 2010 the Veterans Administration launched the first Blue Button to make Veterans personal health information available through a simple click of a digital button. In October 2010, head technology officers of HHS and VA announced that VA and HHS's Center for Medicare & Medicaid Services were offering Blue Button downloads to Veterans and to Medicare beneficiaries. Veterans Administration has been a leader in PHRs with the development of MyHealth*e*Vet web site and services.

Then "Data Liberation' became a popular mantra established by former HHS CTO Todd Park as a way to stimulate innovation, empower patients with their own data, and support data liquidity across healthcare organizations. As of the publication of this book, thousands of healthcare leaders from Aetna, United Healthcare and Walgreens to Banner Health, Mayo Clinic and hundreds of other leaders, have embraced the empowerment vision.

Early in 2013, the Office of the National Coordinator for Health IT (ONC) announced the arrival of BlueButton+. The purpose of the Plus was to make consumers' health data even more accessible through the implementation of interoperable standards that can push and pull structured electronic medical record (EMR) data between a third-party consumer health data application in an unstructured format. The Blue Button idea is now a movement catching the imagination of the developer community including the innovators at GenieMD.com, iBlueButton.com and CareTracker, enabling patient empowerment and better health, and thus moving the needle toward health information-assisted person/patient-centered healthcare and data interoperability.

Clinical Complexity

mBarrier: Implementing clinical health information is difficult due to the complexity of medicine, the fragmented nature of the current health information ecosystem that exists in healthcare organizations, and variability of the human body. Failure in adopting clinical technology is frequently due to execution issues, which range from a lack of participation in planning and selection, poor process re-engineering, insufficient training and resistance to changing how work is done.

The paper-based and manual processes that have evolved over the past 100 years do not change easily. It's impossible for healthcare organizations to extend their services from the hospital and clinic to mobile devices if their back-end systems are *not* harmonized across the ecosystem and fully digitized. For the past 10 years the focus has been to fully implement EMR systems, digitize the infrastructure, and deliver functionality and outcomes in a web world first within a hospital, then by reaching the ambulatory client, and finally reaching out to the home via the web.

Then suddenly, in the span of five or six years, 85 percent of customers are intermittently managing their lives through mobile devices and 50 percent are using smartphones, while the requirement to meet the mobile demands of customers and patients escalate rapidly. Legacy IT vendors are focused on getting their core systems to work and thousands of mHealth IT solutions pop up and seek to integrate with core IT systems amidst vendor and processes and priority resistance. In the end, mHealth deployment is more likely to fail due to human, timing and environmental factors rather than a failure of the technology itself. As with health IT overall, there will be a high failure rate of mHealth apps, services and solutions.

Innovate Now Direction — The Right Teams and Processes Can Address the Complexity Challenge. The complexity demands the application of collaboration and innovation tactics focused on teamwork, process-improvement methodology, and an empowered knowledge-transfer effort to rapidly spread better ways of delivering care.

Experts in clinical computing must provide effective solutions via seasoned application of the concepts, techniques, knowledge and processes of medicine, and display an expert level of critical thinking in applying principles, theories, and concepts on a wide range of issues that are unique to clinical settings. By tracking emerging mHealth applications, services and practices that are easy to use for the clinician or patient, meet regulatory requirements and demonstrate initial results and outcomes, organizations are in a position to support customers wherever they may be. In the end, addressing the complexity factors requires extreme focus on people, process, appropriate technologies (including mHealth), money and the ability to execute better. This approach can help "get it right" to achieve the operational imperatives and the Triple Aim.

Not Invented Here

mBarrier: Healthcare is an insular, top-down and hierarchical culture. The "not invented here" attitude is widespread throughout the industry. This is also true of health IT functions and is one of the reasons that health IT lags five to 10 years behind advances in banking, telecommunications and other sectors. There are some good reasons to account for part of the lag. These include clinical complexity, regulatory requirements, nature of treating medical conditions and other factors. But the extent of the lag is exacerbated by the fact that health IT has generally been an outsourced business. Health IT management teams generally spend their time managing major vendors in the deployment and operations of their disparate systems. The number and capabilities of IT developers inside healthcare organization lags other industries.

With the rapid uptake of mobile devices and services by professionals, patients and customers, we're witnessing the entry into healthcare by non-healthcare players with deep pockets. This includes the major telecommunications companies Verizon, AT&T and Sprint, and other entities such as Google, Microsoft and a range of defense contractors. Until recently, hospital systems, health plans, organized medicine, big pharma or even device manufactures were the lead sponsors of healthcare conferences. Today, we see an expanded cast of characters with direct interest in enabling IT infrastructure and generating significant revenue streams from technology sales and services subscriptions.

Innovate Now Direction — Collaborate to Achieve Diversity by Applying Expertise and Technologies from Other Industries. The sustainability and efficacy of ecosystems comes from collaboratively sourced diversity. The same principle applies to human engineered systems. The strength of the future sickness treatment and true health promoting systems is in collaboration and cross industry diversity through appropriate technology adoption and innovation acceleration. Just like process improvement sciences such as Six Sigma and LEAN developed in other industries were adopted to improve healthcare, the same is needed for mHealth technologies and services.

In times of rapid change when we have been living inside an insular, "not invented here," and "this is the way we have always done it," world, there are some key strategies to take. It's important to find leadership experienced in change and innovation that can infuse a new open and collaborative culture into organizations. As this culture evolves through rapid cycle learning, accelerated knowledge transfer, and a "can do" spirit, it is important to add mobile innovation structure to the IT organizational chart and within the budget to allow for piloting, testing, results, integration and scaling.

To meet our professionals, customers and patients where they are at, health IT leadership and their teams must apply the proven technologies, software development models, etc., often borrowed from other industries to overcome the mHealth barriers.

Slow Adoption of 'Open' Information Technology

mBarrier: The vast majority of the private sector's health IT systems are based on closed proprietary health IT. It was only after the 9/11 terrorist attacks that the push for open standards, open architecture, open data and open interoperability got some traction. This push is still underway as the requirement for open data exchange continues based on requirements of the formal regulations such as Affordable Care Act, HITECH, HIPAA, and Meaningful Use and the widely promoted Blue Button initiative.

The world's most widely adopted health IT system for health systems — VistA (Veterans Administration VistA, not Microsoft's) is essentially "open." The source code for VistA operates as Open Source Software (although it technically is public domain and available through FOIA). Versions of VistA run the Veterans Health Administration, DoD Military Health Services and hospitals worldwide including Mexico, Egypt, Jordan and many other countries. For current information on deployments visit www.openhealthnews.com. Open technology, solutions and software are driving innovation and competition across nearly all industries globally with Gartner projecting it as an industry in excess of $68 billion.

Innovate Now Direction — Open is the Way to Interoperability & Improved Outcomes. So can a culture of "open" sail amid a sea of legacy and walled healthcare islands? The answer is yes! It is estimated that 50 percent of mobile apps are built with open technology and structured for an open ecosystem. It's working in other industries such as the ATM system worldwide, which is built on an open standard and infrastructure. It can and has to work in healthcare to achieve our Triple Aim goals.

There are many flavors of "open." On the technical side there is: open data, open architecture, open APIs, open standards and open-source software. On the business side there is open science, open innovation, open collaboration and others. Interoperability success doesn't necessarily require open-source software, but does demand open standards for the exchange of health and medical information. Open supports interoperability, data liquidity and most of all will support improved outcomes.

Security & Trust Chasms
mBarrier: In healthcare, security is a top priority. mHealth technologies that deliver security whether it's HIPAA, FDA or FIPS 140-2 (military grade security), is available and delivered to mobile devices. The issue of who in the healthcare spectrum of interactions do people trust is another matter. People tend to trust doctors and hospitals before they trust health plans and pharmaceutical companies, but overall there are regional, cultural and individual preferences that need to be understood.

Innovate Now Direction — Do It Right In an Expedited Fashion. These mHealth barriers exist for good reasons, so the issue here is not overcoming or erasing them but to address them in a rigorous, deliberate and secure manner that considers internal and external threats to security of protected health information and vital data.

Wrong Thinking
mBarrier: To be patient-centered (vs. hospital- or doctor-centered) is an essential shift. However from a person-centric perspective, most people don't view themselves as "patients" if they are sick. Many times in healthcare we call people "consumers," but again this is a bit dehumanizing. The diabetes and obesity epidemic which is driving many chronic diseases is a result of "overconsumption." So in essence we are calling people and customers "consumers" and trying to educate and counsel them to not eat so much! And while perhaps best expressed by Shannon Brownlee, Vice President of the Lown Institute, while at a recent conference on ACOs chairing a panel on patient engagement, she advised the audience, embracing the sensibilities of many, that "I'm not my disease, and I don't want to be managed."

The medical world has some of the best and brightest people on the planet driving advances in the understanding, diagnosis, and treatment of complex disease and illness. Clinical professionals are also at the forefront of technology adoption if it's proven to be effective and is easy to use. Witness the rapid adoption of tablets in the form of iPads or Android-driven technology by doctors for personal use. Adoption for professional use is accelerating based on the secure connectivity to EMR and other health information systems.

However, paternalism runs deep in healthcare; in fact it's in the DNA of a culture forged via a rigorous and at times unforgiving physician-in-training initiation process, generalized into mainstream healthcare operations and codified by the payment system.

Innovate Now Direction — Sustained Activation for Better Health Depends Upon Knowing a Person First, Not Just their Medical Conditions. It's time to go beyond patient-centered care. It's time to reinvent the human healing experience to a person- and family- and community-centric view. Mobile devices and environmental sensors applied for mHealth which capture data explicitly or passively in the background 24x7 delivers a whole new context of service and support.

In The Society for Participatory Medicine and emerging communities of empowered people everywhere, there is talk of focusing on people first and their life, fitness and healthcare needs, not just their patient-centered needs. Few institutions walk the talk let alone deliver the experience so this can be a true differentiator for today's leaders.

It's about the human healing, customer experience and satisfaction, and while service and convenience matter, both quality and value are important as well. Whether seen as nuanced semantic differences between the well-intended "Partnership for Patients" and the subsequent spinoff generated by the likes of art-as-message e-health activist Regina Holliday's "Partnership <u>With</u> Patients," there is an undeniable qualitative differential placing the human person first, not just a patient in the conversation as principal vs. organizing systems with their input.

Until the entire wellness and healthcare IT and mHealth ecosystems emerge that effectively recognize and support a person, family and community based and truly "people vs. patient-centered" health and wellness agenda, we're still playing to and at the margins of making this work.

Not Enough Vital Signs

mBarrier: Bending the cost curve and improving outcomes is not just about technology and mHealth technology in particular. It's about connecting with, activating and supporting people to be more fit, happier and healthier. It's about helping them solve life problems which so often get in the way of dealing with their medical issues.

The unique thing about mHealth versus previous technologies is that it is very addictive. For many, many people it's almost always in our pockets, next to our nightstands and with us 24/7. When we are on the go, we check keys, wallet and phone before we go. Plus, these mobile devices have sensors and apps that can take direct input from us and also passively monitor where we are and what we do.

Traditional medicine monitors vital signs, including your heart beat, breathing rate, temperature and blood pressure when a person is in the presence of their doctor. Normal vital signs change with age, sex, weight, exercise tolerance and overall health. Remote monitoring of vital signs of a small group of patients whose conditions warrant traditional vital sign monitoring has been a core part of the telemedicine. Until recently the remote patient monitoring devices that were used were specialized and more expensive than the off-the-shelf monitoring devices of today.

The paradigm shift now is that devices and sensors that can monitor the traditional vital signs are consumer off the shelf devices such as Bluetooth enabled scales that are now available via Best Buy, Target, Amazon and tens of thousands of online and offline vendors. Prices of the hardware have been driven down and investment is in the services and infrastructure to deliver supported self-care and empowering accountable health.

The big mHealth barrier here is that the healthcare industry because of regulation and lack of digitized infrastructure is doing business like we did in the 20th century. Meanwhile our patient customers are mobilizing their lives and we are missing a huge opportunity to connect with people where they are at. Our imperative is to figure how to address the barriers effectively and deliver supported self-care services through mHealth technologies that empower, are easy to use and deliver results for improved outcomes and satisfaction.

Innovate Now Direction — New Vital Signs for the 21st Century: Nutrition, Activity and Sleep. Most medical conditions depend on multi-modal interventions such as medications plus the right nutrition and physical activity. Engaging and activating a person has a greater likelihood when the health messaging is tailored to an individual patient's psychographic, demographic and technographic profile and their specific communication preferences (e.g., texting alerts vs. phone calls or other). Most health and medical conditions and treatment improve if the person combines pharmaceutical/surgical and other conventional treatment with proper diet/nutrition and physical activity adjusted for their personal profile and preferences. Diabetics who take their medication, eat the proper foods in the proper amount and get the right amount of exercise, physical activity and sleep enough will almost always have improved outcomes. Just taking the pill is not a silver bullet cure, but just one part of the equation for health and happiness.

The growth of the quantified self-movement and research from the Pew Internet Life survey indicates that a majority of people do track some aspect of their health, they just don't always use technology. We believe that adoption of tracking health technology across all population sectors is on the rapid uptake because it's getting easier and cheaper to do. People are engaging in fitness and health and tracking with technology and other means is much greater than in the past.

The time has come for the healthcare industry to expand their "vital sign" monitoring to include physical activity, nutrition, and sleep, and provide effectiveness scores to people tailored for their conditions, lifestyle and preferences. mHealth technology delivers affordable approaches to provide both traditional and 21st century vital signs monitoring on a regular, continuous basis, in ways that are convenient and non-invasive to a person's work and lifestyle. The 21st century vital signs to integrate into the healthcare experience are:

1. Physical activity
2. Sleep quality
3. Nutrition

Do-What-You-Are-Told Mentality

mBarrier: For many years the disease management industry complained about low adoption rates for their programs. Patients don't do what they "should" be doing was the mantra. For instance, patients with diabetes eat too much of the wrong things and our program will educate them to be healthier. We live in a society of consumerism and the underlying consumption messages from the packaged/processed food and alcohol industries are difficult to overcome. The desired outcome was rarely achieved and many condition management programs came across as what a patient "should be doing."

Unfortunately, some of the "I know what is right for you" is still going based on the work of determined idealist innovators with one-off "solutions," often without the involvement of patients and doctors. This has resulted in thousands of mobile apps disconnected from the healthcare services ecosystem that get downloaded but rarely used. It's not about the app, but about whether the service delivered is compelling and

the app is used every day. Research from Pew Research Center's Internet & American Life Project indicated the following:
- 60 percent of U.S. adults say they track their weight, diet or exercise routine.
- 33 percent of U.S. adults track health indicators or symptoms, like blood pressure, blood sugar, headaches, or sleep patterns.
- 12 percent of U.S. adults track health indicators or symptoms for a loved one.

However, their tracking is often informal:
- 49 percent of trackers say they keep track of progress "in their heads."
- 34 percent say they track the data on paper, like in a notebook or journal.
- 21 percent say they use some form of technology to track their health data, such as a spreadsheet, web site, app or device.

Technology is part of the solution but not all of it. Program success is highly dependent on how it's applied based on people, process and technology. Truly understanding what motivates a person in the context of their family, community and their cultural differences is frequently the deciding factor whether a technology is first engaging and then supports continuous activation and interaction in managing chronic conditions.

Innovate Now Direction — Make it About Fun, Friends, Fashion & Fitness. In 1989, the book *"Healthy Pleasures, Discover the Medical Benefits of Pleasure and Live a Longer, Healthier Life,"* David Sobel, MD, and Robert Ornstein, PhD, wrote: "Imagine a medical treatment that can decrease heart disease, boost immune function, relieve depression, and block pain — whose only side effect is that it makes you feel good. It's safe, inexpensive, and readily available, No, it's not a miracle drug; rather, these benefits come from the experience of pleasure itself. And this pleasure prescription is filled in the internal pharmacy of the brain."

This finding was reinforced in the *"Health eGames Market Report"* authored by Douglas Goldstein with Physic Ventures in 2008. The report documented the multi-billion dollar expenditure by consumers for video games, social media and other experience that deliver "productive entertainment" as Nintendo calls it. The majority of this multi-billion expenditure directly out of people's pockets has been for exer-gaming and cognitive brain games. Remember the spontaneous adoption of Wii bowling in senior centers across the country. There have been hundreds of studies on the effectiveness video games and immersive learning video experiences in supporting improved health behaviors across a number of conditions. This research in part has been underwritten by the Robert Wood Johnson Foundation. Human beings for the most learn through doing and experiential learning and gamification: video gaming, immersive learning simulations and new entertainment forms are the 21st century vehicles for education and changing behaviors.

Mobile is not a magic solution, the specific engagement ingredients are different for everyone. However today we know the ingredients, the winners will know how to cook the recipe different for each person and family we care for anywhere, anytime, any condition, any place. The key in engagement is converting a "have to" to a "get to." Overall, success depends in promoting wellness and chronic disease management. With chronic disease driving healthcare costs, success requires understanding how to motivate each person based on their preferences and then configuring the right mix of engagement ingredients (e.g., fun, family, fashion and fitness) in the solution.

Fee for Service Inertia

mBarrier: The No. 1 barrier to mHealth adoption is that the vast majority of payment for health services still depends on the "CBUOS" or covered billable unit of service (i.e., the face-to-face visit). Today, only a fraction of payment from Medicaid, Medicare and commercial insurers would pay for a visit or service provided via a mobile phone or some type of telehealth/telemedicine services. This is changing, but again only slowly.

Follow the money... Trillions of dollars of healthcare risk is shifting from payers to providers over the next ten years. Today, however, the entire infrastructure of health systems still depends upon admissions and filled beds. Yes there are hundreds of risk shifting demonstration projects underway and the next age of capitation and risk shift is underway. Nonetheless, today the vast majority of doctors and hospitals in the country are still paid for disease care, not to keep a population healthy. It's not a question of whether it's changing but how fast and how it varies by geography and payer.

While conventional wisdom holds that U.S. healthcare is broken, truth be told, and as is often noted by John Mattison, MD, CMIO, Kaiser Permanente Southern California, it's actually working and delivering precisely on the unit profit maximization incentives that drive industry performance from a disease-care perspective. Nevertheless, the reactive sick care model and continued reliance on face-to-face care for payment is leading the entire ecosystem closer to the tipping point of unsustainability. People are demanding the convenience of mobile health and medical service delivery whenever feasible. Healthcare must step up to accelerate payment systems reform to reward and pay for the delivery of appropriate healthcare services through mHealth and new emerging modalities.

Innovate Now Direction — Pay for Health of Populations, Not Piece Work Disease Care. Mobile fitness is being rapidly adopted by people across the planet, however, it tends to be led by the younger, already healthier populations. For mHealth and mobile medicine to be adopted by broader sectors it will take time and it will also take payers figuring out effective methods of reimbursing for appropriate mHealth that saves time and money for both the customer patient and the payer. Across many conditions the mobile solutions deliver a value proposition that justifies either payers paying or people paying for the mHealth services directly in the new era of retail medicine.

mHealth is convenient, effective and demanded by many people we serve. But mHealth has three major parts — fitness, wellness (health) and medical care. The application of mHealth is occurring fastest in the fitness and wellness realm because of the lack of regulation by FDA, HIPAA and other regulations. Growth in the fitness sector is a direct to consumer payment model that is working because of the "value" delivered by the off the shelf devices.

Billions of dollars are being invested in mobile medicine services and they will become a major channel for the delivery of services because it's convenient; over time it will lower per capita healthcare costs and it is a major patient satisfier, delivering a better patient experience (as long as the mobile service designed with the person in mind). Delivering mobile medicine in the context of the right service and right business model just takes longer than enabling mobile fitness. It is happening and the pace is increasing because of the customer demand and need to deliver more services efficiently with less financial resources.

We just described the top 10 mBarriers along with a direction for innovating our way through and around them. Clearly this is not an exhaustive list but a good start. Certainly it will provide guidance to leaders and innovators as they build their strategic, clinical and operational plans for this year and into the future. The clock is ticking and "business as usual" with modest tweaks here and there just won't cut it this time if we are to meet people's needs for better health at lower costs.

Innovate Now is the Cure for Barrier-itis

Across the industry today there is an explosion of solutions that reorganize the ingredients of people, process, workflow, supported self-care programs or emerging accountable systems that comprise effective solutions. "Innovate Now" is a systematic approach to understand the top barriers and harness the power of mobile digital health and other disciplines on an integrated basis to create these solutions and build the tech enabled sustainable ecosystems of the future. Some product and services generated will be point solutions and others will require public-private sector collaboration to create systemic solutions. The goal or change imperative is to enable the Triple Aim and transform the fitness, health and medical care industries.

The 'Innovate Now' Ingredients

mHealth technologies are essential but are only part of the solution because every person has their preferences about how they apply the vast array of mobile products/services to manage different aspects of their lives. Therefore, the imperative is to understand the fundamental, motivational, behavioral and technology literacy and preferences of each person whose behavior or productivity we wish to influence through mobile technologies and services.

- **Mobile.** Everyone is connected through Internet enabled mobile devices as the speed and reliability of broadband access is increasing with 4G & beyond. Plus, both Smartphone and app use adoption is rapid as more and more service functionality is being added to apps from doctors, health systems, health plans and other players like drugstore chains. People love it because it saves time and it's addictive, in a fun way. Mobile delivers a technology imperative blending ubiquitous computing, the cloud, convenience and coolness (4 Cs).
- **Social Media.** Connected, real-time virtual social experiences ranging from Facebook and Twitter to Instagram, JoinMe, SnapChat, Google+ and many others, to a person's apps used regularly and their compelling game experiences (e.g., Angry Birds and your sponsored immersive learning experiences) that deliver the place to hang out, play, learn and do collaborative activities.
- **Gamification.** The process of turning work into play is *Gamification*. Gamification takes what is considered work and turns it into a fun, engaging experience that builds healthier behaviors and skills in a more effective and engaging approach than other learning methods. It structures progressive and socially connected rewards in a way that supports positive behavior change and empowers daily participation.
- **Big Data Drives Predictive and Prescriptive Analytics.** Structured and unstructured data from across fitness, health and medical care are being com-

bined to drive insights and focused interventions to help the people most in need of care coordination and support.
- **Behavioral Economics.** Personal change science that applies the latest insights from Big Data and along with knowledge from research findings on the power of social media, mobile and gaming to support continuous healthy behaviors.

"Innovate Now" Formula = TIME

It's time to intelligently, creatively and patiently address the mHealth barriers. The "Innovate Now" problem solving formula is future creating process. It combines proven, emerging and appropriate <u>technology</u>, <u>ingenuity</u> (in the form of individual and collaborative team contributions) <u>improvement science</u> focused on processes, <u>money</u> in the form of financial resources and the synergy of <u>Engagement + Activation + Sustained Interaction</u>. Success comes to the leaders and their teams that have extreme focus and understanding of customer needs (patients and professionals) today and tomorrow. With the rapid adoption of mobile across all sectors, it's imperative to rapidly and smartly evolve our strategies by blending digital (online and mobile) and offline interactions with health professionals and patients along their family members to support their life's needs and goals.

TIME is the Formula with the five key Strategies to overcome mHealth adoption barriers

1. **<u>T</u>echnology.** Solutions that with the right UX and appropriate application of technology can work to support positive behavior change when used with the other strategies.
2. **<u>I</u>ngenuity and Improvement** (individual & collaborative teams). The "I" in TIME stands for both Ingenuity and Improvement science. Innovation today is the result of leadership and teams. Human ingenuity at the individual and team level is key. Our team members are problem solvers. Innovation is the process of solving problems. Usually an organization's greatest untapped resource is its own employees. Improvement science for processes: this involves applying the best of LEAN and Six Sigma to streamline processes based on the availability of the appropriate technology.
3. **<u>M</u>oney Resources.** Innovation requires sufficient funding of the endeavors to allow large scale pilot projects needed to test new methods and processes of care delivery at the hospital, clinic, home and wherever patients might be.
4. **<u>E</u>ngagAction**™ is the successful blending of mobile, social media, gamification, big data, behavioral economics to deliver continuous activation and interactions that result in better nutrition, sleep, medication usage, fitness, care transitions and the associated outcomes.

Today we are seeing successful interventions from health plans and others to integrate mobile, social media, gamification, big data and behavioral economics. One leading example of the integration and application of the ingredients and formula is Wellvolution from Blue Shield of California that provides employees with the resources needed to develop and maintain a healthy lifestyle. Started in 2008 with Blue Shield's own employees, it has documented the ability to reduce per capita healthcare costs and improve morale and productivity.

Blue Shield of California has been using a multi-media, multi-modal program to motivate its employees with their branded initiative "Wellvolution," which is a program that uses incentives, games, social media, big data and behavioral economics to promote good health. Wellvolution involved the redesign of the cafeteria to encourage healthy eating, instituting walking (treadmill) work stations, applying principles from the book "Connected" and integrating multiple programs that support the principles of behavioral economics and make fitness the fun and social thing to do. "The most popular features of Wellvolution are those that make it easy, social and fun to engage in wellness," says Bryce Williams, Vice President, WellBeing at Blue Shield of California. Wellvolution's most popular initiatives are Daily Challenge, a newly launched program that allows employees to join colleagues, friends and family to complete a simple daily challenge to promote well-being toward healthy behaviors. Participants can earn health points or badges. It also has seen success with the fourth installment of Shape Up Shield, a social media-fueled challenge that uses an online platform to let employees form teams, post comments in forums, set team and personal fitness goals and give virtual "high-fives" for encouragement.

Since Blue Shield launched Wellvolution, it has seen improvements in diet and lifestyle choices, such as regular physical activity up 33 percent and smoking prevalence falling by roughly 50 percent to only 6 percent. It also has seen significant reductions in cholesterol and high-blood pressure, promising healthcare cost and productivity trends indicative of a 3:1 return on investment. Blue Shield of California has been using the Wellvolution initiative with their own employees and the plan is to offer the program to external employer customers in the future.

Now is the time to act wisely and deliberately. Meet a person's health and medical needs and enable family members' support of activities of daily living as it relates to fitness, health, healthcare and happiness.

Stay tuned — the ride has only just begun!
The next generation of successful EngagActions solutions is taking full advantage of the smart technologies, processes and people. These solutions are integrated with great healthcare teams and personalized based on individual personal needs using the latest multimedia, multimodal strategies driving compelling products and services. This means that mobile, social media, gaming, experiences, along the latest augmented reality tags and billboards, QR codes, virtual reality, geo-location based fitness, health and healthcare offers are sure to keep us entertained and empowered and healthy anywhere if we tailor the solutions to meet the needs, preferences and profiles of the people and communities we serve.

CHAPTER 36

Looking Ahead: An mHealth Roundtable Discussion

By Rick Krohn, MA, MAS, and David Metcalf, PhD

We conclude our examination of mHealth innovation by taking a look ahead. We have compiled — through interviews, personal conversations, formal presentations and published remarks — perspectives on mHealth's future as viewed by a roundtable of mHealth luminaries, including:

- Eric Topol, MD, Director of the Scripps Translational Science Institute.
- Daniel Kraft, MD, physician-scientist, inventor, entrepreneur and innovator.
- Glenn Tullman, mHealth entrepreneur and former CEO of Allscripts.
- Joseph Kvedar, MD, Connected Health, Harvard University.

To bring clarity to the discussion, we have framed the conversation around a series of questions that we believe will direct the course and trajectory of mHealth. We begin by surveying our experts about the current forces shaping the mHealth industry, the barriers to adoption and likely areas of near term growth. We then ask our panel to peer over the horizon and create an image of mHealth in the years ahead.

Please note that previously published remarks are cited.

Do you see specific bright spots in the mHealth landscape? Consumer health? Population health? Chronic-disease management?

Tullman: The entire space of mHealth is about to explode, just as cellphone usage has done, and the number of apps, services, and solutions for health will follow, again, just as it has with mobiles. With the new wearable devices, these will become state-of-the-art solutions and the only real, effective way to bend the cost curve. New technologies, especially mHealth and analytics, will drive real advances in CDM, with patients taking charge.

Kvedar: We were cautious of smartphones for some time in 2008–2009. Then we said we should focus on text messages, because working with populations, we could not see smartphones being the approach, especially for the underserved.

We did a survey within the underserved population and saw that 60 percent were using smartphones. At the end of the study many of the patients came to us and said, "Why are you using text messages? Why don't you have an app?" Sixty percent is a tipping point, perhaps.

Anytime you have free time you pull out your phone. If our sickest patients are doing this, we'd be foolish not to try to engage them.

For text messaging, we have several studies that show that sending people a daily reminder to use sunscreen improved use dramatically.[1] We have also worked with pregnant teens and seen results in adherence to medicine and making more appointments.

There's one study we are just wrapping up with type 2 diabetics, trying to get them to increase their activity level. We asked five questions and integrated electronic medical record (EMR) data. We have twice a day messages and have seen some dramatic results. The study results are still being wrapped up so we are not quite ready to discuss them yet.

The blurring of the lines between Connected Health and mHealth is now complete. So much is wireless now — the two are really synonymous. I'm talking about EMRs and others, but our team is really focused on this area.

Patient monitoring can be huge if we can unlock behavior change. No one wants to look like a slouch in front of their doctor. Having this in the electronic health record would help. I'm really excited to start that study in this area.

In terms of Telehealth, there's a use case that connects me over a tablet, but I think for doctors it may be less useful. I have to be in an enclosed space, so maybe it's more helpful for the patients.

Mobile payments will be interesting because they are a record of where you spend money on healthcare (or things that aren't healthy like your trips to [fast food]).

Topol: There are already a few but let me just describe the impact of one. I believe the portable high-resolution ultrasound (Vscan or Mobisante) represents a home run in replacing the stethoscope for heart, abdominal and fetal examinations. We validated the Vscan compared with the standard hospital lab echocardiogram.[2] To have such high-quality imaging done anywhere 'flattens the earth'—from a paramedic in the field to an emergency room doctor — this technology enables us to simply acquire the image and transmit the video loop to a radiologist or cardiologist expert with a rapid read and text back.[3]

Do you see pre-eminent classes of mHealth industry solutions (remote patient monitoring [RPM], telemedicine, self-care, mobile finance, emerging markets, patient engagement/behavior modification and workforce optimization)?

Tullman: RPM will become the most important and transformational — not the devices, but the middleware (algorithms) that allows us to manage the data inflow and turn it into information that can be acted upon. Telemedicine is simply a tool to add efficiency. Not a game changer. Self-care will be performed by people using great information and tools available at home or that they purchase at the pharmacy (think pregnancy tests). Mobile finance is simply a tool to add efficiency. Not a game changer. Emerging markets will have the same issues as we will, creating a global market for solutions developed here. Patient engagement/behavior modification will increase because the cost will more and more be assumed by the patient, aka the health consumer. So it's their problem, not someone else's.

Workforce optimization — I think the improvement in our health and management of people using remote patient monitoring and making effective use of technologies like Telemedicine will add both efficiency and productivity to the economy.

What are some scalability factors that could help mHealth live up to its promise?

Tullman: The more pressure on costs for healthcare and the more risk hospitals (through ACOs), payers, and self-insured employers assume, the faster they will embrace technologies that improve care and reduce costs.

Kvedar: I've been very disappointed in 4G so far. Maybe it is because of the first generation. I find a combination of limited data plans and spotty service makes it so I am not truly liberated. For example, at first when we had to pay for every text message it was limiting. Today, I'd like snappy service and unfortunately, even with (unlimited plans) it is still limiting. iOS and Android fighting is a pretty good thing for the industry. There is lack of clarity on payment models. Here in Massachusetts, we are full steam ahead, but around the nation, no one will invest in this as a fee-for-service model.

Is mHealth poised to become a genuinely transformative force in healthcare, or will it become another "tool in the toolbox"?

Tullman: mHealth will be absolutely transformational. That said, remember Amara's Law: we tend to *overestimate the effect* of a *technology* in the short run and *underestimate the effect* in the long run. Think about it, Google reports that close to 1.5 million new Android devices come online every day. Putting the power of a computer into the hands of customers who will make purchasing decisions, and flipping the "information disparity" to provide health consumers with more information than physicians, practices and hospitals, will turn the tables in a dramatic fashion. This is not a tool… this is an entirely new way of conducting the business of healthcare.

Kvedar: mHealth is transformative and a compliment to traditional healthcare when used correctly, especially in relation to population health.

Topol: We are in a hyper-innovative stage of healthcare and we have an opportunity to drive the future of medicine. It's going to be a Darwinian process, and every chronic disease can potentially be transformed — more optimally managed — through a digital health system and solution.

Kraft: I guess I would say that healthcare is going to go mobile and local. There's the mobile element where you can take health with you. It can be combined with different groups. We have a company called Amata Health that's doing eBooks for the pre-diabetic, putting them on social networks and linked to a scale, and other elements. So mobile is something that affects all of healthcare.

Going forward, what will be the key drivers of mHealth in terms of stakeholders and solution categories? Will consumerism remain the engine of growth or will other forces like standards and regulation, incentives and reimbursement, or population health rise to the surface?

Tullman: All of the above will drive aspects of the growth of mHealth. Consumerism will be key, but implicit in all consumer behavior and what drives it are incentives and reimbursement. I would also add the term "risk." Going forward, whoever owns the risk will employ technology and strategies like population management to better manage the risk. And, no healthcare operates in a vacuum without assessing the impact of the government (both federal and state) and government programs like Medicare and Medicaid. Obamacare has provided choice for a huge number of consumers. Next up will be whether the government decides to privatize some parts of Medicare, as they have done with the VA.

Kvedar: Connected Health is starting to look like a tablet with vital sign measurements, and the measurements in the cloud lead to a center with nurses that are responsible for population health. Now the same labor force from home health can look over 80–100 patients rather than just five by driving around. You can follow management by exception and have a better business model that costs less and manages more patients.

Topol: We are ending the era of medical information asymmetry, with most/all information in the doctor's domain. The consumer is now center stage — he/she will drive this new medicine with a rebooted model of physician partnership. It is the consumer's data, the consumer's smartphone, and the consumer's choice of who, when and how to share.

The main thing is that there are these remarkable new tools that are hyper-innovative. People are already putting data on social networks, comparing genomic data and competing for the best quality sleep, best blood glucose. It will really take off if consumers are driving this via the power of their social networks. This radical transformation to a higher plateau of medicine is inevitable.[3,4]

What attributes of mHealth will likely lead to economic sustainability — accountability and affordability? Value-based purchasing? Healthcare democratization? Patient-centric or a new provider/patent paradigm? Care coordination and workflow efficiencies?

Kvedar: There are two emerging markets. Doctors are rapid adopters of mobile technology. I know you are aware of the large increase in doctors using smartphones. Travel to the office and pull up relevant data and make physicians more effective. Fitness devices have an audience that is educated, quantitative, motivated and cares about health, and all of the 15 or so monitors on the market are doing pretty well with a small segment of our population.

There is a third audience that is chronic care management and prevention. Feedback loops are used and seem to be growing. An example is Cardiocom, which was just acquired for $200 million. It is taking off where we have full-on managed care reimbursement. Until we have uniformity in this (rather than fee for service models mixed in), it could be a challenge.

Are doctors accepting of the information patients bring in? There is a bell shaped curve of doctors who do not want to accept anything that the patient brings in as useful, whether technology or even a paper-based journal. In the past much of the documentation in patient interviews has just been qualitative and was really crap. There is a change in mindset that needs to happen to even use a spreadsheet or blood pressure cuff measure that the patient took because of the potential for calibration issues.

Tullman: If the question is economic sustainability for healthcare for our country, the answer is all of the above. If we look at healthcare markets where competition is allowed (e.g., Lasik surgery), we see a clear track record of higher quality, more access, more choice and lower costs. So, mHealth and the new healthcare ecosystem will drive both accountability (through better access to information on quality and cost), affordability (through competition) and access (what you call democratization). New services (think Concierge for All) and proactive population health management will drive higher engagement, satisfaction and better outcomes. If the question is how does mHealth stay sustainable, that answer is easy. We all have mobile phones and tablets today, so there is no added cost… mHealth is a free rider. And, new apps will be judged solely by value added by whoever is paying for them, so it's a beautiful model.

What are the biggest challenges facing mHealth?

Kvedar: We are at the top of the Gartner hype cycle. I retain my academic hat, but I have spun out companies, hang out with VCs and see many companies. I think there is too much that is fast moving, not well-thought-out and just chasing the fast money. I feel that the app market has failed. There are so many apps that are only opened once and 30 days later never opened again. There are so many apps that they grind to a halt. Many consumers have too many apps so they ignore them. Consumers are overwhelmed by the choices so they do nothing. Failure B is that we collectively haven't discovered what apps are truly engaging. If you go into your web browser, your experience will look much different than mine. The advertising content is personalized. The marketing industry is moving to personalized; healthcare is still thinking about population-level. We haven't delivered yet in relation to apps.

Tullman: Traditional healthcare providers (organizations and physicians) will fight mHealth from an access and choice standpoint. Their survival will depend on it. Change never feels good when it's done to you. People, acting as health consumers, want 24/7 access through their phones. Doctors' hours were and still, for the most part, are 9 to 5 with a one-hour lunch break. Similarly, organizations that are not producing quality results cost-effectively will now be clearly visible to the healthcare consumer, and that will speed their demise.

Topol: A core problem is the medical profession. The average time it takes for a significant innovation to become standard clinical practice is 17 years. *The Wall Street Journal* had a piece about how 62 percent of doctors don't use e-mail with their patients. This is resistance. But what has really gotten me stirred up is the issue of whether patients should have access to their own health data. The American Medical Association (AMA) was lobbying the government that consumers should not have access directly to their DNA data; that it has to be mediated through a doctor. The AMA did a survey of 10,000 doctors, and 90 percent said they have no comfort using genomics in their clinical practice. So how could they be the ultimate mediator by which the public gets access to their DNA data? That really speaks to medical paternalism. The fact that consumers will have this ability to have it themselves — their genome sequence, their lab tests, their tissues — digitized on their smartphones and their social networks will reboot the way doctors interact with patients.[4]

In terms of barriers to adoption, one of the biggest is the reimbursement question. Who will pay for the device itself? For the data interpretation? And perhaps some mHealth-based procedures won't warrant reimbursement. For example, though stethoscope use is routine during the physical exam, physicians are not reimbursed each time they use their stethoscopes. Primary care doctors at Allina Health in Minnesota are being taught to do head-to-toe ultrasound exams, so how should/will that be reimbursed? Another barrier to adoption is the need for evidence, which goes back to why we launched the Wired for Health study and have a few other trials in planning.

A third factor is lack of awareness and education. There is still a very large number of physicians who do not know about the progress that mHealth is making.[5]

Kraft: One is the huge amount of data. If I'm wearing a patch and you're my doctor, do you want to be looking at my EKG 24/7? No. Are you liable if you miss something? Yes. If I have some funny cough and nothing picks up on it, or the AI doesn't diagnose and I come back later with TB or lung cancer, am I going to sue the patch, the device, the doctor who didn't look at it? There are a lot of questions there. Just like the Google self-driving car does a great job, the only accidents have been when it was stopped at a light. So part of it is the extensive amount of data, how do we filter it? Who's going to pay for it is another question. How do we regulate it? How do we make the data smart — actual information? How do we not turn people into hypochondriacs? Hopefully it might reassure people; some folks who are super attentive might be reassured and not have to feel so anxious.

What can we learn from mHealth's failures?

Tullman: While it's very early for mHealth to have failures (it's just getting started and most of it has yet to be invented), we do see that consumers are confused, generally, with too many apps to choose from. Organizations, and the CIOs that run them, have told me they don't want one more unconnected solution, so we have to find ways to guide the new healthcare consumer and the organizations as well. New consulting and research organizations are springing up to fill that need.

Topol: I worry about the hype. But the innovative, and in many cases ingenious, technology is emerging very rapidly and what we must do is validate that it works well in real individuals/patients, that it improves outcomes and lowers cost. We absolutely need to invest our efforts and resources in such validation initiatives to transcend any hype or false illusions of progress.[3]

Kvedar: The very nature of apps is that they are small bits of software that do one or two things well. (The developer's) motivation is they get you to pay your 99 cents and download the app. [They] don't really care if it leads to outcomes. People who care about health need to move beyond that. People checking their mobile phone 150 times a day is such an opportunity. I think our behavior will change, but it is not there yet. I think we're just getting over the hump in the Gartner Hype Cycle curve. In the famous words of Yogi Berra, "It is dangerous to make predictions, especially about the future."

So many things out there are garbage and everyone is looking for funding. There will be some abrupt examples of firms not even looking at mHealth deals. Right now there are lots of angel investments without much due diligence, but the market is so elastic and the costs of app development can be so low that after a meeting or two they write a check for $50k and spread it around. Some may shy away, except maybe the young angels.

Predictions...

Kraft: With 3-D printing systems coming out, it's going to be instructive across all kinds of fields from manufacturing and beyond. For example, there are ones going into the operating room to make personalized tools and devices for knee and hip implants. That's going to be quite interesting I think, in healthcare to a large extent, one that people can kind of touch and feel. The other is probably going to be the Internet of things, you know Google and Facebook put up ads, using the ability to put different streams together and say "Gosh, Daniel, all these signs point to X." I think artificial intelligence (AI) is going to be very tricky. We're hearing more about that — what's happening at the cutting edge with IBM Watson, for example — and what happens when you can take AI mobile via smartphone. Siri is already doing that, even though it's in the very early stages, it knows you, it knows your voice.

Tullman: Healthcare is hard to understand, even for those who have spent many years working in and around it. That said, today there is less comprehension of what the future will look like than ever before, in part because it will be so different. Imagine you were trying to predict the impact of the Internet and cellphones on how we would buy things (Amazon), communicate (Facebook) and search (Google). Billions of users and billions of dollars of value created. That's what's coming in health and healthcare because we have a broken industry and we are employing both the Internet and mobile technology. So, expect a lot of dislocation, change, and challenge, but expect big changes to come. Five years from now, health and healthcare will be largely fixed and a series of new players will dominate the new landscape.

Topol: Eighty percent of doctors will become unnecessary. We will soon hear: "the robot will see you now." The idea of going to the doctor's office will be as foreign as going to the video store. The diminishing need for hospitals and physical office visits. The stethoscope eventually becoming a relic. I believe that DNA sequencing and other omics (RNAseq, microbiome, epigenomics, metabolomics) will be used up front for most cancers, serious, difficult-to-diagnose conditions, and as the mainstay for new drug development. Perhaps one of the biggest will be embedded nanosensors, in our bloodstream, that put our bodies under constant surveillance and prevent particular conditions such as autoimmune, cancer or heart attacks — by capturing a specific bio-signal and transmitting that to the smartphone. It's a little ways off, but might be especially transformative. It brings a lot of digital medicine together and exemplifies what all this technology can achieve.[3,6]

CLOSING THOUGHTS

As you can see many of the trends identified in the case studies and special topic chapters throughout the book have been reinforced by our expert panel. An understanding of trends and a look over the horizon will help make sense of the fast moving world of mHealth Innovations and the links between evidence, scalability and innovation.

In these pages we have examined the wave of innovation that is shaping the mHealth marketplace — a market whose transformative effects are sending shock waves throughout the spectrum of healthcare services. We have seen, through case studies and expert commentary, that mHealth is more than simply a technology play — it's an evolving ecosystem whose ingredients include a vast array of devices, processes, integrated solutions, and perhaps most significantly, new touchpoints of care.

We have given witness to the wellspring of innovation that is defining mHealth, innovation that is being driven by an explosion of entrepreneurship, by the marriage of technology and opportunities to reimagine care delivery, and by pent up demand for healthcare solutions that are affordable, accessible — and that deliver value.

In the months ahead, we are likely to see mHealth loom ever larger in the healthcare marketplace — not only integrating with, but in many instances displacing traditional care delivery. And that's a good thing. It's a new era in healthcare, one in which consumer choice, product and service efficiency, and value are going to determine how care is delivered, how frequently, and by whom. It's a foundational shift that is going to impact every stakeholder and every process, and we are still only at the beginning.

REFERENCES

1. Kvedar, 2011.
2. Liebo MJ, Israel RL, Lillie EO, Smith MR, Rubenson DS, Topol EJ. Is pocket mobile echocardiography the next-generation stethoscope? A cross-sectional comparison of rapidly acquired images with standard transthoracic echocardiography. *Annals of Internal Medicine*. 2011;155:33-38. [On the Internet] www.stsiweb.org/images/uploads/Vscan.pdf.
3. Nosta J. The STAT Ten: Eric Topol, MD, Speaks Out on Digital Health. *Forbes*. January 30, 2013. [On the Internet] http://www.forbes.com/sites/johnnosta/2013/01/30/the-stat-ten-eric-topol-md-speaks-out-on-digital-health.
4. Winslow R. The wireless revolution hits medicine: Eric Topol talks about the upheaval that's coming as the digitization of health care meets the smartphone. *The Wall Street Journal*. February 14, 2013. [On the Internet] http://online.wsj.com/news/articles/SB10001424052702303404704577311421888663472.
5. Gaglani S. Wired for health: An interview with Dr. Eric Topol. *CardioSource*. American College of Cardiology. September 2013. [On the Internet] http://www.cardiosource.org/News-Media/Publications/CardioSource-World-News/2013/September/Wired-for-Health-An-Interview-with-Dr-Eric-Topol.aspx.
6. Topol E. Keynote address. 2013 HIMSS Annual Conference & Exhibition. New Orleans. March 5, 2013.

Appendix A

mHealth Apps: Functional Comparisons

By Muhammad Nauman, MD, MS

OBESITY

Over the past 30 years, the rate of overweight children has doubled, while the rate of overweight adolescents has tripled in the same period. Currently about 60 million adults — about 30 percent of the adult U.S. population — are obese. These are alarming statistics because the prevalence of obesity can lead to a myriad of other diseases like diabetes, hypertension, heart failure and stroke. The two major causes of obesity are physical inactivity and unhealthy diet, but apps can help prevent this continued epidemic by making it easier to track one's activity and dietary habits. This section looks into different apps that can be used for weight management and increasing physical activity to help consumers understand what may be helpful in achieving their individual goals. See Table A-1 on page 338, for functional comparisons of apps, and Table A-2 on page 339, for wrist band comparisons.

Lose It

This app is available for free in both iOS and Android platforms. It starts by helping users develop a plan based on their current weight and profile information and gives them a daily caloric budget. Once the calorie intake is established, different features in the app make it easier for the user to stick to his or her daily budget. Food intake can be logged easily by using the bar code scanner or the search function. It also has a food database with a wide variety of supermarket and restaurant foods, as well as their available nutrient compositions, which can be added easily to the user's daily log. It can also produce a record of favorite foods and previous meals to provide users with a record of calorie intake during different times of the day.

The app also helps calculate the daily calorie budget by providing the calories that would be offset by substituting physical activities like walking, jogging, playing basketball, etc., thus providing a net calorie intake. The data can be shared with friends and other users to keep people motivated to achieve their goals through community support. The app also allows users to join public groups and take part in health challenges with other people. It can be connected to the Nike FuelBand to track activity and connect with social media apps like Facebook and Twitter to publicize progress.

The premium version of the app costs $39.99 per year and has many additional features to help improve the overall health of an individual. It can track body fat, hydration and sleep goals, in addition to weight goals, and works with devices like Withings Blood Pressure Monitor. Lose It connects with different other apps like Map My Fitness and Run Keeper that create a log for daily activity. It can also include different body measurements as well as blood glucose measurement, steps taken, and exercise regimen of an individual thus providing the overall health picture.

Fooducate

Fooducate is an informative and educative app regarding quality of food and calories provided per serving. The app assigns different nutrition grades from A to D and also provides points by calculating the amount of fats, carbohydrates, fibers and proteins in the desired food. It also gives additional information regarding the presence of artificial preservatives, amount of trans fat, excessive sugar and processing status of foods, and whether healthier alternatives are available. It has the largest database with more than 200,000 UPC labels that can also be browsed by 15 different categories. The health tracker can be a useful tool for weight management, providing the user with daily calorie goals, food points and carbohydrate levels. It also has a daily tip section that provides the latest food stories from the Fooducate blog.

ARGUS

This is the latest free app by Azumio and it helps consumers take control of their health by giving them the opportunity to record their meals, map their physical activity and understand their sleep, all in a single app. The dashboard is a honeycomb that shows your daily activities from walking, running, weight, heart rate and meals, as well as your pattern of sleep. It can also be connected with third party devices like LifeTrak and Withings scale, making it possible to gather data from different resources rather than relying on only one source. It can also help you set goals for activity, sleep and hydration. While there is no way to measure calories that can be consumed with daily meals or fluids intake, ARGUS does show calories that can be burned with any certain activity. The app supports only pictures taken of the food without calorie or nutrient information, thus missing a big opportunity to make photography a bigger aspect for the overall user experience.

Table A-1: Functional Comparison for Free-Standing Fitness Apps.

App	Lose It	Fooducate	ARGUS
Price (US$)	Free	Free	Free
Caloric intake	Yes	Yes	No
Calories burned	Yes	Yes	Yes
Barcode Scanning	Yes	Yes	No
Food Grades	No	Yes	No
Alternatives	No	Yes	No
Social media	Yes	Yes	Yes

Nike+ FuelBand

The Nike Fuel wristband uses a sports-tested accelerometer that captures and displays four different metrics: time, calories, steps and "NikeFuel," a proprietary measure of physical activity. NikeFuel measures physical activity through the movement of the user's wrist and uses algorithms based on oxygen kinetics. NikeFuel awards all participants equal scoring for the same activity regardless of their gender and physical makeup. Nike FuelBand users also can choose to receive a calorie count to better understand how many calories are burned versus how much NikeFuel is earned. The wristband can sync with the Nike+ FuelBand app and the Nike web site through a built-in USB port to record the user's activity each day and track progress.

FitBit Flex

FitBit Flex Wireless Activity and Sleep wristband from FitBit tracks steps, distance and calories burned during the day and tracks your sleep quality at night. It can sync wirelessly with your computer, iPad and smartphone through Fitbit's free mobile app, and the free online dashboard. FitBit Flex gives achievement badges and sends weekly stats e-mail so that users can follow their progress. Users can also connect with family and friends through Fitbit.com, where they can compare stats, share progress and motivate each other. Fitbit online tools also provide users the ability to log meals, water, workouts and weight measurements. The food and activity data can help users lose weight by tracking daily caloric intake. Fitbit data can also be exported to other apps like Lose It and MyFitnessPal so that these users can also track their health in these apps.

Jawbone UP

The UP wristband from Jawbone tracks users' sleep activity, steps taken, and food and drink usage with calorie measurement. It can capture mood levels and has an idle alert that reminds users to move if they have been inactive for too long. The smart alarm can distinguish between light and deep sleep and could help users feel more refreshed by waking them up at the right moment in their sleep cycle. The Stopwatch Mode lets users specify activity periods that help them reach their goals. The Barcode Scanner can help scan and log almost any food and drink with a barcode, and the search function can help consumers enter dishes from different restaurants and their ingredients from the nutrition database. The UP insight engine discovers hidden connections and patterns in daily activities to deliver powerful analytics that could help users develop new behaviors and healthier habits.

Table A-2: Functional Comparison of Different Wrist Bands.

Equipment	Nike+Fuel Band	FitBit Flex	Jawbone UP
Price (US$)	149	99.95	129.99
Steps Counter	Yes	Yes	Yes
Heart Rate	No	No	No
Sleep Tracking	No	Yes	Yes
Calories Burned	Yes	Yes	Yes
Distance	No	Yes	Yes
Social Media	Yes	Yes	Yes

DIABETES

Diabetes affects over 26 million people alone in the United States and 2.2 million new patients are diagnosed with this epidemic each year. It is a major cause of heart disease, blindness and kidney failure, and associated with other major diseases and significant number of deaths. There are 685 diabetes apps available in the Apple Store. Most of them are used to log and track blood sugar levels recorded during different times of day and before and after eating and exercise. There are some apps that are approved by the FDA as a medical device and can also measure blood sugar levels when used with other equipment. See Tables A-3 and A-4 on page 341 for functional comparisons.

Diabetes Tracker

This app was developed by MyNetDiary. It provides a lot of features that can help patients track their diabetes in depth. The app is easy to use and has comprehensive features that can make it easier to track blood glucose, insulin usage, exercise and food. The food database provides an easy tool to track carbohydrate consumption and other nutrients. The quality of food database is ensured by MyNetDiary's PhotoFood Service. The foods that are not included in the food database can be uploaded directly by the consumers and added into food database to ensure accuracy and efficiency. It also allows users to record time for everything from frequent small meals to insulin dosages and medication regimes, as well as daily exercise schedule. It also has daily and weekly charts, bar scanners and diet planning tools.

Glucose Buddy

Glucose buddy is another diabetes management app that can be used by patients to take control of their diabetes. It can help monitor blood glucose as well as insulin units taken by the patients. It also provides charts and graphs for glucose readings and all medications taken by the patient, and helps patients achieve desired blood glucose levels. Glucose Buddy doesn't provide relationship between glucose readings and carbohydrate consumption, and also doesn't include any connection with individuals' exercise regimen. It also doesn't have any food database that can help patients track their calories or any food intake.

Wave Sense Diabetes Manager

This app helps with diabetes management by providing different quality features. The information can be entered quickly, and results in charts and graphs of glucose readings for up to 90 days. It also allows users to set goals for blood glucose measurement, can help patients schedule meals and activities, manage medication, and e-mail recorded information to healthcare providers. The logbook is color-coded to clearly identify highs and lows of glucose reading. It can also put your glucose recordings in context by tagging it with food, exercise, medicine or health issues. The most interesting feature of this app is award-winning, educational diabetes video content delivered courtesy of dLife.

Table A-3: Functional Comparison for Free-Standing Diabetes Management Apps.

App Name	Diabetes Tracker	Glucose Buddy	Diabetes Manager
Price (US$)	9.99	6.99	Free
Blood Glucose	Yes	Yes	Yes
Carbohydrate	Yes	No	Yes
Insulin Dosage	Yes	Yes	Yes
HbA1C	No	Yes	No
Weight Tracker	Yes	Yes	No
Calorie Counter	Yes	No	No

iBG Star Diabetes Manager

iBG star is the first glucose meter that connects directly to the iPhone and iPod touch, thus managing a patient's diabetes anywhere in the world. The iBG Star Diabetes Manager app syncs directly with iBG Star and tracks glucose, insulin and carbohydrate intake, and provides graph and statistics to understand glucose pattern over a long period of time. iBG star can only be used with the iPhone 5 only after connecting authentic Apple Lightening to 30-pin Adapter which costs $29.99. The device costs $74.99 and 50 test strips are $64.99.

Glooko Logbook

Glooko logbook is an FDA 510(k) certified diabetes management system that can upload blood glucose readings from 19 FDA-approved glucose meters directly to a mobile device. It costs $39.95. Once it has synced with a glucometer, it is easy to understand the importance of the reading. Whether the reading is before or after meal, what is the daily insulin intake, what is the target blood glucose range, what is the daily exercise routine, and other findings could be helpful in encouraging patients to undergo lifestyle changes. The built-in food database provides nutritional information on food distributed by more than 5,800 food manufacturers, 700 restaurants and 250 supermarkets. Glooko dashboard gives providers the ability to look at the frequency of blood glucose readings and whether the patient is complying with the prescribed management regimen.

Table A-4: Functional Comparison for Different Blood Glucose Measurement Systems.

Equipment	iBG Star	Glooko Sync Cable	One Touch Ultra Mini
Price (US$)	74.99	39.95	19.99
Sample Size	0.5uL	Varies	1.0uL
Test Time	6 sec	Varies	5 sec
Memory	300	Varies	500
Battery Life	Rechargable	Varies	1000 tests
Downloadable	Yes	Yes	Yes
Coding	No	Varies	Yes

BLOOD PRESSURE APPS

According to World Health Organization, one in three adults have high blood pressure and tracking blood pressure is important in preventing heart disease and stroke. These blood pressure (BP) apps can help achieve these goals by providing ambulatory monitoring for users suffering from high blood pressure. In this section, these apps have been divided into two categories: a) blood pressure measuring apps that work with blood pressure devices and convert your mobile phone or tablet into blood pressure monitor; and b) blood pressure tracking apps that don't work in conjunction with medical devices and can only be used for tracking purposes. The latter have some additional features like weight management and blood sugar trackers that can be useful for overall management of chronic diseases. See Tables A-5 and A-6 on page 343 for functional comparisons.

Blood Pressure Monitor — Family Lite

This is a free app designed for iOS platform by Taconic System can help users manage their blood pressure and weight. It comes with lifetime data visualization, statistics reporting, medication correlation, e-mail import/export and built in reminders with a very simple user interface. The medication correlation can help patients understand the effects of their medications on their blood pressure. The graphical charts can show warning signs if the readings are very high or low. There are built-in reminders so patients check BP on time and control it properly. The readings can be sent to your doctor through e-mail with different available options from plain message to PDF attachment with charts included in it.

HeartWise Blood Pressure Tracker

This app was developed by SwEng LLC and available on iOS platform for $.99. It tracks systolic and diastolic blood pressure, resting heart rate and weight. It also automatically calculates mean arterial pressure, pulse pressure and body mass index. It has a reminder that can alert users regarding their medication time or blood pressure reading measurement. The graph shows blood pressure and other measurement changes over time and also has a weight measurement available both in pounds and kilograms. The camera features also stores information in photo library and can help keep high resolution copies at your fingertips, putting users in charge of their own health. The app also sends reports as a spread sheet or plain forms directly from your phone and also have support available in French, German and Spanish language.

Health Tracker Pro

Health Tracker Pro was developed by XLabz Technologies Pvt. Ltd. for the iPhone. For $3.99, the app can track three common health problems by monitoring weight, blood pressure and blood sugar measurements. The dashboard shows body mass index, blood pressure and sugar as categories. The body mass index also includes height and weight of the individual, while the blood pressure readings show both systolic and diastolic measurements, as well as beats per minute and mean arterial pressure. Each recording has an individual timeline and users can also keep notes with them so that it can be easier to understand the context of the reading in case of any abnormal findings. The app's e-mail feature has the flexibility to send the entire recorded values or selection from a specific period of time, which can help healthcare professionals understand a snapshot or the entire data collection period.

Table A-5: Functional Comparison of Free Standing BP Measurement Apps.

App	Family Lite	Heart Wise	Health Tracker Pro
Price (US$)	Free	0.99	3.99
Blood Pressure	Yes	Yes	Yes
MAP	Yes	Yes	Yes
BMI	No	Yes	Yes
BPM	Yes	No	Yes
Blood Sugar	No	Yes	Yes
Medication	Yes	Yes	No

Withings Health Mate App

This free app from Withings lets patients set goals and receive reminders to achieve those goals. The app starts with a butterfly with four wing sections each associated with a different health factor. The idea is to fill each wing to reach one's goals. The app helps users by dividing these goals into small achievable targets that can be easily reached. The app can work with Withings weight scale and also with Withings Blood Pressure monitor with a universal dock connector that plugs into iPhone, iPad and iPod. The blood pressure cuff is a little rigid and less convenient but has the advantage that the readings can be directly added to an electronic medical record (EMR) such as EPIC systems, or a personal health record (PHR), like Microsoft Health Vault.

iHealth Mobile App

This app works with different health devices including different blood pressure monitors from iHealth labs. There is a wireless blood pressure monitor, wireless blood pressure wrist monitor, and a blood pressure dock that can turn the iOS device into a blood pressure monitor when connected to a blood pressure cuff. It can also work with a wireless scale, wireless activity and sleep tracker, wireless pulse oximeter and wireless body analysis scale that can measure nine different body components including body weight, body fat, lean mass, muscle mass, bone mass, body water, daily calorie intake and visceral fat rating. The great feature of this app is that it can submit data to a personal health record solution and helps patients manage all aspects of their health.

Table A-6: Functional Comparison for Different Blood Pressure Management Systems.

Name of Equipment	iHealth BP	Withings BP Monitor	Walgreens Manual BP Kit
Price (in US dollars)	99.95	129.99	19.99
Time Needed	31 seconds	35 second	Varies
FDA Approval	Yes	Yes	Yes
Persons Required	1	1	2
Social Media	Yes	Yes	No
EHR Connectivity	Yes	Yes	No
mHealth Apps	Yes	Yes	No

APPENDIX B

MAMA Community Spotlights
By Joanne Peter, MBChB, MPhil

COMMUNITY SPOTLIGHT: LIGA INAN, TIMOR-LESTE

The Liga Inan ("Mobile Moms") project is using mobile phones to connect expectant mothers with healthcare providers in the southeast Asian country of Timor-Leste to improve the likelihood of a healthy pregnancy and birth. Funded by USAID's Child Survival and Health Grants Program, Liga Inan is implemented by Health Alliance International (HAI) and Catalpa International, in partnership with Timor-Leste's Ministry of Health (MOH).

Many women in Timor-Leste live in remote and rural areas, which makes it challenging for them to access health facilities and midwives. Liga Inan sends maternal health-related text messages twice weekly to pregnant women, who are enrolled in the project by midwives at the time of their first prenatal visit. The system also sends messages to midwives to encourage phone contact with pregnant or postpartum women, especially around the time of delivery.

Using the MAMA Messages

The MAMA adaptable mobile messages were translated into Tetum, the local language, and edited to 160 characters to fit within a single SMS. Messages were chosen to align with the priorities of the MOH and address the needs of the rural population. The messages were reviewed in stakeholder meetings with the MOH at both national and district levels. Pregnant women in the project area were enrolled in further pretesting to determine comprehension and acceptability.

The messages emphasize attendance at prenatal clinic appointments, using a skilled birth attendant, nutrition, birth planning, and danger signs in pregnancy, delivery and the newborn period. Messages also address the postpartum tradition of tuur ahi (literally, "sitting fire") where the new mother and newborn are sequestered in the home for several weeks next to an open fire because the heat is believed to have beneficial healing effects. The messages included information on the harm of open fire smoke to newborns, with advice to prevent this.

Program Specifics

An initial household survey showed that household ownership of mobile phones was high, text messaging was common, and 73 percent of women could read the local Tetum language.

Midwives use smartphones provided by the project to enroll women into the Liga Inan service during their first prenatal care visit. The midwives receive text reminders about women who are near their due date and are responsible for calling to check their health status, discuss birth planning, or confirm whether the woman has delivered. Midwives also answer questions from pregnant or postpartum women and identify emergencies.

T-shirts and caps with the Liga Inan logo and tagline, "Your health is in your hands" were distributed to project staff, health staff and community health workers to promote the project.

HAI decided on a phased rollout starting in the largest and most densely populated sub-district of Same. Stakeholder meetings including village chiefs, health facility managers and staff, community health workers, teachers and pregnant women were carried out in communities throughout Same to provide information on the service.

Evaluation and Results

Liga Inan was launched in the last week of February 2013 in the sub-district of Same. It rolled out to two additional sub-districts in July and a final sub-district in August 2013. There has been a very enthusiastic response to the project by both the health staff and the communities they serve. In the first six months, 533 women enrolled in Liga Inan and 221 births were recorded among enrollees. Although it is too early to assess the project's health impact, the data is encouraging. In the first full month of Liga Inan implementation there were 56 births attended by a skilled provider (average in 2012 was 38) and 38 deliveries at the health facility (average in 2012 was 27). Over the first six months of the program, the number of midwife-attended births has consistently increased. The project is still in its early phase, however, and HAI staff will be working hard over the next year to assure data quality and effective monitoring. Learn more at www.ligainan.org.

COMMUNITY SPOTLIGHT: LIVING GOODS, UGANDA

Living Goods operates networks of micro-entrepreneurs who go door-to-door selling a wide range of life-changing products, including treatments for malaria and diarrhea, fortified foods, clean cook stoves and solar lights. Networks of franchised micro-entrepreneurs leverage Living Goods' brand, buying power and marketing tools to deliver vital products at accessible prices to the people who need them most.

Cellphones are quickly becoming the single most transformative tool for Living Goods' success. They have built a mobile platform designed to drive demand, increase access, and reduce costs for delivering products that save and change lives.

Living Goods is building a powerful client database across the regions they serve; to date, they have over 35,000 registered cellphone numbers in Uganda. They're leveraging their database and the speed and efficiency of mobile to drive better health through services such as real-time treatment reminders, community agents on call, and pregnancy and child care messages.

Using the MAMA Messages

Living Goods used MAMA's maternal health messages to inspire a set of automated SMS messages for pregnant women and new mothers called the Happy Baby service. Once enrolled by their agents, clients receive automated weekly stage- and age-appropriate SMS messages to encourage a healthy pregnancy and delivery.

To support the agents on the ground and increase their sales, the messaging service includes several messages with a clear call to action, including the name and mobile number of the client's agent.

Living Goods integrates specific product recommendations that support a healthy pregnancy into the messages, like iron and folate tablets, clean burning cook stoves and safe delivery kits. These are all available through community agents.

Example: "Dizziness, headaches, tiredness are all symptoms of low iron. Take a daily iron supplement. Need iron? Call Living Goods (Nakamya Rebecca 077xxxxxxx)."

The Happy Baby service also includes MAMA's educational messages on how to ensure a healthy pregnancy, and emotionally engaging messages to keep clients interested in the service throughout their pregnancy and beyond.

In less than one year since the use of MAMA messages began, more than 7,300 pregnant women have been registered.

Challenges

At the program outset, texting was still foreign to many agents. Living Goods provided intensive training and an incentive plan to drive adoption. In addition, many agents shared phones with their family members and did not always carry them in the field, making it difficult to register clients on the spot. In response, Living Goods offered their agents financing for a good-quality, low-price phone, and more than 40 percent of agents bought one. Learn more at www.livinggoods.org.

COMMUNITY SPOTLIGHT: HEALTHY PREGNANCY, HEALTHY BABY — TEXT MESSAGING SERVICE, TANZANIA

Women in Tanzania have a lifetime maternal death risk of 1 in 38, and every year Tanzania sees the death of 48,100 newborns, ranking it 10th highest in the world. Seventy-five percent of the Tanzanian population lives in rural areas, often far from well-equipped health facilities with trained personnel. This broad portion of the population has limited access to face-to-face coaching on healthy pregnancy.

Wazazi Nipendeni (Parents Love Me) is a national multi-media campaign on healthy pregnancy. The Healthy Pregnancy, Healthy Baby Text Messaging Service supports and strengthens this campaign with a nationwide text messaging service, offering free healthy pregnancy and early childhood care information. The content of all messages is in accordance with current Tanzanian public health guidelines and Tanzanian culture.

Using the MAMA Messages

The Ministry of Health and Social Welfare led the development of the Healthy Pregnancy, Healthy Baby text message content, in collaboration with the mHealth Tanzania Public Private Partnership (led by the CDC Foundation, with financial support from the U.S. Government Centers for Disease Control and Prevention), and several key technical partners. The text messages, based on the Tanzanian public health guidelines, were further developed in response to expert feedback and augmented with content based on the MAMA messages in the areas of post-partum care, fetal development and parent tips. Moreover, the mHealth Tanzania Partnership found significant value in pre-testing the messages at different stages of the content development process. The mHealth Tanzania Partnership learned valuable lessons around developing and translating messages to preserve the original message intention, maximize comprehension among rural users, and respect cultural norms.

Program Specifics

The Wazazi Nipendeni multi-media campaign includes promotion of the free (reverse-billed) text messaging service by listing the short-code (15001) and the registration keyword 'mtoto' ('baby') on all campaign materials. Healthcare professionals in trained health facilities also offer registration assistance to pregnant women as part of the women's routine prenatal clinic visits. The service provides Tanzanians free text messages in Swahili for pregnant women and mothers with newborns up to 16 weeks old, as well as supporters of pregnant women and new mothers (partners, friends and relatives). The service also offers enrollment as a "general information seeker," providing Tanzanians with a wide range of information concerning healthy pregnancy and early childhood care.

Evaluation and Results

In the first six months, the text messaging service registered more than 150,000 active subscribers and sent more than nine million text messages to subscribers. Anecdotal evidence from health professionals working in the facilities indicates that women and partners are requesting HIV/AIDS testing and malaria prevention medication based on encouragement from the messages and timed reminders. The program will capture data on uptake of services such as prenatal care and HIV testing among subscribers. In addition, the mHealth Tanzania Partnership will continue to connect with stakeholders and new partners to sustain and expand the existing service.

Index

A
Acute condition management, 288–290
Adolescent Pregnancy Prevention Campaign of North Carolina (APPCNC), 32–35
    BrdsNBz, 32–35
Advanced Encryption Standard (AES), 192
App ecosystem, 80
    security monitoring, 200–201
    super apps, 80–81
App stores, 80, 233
AppAppeal, 235
ARGUS, 238, 338
Authentication strategies, 204

B
Behavioral design framework, 21
Blood pressure apps, 242–244, 342–343
    Blood Pressure Monitor—Family Lite, 242, 342
    Heartwise Blood Pressure Tracker, 242, 342
    Health Tracker Pro, 243, 342
    iHealth Mobile App, 243, 343
    Withings Health Mate App, 243, 343
Blood Pressure Monitor—Family Lite, 242, 342
Blue Button, 57–73, 195, 219, 318
    behavior enhancing applications (BEA), 65
    case studies, 66–71
    implementation guide, 63–64
    increasing awareness of, 60–61
    Meaningful Use Stage 2 requirements, 62
    and personal health information technology (PHIT), 59–60
    Pledge community, 71
    Pledge Program, 58
Body Media, 14
BrdsNBz text message, 32–35
Bring Your Own Devices (BYOD), 207
    acceptance testing, 209
    corporate policies and procedures, 208–209
    encryption, 211
    identity management, 212
    penetration testing, 209
    physical security, 212
    policy enforcement, 212, 219–220

protective devices, 210
risk reduction, 208
secure socket layer, 211
security incident response, 210
tracking, 211
user access, 207–208
Brothers for Life Campaign, 279–283
  Voluntary Medical Male Circumcision (VMMC), 279–283

C
Case studies
  Adolescent Pregnancy Prevention Campaign of North Carolina, 32–35
  Blue Button, 57–73
  Denver Health, 126–127
  Ghana HIV HelpLine, 273
  ISMETT liver transplant, 149–155
  mDiet, 19–27
  mHealth apps quality, 233–245
  Mobile Alliance for Maternal Action (MAMA), 255
  mobile-to-mobile, 173–179
  mobile prescription therapy, 131–140
  Mobile for Reproductive Health (m4RH), 263–271
  Pew Internet Project, 29–32
  Re-Mission, 95–100
  ScanAvert, 37–43
  St. Clare Health Mission, 183–184
  text4baby, 127–129
  Toshiba America Medical Systems, 111–115
  Voluntary Male Medical Circumcision, 279–283
  Volunteers in Medicine Clinic, 181–183
  Zombies, Run!, 103–109
Chronic disease management, 131–134, 290–291, 332
  barriers, 132
Client-server pattern, 190
Combat Medic Card Game (CMCG), 299–301
Communication patterns, 190
  client-server, 190
  peer-to-peer, 190
  server-mediated, 190
Connectivity constraints, 191
Consumer engagement technologies, 11–16
  health games, 14
  mobile health applications, 12
  mobile technology challenges, 15–16
  recommendations, 15–16
  remote health monitoring, 13

    social networks, 14–15
    text messages, 12
    wearable devices, 13–14
Continua Health Alliance, 189–190

D
Diab, 87
Diabetes management apps, 240–241, 340–341
    Diabetes Tracker, 240, 340
    Glooko Logbook, 241, 341
    Glucose Buddy, 240, 340
    iBG Diabetes Manager, 241, 341
    Wave Sense Diabetes Manager, 241, 340
Diabetes Tracker, 240, 340
Disruptive innovation, 119–121

E
Elaboration Likelihood Model (ELM), 87–88
Electronic medical record (EMR), 143–144
    and data capture standards, 144
    and data collection, 144

F
Facebook, 14, 126
FitBit, 14, 15, 239, 339
Food and Drug Administration (FDA), 224
    and FCC joint efforts, 218
    guidance document, 217–218
    Safety and Innovation Act, 217
Fooducate, 238, 338

G
Gamification, 14, 23, 89
GeckoCap, 89
Ghana HIV HelpLine, 273–277
Glooko Logbook, 241, 341
Glucose Buddy, 240, 340
Google Glass, 191, 199, 300
Greatist, 235–236

H
Happtique, 224–225, 230, 231, 234, 317
Health and fitness apps, 237–238, 317, 323, 337–339
    ARGUS, 238, 338
    FitBit Flex, 239, 339

    Fooducate, 238, 338
    Jawbone, 239, 339
    Lose It, 237–238, 337–338
    Nike+FuelBand, 238–239, 339
Health games, 14
Health Insurance Portability and Accountability Act (HIPAA), 58
    and Blue Button, 219
    compliance guidance tools, 227
    and mobile security, 200–201
    updates, 218–219, 243
Health Level 7 (HL7), 195, 298
Health Record Banking Alliance (HRBA), 59
Health Tracker Pro, 243, 342
HealthTap, 235
Heartwise Blood Pressure Tracker, 242, 342
HopeLab, 91, 96

I

iBG Diabetes Manager, 241, 341
Identity Services Engine (ISE), 203
iHealth Mobile App, 243, 343
Information technology standards, 189–196
    adoption, 320–321
    communication patterns, 190
    networks, 189–190
    security and privacy, 192
    share capabilities, 190–192
    syntax, 192–193
Intelligent Home, 301–303
Intrusion detection monitoring, 203
ISMETT, 149–155

J

JawBone, 15, 239, 339

L

Legal regulations, 201
    mobile security, 201
Lose It, 237–238, 337–338

M

mBarriers to mobile technology, 316–326
    Innovate Now, 326–327
Meaningful Use
Stage 2, 62

Index 353

Stage 3, 216
Medical Body Area Networks (MBAN), 218
mHealth, xxiv–xxvi, 119, 325
    apps, 223–231. See also Mobile health applications
    attributes of, 8–9
    benefits of, 169–170
    business models, 122–123, 165–172
    and chronic condition management, 290–291
    and complimentary technologies, 10
    congressional activity, 216–217
    and diagnosis of acute conditions, 288–290
    economic impact, 177
    ecosystem, 3–10, 250, 320
    evolution of, 166–167
    financial services, 169, 170–171
    global, 170–171, 249–253
    goals, 143
    and government agency involvement, 217–219
    and healthcare providers, 291–292
    innovations, 79–82, 119–124
    key drivers, 81–82
    management, 159–163
    mobility, 173–179
    patient-centered healthcare, 4
    regulation, 123–124
    roundtable discussion, 329–336
    sustainability, 122
    uniqueness, 8
mHealth ecosystem, 3–10, 119
    characterization of, 5
mHealth management, 159–163
    product development strategies, 162
Mobile Alliance for Maternal Action (MAMA), 251, 255–261, 345–348
    Bangladesh, 257
    history of, 256–257
    mobile messaging translations, 259
    South Africa, 258
    Tanzania, 347–348
    Timor-Leste, 345–346
    Uganda, 346–347
Mobile device management (MDM), 199–200
Mobile devices, 79
    apps, 80
    and Brothers for Life Campaign, 279–283
    cost structure, 80

Mobile Diabetes Intervention Study (MDIS), 137–138
Mobile health applications, 12, 15–16, 25, 223–231, 233–245
    advertising process, 224, 225–226
    ARGUS, 238
    Blood Pressure Monitor—Family Lite, 242, 342
    certification process, 224, 225–226, 230, 231, 234–235
    classification methods, 236–237
    connectivity constraints, 191
    data ownership, 229
    design considerations, 25
    Diabetes Tracker, 240, 340
    FitBit Flex, 239, 339
    Fooducate, 238, 338
    Glooko Logbook, 241, 341
    Glucose Buddy, 240, 340
    Health Tracker Pro, 243, 342
    Heartwise Blood Pressure Tracker, 242, 342
    iBG Diabetes Manager, 241, 341, 343
    iHealth Mobile App, 243, 343
    Jawbone, 239, 339
    Lose It, 237–238, 337–338
    Nike+FuelBand, 238–239, 339
    security and privacy, 192, 226–229
    sharing capabilities, 190–192
    and SMS, 25–26
    Wave Sense Diabetes Manager, 241, 340
    Withings Health Mate App, 243, 343
Mobile health games, 85–92
    advantages, 90
    behavioral change theories, 87–88
    development strategies, 90–92
    Diab, 87
    history, 85–86
    Re-Mission, 91, 95–100
    statistics, 86–87
    Zamzee, 87
    Zombies, Run!, 91, 103–109
Mobile health messaging, 19–27, 81, 125–130. See also Text messaging
    advanced capabilities, 24
    and behavioral change design, 20–24
    health programs, 20
    implementation of application, 26
personalization, 22
    program integration, 23–24
    systems integration, 23–24
    user engagement, 22–23

Mobile medical apps, 224
Mobile prescription therapy (MPT), 131–140
    and apps, 135–136
    and chronic disease, 131–134
    Mobile Diabetes Intervention Study (MDIS), 137–138
    solution characteristics, 134–135
    value proposition, 136–138
Mobile for Reproductive Health (m4RH), 263–271
    pilot results, 268–269
    program implementation, 266–268
    and text messaging, 264–266
Mobile security, 199–213
    apps, 200–201, 226–229
    authentication process, 204
    Bring Your Own Device (BYOD), 207–212
    intrusion detection, 203
    legal regulations, 201
    near-field communication devices, 205–206
    physical security, 204–205
    protection software, 204
    radio frequency identification tags, 205
    resource monitoring, 204
    risk assessment, 202–203
    risk management, 202
    Security Rule, 199
    smartphone medical devices, 206–207
    technology, 199–200
Mobile technology, 12–16
    challenges of, 15
    health apps, 12
    and healthier dietary practices, 37–43
    mBarriers, 316–326
    recommendations, 15–16
    remote health monitoring devices, 13
    ScanAvert, 37–43
    text messages, 12
    wearable devices, 13–14
Mobility model, 173–179
    benefits, 177–178
    and healthcare, 175–176
    implementation costs, 177
    and telehealth, 177
Mosio, 30–32
    hotlines/help lines, 31–32
    text messaging, 31
    text speak, 32

time-shifting, 32
My Fitness Pal, 146

N

Near-field communication devices, 205–206
Networking constraints, 191
Nike+ Fuel Band, 146, 238–239, 339

O

Obesity apps, 337–339
Omnio, 305–312
OpenNotes, 59
Organ transplant home monitoring, 149–155
    and Care Innovations Guide, 152–153
    clinical protocol, 153–154
data requirements, 152
    implementation procedures, 150–153
    liver transplantation, case study, 149–155
    telehealth monitoring, 150–153

P

Patient engagement, 45–53, 126
    definition of, 46
    design of, 48–51
    and personal health information technology (PHIT), 59–60
    studies results, 52–53
    testing methods, 49–51
    and text messaging, 128
Peer-to-peer communications, 128, 298
Personal health information technology (PHIT), 59
Pew Internet Project, 29–30, 323, 324
    teen survey on smartphones, 29–30
Privacy, 192, 226–229
Public policy principles, 215–216
    Meaningful Use Stage 3, 216
    mobile technologies, 216

R

Radio frequency identification (RFID), 205
Re-Mission, 91, 95–100
    and cancer prevention, 97–98
    design challenges, 96, 99
    and medication adherence, 97
    theories of, 97
Remote health monitoring, 13, 330

Index

Telcare Blood Glucose Meter (BGM), 13
Resource monitoring, 204
Risk assessment, 202–203
Risk management, 202

S

ScanAvert, 37–43
    interface development, 42
    recall auto-notification, 39–40
    registration process, 38
Security, 192, 199–213, 226–229, 321. See also Mobile security
Self-Determination Theory, 87–88
Server-mediated pattern, 190
Smartphone medical devices, 200, 206–207
Social Cognitive Theory (SCT), 20–21, 87–88
Sonic Boom Wellness, 111–115
    financial benefits, 113
    Sonic Striding, 112
    SonicPed clips, 112, 114–115
    success story, 114–115
    Wellness Incentive Management System (WIMS), 113
St. Clare Health Mission, 183–184
Super apps, 80–81
Syntax, 192–193

T

Telcare Blood Glucose Meter (BGM), 13
Telemedicine system, 152–153
    organ transplant monitoring, case study, 149–155
Text messaging (SMS), 12, 29–35, 80, 125. See also Mobile health messaging
    BrdsNBz, 32–35
    challenges, 128–129
    and changing social behavior, 29–35
    Denver Health, case study, 126–127
    Ghana HIV HelpLine, 273–277
    Mobile for Reproductive Health (m4RH), 263–271
    Mosio, 30–32
    and patient engagement, 128
    Pew Internet Project, 29–30
    security and privacy issues, 128
    text4baby, case study, 127
TIME Magazine, 235
Toshiba America Medical Systems (TAMS), 111–115
    Sonic Boom Wellness, 111–115
Transport Layer Security (TLS), 192

Transportation Theory, 87–88
Twitter, 14

U
Underinsured treatment, 181–184

V
Volunteer providers, 181–184
Volunteers in Medicine (VIM), 181–183, 184

W
Wave Sense Diabetes Manager, 241, 340
Wearable devices, 13–14, 300
    FitBit, 14
Wellness apps, 143
    and data capture, 144–147
    My Fitness Pal, 146
    Nike+ Fuel Band, 146
Withings devices, 15
    Withings Health Mate App, 243, 343

Z
Zamzee, 87
Zombies, Run!, 91, 103–109
    cost of, 108
    data collection, 108
    game play, 104–105